Old Labor and New Immigrants in
American Political Development

Old Labor and New Immigrants in American Political Development

UNION, PARTY, AND STATE, 1875–1920

GWENDOLYN MINK

Cornell University Press ITHACA AND LONDON

First published 1986 by Cornell University Press.
First published, Cornell Paperbacks, 1990.

International Standard Book Number 0-8014-1863-1 (cloth)
International Standard Book Number 0-8014-9680-2 (paper)

Library of Congress Catalog Card Number 85-30963
Printed in the United States of America
*Librarians: Library of Congress cataloging information
appears on last page of the book.*

*The paper in this book is acid-free and meets the guidelines for
permanence and durability of the Committee on Production Guidelines
for Book Longevity of the Council on Library Resources.*

For my grandmothers,

Mitama Tateyama Takemoto

and Helen Hlavaty Mink

Contents

Preface

Immigrants and workers figure prominently in this book, but it is not a book about them. It is about the political development of American trade unionism—and about the centrality of immigration to that development. In the following pages I outline the trade-union response to the migration of southern, central, and eastern Europeans to America after the Civil War, and thence into the American labor market; and I connect that response to the course charted by the American Federation of Labor in national politics. In particular, I show how the admixture of race consciousness and job consciousness within the AFL generated strong but narrow organizational and political interests for unions. That combination helped produce an early but subaltern position for the AFL inside the Democratic party during the industrial period. My purpose, then, is to explore the AFL's subordinate, but important, political role in the two-party system and the state prior to the New Deal and to assess the impact of union labor on the political order that emerged in the first two decades of the twentieth century.

Those who study why American politics developed differently from politics in Europe are generally motivated by common concerns: why an autonomous labor party did not emerge in the United States, why a party-class alignment did not materialize, and why ideological opposition to liberal capitalism did not play a central role in American politics. I share these concerns.

Like many scholars, I have been fascinated by the varied efforts to explain American exceptionalism. My fascination stems from a desire to understand the weakness of social democratic tradition in the United States. But I am also uncomfortable with previous work. My discomfort is provoked by the tendency of exceptionalist scholars to ask what did not happen at the expense of what did, and to tie their answers to seemingly static legacies (e.g., the liberal consensus), or to ad hoc and idiosyncratic factors (e.g., the disposition of certain labor leaders), or to purported peculiarities of the American political economy which do not stand up under comparative scrutiny (e.g., "job consciousness"). At bottom, my discomfort is caused by the fact that exceptionalist scholarship hasn't fully sorted out how to explain what it wants to explain.

I want, therefore, to frame the problem of American historical experience somewhat differently, to ask why conservative trade unionism was the central labor force in American politics and what difference this made. I also seek explanations for American exceptionalism, therefore, but I find them in the purposeful organizational strategies and political choices adopted by the AFL in response to the demographic and economic dynamics of late nineteenth- and early twentieth-century America.

Conservative, group-centered labor politics clearly stalked American political development. The conservatism of union labor held class politics in check; it held even unionism itself in check. What was politically the most ripened stratum of the American working class—native-born and northwest European, or "old," labor—abjured labor-based politics and a welfarist agenda. Through its national institution, the AFL, it articulated a political program not in opposition to, or critical of, liberal capitalism but in defense of its own institutional position vis-à-vis class and state. Why did it do so?

To explain the unique role played by union labor in American politics, I focus on the relationship between the organizational interests of the country's most durable union formation and a national political issue—immigration—that defined the very boundaries of the American working class. Immigration played, I argue, a decisive role in the formulation of an American version of labor politics. Hence I explore the political impact of a split between union and nonunion, old and new immigrant workers; of dramatic demographic change; and of nativism and racism. I do so in order to elucidate the development of trade-union ideology, the movement of the AFL into established state and party structures, and the consequent separation of the AFL from the wider working class. Ultimately, old labor's response to industrial-era immigration underlay its ties to the Democratic party and to the emerging pluralist state. From these ties flowed Democratic decisions about the extent, method, and role of the American state under Woodrow Wilson.

During the long years in which this manuscript was written, I enjoyed critical support from a variety of quarters. Though I can never repay my intellectual debts, I find solid pleasure in thanking those who challenged and inspired me to see this work to completion.

First, I thank my parents, without whose support and influence I would not have had the time, the patience, or the discipline to carry on. I credit them, in good measure, with shaping my ideas and concerns. Though I have not answered questions as they might, I surely have raised questions that concern them and have explored issues with the care and passion that they taught me. Beyond this, they deserve thanks for blessing me at birth with a topic for my first book: I am a coalminer's granddaughter and the great grandchild of sugar plantation contract laborers. However subliminally, my Slavic and Japanese immigrant heritage certainly guided me toward this research.

But no amount of parental interest or faith could have pushed me over the intellectual hurdles raised by my subject. That debt I owe to my teachers, colleagues, and students.

At Cornell University, E. W. Kelley, Isaac Kramnick, and Theodore J. Lowi guided and challenged me, and each introduced me to difficult but rewarding arenas of scholarly inquiry. Professors Kramnick and Kelley were irreplaceable advisers, pushing me to confront complexities, develop ideas, and argue rigorously. Professor Lowi scrutinized the predecessor of this book, helping me fit the pieces of my puzzle together and teaching me to balance creativity with disciplined thinking. He gave critical encouragement to my project, always pushing me in fruitful directions.

Colleagues and friends played a crucial role in the development of this book, as well. The book could not have been written without the steady attention of Jeremiah Riemer to my ideas and argumentation. I made great use of his intelligence and erudition. Aline Kuntz, Mark Silverstein, Nancy Love, and Jim Curtis are part of this book in ways that they know best. Elizabeth Sanders provided insightful reactions to a draft of Chapters 6 and 7. In the true spirit of professional collegiality, Michael Rogin shared his reactions to an early draft, and J. David Greenstone and Nick Salvatore offered instructive guidance in the final preparation of the manuscript.

At the University of California, Santa Cruz, more people than perhaps wish to be incriminated were generous with suggestions and criticism. Grant McConnell gave a thorough and very helpful reading. Michael Brown, Peter Euben, Wally Goldfrank, Isebill Gruhn, Robert Meister, and Alan Richards were always ready to read and forthcoming with pertinent and incisive comments as the manuscript developed. I am grateful for their energetic, if sometimes conflicting, advice. Conversations with Robert Hawkinson and Richard Gordon, as well as the experience of coteaching with each of them, exposed me to perspectives and discoveries that greatly enriched my own thinking. The Comparative and International Studies group and the Institutional Analysis and Social Policy group provided arenas for discussions that both tested my own ideas and enabled me to learn from the work of others. In this connection, Robert Alford, Linda Berthold, G. William Domhoff, William Friedland, and Paul Lubeck contributed useful criticism to several chapter drafts. The Institutional Analysis and Social Policy group, the Faculty Research Committee, and the Affirmative Action Grants Committee have been generous in funding this project.

Bill Walsh brought me good cheer. Elizabeth Jones offered editorial insight and spirited friendship. Anne Carr performed valuable detective work. Scott James provided indispensable research assistance and critically astute advice. My students in Politics 120B and Politics 125 have tested, grilled, and challenged me over the years to the betterment of the book. At Cornell University Press, Peter Agree gave much-needed encouragement during the final stages of revision. Roger Haydon was thorough and professional in helping me bring some clarity to my prose.

Most important, Bill Tetreault deserves credit for any crisp formulations that manage to surface. He saw me through every phase of this enterprise, lending moral support when I needed it and withholding it when my logic became flaccid and my writing unintelligible. His meticulous reading and rereading of each chapter, his sugarcoat-less criticism, and his own sweeping knowledge have influenced every page. And, obligingly, he accepts full responsibility for any imperfections in the text.

GWENDOLYN MINK

Santa Cruz, California

PART I

The Political Side of American Trade Unionism

Immigration, Organization, and the

Nationalization of Labor Politics

CHAPTER I

Labor in American Politics, 1875–1920

Between what matters and what seems to matter, how should the world we know judge wisely?

—E. C. Bentley, 1913

The relations between states and unions have come under increasing scrutiny by contemporary scholars, as unions have been folded into the political structures of advanced capitalism and as labor-based parties have moved in and out of power.[1] The relationship between unions and labor-based parties has engaged more extensive scholarly inquiry, particularly with respect to the early twentieth century, when unions and labor-based parties developed institutionalized oppositions to established regimes. But with the exception of J. David Greenstone's seminal book, *Labor in American Politics,* most analyses of relations between union, party, and state have been formulated with respect to, and empirically grounded in, the historical experience of Western Europe.

This book offers a bridge across the disciplinary divide between students of the comparative politics of advanced industrial societies and students of American politics. It charts the mutual interaction and institutional development of union, party, and state during the industrial period in the United States. Even if, as some observers argue, American and Western European unions can now be said to be similarly situated in the

[1]See, e.g., Peter Gourevitch et al., *Unions and Economic Crisis: Britain, West Germany, and Sweden* (1984); Suzanne Berger, ed., *Organizing Interests in Western Europe* (1981); Andrei Markovits, *The Political Economy of West Germany: Modell Deutschland* (1982); Philippe C. Schmitter and Gerhard Lehmbruch, eds., *Trends toward Corporatist Intermediation* (1979); and John Goldthorpe, ed., *Order and Conflict in Contemporary Capitalism* (1984).

politics of advanced capitalism, they surely reached this point along different historical routes.

Trade unions have been critical agents of both change and impasse in the political universe of what are now advanced capitalist societies. In Europe and Australia, for example, unions were essential to the emergence of labor-based, social democratic parties in the first decade of the twentieth century. Often the problematic legal status of unions prompted either the creation of a political arm for unions, as in the labor parties of Britain and Australia, or fusion with established oppositional parties, as happened with the Free Trade Unions and Social Democratic party (SPD) in Germany. Even in France, where the disappointments of 1848 and under the Third Republic helped produce syndicalist anti-politicalism among unions, the radicalism of the Conféderation Générale du Travail was associated with the eventual ascendance of radical parties into which the CGT eventually moved. In France, then, radical unions waged opposition from the left; while unions in Germany moderated SPD radicalism, and unions in Britain and Australia built reformist political alternatives in loyal opposition. In all of these cases the working-class movements and parties that took shape during the industrial period reflected patterns of class politics which were mediated by the institutional struggles of trade unionism.[2]

In the context of emerging mass democracy and under the strains of developing capitalism, trade unions and labor parties exerted substantial pressures on industrializing states to develop or expand policies and politics to reach—sometimes to accommodate, sometimes to coopt—the wage-earning class as a whole.[3] In the United States, by contrast, neither a labor party nor a social democratic agenda grew up alongside, out of, or in response to the trade-union movement. In fact, American trade unionism explicitly rejected the idea of an independent labor politics and, until the late 1930s, vetoed most social democratic claims upon the American state. Correspondingly, the American state neither responded to nor anticipated working-class political pressure with social welfare innovations.

[2]Maurice Duverger, *Political Parties* (1960); Paul Adelman, *The Rise of the Labour Party* (1972); Henry Pelling, *Origins of the Labour Party* (1965); Carl Schorske, *German Social Democracy, 1905–1917* (1955); Walter Galenson, ed., *Comparative Labor Movements* (1952); Val Lorwin, *The French Labor Movement* (1954); David Thomson, *Democracy in France since 1870* (1946); and Harvey Mitchell and Peter Stearns, *Workers and Protest: The European Labor Movement, the Working Class and the Origins of Social Democracy, 1980–1914* (1971).

[3]See John Stephens, *Transition from Capitalism to Socialism* (1979); Peter Flora and Jens Alber, "Modernization, Democratization, and the Development of Welfare States in Western Europe," in Flora and Arnold J. Heidenheimer, eds., *The Development of Welfare States in Europe* (1981), 37–81; and Harold Wilensky, *The Welfare State and Equality* (1975), chap. 3.

In the United States, then, labor politics took a different route, and the political universe looked rather different than it did in Europe. Still American trade unionism, though it rejected class politics and independent laborism, did not reject politics altogether. Nor was its role in politics insignificant. Rather the trade-union mainstream, through the American Federation of Labor (AFL), elaborated a "politics without class" that, by the turn of the century, had both consolidated the power of the AFL and given to conservative trade unionism a preemptive control over labor's political space. Further, in national politics—my concern here—the AFL cultivated pockets of labor privilege, helping set the stage for and then helping shape the political transformations that distinguish the Progressive Era as one of remarkable political realignment and institutional innovation.[4]

The AFL's rise to prominence in national politics reflected its accommodation to existing political arrangements. This accommodation, I shall argue, developed from the politics of a split labor market, which displaced the politics of class during the industrializing period.[5] The politics of the split labor market expressed antagonisms *within* the wage-earning class, antagonisms that became salient, particularly for settled workers, under the concurrent impacts of immigration and industrial expansion. Ethnic differences and skill differences converged within an expanding labor market to precipitate organizational and nativist anxieties among more skilled, unionizing workers of older immigrant stock. Trade unionism absorbed and articulated these anxieties, isolating American unions from workers below and institutionalizing group antagonisms among wage earners. The AFL spoke as the only organized representation of the working class until the rise of the Congress of Industrial Organizations in the 1930s, but it was the preeminence of the AFL's group concerns which provided the basis for its participation in politics. This trade-union politics led, as we shall see, to relatively early union mobilization within established apparatuses of party and state. It also supported an organization-centered political strategy aimed at securing the autonomy of trade unions from the working class, as well as from employers and government.

American labor, though certainly as militant as—and sometimes more

[4] These changes are insightfully discussed in Martin Shefter, "Party, Bureaucracy and Political Change in the United States," in Louis Maisel and Joseph Cooper, eds., *Political Parties* (1978), 229–37, and in Stephen Skowronek, *Building a New American State* (1982).

[5] Edna Bonacich argues the significance of job competition from lower-priced and "foreign" or culturally different workers in generating ethnic jealousy, racism, and nativism. See Bonacich, "A Theory of Ethnic Antagonism: The Split Labor Market," *American Sociological Review*, 37 (1972), 547–59.

violent than—its European counterparts in its struggles to unionize, never took its militancy outside the workplace to build political opposition or to challenge established political structures. Rather, it mobilized within the middle-class bias of the U.S. political system, moving into coalition with classes above, defending the Tocquevillian ideal of voluntary association, and promoting the Jacksonian vision of a limited American state.

The consequences of this "internal mobilization" were threefold.[6] First, the politics of class was neutralized, and a party-class alignment avoided, when organized labor began to forge strong and early ties to the ruling middle-class party system in the 1890s. The union-party tie transformed the Democratic Party in national politics into a coalition among the AFL, segments of the entrepreneurial and farming classes, and the South; the party of capital, meanwhile, came to power in many areas on the votes of nonunion industrial workers. Different wage-earning constituencies were organized differently in American politics, then, to reduce, in V. O. Key's words, "the coincidence of class affiliation and partisan inclinations."[7] Second, the fastening of the union-party tie during this crucial era precluded alternative political patterns from making headway. Third, the relationship between group and party on the Democratic side, and the disorganization and demobilization of industrial workers on the Republican side, enabled the AFL to seize an "opening to the middle" and forge ties to the state under Woodrow Wilson. Through its association with the Democratic state, the AFL helped influence the method of state intervention which developed during the Democratic decade: in particular, it helped national policy-making institutions emerge as the broker among interests in combat in the courts and in the economy, and it helped secure the policy silence of national government with respect to worker-friendly social welfare reforms.

American labor adapted to the two-party system without first threatening an alternative to it, and it developed ties to the state without first mobilizing against it. Clearly the United States did not experience European patterns of class and party association. Two generations of scholars have analyzed this difference. In the main they have pursued and refined Werner Sombart's blunt question, "Why no socialism in the United States?"[8] to ask: Why no class-coherent, labor-based movement in opposition to the parties and the regime; Why no effective political re-

---

[6]I borrow this concept from Martin Shefter, "Party and Patronage: Germany, England, and Italy," *Politics and Society*, 7 (1977), 403–51.

[7]V. O. Key, "A Theory of Critical Elections," *Journal of Politics*, 17 (1955), 15.

[8]Werner Sombart, *Why Is There No Socialism in the United States?* (1976).

sistance to capitalism in its most ruthless phase; Why no ideological interpretation of inequality to challenge laissez-faire liberalism, corporate liberalism, or liberal reform; Why no labor party?

Perspectives on American Labor

The first of four general categories of answers to these questions connects liberal political values and consensual political forms to certain American material realities and to the circumstances of colonial and early constitutional America. Friedrich Engels and Frederick Jackson Turner argued that the frontier provided American workers with an effective escape from proletarianization and protected American democracy from class politics, because it promised geographic and economic mobility.[9] Both were skeptical that political and economic conflict could be avoided once the frontier disappeared, but others have drawn from the frontier experience a metaphor for American opportunity and abundance. Werner Sombart warned that "roast beef and apple pie" limited the incentives for American labor to engage in politics; David Potter suggested that free land was only one aspect of the bounty that sustained the optimistic and individualistic American national character.[10]

Others have rejected the frontier thesis altogether while embracing its emphasis on possibility and mobility. Louis Hartz—for whom all of America was a frontier—and Seymour Martin Lipset combine both the myth and the reality of opportunity with the political culture and social structure of early America to argue that Americans were locked into a liberal consensus.[11] That consensus, developing unencumbered by the vestiges of a sharply stratified feudal society, disposed America to reject class bases for political association. An ideology of mobility substituted for class identity because the liberal tradition created and celebrated "open society" when it rejected the connection between birth and rank. In the absence of feudal

[9]Engels wrote that "land is the basis of speculation, and the American speculative mania and speculative opportunity are the chief levers that hold the native-born worker in bondage to the bourgeoisie. Only when there is a generation of native-born workers who cannot expect *anything* from speculation *anymore*, will we have a solid foothold in America." See Karl Marx and Friedrich Engels, *Letters to Americans* (1953), 239, and Frederick Jackson Turner, *The Frontier in American History* (1920).

[10]Sombart, 237; David Potter, *People of Plenty* (1954, 1966), 155.

[11]Louis Hartz, *The Founding of New Societies* (1964), esp. 10, and *The Liberal Tradition in American* (1955), chaps. 8, 9; Seymour Martin Lipset, "Trade Unions and the American Value System," in Lipset, *The First New Nation* (1979), 170–204.

"remnants," moreover, capitalism had the field to itself. Material life thus reinforced the ideology of mobility because, in Lipset's words, a "market economy operates best under conditions of free competition, recognizing neither family background nor social limitations."[12]

A second, overlapping, set of arguments focuses on the development of democratic processes and the structure of the American state. The argument holds that the timing and conditions of suffrage, along with the relative weakness of the American state, produced mass electorates that did not have to threaten opposition to be "let in" to American democracy. Engels, Hartz, and Lipset agree that the resilience of the liberal consensus can, in significant measure, be explained by the early extension of the franchise in the United States. Political rights and economic position were divorced in the United States so early on as greatly to weaken the basis for building political organization around economic inequalities understood in class terms. Given the vote before a working class was sufficiently developed to demand it, wage earners did not have to struggle as a class to win political rights elsewhere denied to workers as a class. Franchise extension, decided in the absence of ideological resistance to democratic claims, validated the liberal consensus and proved mobilization against the state unnecessary.

Other, more recent, versions of this argument look to democratic realities, rather than to liberal values, to explain the relationship between early mass democracy and the weakness of class identification in politics. For this view, early suffrage meant early organization of participation within electoral and state structures that scattered arenas of politics and power, that separated work from political life, and that defined the stakes of participation largely in distributive terms. More concretely, the timing of suffrage enabled the ruling political parties to forge a generation of party loyalties before industrialization fully created a working class; to diffuse political participation and identity among the decentralized centers of public authority with which workers came into closest proximity; and thereby to develop in workers an early sense of "belonging" in the political system, chiefly on the basis of geographic and communal attachments. Significantly, too, early suffrage resulted in workers being included in the Civil War realignment that intensified and invigorated sectional, ethnocultural, and particularistic bases for political association for another generation. Hence the diffuseness of the American state, the vigor of local governments, the strength of patronage parties at the local level

[12]Lipset, "Trade Unions," in David Brody, ed., *The American Labor Movement* (1971), 11.

and of cross-class appeals at the national level, all shaped a mass democracy in which the class identity and the national political focus around which workers might have organized both lay dormant.[13]

A third, and related, school of arguments looks at the American electoral system. It asks why the same two parties have dominated national politics since 1860; why the substance of two-party competition did not change to reflect the rapid transformation of its socioeconomic base, especially during the Gilded and Progressive decades, when the Populist party, the Socialist party, and trade-union militancy presented their assaults on industrial capitalism; and why a party-class alignment did not materialize to displace one of the major parties, as the Republicans displaced the Whigs after 1854 and as happened in Great Britain?

Explanations of the dominance of the same two parties since 1860 have largely been developed, beginning with V. O. Key's work, within critical election analysis.[14] The two parties periodically respond to cultural, moral, and economic strains, as well as to the entry of new voters—so the argument goes—by distinguishing themselves along new issue cleavages; voters then react to these same issues by reassessing their partisanship, with crucial voting blocs shifting dramatically and durably.[15] These upheavals tend to substitute for and displace conflict[16] while acting as what Walter Dean Burnham calls America's "surrogate for revolution."[17] Critical elections, that is to say, deflate oppositions while providing openings to new groups; they defuse explosive issues while purging the party

[13]Frances Piven and Richard Cloward, *Poor People's Movements* (1979), 15–18; Piven and Cloward, *The New Class War* (1982), chap. 3; Ira Katznelson, *City Trenches* (1981), 55, 64, 70, 118. Most recently, Amy Bridges charts the significance of early and widespread suffrage for politics in *A City in the Republic* (1984).

[14]Key, "Theory of Critical Elections."

[15]For work on electoral realignments since V. O. Key's see, e.g., Walter Dean Burnham, *Critical Elections and the Mainsprings of American Politics* (1970); James L. Sundquist, *Dynamics of the Party System* (1973); Richard Jensen, *The Winning of the Midwest* (1971); Paul Kleppner, *Cross of Culture* (1970), and *The Third Electoral System* (1979); and Kristi Andersen, *The Creation of a Democratic Majority, 1928–1936* (1979).

[16]E. E. Schattschneider, *The Semi-Sovereign People* (1960).

[17]Walter Dean Burnham, "Party Systems and the Political Process," in William Nisbet Chambers and Burnham, *American Party Systems* (1975), writes, "The critical realignment, to be sure, drastically reshuffles the coalitional bases of the two parties, but it does far more than this. It constitutes a political decision of the first magnitude and a turning point in the mainstream of national policy formation. Characteristically, the relationships among policy-making institutions, their relative power and decision-making capacity, and the outputs they produce are profoundly affected by critical realignments. . . . With characteristic properties such as these, the critical realignment may well be regarded as America's surrogate for revolution. One of these experiences led directly to the outbreak of civil war, and every one of the others has been marked by acute political tension" (289).

system of the cumbersome contradictions that gave rise to those issues in the first place. Critical periods of electoral reorganization also bring about changes in party programs and party coalitions. Nevertheless the various transformations of partisanship over the past century have not moved American politics much off dead center.

Periodic electoral upheavals, as Burnham, among others, shows, have homogenized oppositions at the same time as they have reconstituted electoral politics to protect ascendant political and economic arrangements. Even as he invokes the metaphor of revolution to describe moments of electoral change in the United States, Burnham points out that realignments have brought into being electorates and party systems heavily skewed toward the middle class and well disposed toward prevailing economic interests. Burnham's principal example is the "system of 1896," which governed industrializing America. That system institutionalized the ascendancy of capitalism over democracy.[18] Party competition disappeared throughout much of the country, voter demobilization insulated elites from mass pressures, and political power passed to the party of capital and to a judiciary intent on restraining the outcomes of democratic political action. In Burnham's view, the early democratization of politics in the United States and the resilience of democratic routines gave constitutional legitimacy to the demobilization of democracy during the industrial period while efforts to defuse politics during the Progressive Era rendered the organization of alternatives rather difficult. Further, Burnham tells us, the "system of 1896" was marked by sectional and ethnocultural "pseudo-conflicts" that heightened antagonisms among have-nots, leaving business and political elites, and middle-class values, unchallenged by the victims of the industrializing process. These developments created a "hole in the electorate" where a labor party, or some other working-class movement, might have congealed.[19]

Fourth and finally, scholars have looked inside the labor movement to examine the organizational sources of labor's political pragmatism. The starting point has been the preoccupation of American labor with unionization,[20] and the approach has led to many rich histories of the workplace struggles of organizing workers. The more recent of these studies have

[18]Walter Dean Burnham, "The Changing Shape of the American Political Universe," *American Political Science Review*, 59 (March 1965), 7–28.

[19]Ibid.; Burnham, "Party Systems," 301.

[20]Unions generally have been preoccupied with unionization. See Ruth Horowitz, *The Ideologies of Organized Labor* (1978), 31–39; G. D. H. Cole, *British Working Class Politics* (1941), 169, 186; George Dangerfield, *The Strange Death of Liberal England* (1961), chap. 4; and Mitchell and Stearns, 99ff.

tried to show that such struggles were often animated by the class consciousness of workers, though class consciousness may not have reached into politics.[21] Others have stressed the conservative, oligarchic consequences of organization to explain why that consciousness did not find broad-based political expression.[22] Some have supplemented this view with the argument that political coercion—a hostile state—limited workplace successes and foreclosed political opportunities.[23]

Different answers have been developed by those who emphasize the internal logic of trade unionism in explaining its political ambivalence. Selig Perlman made this connection, one now challenged by the new labor history,[24] more than a generation ago, when he suggested that isolation from intellectuals and an expanding labor supply accounted for the political behavior of American labor.[25] In the absence of disinterested theoreticians, Perlman argued, economic and organizational interests took precedence over political and ideological ones: when trade union ideologues come from the rank and file—as did Samuel Gompers, for example— immediate, job-oriented demands dominate both trade unionism and trade-union politics. American labor differed from its European counterparts in being isolated from intellectuals and, accordingly, took a different political route. Perlman further argued that the job-oriented demands that gave substance to labor politics flowed from conditions in the labor market. Trade unions rejected political independence and embraced job-conscious pragmatism, because pessimism with regard to job opportunities and economic security was endemic among organized occupational groups. The steady expansion of the labor supply through immigration and the abrupt displacement of many crafts through mechanization sus-

[21]E.g., Alan Dawley, *Class and Community: The Industrial Revolution in Lynn* (1976), and David Montgomery, *Workers' Control in America* (1980).

[22]E.g., Piven and Cloward, *Poor People's Movements.*

[23]Ibid. This view has been tied to the fact of judicial harassment of American unions during the industrial period as well as to the observation that American unions and their activities remained outside the law, at least in principle, far longer than unions in Europe. For a comparative perspective see Charles Tilly, "Collective Violence in European Perspective," in Hugh Davis Graham and Ted Gurr, eds., *The History of Violence in America* (1969). Christopher Tomlins, *The State and the Unions* (1985), analyzes the "legal twilight zone" in which American unions were forced to operate (Part I). The legal status of unions in Europe was nevertheless quite problematic. See Seymour Martin Lipset's discussion of the relationship between states and labor in "Radicalism or Reformism: The Sources of Working-Class Politics," *American Political Science Review,* 77 (March 1983), 1–19.

[24]The new labor history has been debated by David Brody, "The Old Labor History and the New," *Labor History,* 20 (1979), 111–26, and Robert Ozanne, "Trends in American Labor History," ibid., 21 (1980), 513–21.

[25]Selig Perlman, *A Theory of the Labor Movement* (1928, 1978), chaps. 5, 7.

23

tained fears of job scarcity, fears that led unions to concentrate on securing job control for skilled workers by organizing the workplace and the
work process. Politics was largely irrelevant to this struggle because,
under laissez-faire capitalism, government had little to say about employment policies, wage levels, and conditions of work. The political
demarcation between classes having been eliminated before the labor
movement really started in the United States, moreover, workers were
unlikely to translate their economic worries into political action.

Michael Rogin follows Perlman to analyze the substance and consequences of trade-union ideology.[26] Rogin's interest is not in the origins or
theoretical bases of the ideology but in the political and organizational
purposes that it served. That ideology, voluntarism, spelled out the instrumental logic that underlay the conservative course charted by trade-union
leaders and followed in general by the trade-union mainstream. At one
level, voluntarism was a pragmatic doctrine that responded to the political
conditions of industrializing America. As suffrage came early, partisanship—and political integration—preceded mobilization of a trade-
union movement. Moreover, the organization of partisanship and the intensity of the Civil War partisan cleavage meant that party loyalties were
both deep and long-standing—and unrelated to class experience. The
leaders of the developing trade-union movement were understandably
fearful of becoming partisan and of demanding partisanship of their members, for the distribution of political loyalties among workers threatened to
undermine the unity of economic identity which trade unionism vigorously asserted. In many cases, workers loyal to the same union were
also loyal to different parties. Further, the state in industrializing America
was generally hostile to labor: when it intervened, it did so decisively and
coercively, to obstruct the organization of labor through injunctions and
the denial of legal status. Trade-union leaders thus viewed the state as an
inevitable antagonist of the labor movement. Their response to this combination of political conditions was to demonstrate that labor did not
threaten traditional politics, on the one hand by insisting that unionists
were traditional partisans and on the other by showing that labor *qua* labor
eschewed politics.

But there was more to voluntarism. Voluntarism was, as Rogin demon-
strates, an ideology developed to protect the organizational interests, and
the small constituency, of the American Federation of Labor. As a theory,

---

[26]Michael Rogin, "Voluntarism: The Political Functions of an Anti-Political Doctrine," *Industrial and Labor Relations Review*, 15 (July 1962), 521–35.

voluntarism invoked traditional liberal principles—individual liberty and economic freedom—as labor's defense against political and governmental coercion. Yet in practice, voluntarism concealed the coercive weapons of trade unionism in the economic arena (strike violence, boycotts, and closed shop)[27] while rationalizing the AFL's claim to speak for the whole class. In principle, voluntarism defended the collective power of workers through voluntary association and defended those associations from political interference. In practice, Rogin tells us, voluntarism promoted the institutional position of a narrowly constituted trade unionism, widened the chasm between unionists and the larger working class, and justified the AFL's political opposition to positive state action designed to enhance the economic welfare of the working class as a whole (e.g., the minimum wage and social insurance). Though antipolitical and individualist in theory, voluntarism was neither in practice. Indeed, it provided the rationale for the AFL's political interventions against the working class and against innovations in social policy, as well as for the AFL's internal regulation of the labor movement.

Voluntarism, then, was a doctrine of union preeminence. As it warned against involvement with the state and politics, so it served a political purpose: promoting the AFL's autonomy in the workplace, in the labor movement, and at the intersection of state and society. The only organized segment of the working class rejected both political independence and worker-oriented state intervention. In doing so, it made economic action through (and therefore membership in) trade unions the sole vehicle for pursuit of occupational and economic security. And when it limited entry into trade unions, it put the trade-union monopoly of organization and representation in the service of the most privileged stratum of the wage-earning class.

The Perspectives in Perspective

These various perspectives provide useful insights into labor's role in American politics; but each has its limitations. The frontier thesis and the liberal consensus suggest the importance of political culture and material life in limiting the means and incentives available to labor in politics. The abundance of free land and the presumption of political equality in nine-

---

[27]James Q. Wilson makes this point in *Political Organization* (1973), chap. 7, as does Mancur Olson, *The Logic of Collective Action* (1971), 70–72, 76, 88.

teenth-century America tended to focus attention not on property relations but on the preservation of economic opportunity through the equitable distribution of land.[28] Together, the expectation of social mobility, the preindustrial extension of the franchise to adult white males, and the mobilization of mass electorates within a permeable regime helped obscure connections between politics and class. But the frontier closed; a working class settled into place; immigrants from feudal and semifeudal traditions created an industrial working class; and the federal judiciary removed economic questions from political arenas more vulnerable to popular majorities and nationalized them under judicial surveillance.[29] What happened then?

Part of the explanatory power of the frontier thesis lies in the durability of the frontier *myth*; belief in the possibility of opportunity and advancement persists long after the geographic reality disappears. But the millions of new immigrants who arrived during and after the closing of the frontier lacked experience with the frontier reality and thus could not have fully internalized the frontier myth. Nor could they have experienced the democratizing influences of the frontier community which helped reproduce the American national character and dilute feudal identities imported from Europe.[30]

By the same token, most accounts of the experience of new immigrants in America do not suggest that these workers shared in the abundance and material comfort that supported the liberal faith. Though they were in important ways "better off" once in the United States (e.g., they had jobs), most lived in poverty, many in squalor, and some in feudal dependence upon industrial employers.[31] It is not clear that the promise of

[28]This is borne out by National Labor Union and Knights of Labor support for the land theories of George Henry Evans and Henry George. See Marx's critique of Henry George in Marx and Engels, 12.

[29]Arnold Paul provides a lucid analysis of the transformation in constitutional jurisprudence in *Conservative Crisis and the Rule of Law* (1960).

[30]With the closing of the frontier, Turner warned, "It is not surprising that socialism shows noteworthy gains . . . that the demand for primary elections, for popular choice of senators, initiative, referendum, and recall, is spreading. . . . They are efforts to find substitutes for that former safeguard of democracy, the disappearing free lands. They are the sequence to the extension of the frontier." Turner, "Social Forces in American History," in Turner, 321. Charles Howard Shinn, scooping Turner, celebrated the democratizing influence of the frontier community in *Mining Camps* (1884). For a more pessimistic treatment of democracy and the frontier see Josiah Royce, *California from the Conquest of 1846 to the Second Vigilance Committee: A Study of American Character* (1886).

[31]See W. J. Ghent, *Our Benevolent Feudalism* (1902); Jane Addams, *Philanthropy and Social Progress* (1893); Jacob Riis, *How the Other Half Lives* (1890); and Peter Roberts, *Anthracite Coal Communities* (1904).

26

opportunity was realized fully and repeatedly enough to insulate the psychology of abundance and mobility from the effects of economic insecurity, of irregular employment in many industries, of piece-rate or volume-based pay, and of old-age, health, and disability dependency. Indeed, Frederick Jackson Turner associated late nineteenth-century demographic change itself with the degeneration of material conditions necessary to sustain the promise of opportunity. He lamented the coming of southern, central, and eastern Europeans as a "loss to the social organism of the United States," because the immigrant influx "counteracted the upward tendency of wages" and supported "the sweatshop system."[32]

In this connection, the view that occupational and intergenerational mobility was sufficiently high in the United States to explain the "failure of working-class-based protest movements to attract a mass following"[33] has been recently reexamined. Occupational mobility at the bottom of the working class, Stanley Aronowitz argues, did not mean unskilled, immigrant workers achieved social mobility because such mobility did not produce real movement between classes. Nor was it connected to any substantial increase in the number of skilled workers—an increase arguably necessary if semiskilled and unskilled immigrant industrial workers were to penetrate the hold of old-stock labor on the "better class jobs." Occupational position often went hand in hand with ethnic position—70 percent of Slav, Italian, and Hungarian immigrants were unskilled in 1910 and 75 percent of the unskilled labor force in steel was comprised of southern and eastern European immigrants. While new immigrants occupied significant proportions of unskilled and semiskilled jobs during the industrial period, old labor controlled equally significant proportions of skilled work and often moved into supervisory positions. Such labor-market segmentation suggests that occupational status and occupational mobility were more accessible to certain groups of workers than to others. If so, occupational mobility per se cannot explain the asserted docility of industrial workers; nor can it account for the organizational disparity between new immigrants and occupationally more mobile old labor. The idea that intergenerational mobility subdued class consciousness is similarly problematic. New immigrant children did not move easily into skilled positions—or into unions—until the late 1930s. Equally important, intergenerational mobility takes time to be demonstrated; it is not the

---

[32]Quoted in Thomas R. Gossett, *Race: The History of an Idea in America* (1963), 292.
[33]Stephan Thernstrom, "Socialism and Social Mobility," in John Laslett and Seymour Martin Lipset, eds., *Failure of a Dream?* (1974), 551; Thernstrom, *Poverty and Progress* (1974).

27

kind of personal mobility experience that verifies the individual's freedom to rise in the world and that thereby vitiates class thinking. Finally, the mobility argument is not fully persuasive in comparative perspective. Some critics point out that mobility rates among blue-collar workers in industrial America were not distinctly higher than in industrial Europe and sometimes were even rather low. These critics maintain that widely drawn occupational and class boundaries can exaggerate mobility and conceal labor stratification.[34]

Quite apart from the flaws of mobility studies is the fact trade unionism developed notwithstanding the cultural ethos of social mobility. The job-conscious focus of American trade unionism indicates that workers generally accepted their wage-earning status rather than anticipating escape; it was *within* that status that workers sought to win protections and improvements. The ethos of social mobility thus cannot tell us why workers organized into unions at all. Because it cannot tell us that, it cannot explain why workplace politics was never complemented by a workers' politics off the job.

There are similar limitations to consensus theory. At the center of Hartz's explanation of American exceptionalism lies the argument that America was settled by liberal colonizers. America thus stands in stark contrast to Western Europe, where vestiges of feudalism remain resilient, as well as to Latin America, settled by a "feudal fragment," and Australia, settled by a "radical fragment."[35] But although the "bourgeois fragment" of England brought with it its characteristic bourgeois ideology—liberalism—when it settled America, it did not have the field to itself in America once industrialism took root. American political futures were not, in fact, settled by America's earliest settlers.

Hartz's logic rests on the assumption of bourgeois homogeneity. It works for the constitutional period; then, in the absence of feudal institutional and social structures that bourgeoisies elsewhere had to fight, early Americans crafted a classically liberal state. But it does not work for the industrial period; then, homogeneity gave way to diversity under the impact of immigration, and then, in the words of Gompers, "the views [were] gaining upon every side that the classes in society [were] becoming decidedly more distinct . . . and this feeling . . . intensified."[36] By

---

[34]Stanley Aronowitz, *False Promises: The Shaping of American Working Class Consciousness* (1973), 149–51; see also Katznelson's discussion in *City Trenches*, 13.

[35]Hartz, *Founding of New Societies*, pt. 1.

[36]Samuel Gompers to the U.S. Senate, Committee on Education and Labor, *Relations between Capital and Labor*, Hearings, 49th Cong., 1st sess. (1885), 1:374–79.

Hartz's own definition, those born into vestigially or actually feudal societies carry with them feudal "remnants" that do not easily surrender to
the liberal assumption that social and property relations are irrelevant to
economic opportunity and freedom. If the "bourgeois fragment" carried
with it the egalitarian ideal, other fragments carried the patterns and
hostilities associated with stratified social orders. The immigrants who
came to industrial America in the late nineteenth and early twentieth
centuries—nearly twenty-five million by 1920—were quite different from
the yeomen, traders, and Protestants who first colonized America. Peasants, laborers, and Catholics from ascriptive societies, they were the very
strata most likely, according to Hartz, to combine political with corporate
identity.

Even if these workers came to the United States not only to escape
poverty, drought, or persecution but also to acquire a place in "open
society," their expectations of "open society" were compromised when
immigrants were denounced as congenitally antidemocratic,[37] when they
were proletarianized, and when they were excluded, on the basis of race
and occupational position, from trade unions. Many of these workers may
have sustained their faith in open society nonetheless, but they did so most
likely as a result of the material instrumentalism that brought them to the
United States to begin with.[38] Hence it may have been economic self-
interest rather than liberal values that discouraged the political articulation
of a common economic and social experience. Still, the militancy of some
of these workers during the Progressive Era suggests that economic self-
interest, in time, could lead to mobilization and protest as much as to
docility and silence. Further, when these new Americans participated in
politics, their participation did not always conform to the individualist
premises of the political culture. Indeed, the strength of communal appeals in politics intimates the resilience of cultural identities and the
persistence of associational habits brought over from Europe—habits that
were at odds with liberal patterns of politics.

If common liberal values cannot explain the durability of middle-class
politics, perhaps democratic realities can. The argument that early suffrage depoliticized property relations and generated political loyalties
based *not* on class is intuitively satisfying. So is the idea that mass electorates mobilized inside patronage democracy lack both the discipline and

[37]Cf. James Bryce, *The American Commonwealth*, vol. 2 (1910), 103–4; John Commons,
Races and Immigrants in America (1967); and Elmer Cornwell, "Bosses, Machines and Ethnic
Groups," *Annals of the Academy of Political and Social Sciences*, 353 (May 1964), 22.
[38]Gerald Rosenblum, *Immigrant Workers: Their Impact on Labor Radicalism* (1973).

the programmatic justification to consolidate opposition. So is the suggestion that a combination of vigorous local government and a weak federal state left workers with no national focus for political mobilization. And so, too, is the argument that machine politics generated personalistic and distributive expectations from political life, at the expense of programmatic and redistributive ones.

Yet even this line of analysis begs certain questions. Early suffrage may have depoliticized property relations, but it did not abolish them.[39] It became clear, as industrialism advanced, that property relations governed the relations of production as well as the distribution of political power and the relationship between employers, workers, and the state. As government—especially the federal judiciary—dispensed its favors to capital, sanctioning and legitimating employers' repression of labor, so property relations ought, at least in theory, to have been repoliticized. Early suffrage had desultory effects on labor-based politics. But elsewhere the state refocused labor-based politics after suffrage, because it could not be neutral about relations between labor and capital. Thus in Britain, for example, labor decided to build its own party and pursue a parliamentary strategy in response to actions of the British state (notably Taff Vale). Even in the United States unions expressed political complaints against the state—for allowing Chinese immigration, for facilitating employers' recruitment of European immigrant labor, for failing to enforce the federal eight-hour law, for refusing legal recognition for unions.[40] From these complaints, however, American unions developed a group-centered politics that fitted in with middle-class structures of politics.

The argument that early suffrage meant early—and presumably deep-seated—partisanship is also problematic. Workers who immigrated after

---

[39]Marx argues this point in "On the Jewish Question": "But the political suppression of private property not only does not abolish private property; it actually presupposes its existence. The state abolishes, after its fashion, the distinctions established by birth, social rank, education, occupation, when it decrees that birth, social rank, education, occupation are nonpolitical distinctions; when it proclaims, without regard to these distinctions, that every member of society is an equal partner in popular sovereignty, and treats all the elements which compose the real life of the nation from the standpoint of the state. But the state, nonetheless, allows private property, education, occupation, to act after their own fashion, namely as private property, education, occupation, and to manifest their particular nature. Far from abolishing these effective differences, it only exists so far as they are presupposed; it is conscious of being a political state and it manifests its universality only in opposition to these elements. . . . Where the political state has attained to its full development, man leads, not only in thought, in consciousness, but in reality, in life, a double existence—celestial and terrestrial. He lives in a political community, where he regards himself as a communal being, and in civil society where he acts simply as a private individual, treats other men as means, degrades himself to the role of a mere means, and becomes the plaything of alien powers." In Robert Tucker, ed., *The Marx-Engels Reader* (1972), 31–32.

[40]U.S. Senate, *Relations between Capital and Labor*, 1:279–82; 296–300; 374–79.

the Civil War clearly did not inherit these loyalties. Nor, when they developed party loyalties, did they do so on the same bases as workers before them. In Irish-dominated cities, for example, the incentive that stimulated new immigrants to partisanship tended to be services rather than access to political power.[41] With politics closed off as a route to mobility, moreover, new immigrant voters tended to be less consistently partisan, less politicized, and less integrated within patronage democracy. Both the size of the new immigrant population in industrializing America and the changes which that population produced in patronage democracy raise doubts about the decisiveness of early suffrage for politics in the industrial period.

Even if early partisanship created insuperable barriers to political independence or common partisanship among settled workers, early party loyalty did not mean fixed party loyalty. Election studies show that partisanships can change dramatically and that they indeed did during the critical realignment that punctuated the industrial period. Moreover, these studies show that parties can change: the Republican Party displaced the Whigs during the Civil War realignment, for example. We are left with a nagging problem: why were workers apparently willing to move between the established parties—and unionists generally willing to move into the same party—but apparently either unwilling to build or uninterested in building an alternative party?

Partisanship itself was, we must recognize, considerably less important than the fact that preindustrial democratization engaged workers in the political system as individuals, as members of loosely federated clienteles, and as supporters of parties that did not represent specific class interests.[42] This fact underlay the antiparty tenets of voluntarism as well as the trade-union belief in the possibility of separating politics from workplace. But how do we explain why voluntarist unions eventually abandoned nonpartisanship, staking out a presence in national politics and developing ties to the national Democratic party? Unions may have struck a modus vivendi in local politics, leaving politics to political machines in exchange for union autonomy in the workplace.[43] These same unions did

[41]See Steven P. Erie, "Two Faces of Ethnic Power: Comparing the Irish and Black Experiences," *Polity*, 13 (1980), 262–74.

[42]Werner Sombart observed that the party system "makes it extremely easy for the proletariat to belong to traditional parties. In attaching himself to one of the two parties, even the class-conscious worker need never go against the dictates of his intellect," because partisanship was not organized around class identities or explicit class goals. Quoted in Katznelson, 70–71.

[43]Martin Shefter, "Trades Unions and Political Machines," in Ira Katznelson and Aristide Zolberg, eds., *Working Class Formation: Nineteenth Century Patterns in Western Europe and the United States* (1985).

not, however, concede the national political arena to hostile employers, incoherent electorates, and state and party managers. In national politics, unionized workers mobilized around union-related goals.

This brings us to the contention that labor could not build a political movement and workers could not share a common political perspective because politics in the United States was so diffuse. Certainly American politics was complicated by federalism, the primacy of local regimes, the lack of bureaucratic autonomy, and the dominance of highly decentralized political parties. These features of the American system during much of the nineteenth century had several implications. First, government here seemed more accessible and more permeable to popular influence than governments of more centralized or more stratified political orders. Second, the relationship between government and workers and the impact of public authority on unions varied among states and localities. Third, the agents and agencies of repression with whom workers came into contact were likely to be not those of national government but those of employers and localities: industrial police, labor spies, state troops, magistrates, municipal police. Often, electoral constraints and cross-cutting indentities undermined the use of local public power against organizing workers, resulting in the privatization of coercion through industrial armies.[44] In other cases the political influence of capital won swift and unambivalent excercise of public power against labor—as, for example, when governors dispatched state militias to quell labor disturbances. The plethora of arenas and policies obscured the class bias of government, and union struggles for relief from coercion were dispersed across a confusing universe of governmental and economic entities. The national and political foundations for class-based political mobilization were extremely weak.

The problem with this line of argument is that these political arrangements were altered significantly during the late nineteenth century. The growth of large industry, railroads, cartels, and trusts nationalized the economy, and in important sectors—such as steel and coal—it centralized labor policy. National markets and the anti-union activities of capital brought workers into closer proximity with one another. Cigar makers in New York and cigar makers in San Francisco developed common interests, for example, notwithstanding geographic separation and differences of political experience.[45] Even private weapons and techniques

---

[44]Cf. Bruce C. Johnson, "Taking Care of Labor: The Police in American Politics," *Theory and Society*, 3 (1976), 94ff.

[45]Alexander Saxton, *The Indispensable Enemy* (1971).

of discipline and coercion became nationalized, as lockouts and blacklists spread within industries and as labor spies—for example, the Pinkertons—moved among them.[46]

Immigration meanwhile produced dramatic demographic change in the labor market across sectors of industrializing America.[47] It gave settled workers a common workplace experience. The immigrant scabs who broke strikes and the unskilled immigrants who "degraded" the production process provided unionists with a common and national nemesis. Finally, the Supreme Court began, in the 1890s, to nationalize many political questions and to centralize political power.[48] The Court's nationalizing decisions were designed to promote laissez-faire rather than to expand governmental authority, to relieve capital from the decisions of legislatures as well as from the activities of unions. But laissez-faire constitutionalism made the Court the superintendent of politics and the economy, thus confounding the constitutionally structured conflicts between institutions and domains of public authority and creating an identity between Court and state. This new jurisprudence lent the weight of the state to the side of capital—and against labor—and accordingly gave unionists a common political opponent. These developments nationalized American politics. They underscored the national political problems that overrode localism and pushed labor into the national political arena.

The central importance of the national political economy is recognized in critical election theory, developed most brilliantly and completely by Walter Dean Burnham. From Burnham we learn that each party system is in its day national in scope; each aligns competing national electorates according to salient national divisions: Hamiltonian-Jeffersonian, sectional, urban-rural, ethnocultural. New national coalitions are usually brought into being under two conditions: when political structures and

[46]James Horan, *The Pinkertons* (1967). According to Horan, the Pinkertons helped break seventy-seven strikes between 1869 and 1892. They continued their industrial espionage well into the Progressive Era. They were associated with some of the most famous repressions of labor: the Molly Maguire episode (1875–77), the Homestead Strike (1892), and the Ludlow Massacre (1914).

[47]Immigration between 1881 and 1890 nearly doubled the previous decade's figures. With this decade the sources of the immigrant waves changed sharply to points east and south of industrial Europe. The preponderance of these "new" immigrants moved into unskilled and semiskilled occupations. See U.S. Bureau of the Census, *Statistical Abstract of the United States: 1950* (1950), 97; U.S. Bureau of the Census, *Immigrants and Their Children: 1920* (1927), 62; and Thomas Sowell, ed., *Essays and Data on American Ethnic Groups* (1978), 117.

[48]See Paul, *Conservative Crisis*. Of particular concern to labor was the development of the labor injunction—see Paul, chap. 6, and Felix Frankfurter and Nathan Greene, *The Labor Injunction* (1930), chap. 1—and the application of the Commerce Clause, the Sherman Act, and the Fourteenth Amendment against labor and labor legislation.

33

processes lag behind economic organization and power, and when party alignments cease to reflect dominant economic and political cleavages. The "system of 1896," for example, arose from the impact of industrialization and rested on the tensions between the needs of capitalism and the expectations of democracy. The regime itself did not come under assault, but older political coalitions did. Electoral politics was, as a result, reconstituted to reflect tensions between centralizing capital and decentralized government, between metropole and countryside, between creditors and debtors, between Court and legislatures, and between propertied minorities and popular majorities.

Changes in the national political economy, as Burnham shows, changed the electoral universe and provided the basis for national political mobilization. Those changes exposed the insufficiency of established channels of political representation and precipitated revolt from below. But while that revolt, Populism, questioned liberal capitalism and upset old coalitions, it was the party of capital which rose to power in its wake. Liberal capitalism thus achieved hegemony.

The Republican triumph has been taken to support Burnham's view that the industrial-agrarian cleavage was preeminent in the electoral upheaval of the 1890s. The parties reorganized to correspond to that cleavage: the Republican party became not simply the party of capital but the party of industrialism, while the Democratic party became the party of the rural periphery and the South. As the party of industrialism, the Republican party dominated national politics and worked to promote capitalist industrialization, supporting the jurisprudential and administrative expansion of central government, and demobilizing lower-class electorates through assaults on the substantive, procedural, and patronage bases for political association and participation.[49]

Burnham thus connects the "system of 1896" to the creation of a "hole in the electorate," an empty political space occupied in other countries by socialist or social democratic parties. But the "hole in the electorate" which Burnham describes obscures the union-party tie that first emerged in 1896, because the broad contours of the industrial-agrarian cleavage conceal a realignment that took place among wage-earning constituencies. Though industrial workers were not coherently mobilized

[49]See Burnham, "Changing Shape," reprinted in Walter Dean Burnham, *Current Crisis in American Politics* (1982), 48–51, and his "Party Systems." Samuel P. Hays treats the bias of Progressive Era political and administrative reform against the working class in "The Politics of Reform in Municipal Government in the Progressive Era," *Pacific Northwest Quarterly,* 55 (1964), 157–69.

34

during this critical period, trade unions were: industrial workers voted Republican while trade unions sided with the Democrats. The result, I shall argue, was that unions preempted labor's political space. The hole in the American electorate was not a political vacuum but the area in which the trade-union mainstream would craft a "politics without class."

Again we face the question of why class politics did not materialize in the United States. The assumptions underlying this question have been assailed by some students of the labor movement. Some writers, notably Alan Dawley and David Montgomery, insist that the potential for such a politics was clearly there, because class struggle at the time was both measurable and irreconcilable.[50] Highly specialized studies have tried to elucidate these struggles, arguing the preeminence of worker hostility toward employers. Some have described the class-based intensity of union-employer struggles, others have stressed the struggles of workers rather than of institutions (unions).[51] If these struggles did not sustain explicit political expression, it was because they were stifled from above: by employer repression, union busting, Taylorism, labor elites, and the state.

There are several problems with this interpretation. First, unions were clearly politicized by their workplace struggles, but equally clearly they were politicized on the basis of institutional, rather than class concerns. If class conflict dominated the workplace, one would expect unions to represent the class, either at work or in politics. In practice, however, unions limited access to union membership, expressed antagonism toward new workers, and moved into political coalition with classes above rather than workers below. Second, if labor oligarchy explains union conservatism, one would expect unionists to have ousted that oligarchy in the elections that gave them periodic opportunity to do so. In practice, however, unionists from Lynn to Lawrence and New York to San Francisco expressed the prejudices and reproduced the agenda championed by the AFL in national politics. Institutional self-interest was the cornerstone of labor politics, but in significant respects that self-interest reflected the grievances and interest of the institution's constituency. E. E. Schattschneider's axiom is more useful here than Robert Michels' strictures: organization, in the first place, is the mobilization of bias.[52]

A third problem with this general perspective is the contention that the

---

[50]Dawley, 143, 181, 182; Montgomery, *Workers' Control.*
[51]E.g., Herbert Gutman, *Work, Culture and Society* (1977), 10–11, chap. 5.
[52]Schattschneider, 69.

state coerced labor into submission. In fact "the state" did not begin to deal systematic blows to labor until the Court invented antilabor jurisprudence in the mid-1890s. By then, as I shall show, the patterning of group-centered labor politics was already in process. Before the Supreme Court centralized and empowered the law against labor, state courts and local police were commonly invited to repress striking or organizing workers. As a result, state action against labor varied geographically, depending upon local statutes and the interpretation by local courts of the common law.[53] The effectiveness of state action also depended upon the willingness of local police to enforce legal sanctions against workers with whom they lived in close proximity. Indeed, because of the community roots of the local public police, enforcement of court rulings and protection of capital were by no means automatic: the police on occasion refused to wield clubs against strikers, sometimes deputized strikers, and even arrested strikebreakers.[54] This unpredictability encouraged industry to bypass localities and invent private instruments of repression; industrialists also solicited intervention from federal courts and federal troops, underscoring the complexity through the 1890s of the relationship between the state and labor.

In comparative perspective, moreover, the idea that a hostile American state repressed class politics looks dubious. States in Europe were surely more centralized, stronger, and at least equally hostile.[55] Workers across Europe mobilized within and against different states in different ways, of course, but the common pattern saw workers and unions becoming politicized as governments showed favor to capital during industrial transformation. Even a family comparison on the spectrum of "stateness" and coercion does not bring American labor into the family of European labor politics: Taff Vale, for example—in which the British High Court and House of Lords enjoined railway strikers and held them liable for strike damages—pushed British labor toward political independence; in the United States, by contrast, analogous applications of the Sherman Act and

[53]In the early 1880s unionists found federalism a far thornier problem than the central government. Thus Peter J. McGuire, long-time secretary-treasurer of the Brotherhood of Carpenters and Joiners and one of the founders of the AFL, appealed to Congress to nationalize jurisdiction over unions by granting general legal recognition to them. U.S. Senate, *Relations between Capital and Labor,* 1:323–26.

[54]Gutman, chap. 5; Johnson, 98–99.

[55]Cf. Lipset, "Radicalism or Reformism." Duverger, 1–60, pursues a similar theme when he connects the struggle for democracy in Europe to the forms of party organization which emerged there. See also Reinhard Bendix, *Nation-Building and Citizenship* (1977), 97–123.

Commerce Clause pushed the AFL more deeply into middle-class, coalition politics.

Perlman and Rogin provide useful insights in this regard, Perlman because he connects job consciousness to political pragmatism, and Rogin because he relates organizational factors to trade-union conservatism. For Perlman, job consciousness made unionization labor's priority; while for Rogin, labor's preoccupation with unionization heightened labor suspicions of government. Job-conscious unionism thus downplayed labor's role in politics. Simultaneously it generated a cautious politics that aimed at keeping the state out of the workplace whether as gladiator for employers (through injunctions) or as friendly surrogate for unions (through social welfare).

Perlman and Rogin, while they develop incisive analyses of the American trade-union mainstream, do not fully explain its tenacious conservatism. Perlman, and John Commons before him, link job consciousness to changes in the labor market.[56] But they cite job consciousness to account for the absence of European-style labor politics rather than to explain the style of labor politics which the AFL actually developed. They thus stop short of seeing changes in the labor market (which, they argue, underlay job consciousness) as the bridge between job-conscious unionism and the purposeful politics of American labor.

Rogin's examination of voluntarism exposes the rationale for trade-union politics and comes closest to explaining why the AFL clung so determinedly, if flexibly, to that rationale. Yet in Rogin's work one misses a sense of how conditions inside the working class at once validated, invigorated, and reproduced the organizational assumptions and interests of the "narrow constituency" he describes. Trade unions in Europe began with a job-focus; bread-and-butter unions, too, they organized better-paid, more skilled workers. But these European unions either built their own, or participated in, labor-based political institutions. They also accommodated, though not painlessly, larger wage-earning constituencies.[57] They also faced hostile states and employers, battling public and private impediments to trade-union autonomy. But they did not resist friendly state intervention—on the contrary, they mobilized in politics to make government friendly. Why was American labor so different? Volun-

[56]John Commons, "American Shoemaker, 1648–1895," *Labor and Administration* (1913), 219–66.
[57]The experience of British labor with the "new unionism" comes to mind; see Adelman, chap. 1, and Pelling, chap. 5.

tarism expressed the difference but does not in itself account for it. Similarly Rogin exposes the practical limitations and ideological inconsistencies of voluntarism but does not, himself, fully explain them.

Rogin's emphasis on the narrow constituency of the AFL nonetheless provides a key to understanding American trade-union politics. The AFL represented a small fraction of the working class while it claimed jurisdiction over the whole. The AFL fraction viewed new workers and a broader unionism as a threat to its own well-being. The very job consciousness that first made unionists out of workers then made unionists into exclusionists.

Job and status jealousies were typical of skilled workers in industrializing states. In the United States, however, these workplace divisions were more visibly and rigidly replicated in the community, because the immigration of the industrial era brought vast numbers of culturally, linguistically, and occupationally different workers into the American labor market. It was Slavs, Poles, Italians, and other "new" immigrants who performed unskilled and semiskilled work in industry. As a result, job-conscious unionism became suffused with ethnic and race consciousness. The constituency of trade unionism, in consequence, was consolidated on the basis both of craft *and* of caste. This combination politicized trade unionism while at the same time depoliticizing the class.

The effect of the new immigration was to make trade unionism resolute in its job consciousness and jealous of its organizational position. This was in part the AFL's response to its own membership. But more important, this was, as Rogin reasons, the result of the AFL's organizational interests and ambitions as AFL leaders understood them: chiefly to secure the autonomy to protect its organization and constituency from the working class as well as from the state and employers. As immigration and mechanization enlarged the "hole" in the labor movement, the AFL worked to maintain it. In so doing, the AFL made antagonisms within the class—and hence the interests of the group—preeminent. Fragmentation within the class, in turn, gave an advantage to the best-organized fragment, enhancing its institutional prospects. The institutional position of the AFL, given the size and bias of its constituency, favored the federation's assimilation into middle-class politics.

Voluntarism gave ideological stature to the group politics of the trade-union mainstream. The question at issue becomes not "Why no class politics?" but "Why group politics?" If the AFL substituted voluntarism for class ideology, what did it substitute for political independence? If it substituted interest-group coalitions for an alignment of party and class, why did cross-class affinities prove stronger than common workplace identities? What, finally, were the consequences of group-centered labor politics—for parties, for the state, and for the workers marginalized by trade unionism?

The Political Development of American Labor

What, in sum, is "exceptional" about American labor politics, and thus about American politics as a whole? Generally speaking the problem has been framed negatively, as the absence of a broad-based constituency behind unionism and the absence of an autonomous labor party. And generally speaking, explanations have rested with static legacies that determined that "it can't/couldn't happen here." We need, however, to recognize the political choices made by union labor as well as the institution building to which those choices were connected. Union labor was not simply narrowly based and politically dependent on middle-class parties; by the early twentieth century it was highly institutionalized and politically purposeful within the two-party system and the state.

My perspective requires analysis at two intersecting levels, the organization and the system,[58] and engages two questions. How and why did a narrowly organized union movement link up to the two-party system? How did union labor, within the confines of its narrow, subaltern status, help shape the political order that emerged in the twentieth century? The first question requires a look at the Gilded Age, when the so-called "second industrial revolution" (extensive growth of capital-intensive industries—e.g., steel, coal, rails) was in the United States and elsewhere accompanied by intense class conflict, challenges to the traditional (craft) organization of labor, and in many countries a "new unionism" linked to the broader solidarity of labor-based political action. We will take such a look at the development of the organizational and political bias of American union labor during the late-nineteenth century in Part II. The second question requires examination of the Progressive Era, when liberal elites in the United States and elsewhere forged alliances with cooperative labor leaders, attempted to create incipient "corporatist" states, and reinforced

---

[58] I thank Jeremiah Riemer for helping with this formulation. Michael Rogin makes a similar point in "Voluntarism," when he distinguishes between the "internal" and "external" purposes of AFL ideology.

labor discipline with new managerial structures for business. I undertake this examination in Part III.

The explanation I shall advance for the role played by labor in American political development hinges on the relationship between the organizational interest of the most durable union (the AFL) and the convergent national political issues of immigration, race, and labor-market policy. The organizational interest and organizing strategy of the AFL narrowed the scope of industrial action. Meanwhile the issues of immigration, race, and labor market established occupational, organizational and political boundaries within the American working class. Further, the relationship between its organizational and its political interests induced union labor to violate the letter of its voluntarist dogma, first by attaching itself at the national level to a nonlabor party and then by participating in government when that party came to power.

Together the organizational interest and the limited politicization of union labor split the working class politically along lines drawn by the overlapping criteria of skill and ethnicity. In contrast to countries where class *competed with* ethnicity (or religion, or language) to determine the political affiliation of workers, in America class *yielded to* political, organizational, occupational, and ethnic segmentation. Segments of the American working class supplied constituencies for existing political parties that did not need to engage in the socialist or countersocialist (linguistic-nationalist or religious-corporatist) appeals required of European labor parties and mass competitors with labor wings. Meanwhile the best-organized segment of the American working class claimed representation of the whole and used its monopoly of organization to forge ties through party to state, where it struggled to secure its institutional position in the name of racial protection and private-sector freedoms.

The fundamental trade-union interest in politics during the industrial period was to win economic and political conditions hospitable to trade-union autonomy. Autonomy meant the right of workers to organize into unions; the right of unions to be recognized by employers as bargaining agents for workers; the control by unions for their members of conditions of work and provision of benefits; the right of unions to engage in activities necessary to secure equal footing with employers in the workplace; and AFL superintendence of the labor movement. In its earliest conception, autonomy also meant independence for international craft unions and their locals, and it emphasized the independence of workers in and through their voluntary associations. These early promises gave way, however, to centralization of power in the AFL leadership and to coercive innovations designed to secure and regulate union presence in the work-place—for example, the closed shop and exclusionary criteria for membership.[59]

Unionists initially viewed the workplace as the appropriate arena and "economic action" as the appropriate method for struggle over the associational rights and autonomy of workers. But the changing political and economic climate of the late nineteenth century moved that struggle into the political arena, where the AFL complemented job-conscious unionism with organization-conscious politics. In fact the development of political and economic constraints to unionism forced the AFL to develop a political strategy while strengthening the AFL's view that trade unionism should be independent from political and governmental interference. The goal of trade-union autonomy mediated the relationship between the AFL's organizational interests and its political strategy. By the same token the ways in which the goal of autonomy became politicized determined the AFL's political strategy. The first and decisive factor to politicize the trade-union movement on a national scale was immigration. Immigration expanded the class, heightening job consciousness, and it fragmented the class, making divisions within it the basis for trade-union politics.

Massive immigration transformed the American labor market, starkly differentiating workers one from another on the basis of culture, language, and skill. Dramatic changes in immigration patterns—in the number and ethnicity of immigrants—coincided with rapid industrial and technological advances. Thus changes in the work process—through the expansion and mechanization of the workplace—coincided with changes in the composition of the labor supply. This increased the leverage of employers in their confrontations with unions while endangering the craft-based form of unionism institutionalized in the American Federation of Labor.

New immigrants were cheap, abundant, and unfamiliar with unions—attractive prospects for employers, especially in industries where mechanization had eliminated skill and experience as occupational criteria. Not only did employers recruit such workers to staff expanding enterprises but, in strike after strike, they replaced unionizing workers with new immigrants. Unions not only lost battles but in many instances lost the

[59]See Stuart Kaufman, *Samuel Gompers and the Origins of the American Federation of Labor* (1973), 168, 199. Membership criteria were established by the affiliates; they included proof of skill, proof of citizenship, and union credentials from the home country.

ground on which to fight those battles: by the mid-1890s, for example, unionism was moribund in steel and extinct in anthracite coal, two sectors that lay at the heart of industrialization.[60]

Equally important, new immigrants in industry raised questions about what kind of unionism and autonomy for whom. The trade-union constituency was made up chiefly of Irish, German, and native-born workers who for the most part were organized into unions by skill and by trade. Their unions fought with employers over the terms and conditions of work: wages, hours, regularity and security of employment, job control. On all counts—composition, structure, and function—trade unions served more privileged workers even though, in their struggles with employers and with government, they claimed to represent the whole working class. The preconditions for union success in bargaining with employers, and thus for the loyalty of the union membership and the strength of the union organization, were a labor market favorable to union control over the allocation of work and political deference to unionism itself.

Absorbing the new industrial workers who transformed the labor market from the 1880s on was not an obvious alternative for the AFL. To do so would have meant embracing the very workers unionists blamed for obstructing unionization (scabs), helping deskill the work process (green hands), and undercutting wage and job control claims of unions (cheap labor). To include unskilled and semiskilled ethnic workers, moreover, would have jeopardized the organizational and jurisdictional apparatus of established unions in the workplace, and would have challenged the monopoly of craft-based unionism over working-class organization. American unions, like their European contemporaries, were concerned with unionization in general, but they were equally concerned with maintaining their position as principal agents of unionization. This self-interest was rendered more acute when "native" trade unionism confronted industrial workers "imported" from abroad.

When the trade unions federated nationally in the 1880s, their national organization, the AFL, reflected these concerns. Organizational maintenance, for unions in the workplace and for the AFL in the labor movement, could be reconciled with a more encompassing, more heterogeneous—and more unpredictable—unionism only by sacrificing the institutional privileges of the AFL and by ignoring the status anxieties and economic jealousies of the constituency it was formed to serve. Nor, race

---

[60]In anthracite coal, employers began displacing old-stock workers with new immigrants in the mid-1870s. In steel, new immigrant scabs were recruited to break the Homestead Strike in 1892.

and craft aside, did a mass strategy promise a better harvest for unionism than did a job-conscious one. Inexperienced with unions and union struggles, newer workers were best known for union busting, both when they became workers beyond the reach of craft discipline and when they crossed picket lines to break strikes.

Immigration thus squeezed trade unionism from below. The trade-union response to this pressure was to mobilize, and then to lobby, for immigration restriction. The Chinese first called forth this response, crystallizing the labor movement in San Francisco. We remember this episode as Kearneyism; Samuel Gompers remembered it as pushing trade unions to affiliate nationally in what became the AFL.[61] On the heels of the Chinese menace came the Slav invasion of the anthracite coal fields. Soon thereafter steel and textiles fell, giving impetus to the centralization of exclusive trade unionism and to trade-union agitation for an exclusive polity.

Pressures from below also conditioned the AFL's attitude and behavior toward the state—toward both its hostile judgments and its friendly initiatives. Antilabor jurisprudence consolidated the group while validating union suspicions of government. Because of the AFL's resistance to a more inclusive unionism, the wider constituency was neither directly affected nor directly aroused by these legal questions. Hostile state action did not, as a result, provide a basis for class opposition. But it did provide an incentive to intensive group pressure on parties and officials to circumscribe the Court. Hence the AFL engaged in a "politics of interested minorities" to bargain for union autonomy from judicial interference as well as for union relief from immigration.

The AFL's suspicions of government, along with its definition of its own group interest, converged during the Progressive Era in AFL opposition to such worker-directed social reforms as wages and hours laws for men and unemployment insurance. The AFL, separated from the working class and shaped by its experience with the Court, viewed even positive government as labor's inexorable adversary.[62] Legislation to socialize uncertainty and to regulate the conditions of work it regarded not as complementary with but as alternative to benefits allocated to union members from union funds and as alternative to the bargain struck in the wage contract. An apparently friendly state was, by this logic, really a hostile

---

[61]Samuel Gompers, *Seventy Years of Life and Labor,* vol. 1 (1919), 216–17.
[62]Samuel Gompers, *Seventy Years of Life and Labor,* vol. 2 (1925), 26; Gompers, "Voluntary Basis of Trade Unionism," AFL Convention *Proceedings* (1924), 5; Gompers, ed., *Labor and the Employer* (1920), 149–51; and *American Federationist,* January 1917, p. 48.

43

one because it would substitute a relationship between worker and state for the still tenuous relationship between worker and union.[63] What is more, friendly state policies would reach beneath trade unionism to the rest of the working class. Not only would union incentives, and hence union autonomy, suffer at work, but union control of labor politics would be likely to suffer as well. The economic relationship between worker and state would also be a political one: a mass politics might develop where a mass unionism had not.

Immigration thus politicized the problem of entry into and competition within the labor market, moving the struggle for trade-union autonomy beyond the workplace and situating it within the politics of a split labor market. As anxieties about organization and labor market became focused politically—in reaction to developments in the class and actions by the state—opposition within rather than between classes came to dictate the political choices of union labor. Intraclass opposition became the basis for a union-conscious politics that defended the group from class and state. Out of this union-conscious politics the AFL would forge ties to the Democratic party under the "system of 1896," ties to capital during the first decade of the twentieth century, and ties to the state under the "decision of 1912."

[63]American unions were not alone in their suspicion of government, but they were unique in the duration and intensity of their suspicion. British unions, for example, were wary of certain proposals by the Liberal government (e.g., unemployment insurance); still, they argued for others (e.g., an improved workmen's compensation act and old-age pensions). In Germany, August Bebel warned in 1893 that "the state system of workingmen's insurance took away from the trade unions that branch of activity, and has in effect cut a vital nerve, as it were. For benefit systems had meant enormously in the furthering of unionism in Britain and among the German printers. Labor legislation has likewise preempted many other lines of activity which properly belong to the trade unions" (quoted in Perlman, 77–78). Despite this reading of the effect of Bismarck's welfare revolution, German unions, including the conservative ones, increasingly favored statist solutions to major social welfare questions. In both Britain and Germany, worker, union, and party pressures favored the incorporation of unions into the administration of those statist solutions.

CHAPTER 2

Old Labor and New Immigrants
The Antagonism

Your great obstacle in America, it seems to me, lies in the exceptional position of native-born workers. Up to 1848 one could speak
of a permanent native-born working class only as an exception. . . . Now such a class has developed and has also organized
itself on trade union lines to a great extent. But still it occupies an
aristocratic position and wherever possible leaves the ordinary
badly paid occupations to the immigrants. But these immigrants
are divided into different nationalities, which understand neither
one another, nor, for the most part, the language of the country. . . . To form a single party of these requires unusually powerful incentives. Often there is a sudden violent elan, but the bourgeoisie need only wait passively, and the dissimilar elements of
the working class fall apart again.

—Friedrich Engels, 1892

In the United States, economic and ethnic unrest were joined in trade
unionism, producing a group-focused labor politics. Industrialization provided the context and immigration the conditions for this patterning of
group conflict within the working class. Industrialization created the need
for an expanded labor force, and immigration filled it. Industrialization
differentiated the production process, thereby differentiating the labor
force according to function. Immigration added a racial and ethnic dimen-
sion to that functional separation by introducing racially and culturally
different workers into American industry. Industrialization gave rise to
worker organization; worker organization heightened employer interest in
securing labor-market conditions that would weaken the bargaining position of organized workers. Immigration provided those conditions, bring-

ing in new workers not only in opposition to settled workers but in opposition to their institutions, as well.

The massive immigration of workers from eastern, central, and southern Europe thus insinuated a very deep race problem within the American working class at the very moment that the trade-union movement was taking off.[1] This race problem increased in intensity, as immigration increased in volume, throughout the decades when trade unions in other countries were making their peace with industrial unionism and moving into labor-based parties.

Racism and ethnic antagonism within the working class is, of course, by no means distinctively American. Labor migration was part of the industrializing process in Europe also, and there too, though largely an internal migration, it produced divisions and hence tensions among workers. Karl Marx warned that hostility between Irish and British workers would be "the secret impotence . . . of the working class,"[2] while Max Weber gave intellectual stature to the resentments of German workers when he rose, in his Freiburg Inaugural, to defend the German national character against the Polish infiltration of the Ruhr. But these divisions were never so extensive in Britain and Germany as to prevent workers from participating in labor-based, reformist or social democratic parties.[3]

In South Africa and Australia, by contrast, where the color and culture lines were drawn far more sharply, racial solidarity among white workers helped consolidate labor parties and invigorated class-based politics. White workers in South Africa founded a labor party in 1910, demanding African exclusion from the capitalist sector: their race consciousness exploded against capital in the Rand Revolt of 1922 when they rallied behind the slogan "Workers of the world unite and fight for a white South

---

[1] I use the concept of race here as it was articulated in the politics of industrializing America. Blacks were clearly central to race theories and the "race problem," but by the late 1870s race thinking covered European ethnic and national differences as well. The Teutonic origins theory, which racially distinguished eastern, central, and southern Europeans from northern and western Europeans, was the chief formulation of race thinking as it applied to immigrants. See Thomas Gossett's fine *Race: The History of an Idea in America* (1963).

[2] Karl Marx and Frederick Engels, *Letters to Americans* (1953), 78.

[3] Celtic integration into British Labour was, to be sure, quite problematic and riddled with ethnic, labor-market, and nationalist enmity. Labour and Liberals often appealed for Celtic electoral support on nationalist grounds. Still, ethnic antagonism was pronounced. As Beatrice and Sidney Webb wrote upon their visit to Ireland in 1892: "We will tell you about Ireland when we come back. The people are charming but we detest them, as we should the Hottentots—for their very virtues. Home Rule is an absolute necessity *in order to depopulate the country of this detestable race.*" Quoted in Michael Hechter, *Internal Colonialism* (1977), 285, n. 2.

Africa.''[4] Australian workers reviled the Chinese and came together, in the 1890s, in a labor party that pressed, as its banner issue, the White Australia policy.[5]

Labor migration has generally been encouraged in opposition to settled workers and their institutions. The political significance and political consequence of that migration vary, however, with timing, scale, and context. Industry, in seeking new sources of lower-priced labor, has made an ethnic choice in favor of people whose experience with capitalist institutions lags behind that of workers already in place.[6] Discrimination by industry has tended either to reinforce or to provoke divisions and antagonisms among workers.

Like white workers in Australia and South Africa, ''old'' labor in the United States developed an exclusionist politics. But exclusionist labor politics produced relationships between unions, party, and state in the United States very different from those in Australia or South Africa, while positioning American labor on a political trajectory rather different from that of its European counterparts. Exclusionist labor politics developed outside the United States where white workers could define class in opposition to race. They were aided in this by sharp political and civil demarcations between class and race. Although class struggle ''for whites only'' contained peculiar contradictions, it nevertheless coexisted with the development of an independent labor politics. But in the United States, class and race interacted uneasily under the impact of class expansion through ethnic differentiation, and in a context of political equality. Ultimately, under the simultaneous weight of industrialization and the steady influx of new European workers, class solidarities in the United States gave way before race and status solidarities.

Organized labor, in adopting a protectionist stand against newer, cheaper labor, joined anticapitalist economic action with anti-immigrant economic and political action in an effort to limit the movement of newer and cheaper labor into the orbit of American capitalism. Significantly, exclusionist unionism in the United States not only was racist, but became increasingly

[4]Noted in Edna Bonacich, ''Capitalism and Race Relations in South Africa: A Split Labor Market Analysis,'' *Political Power and Social Theory*, 2 (1981), 252–55. See also George M. Fredrickson, *White Supremacy: A Comparative Study in American and South African History* (1981), 232–34.

[5]See J. T. Lang, *I Remember* (1950), 32.

[6]Everett C. Hughes, ''Queries Concerning Industry and Society Growing Out of the Study of Ethnic Relations in Industry,'' *American Sociological Review*, 14 (April 1949), 211–20; Bonacich, 245–47; and Fredrickson, chap. 5.

47

conservative as well. While white workers in Australia struggled *against* classes above to isolate and exclude the Chinese minority, for example, old-stock workers in the United States aligned *with* classes above to struggle against new immigrant masses below. And while white workers in South Africa treated their struggles against blacks as part of a class struggle with capital over maintaining a color bar in the capitalist sector,[7] American trade unionists regarded their campaign to create barriers to immigration as part of a group struggle to curtail expansion of the class beneath and thereby to consolidate trade-union autonomy at work and over the labor movement. Racism and progressivism became intertwined in the labor politics of Australia and South Africa, with devastating consequences for the targets of racism. In American labor politics, however, racism bred conservatism and retarded prospects for social democracy.

The immigration of the industrial era created an extraordinary heterogeneity in the United States. Between 1880 and 1920 nearly two-thirds of all immigrants came from outside northern and western Europe: from outside the "bourgeois fragment" that settled America and from outside the ethnic stock that had immigrated to it during the first half of the nineteenth century.[8] This contrasts sharply with other receiver societies: Argentina drew 67 percent of its immigrants from Spain and Italy; Canada drew 50 percent from the United Kingdom and 25 percent from the United States; and Australia drew nearly all from Britain and Ireland.[9] Among industrializers both in the core and on the frontier, moreover, the United States stands first for the proportion of its workforce occupied by immigrants from outside the dominant culture.[10] In the London of 1880, for example, immigrants from foreign countries accounted for only 1.6 percent of the population,[11] while a full 63 percent were native *to London*. In the New York of the same year, by contrast, immigrants and their children comprised 80 percent of the population and by 1890, 59 percent of the city's eligible electorate was foreign-born.

Even in Australia, where race antagonism was pronounced among white workers, the Chinese presence never threatened to displace the white-working class majority. In the United States, on the other hand, new immigrants had come by 1910 to occupy some two-thirds of the labor

---

[7]See H. J. and R. E. Simons, *Class and Colour in South Africa* (1969), 55, 88–90; Sheila Van der Horst, *Native Labour in South Africa* (1971), 171–83; and Bonacich, 253.

[8]U.S. Bureau of the Census, *Immigrants and Their Children: 1920* (1927), 62.

[9]Melvyn Dubofsky, *Industrialism and the American Worker* (1975), chap. 2.

[10]See Hughes, 214; Herbert Gutman, *Work, Culture and Society* (1977), 40–41; and Walter Galenson, ed., *Comparative Labor Movements* (1952).

[11]This does not include the Irish.

force in mining and manufacture. White Australian workers and unions could appeal to working-class majorities to build opposition to the Chinese, but settled American workers could only appeal to a fraction of the class to organize opposition to the new immigration. In South Africa, finally, white workers, and whites generally, were clearly a numerical minority. African absorption into the capitalist economy during the period when unions and parties formed was episodic and incomplete; racial subjugation, white political hegemony, and race barriers in industry gave white workers, however fearful of displacement in industry, the field to themselves in politics. But in the United States, immigration provided a steady flow of new workers into industry and into the political life of the nation.

Group-centered, coalition politics was the offspring of the American demographic dynamic. Immigration created and hardened divisions within the working class, separating settled and organizing workers from an imported proletarian underclass. Immigration was also a political issue that spanned and linked segments of classes in political coalition. Finally, the immediacy of the problem of immigration brought labor to rely on political resources that already existed: the ruling political parties and the electoral competition between them.

Gilded Age immigration aroused a defensive group consciousness in organizing labor because it coincided with blows dealt more frontally by courts and employers. The new immigration—disproportionately of male peasants and unskilled laborers—roused trade unionists against new workers because demographic changes coincided with technological, political, and economic setbacks to trade union efforts to empower workers through association in the workplace. Most new immigrants went directly into the labor market where, notwithstanding rapid industrial expansion, they came into competition with old labor and its workplace institutions. As one Congressman stressed in 1884, during debate on his proposal to prohibit contract labor:

> The percentage of females over fifteen years of age in 1883 from all European countries was 38.8, while from Hungary it was but 14.5, and from Italy, but 8. The percentage of common laborers from all European countries in 1883 was 25.5, while the percentage of common laborers from Italy and Hungary during the same year was over 61. . . . I find in three years a little over 80,000 Italians have been landed on our shores, and of this number nearly 70,000 are males. . . . They come in droves of males.[12]

[12]*Congressional Record*, 48th Cong., 2nd sess., 15 (June 19, 1884), 5349–52.

In important instances, moreover, immigration was directly connected to employers' efforts to police their work forces and obstruct unionization.[13] One of the earliest and clearest examples of this employer strategy occurred in the anthracite coal industry, which I discuss below.

Immigration was encouraged by the central government during the Civil War and courted by industrialists during the 1870s and '80s. It became a chronic handicap for organizing labor as the immigrant wave began to take on a life of its own in the 1880s. While the rise of laissez-faire constitutionalism in the 1890s enhanced the state's ability to police the activities of organizing workers, immigration empowered employers with armies of alternative, lower-priced labor—one flank of a larger industrial army that included labor spies, agents provocateurs, and private police. This dual handicap undercut the advances made by trade unionism in the years immediately after the Civil War. Immigration in particular seemed responsible for the new vulnerability of unions because, by expanding the labor pool and creating a reservoir of potential strikebreakers, it freed employers from the constraints of a tight, unionizing labor market.

Immigration thus heightened group identities based on race, function and organization among old-stock workers who were both more skilled and more organized. The institutional expression of this group consciousness was union structures and membership requirements that for the most part excluded new immigrant workers. This exclusion separated new immigrant workers from the political struggles that elsewhere brought workers into closer coalition with one another: in Germany, for example, following Bismarck's antisocialist laws and the establishment of tiered suffrage, and in Britain after the first surge in "new unionism" and Taff Vale.[14]

Even as American trade unionism began to face the contradictions that the fact of state power exposed in pure and simple unionism, it was confined to a narrow political space by its exclusionism. Raised initially about the Chinese but later generalized to include southern, central, and eastern European immigrants, the immigration question politicized settled workers as trade unionists along a cleavage that derived from their economic and racial position within the wage-earning class. The new immi-

[13]Hughes, 216, 220.
[14]Eric Hobsbawm, "The 'New Unionism' in Perspective," in Hobsbawm, *Workers: Worlds of Labor* (1984), 152–76. In discussing the discontinuous expansions in unionism in Britain and the European continent, Hobsbawm remarks: "If unions are to be effective they must mobilize, and therefore seek to recruit, not numbers of individuals but groups of workers sufficiently large for collective bargaining. They must recruit in lumps" (155). American unions did not recruit in lumps.

gration, unlike questions of wages and hours, could not be resolved through economic action. In theory, unions could win de facto immigration controls from employers through boycotts, strikes, and the union shop. But in practice, employers were unlikely to concede such controls as long as the state held open the doors to immigration and new workers were thereby available to break union efforts. Unions clearly needed laws to restrain immigration and thereby to limit the effectiveness of employers' labor-market remedies for unionism.

The advantage that the new immigration provided to employers—particularly as immigration interacted with mechanization—required a political response from union labor. That political response took the form of legislative struggles to secure a closed-shop society through qualitative restrictions on immigration. Initially unions pursued local remedies, for example, state-level regulations against the Chinese. But once the Supreme Court federalized immigration policy in the mid-1870s, states and localities could no longer resolve the issue.[15] The Court's ruling in effect federalized policy *silence* on the regulation of immigration. In combination with approval by the Congress, in 1864, of employer-recruited immigrant contract labor, federal silence with respect to the regulation of immigration placed the state squarely on the side of capital. As immigration became a national political issue, therefore, it was the state around which trade unions had to mobilize. Immigration accordingly cut against the local, voluntarist political habits that unions had adopted in recognition of the diffuse character of the national regime. As it politicized the labor movement, the immigration question nationalized labor politics. But it also neutralized the politics of class.

Lineages of Trade-Union Nativism

Between 1880 and 1920, 23.5 million immigrants entered the United States.[16] Overall, 63 percent came from countries outside northern and western Europe; during the decade of the most intense immigration, when they came at a rate of nearly a million a year, "new" immigrants ac-

[15]See Benjamin Klebaner, "State and Local Immigration Regulation in the United States before 1882," *International Review of Social History,* 3 (1958), 269–95, and Elmer Sandmeyer, "Anti-Chinese Legislation and the Federal Courts," *Pacific Historical Review,* 5 (1936), 194.
[16]By decade the figures were 2,598,214 (1851–60); 2,314,824 (1861–70); 2,812,191 (1871–80); 5,246,613 (1881–90); 3,687,564 (1891–1900); 8,795,386 (1901–10); 5,735,811 (1911–20). From U.S. Bureau of the Census, *Statistical Abstract of the United States: 1950* (1950), 97.

counted for some 78 percent of arrivals.[17] Of the initial new immigrant wave, close to 70 percent were men between fifteen and forty years of age,[18] and most became industrial workers in American factories and mines. Seventy percent settled in American cities: in 1900, 37 percent of New York City's population was foreign-born and 80 percent of New York City and Chicago were either foreign-born or of foreign parentage.[19]

This new immigration intensified economic and organizational anxieties among settled, organizing workers. The hostile response of old ("native") labor was directed not against immigration per se, however, but against the particular type of immigration that took hold during the industrializing period. Because many old-stock workers were themselves immigrants and because family reunification was contingent upon open frontiers, principled union opposition to all immigration was highly problematic. But new immigrants were visibly different: they moved into industry at lower levels and for lower wages, spoke unfamiliar languages, and carried different cultural baggage. Old-stock immigrants thus differed from the new, allowing "native" labor to specify opposition to immigration in qualitative, racial terms. As a result, racial argument became the dominant way in which labor expressed opposition to immigration. The preeminence of racial argument made nativists out of job-conscious unionists.

While nativism was not new to America, trade-union nativism was. Nativism had been a strong current in American politics before the Civil War, expressing Protestant antipathy toward immigrant Catholics.[20] Anti-Catholic nativism fed on religious stereotypes and articulated the belief that the Irish, in particular, were lacking in the discipline, sobriety, independence, and spirit of achievement that comprised the core of American virtue. Anti-Catholic nativism further celebrated America as "the political aspect of the Reformation," viewing the habits of Catholic foreigners as incompatible with American democracy. Arguing "Anglo-conformity" on the grounds that "the people made this government, and not the government the people," anti-Catholic nativists advocated political nativism, which sought to purify the ballot box by excluding Catholic immigrants from political participation.[21]

[17]Ibid.; U.S. Census, *Immigrants and Their Children: 1920*, 62.
[18]Gerald Rosenblum, *Immigrant Workers: Their Impact on Labor Radicalism* (1973), 34.
[19]Donald J. Bogue, *The Population of the United States* (1959), and Robert Hunter, *Poverty* (1904), 267.
[20]See Ray Allen Billington, *The Protestant Crusade: 1800–1860* (1963).
[21]For an illuminating presentation of political nativism, see Louis Dow Scisco, "Political

This antebellum anti-Catholic tradition persisted after the Civil War among elements of the middle class who battled for Prohibition, anti-saloon laws, and restrictions on parochial education. But a second strain of nativism also developed in the very constituencies targeted by anti-Catholic nativists. This new, race-principled nativism united Catholic Irish with other old-stock workers (and certain political elites) in a movement to restrict the entry of unskilled new immigrants into the American labor market. Among workers, at least, the religious cleavage that had once brought native and immigrant into conflict was superseded.[22] Now an ethnic and racial division brought settled immigrants, many Catholic, into conflict with new arrivals who, in many cases, were Catholic themselves.

A response to the economic and social transitions of the late nineteenth and early twentieth centuries, trade-union nativism developed from the conjuncture of new immigration and disruptive economic change. It was supported by a liberal tradition that was, in many circles, culturally or racially explained, by a nativist tradition that demanded conformity to the political culture, and by a racist tradition that ranked peoples in a racial hierarchy; and it conditioned the direction labor would take in American politics. That direction led toward the elevation of ethnic difference and antagonism to ideological heights and toward political action that put that ideology into practice. Racial nativism became a driving force behind union politics; laissez-faire liberalism (voluntarism) was its principal ideological formulation. Race and liberalism became intertwined in old labor's political argument against the corruption by new immigrants of American virtues, standards, and traditions.

Accelerated industrialization during the Civil War, along with the ferment over economic and social reform associated with the free-labor ethos, generated the context for trade-union nativism. The demand for arms and supplies spurred increased production; the demand for soldiers created manpower shortages. As a result the federal government passed an act to encourage immigration which not only held the doors wide open for labor migration but also allowed the recruitment of contract laborers and helped distribute immigrants upon arrival. Passage of the act led to the

---

Nativism in New York State" (diss., Columbia University, 1901). Michael Holt discusses the political impact of nativism in *The Political Crisis of the 1850s* (1978). See also Milton M. Gordon, *Assimilation in American Life* (1964), 85–98, and Charles E. Norton, ed., *Orations and Speeches of George William Curtis*, vol. 1 (1894), 51.

[22]David Montgomery treats antebellum nativism among workers in "The Shuttle and the Cross: Weavers and Artisans in the Kensington Riots of 1844," *Journal of Social History*, 5 (1972), 411–46.

formation of the American Emigrant Company, which imported laborers upon request by prospective employers, who advanced passage money and paid a commission to the Company.[23]

This wartime immigration act led to America's first systematic effort to import immigrant labor. Although the contract labor provisions of the act did not account for much of the post–Civil War new immigration, it established an apparatus for recruiting immigrants, and for making the expensive journey across the Atlantic affordable to the poor of the European hinterland. By allowing immigrants to mortgage their first year's earnings to pay their passage and providing for enforcement of those mortgages, the act aided employers' efforts to procure labor. In American gateway cities, labor exchanges also assisted employers by distributing immigrants to industry. As the new immigration began to develop momentum in the 1880s, employers were able to rely on this less expensive, direct recruitment of low-priced, and nonunion, workers in the gateway cities.[24]

Business and government continued to cooperate to promote immigration after the Civil War. The Republican party platform of 1868 pledged continued encouragement for immigration; the federal government tacitly endorsed continued immigration; and steamship companies, railroads, and land agencies joined industrial employers in improving efforts to recruit immigrants.[25] For the most part, immigration policy was lodged in the private sector, where it was a function of employers' manpower policies.

In the first few years immediately after the Civil War the American working class enjoyed an unprecedented unity.[26] Unity within union, despite partisan divisions among workers, healed the sharp divide between Protestant and Catholic workers. Labor reformism flourished, sometimes alongside Irish nationalism, sometimes alongside radical Republicanism. Moreover, conditions in the labor market favored labor: immigration rates were no higher than they had been during the decade before the war, internal, westward migration helped reduce the industrial labor supply, and the manpower demands of accelerated industrialization muted job competition. In this context of social and economic possibility, old unions were reorganized, new unions were founded, and separate

[23]George W. Stephenson, *A History of American Immigration, 1820–1924* (1926), 136.

[24]Maldwyn Allen Jones, *American Immigration* (1960), 191, 251, and *Congressional Record*, 49th Cong., 1st sess., 16 (1885), 2:1780–81.

[25]Stephenson, 138, 141. See also U.S. Congress, *House Executive Documents*, 42d Cong., 1st sess., no. 1, and 43d Cong., 1st sess., no. 287.

[26]Cf. David Montgomery, *Beyond Equality* (1967), chaps. 3 and 4.

crafts were amalgamated into national and international unions.[27] In some industries unionism was quite strong, and in some states the strength of labor influenced legislatures to promote the core claims of unions. In Pennsylvania, for example, miners won a maximum-hours statute in 1868. The leading objective of a revived and expanded labor movement was to secure legislation guaranteeing the eight-hour day. Federal passage in 1867 of an eight-hour statute covering government workers testified to the strength of the movement at this time.[28]

But labor's solidarity and ascendancy were short-lived. Capital and its political allies were not prepared to submit to the collective power of unions or to the criticism of northern economy and society implied by labor's organizing activities and its political demands. Expanding industry required new forms of labor discipline, while industrialism itself produced a more settled, less mobile working class. Both developments contributed to a crisis of the free-labor ideology. Labor discipline blunted labor-oriented reformism while generating workplace struggles over who would control that discipline. Moreover, the articulation of class demands through unions and labor-based political associations drew stark lines between "wage slavery" and privilege, cutting to the core of northern liberal egalitarianism.[29] As Democratic Irish workers and Republican German and native-born workers moved into association as unionists, the "harmony of interests" within the Republican free-labor coalition became discordant. At stake were labor and Republican understandings of free labor: for the former, free labor meant freedom from absolute dependence upon employers, if necessary through institutions of collective worker independence, but for the latter it meant individual self-ownership in a free market for labor. To Republican reformers, the collision of ideology and interest and its focus on labor conditions in the North posed a frontal assault on the political economy that the Union had fought to defend and extend.

As Republicans regrouped to defend the emerging economic order, employers developed strategies to resist combinations of workers by themselves combining and by policing their work forces. The principal innovations of capital under Reconstruction were the recruitment of cheap

[27]See George E. McNeill, *The Labor Movement: The Problem of Today* (1892), 125. The coal miners and cigar makers set the precedent when they nationalized their unions, in 1861 and 1864 respectively.

[28]Ibid., 131.

[29]See Montgomery, *Beyond Equality*; Eric Foner, *Free Soil, Free Labor, Free Men* (1970), and *Politics and Ideology in the Age of the Civil War* (1980), chaps. 4 and 6.

labor, rapid mechanization, the creation of industrial police forces, and industrywide cooperation to enforce labor policies. Workers responded with occasional acts of Luddism and frequent antiemployer militancy, but they also commonly expressed hostility to newer, cheaper labor. This last reaction would come to assume preeminence in union labor's political response to industrialism.

The early experiences of workers in two unionized industries are instructive. In shoemaking we can see an early linkage between job-conscious unionism and trade-union nativism. In anthracite coal mining we can see the replacement of a unionized workforce with new immigrant labor. Both cases show the interconnectedness of cheap labor, functionally and ethnically different labor, and union busting.

In the years after the Civil War perhaps the strongest trade union was the nationally organized Knights of St. Crispin, which represented workers in the shoe making industry. By 1870 the Knights claimed a total membership of fifty thousand, the majority concentrated in Massachusetts. Theirs was the largest organized following of any single union in the nineteenth century.[30] The Crispin organization derived its vigor from several sources, one being agitation for higher wages. The purchasing power of wage earners in shoe manufacture had declined precipitously since the antebellum period. Between 1858 and 1870 the cost of living had increased by 90 percent while wages increased only 50 percent; by 1870 the average daily wage for men in shoe manufacture was a scant $1.70.[31] But the most important stimulus to Crispin action was the combined threat from "green hands" and the sewing machine: both displaced skilled workers, intensified job competition, and complicated the position of the union.

The Crispins first expressed their hostility toward "green hands" by incorporating in their constitution a pledge against teaching the trade to new workers. "No member of this order," it read, "shall teach or aid in the teaching of any part or parts of boot or shoemaking," except to his own son, without permission granted by a three-fourths vote of his lodge.[32] But the sewing machine undermined this boycott. Because a new

[30]See John Hall, "The Knights of St. Crispin in Massachusetts, 1869–1878," *Journal of Economic History*, 18 (1957), 161; Don Lescohier, *The Knights of St. Crispin, 1864–1874*, Bulletin of the University of Wisconsin no. 355 (1910); and John Commons, "American Shoemaker, 1648–1895," in his *Labor and Administration* (1913), 219–66.

[31]Noted in Frederick Rudolph, "Chinamen in Yankeedom: Anti-Unionism in Massachusetts in 1870," *American Historical Review*, 53 (1947), 6, 10. Anthracite coal miners, for comparison, earned $2.50 a day.

[32]Quoted in Lescohier, 76.

worker could learn to operate it in a day—and without the help of craft workers—union regulation of training and apprenticeship did not assure union control over access to employment. The Crispins accordingly started to concentrate on the workplace, demanding of employers that the machines be operated only by union men at union wages.

The employers' initial response was to hire nonunion workers, but the typical nonunion worker hired locally became a loyal union member within a year. Consequently employers began to search for atypical workers who could be counted on not only to accept low wages but, more important, to not assimilate into the union. In 1869 a trade weekly proposed the use of Chinese workers. The New England Shoe and Leather Association endorsed the idea, arguing for cheap leather goods whatever the source.[33]

One enterprising manufacturer in North Adams, Massachusetts, acted upon this suggestion and imported seventy-five Chinese workers from San Francisco in 1870. Significantly the Chinese were imported to break a Crispin strike.[34] Unionists reacted to this strike-breaking innovation by denouncing the Chinese. Later, shoe manufacturers in Lynn called for industry cooperation to import more Chinese, and Chinese labor enabled some employers to reduce wages and fire union members. The Crispins responded with a political drive to exclude the Chinese from Massachusetts. They lobbied the legislature and appealed to fellow unionists in New York to restrict the entry of Chinese workers into the Massachusetts labor market.[35]

The Massachusetts legislature eventually refused to prohibit the importation of Chinese labor, but by that time tensions were abating, chiefly because the Chinese menace had itself dissipated—employers found the costs of importation and housing prohibitive.[36] But workers did not swiftly forget the incident. The fact that employers could turn to an alternative work force in the face of trade-union challenges underscored union vulnerability to employer manpower policy. More important, the incident in the Massachusetts shoe industry was not an isolated one. At about the same time the Chinese labor problem was unfolding dramatically in California, and Slavic laborers were being introduced into the anthracite coal industry.

[33]See Hall, 166–67.
[34]Ibid., 165.
[35]According to Lescohier, 37.
[36]Hall, 168. The transportation and housing costs for the seventy-five Chinese had totaled $10,000.

While employers in the Massachusetts boot and shoe industry experimented with Chinese labor, their opposite numbers in the anthracite coal industry undertook what would prove to be a more successful assault on a union. Like the boot and shoe workers, anthracite miners had organized a strong union, the Workingmen's Benevolent Association (WBA), which had dominated the coal trade since 1865. Though concentrated in a narrow, anthracite-rich corridor in northeastern Pennsylvania, the strength of the union reverberated across the state, affecting coal operators and the railroads that carried coal to market. But by 1875 the WBA had been destroyed.

The Civil War had been good to the industry. Between 1861 and 1864 the price of lump coal had more than doubled, from $3.89 to $8.39 per ton, coal operators had opened new collieries, and the railroads had built new lines to haul the coal to market. The end of the war, however, brought an end to the industry's good fortunes. By 1867 demand had slackened dramatically, and prices began to drop, eventually by half. The coal operators were hurt, as were the carriers who had come to depend on anthracite coal production for 90 percent of their freight. Freight profits for the Reading Railroad, for example, declined sharply, from $5 million in 1865 to barely $2 million in 1869.[37] But the coal miners bore the brunt of the industry's losses because their wages were based on the market price of their daily output. Overstocked markets lowered the value of daily output, and led operators periodically to shut collieries down—thus interrupting daily output—to compensate for earlier overproduction.

The miners responded by striking for a different wage basis. (Their strikes also suspended output until supply diminished to levels at which operators could raise prices.)[38] After WBA strikes during the summers of 1867 and 1868, union strength and improved market conditions induced coal operators to negotiate a new wage basis with the miners. The agreement tied wages directly to the market price of coal, but also established a minimum wage for miners at $2.50 per day.[39] The favorable wage scale so invigorated unionizing efforts that by 1870, 86 percent of the workforce belonged to the WBA. Also by 1870 most collieries were closed shops.[40]

[37]See Marvin Schlegel, *Ruler of the Reading* (1947); *Pottsville Miners' Journal* for 1869.
[38]Schlegel, 16ff., and Arthur Suffern, *Conciliation and Arbitration in the Coal Industry* (1915), 204.
[39]Schlegel, 19; Henry Rood, "The Mine Laborers in Pennsylvania," *Forum*, 14 (1892–93), 110–22; and Victor Greene, *The Slav Community on Strike* (1968).
[40]Suffern, 205.

The nature of the wage agreement encouraged the union to use the strike weapon to influence the price fetched by coal in the market. The union suspended work to control overproduction and sometimes to cut production enough to force an increase in coal prices, and thereby in miners' wages.[41] The situation was economically untenable for the railroads, whose profit from freight rates depended on the availability of freight rather than on the market price of freight. Led by the Reading, the carriers identified the union as the source of their troubles. To break the union, however, they needed to control the mines. Hence the Reading trebled freight rates in 1870, forcing the independent operators either to sell out or to accept oversight by the railroads. By the end of 1871 the Reading owned 70,000 acres of coal lands; by the end of 1873 it owned upward of 100,000 acres, or one-third of the coal lands in the entire anthracite basin.[42] Other carriers followed suit: by 1871 the Delaware, Lackawanna & Western, for example, controlled 17,000 acres in the northern fields. Railroad ownership of the mines made it possible for a handful of employers to consolidate labor policy against an industrywide union. It also gave the Reading sole control of the Schuylkill fields, the hotbed of unionism and labor militance.

Once in the business of coal production, the railroads, led by the Reading, set about destroying the union. They did this in a number of ways. An industrywide strike in 1871 provided an occasion to cut wages and to substitute for the minimum wage a minimum price per ton below which wages would not fluctuate with market price.[43] Employers now orchestrated periodic suspensions and lockouts to control for overproduction.[44] These suspensions and lockouts were deliberately unscheduled, keeping work and wages unpredictable, though in practice they ensured that workers would average fewer than one hundred sixty days in the mines during any single year. Further, the industry exercised political and police functions over the miners. Industrial communities became company towns. The Coal and Iron Police was organized to break strikes and otherwise maintain order. The Pinkerton Detective Agency was brought in, to spy on, provoke, and then to expose union activities.

The industry delivered its final blow to the WBA in the winter of 1875, during the five-month "Long Strike." The strike itself was probably lost

---

[41]Schlegel, 26.

[42]Eliot Jones, *The Anthracite Coal Combination in the U.S.* (1913), 29.

[43]U.S. House, *Labor Troubles in the Anthracite Regions of Pennsylvania, 1887–88,* 50th Cong., 2d sess., Report 4147 (1889); Suffern, 211.

[44]Henry D. Lloyd, *A Strike of Millionaires against Miners* (1890), 11.

even before it began: the union had disappeared from the northern fields after 1871, internal divisions had reduced enrollments elsewhere, and the remaining unionists were divided over whether to strike at all. The strike was, in effect, the last act in the struggle for union survival, and the industry worked to ensure that it was, in fact, the union's last act. Employers evicted families of strikers from company houses, fired and black-listed strikers, and drove union leaders from the state. Both the courts and the Catholic church came to the aid of employers, the courts by ruling union activity to be conspiratorial and criminal, the church by abusing the confessional and by excommunicating many strikers.[45] Where church and courts were impotent, employers relied on the Coal and Iron Police to enforce peace and discipline. The police also flanked the two thousand Slavic peasants imported by the industry to scab.[46]

The dispute that felled the union in 1875 occurred alongside the more violent struggle between the industry and the Molly Maguires. The campaign against the Mollies, masterminded by the Reading, had been set in motion after the strike of 1871. Initially the idea had been to sensationalize the Mollies, to underscore their Irishness, and thereby to create divisions within the union to which the Irish, Welsh, English, and Scots commonly belonged.[47] By 1875 the strategy had had some success, if we can judge from antagonisms between unionists and from the cautions of British miners against the union militancy that brought about the Long Strike.

In some respects the suspicions shared by British and Welsh miners toward the Irish—who were becoming the majority of the work force—were a carryover from Britain. More important, however, was the reinforcement of ethnic suspicion and antagonism by the functional and status differentiation of the anthracite coal work force. The British and Welsh had been brought in as skilled workers, and the few ''American'' miners were American-born sons of contract miners recruited in Britain and Wales.[48] The Irish, by contrast, were mere immigrants to the United States hired as unskilled manpower. The British and Welsh had been invited from their homeland where the Irish had been collected from the charities and labor exchanges of America's gateway cities, and such distinctions were reflected in the wages and categories of employment. Still,

[45]Greene, *Slav Community on Strike;* Anthony Bimba, *The Molly Maguires* (1965).
[46]See Rood, 112, and Greene, 61.
[47]Bimba, *Molly Maguires,* passim, and Wayne Broehl, *The Molly Maguires* (1965).
[48]Cf. Charlotte Erickson, *American Industry and the European Immigrant* (1957), 42, and Clifton Yearley, *Enterprise and Anthracite: Economics and Democracy in Schuylkill County, 1820–1875* (1961), 166.

British, Welsh, and Irish miners worked side by side in the same mines and over time joined the same union. Proximity and shared hostility toward employers bound unionists together until the popular identification of the Irish, the Mollies, and the union drove wedges into the union movement.

These divisions did not destroy the union, however, for the Irish were both the core of the labor force and the backbone of the organization. Hence employers, chiefly the Reading, were driven to other tactics. One was to arouse enmity toward the Irish by singling them out as targets of discrimination. Signs reading "Irish No Need Apply" (*sic*) were posted at Reading collieries and at others throughout the region. Another was to infiltrate the Mollies, incite them to violent acts, and then publicly to equate Irish violence and union activity. A Pinkerton detective did this, and on his testimony a dozen Mollies were sentenced to death in 1877.[49]

Once the union was dismantled, in 1875, the Molly Maguires were the only organized power left among the miners. Their destruction eliminated worker organization from the industry. The only remaining impediment to employer autonomy in anthracite coal was the possibility that the union would reappear. Employers accordingly set about constructing a union-free environment.

Employers had learned in 1871 the value of oversupply in the labor force.[50] Competition between workers for a day's wages promoted docility, particularly when work was irregular. One problem, then, was how to achieve that favorable balance in the labor supply.[51] A second problem was how to manage job competition so that docility did not yield to job consciousness and, through job consciousness, to unionism. The solution, it would turn out, lay in a joint manpower policy for employers in the anthracite coal region. The core of that policy was to build cheapness and heterogeneity into the labor supply—and thereby to weaken the position of English-speaking and organizationally skilled miners—by recruiting the kind of worker who had readily crossed picket lines in 1871 for a wage of ten to sixty cents a day. The central European peasant, so steeped in deference, so poor, and so desperate for the American dream that in Father James Huntington's words he "knelt down and kissed the hand of the boss who sent him to work," was that kind of worker.[52]

---

[49]Broehl, *Molly Maguires*. Allen Pinkerton tells his version of a Pinkerton's "evidence gathering" in *The Molly Maguires and the Detectives* (1877).

[50]Lloyd, 32, 48, 69.

[51]Cf. Erickson, 108.

[52]Quoted in Jane Addams, *Philanthropy and Social Progress* (1893).

Central, southern, and eastern European peasants were targets for recruitment for several reasons: they did not speak English; they had no experience with unions; they came from feudal or semifeudal societies; and they were refugees from an ascribed poverty. All of these characteristics set them apart from the established labor force and made them choice material for the building of a union-free industry. Low in cost and low in trade consciousness, these peasant immigrants would circumscribe unionism: they were, according to contemporary testimony, "as a matter of course, favorites with operators, as they never grumble about wages, and take what is given them by the company stores without murmuring, and . . . never strike."[53] Furthermore the barriers of language, of communal ties, of work habits and work experience, would retard trade-union expansion. These recruits were not part of the informal, international nexus of unionists which expanded with the arrival of every skilled worker from western Europe. Nor were they likely to undermine the anti-union strategy of employers as British recruits had done, twice in 1866 and repeatedly thereafter—by flatly refusing to work as scabs.[54]

The anthracite coal industry started actively to advertise for and to recruit such workers in the mid-1870s. It asked American consulates in Europe to place notices in local newspapers promising a minimum miner's wage, housing, and regular work.[55] Where American standards of living were insufficiently known, the industry hired recruiting agencies or sometimes sent its own agents to canvas the eastern European countryside for potential workers.[56] In 1884 the American consul at Budapest described the situation thus:

> There seems to be an agency at work which, by misrepresentations, induces people to leave their homes who will not better their condition thereby, nor benefit the country which receives them. People inquire by letter and in person at the consulate about this agency of which they have heard or read. . . . I have information that agents are managing the business a good

[53]Testimony of Captain Schoonmaker, brother of a large coke manufacturer, reported in the *Congressional Record,* 48th Cong., 2d sess., 15 (June 19, 1884), 5360.

[54]Erickson, 50.

[55]Ibid., 42. Samuel Gompers complained that, in fact, American consulates did far more than this. In 1883 he told a Senate committee: "I am complaining that the persons who were consuls abroad of this country should have permitted their personal and official signatures," certifying the trustworthiness of prospective American employers, "to be used in furtherance of private interests in the struggle between capital and labor, and should have thrown their influence into the scale in favor of capital." U.S. Senate, Committee on Education and Labor, *Relations between Capital and Labor,* Hearings, vol. 1 (1885), 279–82.

[56]W. J. Ghent, *Our Benevolent Feudalism* (1902), 35.

deal in the manner of the coolie trade, and that these immigrants are shipped to the United States like so many cattle.[57]

Beginning in 1875 and for at least a quarter-century thereafter, central, southern, and eastern European laborers flowed steadily into the anthracite coal basin of Pennsylvania. They came at a rate of twelve a day.[58] By 1890 they numbered 43,000—only a few thousand below the Irish population. By 1900 they totaled 89,000, outnumbering any single old-stock group by three to one and falling only 10,000 short of the combined total of Irish, English, Welsh, Scots, and Germans.[59] This wave of new immigrants doubled the labor supply, reinforcing competition for jobs with competition between cultures and organizational position. The new immigrants received lower pay, exacerbating cultural and occupational tensions, particularly because mechanization was simultaneously depressing the value of skilled career miners. They were associated with strike breaking and union busting, heightening organizational anxieties. In a sense these various tensions were also institutionalized by the industry, which cordoned off new immigrants in separate communities. Competition and isolation segmented identities, nourished resentments on both sides, and mixed anticapitalist feeling among unionists with ethnic antagonism between workers. As a measure of the employers' success in this work force reconstitution, a work force that had once been well-unionized fell into disarray: the union was moribund for twenty-five years while wages fluctuated downward in some areas and remained stubbornly fixed at 1875 levels in others.

The successful use of new immigrant labor to deflect unionization and promote discipline in anthracite coal invited imitation elsewhere, especially as the new immigration developed its own momentum. As Terence Powderly, Knights of Labor leader, recalled:

The immigration from Poland began to make itself felt in 1872. . . . The tide from Hungary began to set in in 1877. The railroad strike of that year created a desire on the part of the railroad operators to secure the services of cheap, docile men, who would tamely submit to restrictions and imposition. Hungary was flooded with advertisements which set forth the great advantages to be gained by emigration to America.[60]

[57]*Congressional Record*, June 19, 1884.
[58]Frank Julian Warne, *The Slav Invasion and the Mineworkers* (1905), 51.
[59]Ibid., 58; Suffern, 232.
[60]Terence V. Powderly, *Thirty Years of Labor* (1889), 428–29.

The employers' manpower policy, furthermore, invited union hostility toward new workers, whose social and occupational position and experience seemed to enhance the advantage of employers against unions. In testimony before a congressional committee investigating the relations between capital and labor, for example, Samuel Gompers explicitly associated the recruitment of immigrant workers with strike breaking.[61] In consequence, as the AFL and its unions were pressed to assume a defensive posture against employer assaults on a variety of fronts during the 1880s, they developed a protectionist stance with respect to their own constituency. As Gompers put it, "it is a question whether the workingmen of America shall eat rats, rice, or beefsteak."[62]

Equating the low wages and low union consciousness of new immigrants with "lowness on the scale of intelligence," old labor distanced itself from new immigrants using racial and ideological criteria. Describing new immigrants as "probably the offspring of serfs and slaves" and new immigrant workers as "willing slaves . . . willing to submit to almost any conditions," old labor and its political allies appealed to the free-labor ethos against degradation by new immigrants.[63] Where, before the Civil War, the ideology of free labor had produced labor support for abolition of slavery, in the Gilded Age it produced union demands for abolition of the new European labor migration. And where, before and during the Civil War, labor-market anxieties and race hostilities had produced profound ambivalence (and sometimes violence) toward free black labor, in the Gilded Age the free-labor market produced deep antagonism from old labor toward "servile" new immigrants.

Employers committed the first act of discrimination when they favored newer, cheaper labor that was, at least initially, socialized poorly if at all into the capitalist political economy. Unions responded to that discrimination by articulating an exclusionist politics.

Trade-Union Nativism and Labor Politics

Several students of American labor and American politics have commented on the significance of immigration for the "politics without class" that characterized American political development. Most agree that the presence of a vast imported proletariat undermined the chances for

[61]U.S. Senate, *Relations between Capital and Labor*, 1:279–82.
[62]Ibid., 282.
[63]*Congressional Record*, June 19, 1884.

class identity because, in politics, ethnic and religious identification took precedence.[64] A web of pseudo-conflicts thus limited the political significance of labor militancy. Many also argue that the magnitude of immigration intensified the competition for jobs and disruption in employment which accompanied rapid technological change.[65] This, it is said, underlay the job-conscious pragmatism of unionists, on the one hand, and the job-conscious instrumentalism of disorganized immigrant workers, on the other. Many scholars thus link immigration to jealousies within the class and thus to job-conscious unionism. Nonetheless the connection between the new immigration and the strange career of American trade unionism *in politics* has not been adequately pursued.

Those who analyze the consequences of immigration for politics have concentrated on the immigrants themselves, on their slowness to discover unionism, on ethnic politics, and on urban political machines. Gerald Rosenblum, for example, argues that immigrant workers were isolated from the American labor movement by their job-conscious, instrumental materialism.[66] Those who shared economic opportunity adapted quickly to the individualist premises of liberal capitalism: in their subjective orientation America offered a "second chance." For those who anticipated going back across the Atlantic with the rewards of American economic opportunity, meanwhile, America promised an eventual second chance back home: they were unlikely, therefore, to invest in indigenous American institutions or movements. Though two-thirds of new immigrants would ultimately remain in the United States, many viewed their position in the American working class as a transitional one.[67]

Other commentators have focused not on return migration but on the consequences of immigrant settlement in the United States for American democracy. John Commons, for example, labor's great defender in the early twentieth century, contended that immigrants were the bane of trade unionism and of American democracy.[68] Writing at the height of the new

[64]E.g., John Commons, "Immigration and Labor Problems," in Robert Marion La Follette, ed., *The Making of America: Labor* (1967), 236–61; Marx and Engels, 242–58; John Higham, *Send These to Me: Jews and Other Immigrants in Urban America* (1975), 22–25; and Gutman, 15.

[65]E.g., Selig Perlman, *A History of Trade Unionism in the United States* (1923), and *A Theory of the Labor Movement* (1928). One clergyman commented in 1887: "Not every foreigner is a workingman, but in the cities, at least, it may almost be said that every workingman is a foreigner." Quoted in Gutman, 40.

[66]Rosenblum, *Immigrant Workers*. See also Harry Jerome, *Migration and Business Cycles* (1926).

[67]Gabriel Kolko, *Main Currents in Modern American History* (1984), 69–72.

[68]Commons, "Immigration and Labor Problems," and "Class Conflict," in *Labor and Administration*, 78–79.

immigration, Commons complained that "the peasantry of Europe to-day is in large part the product of serfdom and of that race-subjection which produced serfdom. . . . How different from the qualities of the typical American citizen whose forefathers have erected our edifice of representative democracy."[69] Reformer E. L. Godkin of the *Nation* shared this view, commenting, in 1887:

> There has appeared in great force, and for the first time on American soil, the dependent, State-managed laborer of Europe, who declines to take care of himself in the old American fashion. When he is out of work, or does not like his work, he looks about and asks his fellow-citizens sullenly, if not menacingly, what they are going to do about it. He has brought with him, too, what is called "the labor problem," probably the most un-American of all the problems which American society has to work over to-day.[70]

Commons and Godkin were joined by James Bryce, who maintained that immigrants provided the fodder for patronage parties, corrupted city politics, and debilitated democracy wherever they settled.[71] In the main, such writers regarded immigrants as incapable of appreciating their citizenship rights because they came from unassimilable, inferior stock.

More recent scholars also connect the immigrant presence to the trajectory of American democracy. Ira Katznelson, for instance, explains that mid-nineteenth-century immigrants made possible the patterning of urban politics around communal and community identities at the expense of workplace and class interest.[72] According to this view, the patronage parties that ruled and rewarded loosely federated, largely ethnic clienteles were sufficiently institutionalized to mediate the political impact of industrialism, while ethnic identity was sufficiently resilient to withstand political appeals to workplace experience.[73]

[69]John R. Commons, *Races and Immigrants in America* (1907), 10–11.

[70]Quoted in Gossett, 298.

[71]John Commons, "Race and Democracy," *Chautauquan,* 38 (September 1903), 33–42; and James Bryce, *The American Commonwealth,* vol. 2 (1910), 103–4. For a less charged but related argument, see Elmer Cornwell, "Bosses, Machines, and Ethnic Groups," *Annals of the Academy of Political and Social Sciences,* 353 (May 1964), 22. More recent versions of this general view stress the political culture and political ethos carried by different immigrant groups. See Edward Banfield and James Q. Wilson, *City Politics* (1963), and Nathan Glazer and Daniel Patrick Moynihan, *Beyond the Melting Pot* (1970).

[72]Ira Katznelson, *City Trenches* (1981), pt. 1.

[73]On the importance of the structures of party politics and, more especially, on the role of organizational innovation in institutionalizing the urban political machine, see Martin Shefter, "The Electoral Foundations of the Political Machine: New York City, 1884–1897," in Joel Silbey, Allan Bogue, and William Flanigan, eds., *The History of American Electoral Behavior* (1978), 281–98.

What is needed, however, is a shift in the discussion. Whether or how immigrants were political "laggards" is less important than how the response to immigration made a political laggard of American trade unionism. My argument is that immigration, rather than immigrants, played the decisive role in formulating an American version of labor politics. What makes this American style of labor politics so important, I further argue, is its centrality to the institutional and political realignments of the Progressive Era—the realignments from which twentieth-century patterns of state and party development emerged. Courts and employers may have provided incentives for unions to get involved in politics, but it was segmentation within the working class as a result of immigration which became the *basis* for trade-union mobilization in politics. Labor politics was grounded in only a fragment of the class, but such was its organizational position that the fragment monopolized the political space of the entire class, shutting out other, labor-based alternatives.

Conservative, group-centered labor politics stalked American political development. Its monopoly of representation and organization unchecked by mass unionism or a class-based party during the turbulent industrial decades, old labor held class politics in check and, through its institutions—craft unions—even limited unionism itself. The most politically mature stratum of the American working class abjured labor-based politics and eschewed social democratic collectivism. It articulated a political program not in opposition to or critical of liberal capitalism but in defense of its own institutional position vis-à-vis class and state.

Ethnic and functional anxieties deflected organizing workers away from anti-employer militancy and reform-oriented political action, and toward securing labor-market conditions favorable to trade-union autonomy. The universalist attitudes of the Knights of Labor and the reformist goals of the older National Labor Union were displaced by the particularistic attitudes and defensive goals of the trade-union mainstream. This displacement was facilitated by the nativism and racism that preceded Gilded Age industrialization and by the development of nativist theories that gave scientific validity to racial explanations of poverty, economic conflict, and the degeneration of American democracy.[74]

[74]See Barbara Solomon, *Ancestors and Immigrants* (1956); Edward N. Saveth, *American Historians and European Immigrants, 1875–1925* (1948); John Higham, *Strangers in the Land* (1977); Edward Bemis, "Restriction of Immigration," *Andover Review*, 8 (March 1888), 250–64; Bemis, "The Distribution of Our Immigrants," ibid., 9 (June 1888), 587–96; Robert Hunter, "Immigration: the Annihilation of our Native Stock," *Commons*, 9 (April 1904); Francis Walker, "The Great Count of 1890," *Forum*, 11 (1891), 406–18; and Walker, "Immigration," *Yale Review*, 1 (1892), 125–45.

Immigration and labor markets interacted with race thinking and organizational interest to open the union path into party and state. One step along this path was the organizational isolation of unions from the working class; another was the electoral separation of old labor and new immigrants, which solidified union antistatism and restricted ties between state and class to ties between state and AFL.

Nativism defended craft-based unionism from a more comprehensive unionism, because industrial workers tended to be new immigrants. The craft structure of trade unionism thus "fitted" with the ideology of nativism, because both formalized antagonisms against the class beneath. New immigrants did unionize in exceptional cases (the New York needle trades, for example), but on the whole both employers and unions made an ethnic choice that worked to sustain old labor's monopoly of organization within the class. As a result, nativist trade unionism had the field to itself when it entered politics seeking remedies for demographic and judicial setbacks to its autonomy. Nativism, furthermore, had middle-class origins, and its diagnosis of social and political problems in industrial America had a middle-class appeal. The AFL thus found well-placed friends in national politics.

Where immigration, industrialization, and union building came together, there a combination of widespread suffrage, organizational interest, and race logic conditioned the labor politics of industrial America. These factors lay behind the role played by the trade-union mainstream in national politics. I do not mean to suggest that these factors tell the whole story. But they do complete the complex story of the political relationships that unions forged within and between classes, relationships that include the union–Democratic party tie after 1896, the union partnership with corporate liberals after 1900, and the participation of antistatist unions in the Democratic state under Woodrow Wilson. As the following chapters show in detail, these relationships quarantined the working class from unions and institutionalized opposition within, rather than between, classes.

PART II

The Union-Party Tie

CHAPTER 3

Meat vs. Rice (and Pasta)

Discovering Labor Politics in

California, 1875–85

In 1878, of 40,000 cigarmakers in the entire country, at least 10,000 were Chinamen employed in the cigar industry on the Pacific Coast. . . . Unless protective measures were taken, it was evident the whole industry would soon be "Chinaized". . . . This was an element in deciding the cigarmakers to give early and hearty endorsement to the movement for a national organization of labor unions, for the help of all wage earners was needed in support of Chinese exclusion.
—Samuel Gompers, *Seventy Years of Life and Labor*,
vol. 1, 1919

The first sustained and dramatic instance of union politicization on the basis of labor-market pressures occurred in California when white workers in San Francisco mobilized against the Chinese.[1] From this mobilization San Francisco emerged as one of union labor's strongholds. But the mobilization of union bias against new workers was not limited to California, and the anti-Chinese movement was only the beginning of trade-union nativism. From the mid-1870s a profound racial and nativist strain would be at the political core of trade unionism.

Although the "Chinese menace" was geographically contained, the anti-Chinese movement must be viewed in a national context. It invigorated national union solidarity. It gave racial dress to union interest, endowing traditional job- and organization-conscious unionism with a

[1] Alexander Saxton provides an excellent and complete treatment of the history of this mobilization in *The Indispensable Enemy: Labor and the Anti-Chinese Movement in California* (1971). My discussion follows many of Saxton's insights.

coincident race consciousness. It produced a union logic whereby old labor distinguished itself from new immigrants on the basis of its conformity with liberal tradition, values, and structures. It provided a solvent for the tension between union voluntarism and ethnic partisanship. By 1896 these developments had prepared the way for a union-party tie that sent old labor and new immigrants along separate electoral paths. And by the following year these developments had placed a class-neutral but group-charged demand for restricted immigration at the heart of the trade-union political agenda.[2]

In several crucial respects, then, anti-Chinese agitation in California foreshadowed a more general trade-union nativism, which transposed anticapitalist feeling with anti-immigrant hostility. Although directed against a group that only remotely affected workers in other localities, the California struggle causally associated the dislocations of advancing industrialization with the entry of new workers into the labor supply. While nativist anxieties about the labor market did not displace more traditional labor-capital conflicts in the workplace (over wages, hours, and union recognition), these same anxieties dissipated any movement toward class politics. A mixture of economic, racial, and national arguments against the Chinese provided old labor with organizational and political defenses to use against the more sweeping demographic change brought on by new immigration from Europe.[3] Within the labor movement, ethnic exclusion solidifed craft-based exclusion, stripping union economic action of its class potential. In politics, that class potential was further weakened as unions identified their political priorities in terms of union antagonism toward "undesirable" workers. Later, as injunctions and antitrust liability broadened union political interests, the group structuration of the working class held the pursuit of those interests within the boundaries of group politics.

"Class feeling" fell to "race feeling," but race feeling considerably enhanced "union feeling." Indeed, the coincidence of episodic booms in the San Francisco labor movement and action against the Chinese suggested to labor leaders that race feeling was an important source of soli-

[2]Samuel Gompers defended the plank in 1902, saying: "This regulation will exclude hardly any of the natives of Great Britain, Ireland, Germany or Scandinavia. It will exclude only a small proportion of our immigrants from North Italy. It will shut out a considerable number of South Italians and Slavs and others equally or more undesirable or injurious." AFL *Proceedings* (1902), 21–22.

[3]Saxton, 273–79, and A. T. Lane, "American Trade Unions, Mass Immigration, and the Literacy Test, 1900–1917," *Labor History*, 25 (Winter 1984), 5–25, discuss union analogies between Chinese and new immigrants.

darity within old labor.[4] The interaction of race feeling and union feeling encouraged the internal (organizational) development of old labor. One reason it did so was that among the trades "invaded" by the Chinese in San Francisco was the cigar industry. In addition to being well-organized in the East, the cigar trade was among the leaders in the labor movement. Convinced by colleagues in San Francisco that "unless protective measures [are] taken, it is evident that the whole industry [will] soon be 'Chinaized,'" eastern cigar makers joined the anti-Chinese crusaders in the West. In fact, as cigar unionist Samual Gompers recalled in his autobiography, the Chinese problem was "an element in deciding the cigar makers to give early and hearty endorsement to the movement for a national organization of labor . . . for the help of all wage earners was needed in support of Chinese exclusion."[5]

The Chinese presence helped define not only these internal interests but the external (political) goals of old labor as well. The issues of race and labor market were created by unregulated immigration and demanded an unambiguous political remedy: pass a law. Winning passage of a law, however, drew unions into the orbit of the state, extending bread-and-butter unionism into the political sphere. The solution to the Chinese problem lay with Congress, moreover, and so the anti-Chinese campaign nationalized union politics. While motivating old labor to concerted union action, the Chinese question provided a peculiar bridge between unionism and national politics.

The nationalization of the trade-union movement in the 1870s and '80s thus coincided with its politicization. Its voluntarist pretensions notwithstanding, the national trade-union movement was from its early days concerned with a political goal, one that not only pushed the movement into partisan politics on a national scale, but also demanded state intervention on labor's behalf. The prominence of this political goal had enormous and enormously negative consequences for class-based labor politics in the United States.[6] American workers, like their counterparts in other countries, were shaped by their earliest political struggles. European workers struggled initially for suffrage, however—a dispassionate goal as between workers. American workers, enfranchised without struggle, mo-

---

[4]See Frank Roney, *Frank Roney, Irish Rebel and California Labor Leader: An Autobiography* (1931), chaps. 4–5.

[5]Samuel Gompers, *Seventy Years of Life and Labor*, vol. 1 (1919), 217.

[6]Henry George argued in his reassessment of the "Chinese problem" in 1880 that the use of the Chinese issue in labor mobilization distracted and immobilized labor radicalism. "The Kearney Agitation in California," *Popular Science Monthly*, 17 (August 1980), 433–53.

bilized to restrict immigration—a dispassionate goal as between classes though highly charged within classes. Both European and American labor went on to struggle with state sanctions against working-class activity, but they did so from very different starting points. Suffrage hung on inequality between classes, immigration on racial and ethnic difference within the working class. Labor-based political action reflected this difference: suffrage often required European labor to mobilize outside established political channels where immigration required American unions to mobilize within existing politics. This internal mobilization was first worked out around the issue of anti-Chinese legislation; eventually a more general national accommodation would be struck on the issue of immigration from eastern and southern Europe.

Background to the Anti-Chinese Movement

When a working class coalesced in San Francisco in the late 1860s, it inherited a tradition of antagonism toward the Chinese that had first found expression in the mining frontier.[7] By 1867 the Chinese issue had become central for California workers as well as for astute California politicians, principally because of disruptive changes in the size and the distribution of California's population. Between 1860 and 1870 the population of the city of San Francisco more than doubled, from 57,000 to almost 150,000.[8] Several developments gave the Bay Area labor market nearly one-third of the state's population. First, declining yields in the mines after 1865 sent thousands of white miners into the city to look for work. Second, the construction of the transcontinental railroad enabled fifty thousand people to migrate overland in 1868 and 1869; most of them gravitated to San Francisco. Third, with the completion of the railroad in 1869, another ten thousand white and Chinese workers moved to San Francisco to find work. Fourth, as the mining communities folded the Chinese relocated in San Francisco; by 1871 one of every three workers in the city was Chinese. Fifth, the California population was disproportionately male; the overwhelming majority of those who settled in San Francisco entered the

[7]Cf. Saxton, chap. 3; Mary Roberts Coolidge, *Chinese Immigration* (1909); Hubert Howe Bancroft, *Works,* vol. 38 (1887); and Carl C. Plehn, "Labor in California," *Yale Review,* 4 (1896), 410.
[8]U.S. Bureau of the Census, Ninth Census, vol. 1, *Population* (1872), 15.

labor market, and by 1871 there were four workers for every job.[9] Finally, employers stepped up their efforts to recruit new workers. They organized the California Labor and Employment Exchange and the Immigrant Aid Association to encourage further overland migration from the East.[10]

These labor-market pressures did not develop in a political vacuum. The state and capital (mainly the railroads) seemed to be in league behind the expansion of the labor market, chiefly through the continuing entry of Chinese.[11] Two political catalysts in this regard were the conclusion of the Burlingame Treaty in 1868 and the promulgation of a pro-Chinese hiring policy by the Southern Pacific Railroad in 1870. The Burlingame Treaty established reciprocal most-favored-nation rights between the United States and China. Among these rights was voluntary emigration: the preamble to the treaty expressly affirmed the "inalienable right" of any person to change home and allegiance. The treaty seemed to invite the Chinese, and the arrival of some twenty-two thousand new Chinese immigrants in San Francisco between 1868 and 1871 encouraged white workers to identify joblessness and wage reductions with the Chinese presence. Workers were aroused against further Chinese incursions when the Southern Pacific announced that it intended to rely on Chinese labor in projected railroad construction.[12]

The immediate consequences of the Bay Area's population boom were the reduction of wages and the extension of the working day. These losses combined with the pressure of unemployment to focus worker anxiety on labor-market fluidity. Because the Chinese were a highly visible segment of the San Francisco labor force (13.2 percent in 1870),[13] white workers tended to blame the Chinese for unfavorable wages and working conditions. That the Chinese were racially and culturally different eased this transposition of job consciousness and nativism.

Race consciousness, as an expression of anxieties about the labor market, was prefigured by the race-conscious political heritage of the California mining frontier. But it was also prefigured in the race-conscious political heritage of the antebellum and Civil War working class. In this

[9]Lucille Eaves, *History of California Labor Legislation* (1910), 3; Elmer Sandmeyer, *The Anti-Chinese Movement in California* (1939), 17.

[10]Eaves, *History of California Labor Legislation;* Coolidge, 65, 350; Ira Cross, *History of the Labor Movement in California* (1935), 61.

[11]The railroads were long identified as the importers of Chinese contract labor. Legislation to enforce such contracts triggered the first cries for Chinese exclusion in the spring of 1852. See *Daily Alta California*, March 10, 21, April 12, May 4, 1852.

[12]See Coolidge, 350; Cross, 64.

[13]Ninth Census, *Population*, 768.

regard, the composition of San Francisco's white working class is relevant: the city's population was nearly 50 percent foreign-born. Of the white immigrant population, 41 percent were born in Ireland; of the white working population, 25 percent were Irish born.[14]

The political lineage of Irish immigrants was a complicated one. The Irish (and German Catholics) had themselves been targets of nativists in the East, so a new rationale was required before they could become carriers of nativist unionism. But that rationale was, in a sense, already there, in the Irish political lineage that tied most Irish to the Democratic party. That lineage descended from the Jacksonian producer ethic through urban party systems to Democratic conceptions of race and equality. Both their Democratic heritage and their experience with anti-Catholic nativism separated most Irish from Republicanism and especially from the weakest component of Republicanism—the assertion of equality for blacks. Irish Democratic sympathies had been expressed in wartime elections in New York and Pennsylvania; Irish race hostilities had been demonstrated in wartime riots.[15]

In San Francisco, therefore, a significant segment of the white working class carried a political heritage that interacted easily with race-conscious mobilization against Chinese labor competition. The interaction of race consciousness and job consciousness, Democratic affinities and unionism, meant for the union movement that race offered a new rationale for nativism, following which former victims of nativism would themselves become nativists. Race consciousness was an important precondition for the way in which white labor articulated its labor-market anxieties; meanwhile, interdependent anxieties about race and labor market liberated the

[14]Ibid., 347, 768. When Chinese viceroy Li Hung Chang toured the United States in 1896, he specifically singled out the Irish as carriers of anti-Chinese hatred: "We know that the Geary Act [the 1892 extension of the Chinese Exclusion Act] is due to the influence of the Irish and the laboring classes, who wish to monopolize the labor market. . . . The Chinese can live cheaper than the Irish. . . . Your laboring classes hate the Chinese because they are the possessors of higher virtues than themselves." Quoted in *New York Times*, September 3, 1896, p. 10.

[15]Joel Silbey discusses the potency of race, on the one hand, and of ethnoreligious liberalism, on the other, for Democratic constituencies in *A Respectable Minority: The Democratic Party in the Civil War Era, 1860–1868* (1977). See also Eric Foner, *Free Soil, Free Labor, Free Men: The Ideology of the Republican Party before the Civil War* (1970), 231; Saxton, 28–29; and James F. Richardson, *The New York Police: Colonial Times to 1901* (1970), 130–42. According to Richardson, the New York draft riots of July 1863 erupted as a consequence of social and labor market conditions, specifically the fact that the rich could buy themselves out of the draft and the competition between Irish and black workers. The rioters were generally lower-class Irish. The riots were at one level probably class acts but at another fraught with race feeling. Similarly, though Irish anti-Republicanism reflected race and class feeling, it also expressed a strong and defensive cultural consciousness triggered by Republican-associated anti-Catholic nativism.

immigration question from the constraints of ethnoreligious argument. Race dissolved the antebellum antinativist consensus among old-stock Catholic workers after the Civil War. The Chinese issue was the vehicle for that dissolution; the organizational and political consolidation of old labor against new immigrants was the result.

The Anti-Chinese Movement, 1870–80

After 1870 direct competition from Chinese labor in two critical industries spurred workers to organize around the Chinese issue. The cigar makers and the boot and shoe workers brought anti-Chinese nativism to the forefront of unionism. Their success in mobiling working-class support, in uniting workers in a common cause, and in generating incentives for vigilant anti-Chinese solidarity stemmed from several factors. First, workers in both trades were affiliated with vigorous national unions—the Cigar Makers' International Union and the Knights of St. Crispin. Second, eastern members of both trades endorsed the anti-Chinese maneuvers of California workers because cheap Chinese labor jeopardized the position of eastern products in the national market. Third, both trades focused on the Chinese issue at a time when workers were seeking someone to blame for unemployment and wage cuts. Finally, both trades were, in fact, objectively affected by Chinese labor; anti-Chinese nativism was legitimated by economic self-interest.[16]

In the spring of 1870 the Knights of St. Crispin launched the first of a series of campaigns that would culminate in Kearneyism. In the previous year five hundred Crispins had been defeated in a strike for higher wages,[17] and in 1867 and 1868 many Crispins had drifted away from wage work to establish small cooperatives in competition with manufacturers. Both actions led boot and shoe employers to rely increasingly on Chinese labor in order to become competitive with eastern factories.

[16]In 1870 the labor force in the boot and shoe industry was 19 percent Chinese-born, 26 percent Irish-born, 18 percent German-born, and 3 percent British-born. Twenty percent was U.S.-born, though presumably many of this group were children of old-stock immigrant groups. In 1870, 91 percent of the labor force in cigars and tobacco was Chinese. The labor force in both industries was more than 90 percent male. Statistics compiled from the 1870 U.S. Census in Coolidge, 359.

[17]The total number of boot and shoe workers in San Francisco was 600 in 1868; by 1870 they numbered 1,500. Cross, 57.

Employers were abetted by rapid mechanization of the industry, which allowed them to replace skilled white labor with unskilled Chinese.[18]

Consequently the Knights of St. Crispin precipitated a struggle with employers in 1870, demanding both a wage increase and the elimination of Chinese labor from the industry. Because their protest followed on the heels of the Southern Pacific announcement that it would rely on Chinese labor, workers outside the boot and shoe industry joined the Crispins' cause. A further spur to concerted action was the annual arrival of more than ten thousand able-bodied Chinese men at the San Francisco Custom House.

Anticoolie clubs joined the Crispins and other trade unions in the first Anti-Chinese Convention of California.[19] In support of the strikers the group orchestrated anti-Chinese demonstrations and mass meetings in San Francisco. Workers marched through the city waving placards denouncing the Chinese: "Women's Rights and No More Chinese Chambermaids," "Our Women are Degraded by Coolie Labor," "American Trade Needs No Coolie." In addition, committees of unemployed workers were sent from shop to shop to demand the ouster of the Chinese, and boycotts were organized against Chinese-made goods. By August 1870 the Anti-Chinese Convention had formulated political demands. It condemned the coolie system, urged the immediate abrogation of the Burlingame Treaty, demanded an end to Chinese immigration, denounced public officials who employed Chinese, and opposed the permissive policies that enabled steamship companies to recruit and carry Chinese immigrants.[20]

Eastern labor groups meanwhile sponsored anti-Chinese rallies in Boston and New York City. This anti-Chinese nativism in the East resulted from a combination of imagined and real impingement by Chinese labor. The importation of Chinese labor into the Massachusetts shoe industry was a direct experience for one sector of eastern white labor. But in addition, various commentators had aroused eastern anxieties about the Chinese threat. In an article for the New York *Tribune,* for example, Henry George indicted the "long-tailed barbarians" for "making princes of our capitalists . . . and crushing workers into the dust." After describing the ubiquity of the Chinese in San Francisco, he predicted that "in every case

---

[18]Coolidge, 57. In the East, mechanization encouraged the employment of women and children in the boot and shoe industry. By the early 1870s women constituted 48 percent of the work force. In San Francisco in 1870 the boot and shoe work force was 94 percent male.

[19]Other labor organizations included the Carpenter's Eight Hour League and the Machinists, Stone Masons, Plumbers, and Carpenters' and Joiners' unions.

[20]See Elmer Sandmeyer, *The Anti-Chinese Movement in California* (1939), 47–48.

in which Chinese comes into fair competition with white labor, the whites must either retire from the field or come down to the Chinese standard of living.''[21]

George's prediction was immediately germane for the cigar industry, where the emergence of national markets had brought Chinese-made cigars into competition with cigars made by eastern white labor. Of all trades in San Francisco, moreover, cigar manufacture was the most severely affected by Chinese labor: of 1,800 cigar makers in 1870, 91 percent were Chinese. Cigar makers in California, because of the lower cost of Chinese labor, averaged wages 10 percent lower than in twenty other states. California cigar manufacturers with no little success had shifted to Chinese labor in order to secure an advantageous position in the national market. As a result, eastern cigar makers—notably Samuel Gompers and Adolphe Strasser, president of the Cigar Makers' International Union—defended the anti-Chinese posture of their California colleagues and actively involved themselves in the exclusion movement.[22]

Aside from grooming Samuel Gompers for leadership of the American Federation of Labor, the most durable contribution of white cigar makers to trade unionism grew out of their efforts to reassert control over the cigar-making trade. In 1874 cigar makers revived and refashioned the union label as a certificate for white labor.[23] Chinese-made goods could not bear the union label, which facilitated boycotts. The label turned out to be a potent weapon of trade unionism was well as of anti-Chinese nativism. By 1880 the San Francisco cigar-making industry had been forced to reduce the proportion of Chinese in the work force to 33 percent. So effective was the label as a symbol of trade unionism and instrument of anti-Chinese economic action that manufacturers and merchants produced counterfeit labels. When the state legislature declined to make counterfeit union labels illegal in 1878, and when the U.S. Patent Office refused to copyright the union label in 1879, the fight to protect the label became a focal battle for the trade-union movement. This linkage of union label, white labor, and union shop revealed the organic connection between nativism and trade unionism.[24]

By 1875 anti-Chinese nativism had gripped the white working class in

[21]Henry George, "The Chinese on the Pacific Coast," *New York Tribune*, May 1, 1869, pp. 1, 3.
[22]Coolidge, 359, 366; Gompers, 216–17; Samuel Gompers and Herman Guttstadt, *Meat vs. Rice: American Manhood vs. Asiatic Coolieism: Which Shall Survive?* (1902).
[23]Saxton, 74.
[24]California *Assembly Journal*, 23d sess. (1880), 78; E. R. Spedden, "The Trade Union Label," Johns Hopkins University *Studies*, ser. 28, no. 2, 89 n. 1.

San Francisco, partly because of trade-union campaigns against the Chinese and partly because of new pressures on the labor market following the eastern Panic of 1873. California was spared the immediate economic crisis created by the panic, but between 1873 and 1875 it was forced to absorb 154,300 overland migrants who moved west to escape the eastern depression. Most migrants located in San Francisco where they swelled an already congested labor market.

The economic problems generated by unemployment were aggravated by mining stock panics in 1875 which depreciated stock values and ruined many speculators. Meanwhile the period 1873–76 saw the largest influx of Chinese immigrants in California's history: 20,000 in 1873, 14,000 in 1874, 16,000 in 1875, and 23,000 in 1876. Despite the obvious abundance of white labor created by overland migration, employers continued to recruit specifically Chinese workers. The California Immigrant Union argued in 1875 that "Chinamen are a necessary evil at present, for the reason that most of the young men of our state and newcomers generally, will not work for small wages. As soon as this is remedied by an importation of Eastern and European labor willing to work for $1 to $1.50 per day, the employment of Chinese will gradually be diminished." When a financial and industrial crisis finally hit California in 1876–77, white workers blamed the Chinese.[25] Although the immediate causes of the crisis had little to do with the Chinese, the response singled them out for destabilizing the labor market. Chinese exclusion was presented as a precondition for economic revival.

The Democratic party played the Chinese card to win control of California in 1867 and to secure that control in 1876.[26] During the 1876 campaign, Democratic candidates passionately denounced the Chinese, demanded immediate restrictions on Chinese immigration and immediate deportation of resident Chinese, and advocated changes in the Burlingame Treaty.[27] Nationally the Democratic platform included a forceful denunciation of the Chinese based on their putative racial inferiority and their (racially determined) inability to assimilate.[28] As the party out of power

[25]Cross, 69; Sandmeyer, 16–17; Coolidge, 354.

[26]The Democratic party had, since the late 1860s, pressed the Chinese issue as a means of regaining a competitive position in California politics. The tactic made sense, given popular opinion and the influence of pro-Chinese railroads in the Republican party. The large Irish presence in California, especially in San Francisco, probably eased Democratic rejuvenation, since Irish-Democratic ties from another time and another neighborhood could be strengthened through a common anti-Chinese nativism.

[27]See Sandmeyer, 49.

[28]Kirk H. Porter and Donald B. Johnson, *National Party Platforms, 1840–1960* (1961), 50, 54.

during the 1860s, the Democratic party worked well as a vehicle of protest. But in the 1870s, when the full force of depression inflamed the antagonism of white workers toward Chinese, the Democratic party was the party in power. Though William Irwin, Democratic governor of California, and Andrew Jackson Bryant, Democratic mayor of San Francisco, lent their authority to the anti-Chinese cause (convening anti-Chinese meetings, sending lobbyists to Washington), once in power the Democratic party was compromised as a vehicle of protest. As part of the California political establishment the Democratic party was an unlikely conduit for the worker discontent unleashed by depression, especially when it had not delivered relief from the Chinese. Although the state party's actions were limited by the Supreme Court's decision to federalize immigration policy, white workers generally took the party's failure to effect anti-Chinese policies as indicating that its nativist promises had been hollow.[29]

White workers, particularly the unemployed, were thus ripe for independent political mobilization. During the summer of 1877 Denis Kearney aroused their mass opposition to the Chinese in the sand-lot rallies that shook San Francisco.[30] The Democratic promise was incomplete and the reach of unionism was limited by unemployment, so anti-Chinese furor was not easily channeled through existing social and political institutions. In August, Kearney formed the Workingmen's party of California, an independent political party that occupied the institutional vacuum. The party's purpose was to "extirpate the Chinese"; its constituency united white workers with elements of the middle class, chiefly small property holders like Kearney himself.[31]

The sand-lot rallies now emblematic of Kearneyism were set off not by Chinese issue, however, but by the great railroad strike that began to spread nationwide in the midsummer of 1877. According to Frank Roney, a central figure in the city's trade unionism, San Francisco was drawn into the vortex of labor mobilization when the strike was extended to the Pennsylvania Railroad. Excited organizers invited the city's residents to the sand-lots in front of city hall in celebration. Thousands responded, listening to speeches from "all shades of political thought . . . [but] those who were most vociferously applauded pointed to the Chinaman as the true source of all the trouble."[32]

---

[29]James Bryce, *The American Commonwealth*, vol. 2 (1910), 449.
[30]San Francisco *Examiner*, July 24–28, 1877.
[31]Roney, 300; Ralph Kauer, "The Workingmen's Party of California," *Pacific Historical Review*, 13 (September 1944), 278–91.
[32]Roney, 269.

Denis Kearney, by most accounts, was something of a crank. It is doubtful that he was committed to any kind of political program beyond Chinese exclusion. His working-class roots somewhat obscured by his petit-bourgeois position in Gilded Age society—he was an independent drayman—Kearney was only marginally connected to earlier trade-union struggles against the Chinese. Indeed, some have maintained that Kearney was only marginally a nativist, that the anti-Chinese movement was for him merely an opportunity to embark on a political career.[33] Still, whether a principled or an opportunistic racist, Kearney won a mass following almost instantly—especially from among San Francisco's aggrieved and unemployed workers—when he inveighed against the Chinese. Though neither a labor leader nor a workingman in any class sense, Kearney was a powerful rhetorician of nativism, articulating the labor-market anxieties of white labor in class-neutral terms. He thereby helped redirect conflict between labor and capital into group-charged competition in the political arena.

Kearney's dubious credentials notwithstanding, the Workingmen's party gave political focus to nearly ten years of working-class agitation against the Chinese. It arose confidently, to cleanse California of the Chinese.[34] Speaking for its working-class nativist base, the party's first platform promised to rid the country of the Chinese; to wrest government from the rich (that is, the railroads who recruited and employed Chinese workers); to destroy the power of wealth through taxation; to elect only Workingmen to public office; and to mark as public enemies all employers of the Chinese.[35] In addition, party officers issued a manifesto:

We have made no secret of our intentions. . . . Before you and the world, we declare that the Chinamen must leave our shores. We declare that white men, and women, and boys, and girls, cannot live as the people of the great republic should and compete with the single Chinese coolies in the labor market. . . . To an American, death is preferable to life on a par with the Chinamen.

[33]Ibid., 271; Roney alleges that Kearney's anti-Chinese nativism was disingenuous. He suggests, too, that Kearney's speeches were being written by somebody on the *Chronicle* staff, the *Chronicle* being the San Francisco newspaper that enjoyed widened circulation as a result of the play it gave to the Chinese problem and Kearney agitation. Whatever the case, with each speech, Kearney's rhetoric become more intemperate. By early fall he would recklessly suggest that "a little judicious hanging would be the best course to pursue with the capitalists," while "a few fires would clear the atmosphere." San Francisco *Evening Bulletin*, September 22, 1877.

[34]Cf. Eaves, 33.

[35]Kauer, 280.

Explaining why independent political action was necessary, the declaration continued:

> What then is left to us? Our votes! We can organize. We can vote our friends into all the offices of the state. We can send our representatives to Washington. We can use all the legitimate means to convince our countrymen of our misfortune, and ask them to vote the moon-eyed nuisance out of the country. But this may fail. Congress, as you have seen, has often been manipulated by thieves, speculators, land grabbers, bloated bondholders, railroad magnates, and shoddy aristocracy. . . . Our own legislature is little better. The rich rule them by bribes. . . . We call upon our fellow workingmen to show their hands, to cast their ballots aright, and to elect the men of their choice. We declare to them that when they have shown their will that "john" shall leave our shores. . . . Is this treason? Then make the most of it. Treason is better than to labor beside a Chinese slave. . . . The reign of the bloated knaves is over.[36]

The Democratic party would eventually redirect this anti-Chinese insurgency into its own channels. But at the outset the response of established parties was to collaborate in order to squelch the Workingmen's movement. Mayor Bryant issued a ban on public gatherings. Municipal authorities arrested Kearney and his partners in leadership, Knight and Day.[37] The bipartisan establishment took legislative action to proscribe the movement's activities—especially the violent demonstrations against the Chinese provoked by Kearney and his audiences.[38] The state legislature also increased the size of the San Francisco police force by statute and appropriated $20,000 to be spent at the governor's discretion to protect the public peace.

When Kearney and the Workingmen refused to surrender to law, Republicans and Democrats formed bipartisan vigilance and safety committees to quell social disorder and appealed to Congress for federal action against immigrant Chinese.[39] When the Workingmen began running candidates and winning elections—as they did in the spring of 1878—Re-

---

[36]Quoted in Cross, 98, 99.

[37]See Hubert Howe Bancroft, *History of California*, vol. 7 (1887), 358; San Francisco *Examiner*, October 30, 1877, and *Evening Bulletin*, November 5, 1877.

[38]One of the more notorious legislative enactments was the "Gag Law" of 1878, which prescribed criminal penalties for speaking before groups of twenty-five or more "with intent to incite riots or acts of criminal violence." California Legislature, *Amendments to the Codes* (1877–78), 117.

[39]Kauer, 281.

publicans and Democrats again converged, forming bipartisan slates to consolidate their electoral power against the Workingmen.[40]

Under assault by the ruling parties, the Workingmen's party also came into conflict with unions late in the spring of 1878. Kearney was able to retain control of the movement, but his refusal to compromise with union labor generated union-party conflicts that eventually restored unionism to the organizational center of anti-Chinese nativism. Eventually, too, the Democratic party would resume its position as the political vehicle for anti-Chinese demands.

Trade unionists within the Workingmen's party closed ranks against Kearney, who resisted full union participation in the movement. A permanent schism developed between Kearney and trade-union leaders (most important of whom was Frank Roney) over two issues: union representation on the party's central committee and the unions' role in party decision making.[41] For a brief time the trade-union faction even expelled Kearney and claimed the party for itself. Kearney soon enlisted a personal following, however, to establish a rump party and regain control by invading the ward clubs. By the time of the state constitutional convention, which was convened in June 1878, Kearney and his followers had suppressed the trade-union faction, run a slate of convention delegates, and won one-third of the convention seats (51 of 152).[42] Union-labor and Democratic management of the Chinese issue was still a year away.

The Workingmen were largely responsible for the decisions of the state's constitutional convention, both because their movement had occasioned the call for the convention and because they dominated the proceedings.[43] The three principal issues facing the convention were the railroads, taxation, and the Chinese. The Workingmen traded support for the Grangers on railroads and taxes for Granger support on the Chinese question. This Granger-Workingmen coalition was not unnatural, for small farmers were rapidly growing resentful of the increasing reliance of large farmers on cheap Chinese labor. In Reconstruction America, more-

[40]The Workingmen elected an assemblyman from Santa Clara, a state senator from Alameda, the mayor and city attorney of Sacramento, the mayor, police judge, district attorney, and justice of the peace of Oakland, and municipal officials in Santa Cruz, San Leandro, and Redwood City. Kauer, 282.

[41]Roney, 295–96.

[42]San Francisco *Examiner*, May 8, 15, 1878; Cross, 113; and Eaves, 36.

[43]Kauer, 283–84; Theodore H. Hittell, "Observations on the New Constitution," *Overland Monthly*, 1 (January 1883), 34–41; Eaves, *History of California Labor Legislation*; and George, "Kearney Agitation in California," 446.

over, the labor movement and land reformism were interconnected.[44] Once allied, Grangers and Workingmen formed a controlling plurality of convention delegates.

Although the convention was dominated by representatives of workingmen, the new constitution, according to Henry George, "entrenched vested rights—especially in land—more thoroughly than before, and interposed barriers to future radicalism by a provision in regard to amendments which it will require almost a revolution to break through. It was anything but a workingmen's constitution: it levied a poll tax without exemption, disenfranchised a considerable part of the floating labor vote, and introduced a property qualification. . . ."[45] Indeed, what was in good measure a "Workingmen's constitution" *dis*enfranchised fragments of the working class and politically institutionalized the group bias of urban white labor.

For George, the Chinese presence had once been symptomatic of the monopoly problem. Now, however, the anti-Chinese obsession of politicized workers—though still symptomatic of the problem and though superficially antagonistic to capital—seemed to play directly into the hands of monopoly. As George now reasoned, labor politics built around the race question was ultimately a distraction. Such a politics prevented workers from coming to terms with the fundamental questions of land ownership and the shrinking opportunity for individual enterprise.

But as far as the Workingmen were concerned, the Chinese question *was* fundamental, so the new constitution *was* a Workingman's constitution: it contained at least eight anti-Chinese provisions. It forever barred the Chinese from voting, it denied the Chinese access to employment on public works projects, and it prohibited corporations from hiring Chinese. It also empowered the legislature to impose conditions for Chinese residence and removal, impose penalties on the importation of coolie or contract labor, find ways to discourage or prohibit Chinese immigration, and designate certain geographic limits on Chinese residence.[46] The con-

[44]The symbiotic relationship between the labor movement and land reform, unionism and Irish nationalism, in Reconstruction America is developed by Eric Foner, "Class, Ethnicity, and Radicalism in the Gilded Age: The Land League and Irish-America," in Foner, *Politics and Ideology in the Age of the Civil War* (1980), 150–201, and by David Montgomery, *Beyond Equality* (1967).

[45]George, "Kearney Agitation in California," 446.

[46]Eaves, 37; Carey McWilliams, *Factories in the Field* (1944), 73. The anti-Chinese clauses of the new constitution were challenged in the courts by affected corporations. In a lengthy opinion the U.S. Circuit Court ruled that any provision of the California Constitution and of state

85

vention debate on the Chinese question strongly suggests that these provisions were more than tactical efforts to regulate labor-market competition. Speech after speech betrayed the extent to which the economic rationale of anti-Chinese nativism had been subsumed by popularly held racial prejudice. One speaker decried the "moon-eyed lepers"; others argued that the Chinese race would be the destruction of white civilization: "If clover and hay be planted upon the same soil, the clover will ruin the hay, because clover lives upon less than the hay; and so it is in this struggle between the races. The Mongolian race will live and run the Caucasian race out."[47]

Drawing strength from the popularity of the anti-Chinese cause, the Workingmen were now tempted to broaden their political efforts. The party nominated a complete slate of candidates for the 1879 municipal elections in San Francisco and elected Workingmen to a number of offices, most important the city's new mayor. In the same election Workingmen also offered an "Against Chinese Immigration" entry on the statewide ballot; it was approved by a vote of 150,000 to 900.[48]

After the 1879 elections, however, and despite its strong showing, the Workingmen's party dissipated rapidly. Lack of influence with the San Francisco Board of Supervisors handcuffed the mayor. Although the mayor had pledged to use the city's powers to resolve the Chinese problem and to relieve unemployment, he was unable to do so. With the Workingmen unable to use the law against the Chinese, fears spread that they would take to the streets and pillage Chinatown or massacre Chinese. Public hostility toward rumors of insurgency hardened irreparably when the mayor's son shot and killed Charles DeYoung, editor and publisher of the San Francisco *Chronicle,* in the spring of 1880.[49]

Other developments also helped erode the Workingmen's base. In 1878 union labor, disgruntled with Kearney and unsuccessful in its power struggle within the party, moved its anti-Chinese nativism into union structures. Though established under the auspices of the Workingmen's party, the Representative Assembly of Trades and Labor Unions soon parted

---

statutes which conflicted with the Burlingame Treaty was invalid. The court further held that the California enactments against corporate employment of Chinese violated the due-process clause of the Fourteenth Amendment. *In Re Tiburcio Parrott,* 6 Sawyer 349–89.

[47]See *Debates and Proceedings of the Constitutional Convention of California,* 2 (1881), 700–704.

[48]See Cross, 123; Kauer, 287.

[49]Charles DeYoung had earlier shot the mayor during his campaign for the office. DeYoung, whose newspaper had been a journalistic arm for the Workingmen, had had his own candidate in mind for the mayor's race. He used his paper to discredit Isaac Kalloch during the campaign, and Kalloch retaliated from the pulpit, whence he impugned the reputation of DeYoung's mother.

company with the (largely unemployed) insurgents, directing its anti-Chinese activities into more traditional union channels. This institutionalizing of anti-Chinese labor politics did not in itself destroy Kearney's efforts, but it certainly played a role in the Workingmen's self-destruction. With the movement's demise, unions and the Democratic party moved back into the center of anti-Chinese politics.

Kearney himself helped provoke the collapse of the Workingmen's party. He summarily declared an alliance with the national Greenback Labor party in the spring of 1880, at a time when the electoral futures of both parties were in serious doubt.[50] By 1880, Greenback Labor nationally was losing its labor-based support, in part as a result of craft-union voluntarism and in part as a result of Irish defections back to the Democratic party. The Irish had earlier given critical support to the third-party effort, particularly in Pennsylvania, but their long-standing Democratic sympathies were reactivated when Knights of Labor leader Terence Powderly, Fenian Michael Wood, and union leaders grew wary of the third-party cause.[51] Similarly union suspicion of third-party mobilization, particularly a party under the incorrigible Denis Kearney, and seemingly transcendent Democratic partisanship chipped away at the Workingmen's electoral base.

Most Workingmen, especially the Irish among them, had been and still were basically Democrats.[52] Defection to an independent party at the local level could coexist with general Democratic identification, especially in a relatively new city and in a fledgling urban party system. Even in older Democratic cities, after all, parties and machines were not always able to contain working-class insurgency: Tammany suffered an erosion of working-class support during the mid-1870s and in 1886 was challenged by a third party that attracted many working-class Irish and Germans.[53] Still, such electoral insurgency was usually short-lived, because the Democratic party typically made itself accessible to the influence of local labor and

[50]For the complicated story of Greenback Labor see Ralph R. Ricker, *The Greenback-Labor Movement in Pennsylvania* (1966), especially 124–25.

[51]See Francis G. Couvares, *The Remaking of Pittsburgh: Class and Culture in an Industrializing City* (1984), 67–69.

[52]Roney, 303–4.

[53]Steven P. Erie, "The Organization of Irish-Americans into Urban Institutions: Building the Political Machine, 1840–1896," paper delivered to the American Political Science Association (1983); Martin Shefter, "The Electoral Foundations of the Political Machine: New York City, 1884–1897," in Joel Silbey, Allan G. Bogue, and William H. Flanigan, eds., *The History of American Electoral Behavior* (1978), 263–99. For a history of machine building in San Francisco, see William Bullough, *The Blind Boss and His City: Christopher Augustine Buckley and Nineteenth Century San Francisco* (1979).

managed salient labor issues. If sustained extra-Democratic mobilization was unusual at the local level, insurgency was even more difficult within the national party system. Affiliation with a national independent party required a complete break with intense partisanships based in bitter Civil War experience. Irish-Democratic solidarities in particular were deep and of long standing, because of the party's Jacksonian message, its offer of a shield against anti-Catholic nativists, and, in older urban centers to which large numbers of Irish immigrants flocked, its capture of Irish partisanship through management of patronage and control of naturalization and electoral ritual.[54] A break with existing parties required powerful incentive— not supplied by the Greenback Labor party, which had focused on the currency question and held aloof from the Chinese question and which in any case was beginning its decline. Stronger incentive was provided by the Democratic party, which reclaimed the anti-Chinese banner in 1880 and thereby derailed wildcat politics.

Democrats within the Workingmen's party moved in 1880 to redirect the anti-Chinese movement into Democratic institutions. First, they struck a patronage bargain with Workingmen candidates and bosses in the San Francisco supervisorial elections. Later, Democratic Workingmen called a state convention, expelled Kearney, and announced their support for the national platform and candidates of the Democratic party.[55] Kearney was ultimately forced to retire from politics, under police protection, and to return to managing his business.

Democrats, Unions, and the Yellow Peril

The Democratic party profited enormously from the dissolution of the Workingmen's party. But along with the GOP, it benefited even more from the experience of the Workingmen's movement. Kearneyism taught both parties what can happen when workers, feeling betrayed on all sides by politicians, unite in common cause: it demonstrated the power of the labor vote. But it also showed that the labor vote could be harnessed without conceding class-charged, labor-specific demands such as the reg-

[54]See Lee Benson, *The Concept of Jacksonian Democracy* (1961), especially chaps. 7, 8, 14; Paul Kleppner, *The Cross of Culture: A Social Analysis of Midwestern Politics, 1850–1900* (1970); Joseph Schafer, ed., *The Intimate Letters of Carl Schurz, 1841–1869* (1928); Clifton Yearley, *The Money Machines: The Breakdown of Reform of Governmental and Party Finance in the North, 1860–1920* (1972); and Amy Bridges, *A City in the Republic* (1984), chap. 5.
[55]Cross, 127.

ulation of hours and wages. As a result, both parties were quick to espouse the anti-Chinese catechism after the state's constitutional convention. California Republicans pursued Chinese exclusion in Congress, and in 1880 the national Republican platform included an anti-Chinese plank. But despite this platform provision, Republicans outside California were uncertain nativists. Indeed, Republican President Rutherford Hayes vetoed an 1879 bill limiting any ocean vessel from carrying more than fifteen Chinese; that veto, along with principled opposition to Chinese exclusion from a vocal minority of Senate Republicans, made Republican anti-Chinese rhetoric ring somewhat hollow. Principled Democratic anti-Chinese nativism was more credible. California Democrats formed a majority in the State Assembly behind stringent policies toward Chinese residents, while the national Democratic party dominated a majority in Congress behind Chinese exclusion bills.[56]

For the Republicans, anti-Chinese nativist rhetoric was electorally necessary in California. For the Democrats, the anti-Chinese shibboleth was also electorally necessary—especially if the Democratic party was to hang on to the labor vote.[57] For the Republicans, the Chinese issue was a divisive one: steamship companies and railroads had invested heavily in Chinese immigration, and abolitionist and radical Republicans believed that at the core of anti-Chinese nativism lay race prejudice.[58] The Democrats found anti-Chinese nativism easier to embrace. Though the Democratic party had long sheltered white immigrants against anti-Catholic nativism, its advocacy of ethnoreligious liberalism was not connected to racial liberalism. Indeed, the constituency of ethnoreligious liberalism had often seen itself in competition with, or in opposition to, the constituency of racial liberalism. As long as the Chinese stood in analogy to blacks rather than to old-stock immigrant groups, anti-Chinese nativism did not engage ideological controversy within the Democratic party. The Chi-

[56]In 1880, for example, the Democratic coalition in the state legislature enacted the McCallion Bill, providing for removal of Chinese from nonurban communities whose well-being was jeopardized by the Chinese presence. *Daily Alta California,* April 28, 1882, p. 1.

[57]In April 1882 the *New York Tribune* commented that the Democratic Party hoped to become strong in California through hatred of the Chinese. In his lecture "Politics Makes Cowards of Us All," the Honorable Frank M. Pixley echoed this view of the Democratic Party: "We need not recapitulate the thronging incidents . . . riots against the draft in New York, riots against negroes . . . and the sand-lot uprising in San Francisco—to demonstrate how utterly wanting is the Democratic Party of the element of self-respect and courage. The reason of this cowardice is obvious to us all. These criminal and ignorant classes have votes. They can be used to secure the political ascendancy of the party that secures their adhesion." *Daily Alta California,* August 21, 1882, p. 1.

[58]*Daily Alta California,* March 4, 1882, p. 1, March 9, 1882, p. 1; Saxton, 133–37.

nese-black analogy was quite prominent in the debate over Chinese exclusion, both among abolitionist and radical Republicans and among Democrats. In Meridien, Mississippi, the *Mercury* advocated more Chinese immigration, reasoning both that Chinese and blacks offered equivalent forms of labor and that Chinese habits would be good for blacks.[59] In New York City the *Tribune* assailed Democratic race analogies: "If there is a despicable prejudice anywhere in this land, of which all decent men are heartily ashamed, the Democratic party has not failed to appeal to that prejudice, and to stake its existence upon the strength and permanence of this narrow and contemptible policy."[60] In a way the Chinese issue raised the "bloody shirt." By 1880 it had moved to the center of national politics.

Economic recovery facilitated the absorption of most white workers into the California Democratic party. It also made possible the resurgence of trade unionism in San Francisco. Early in 1880 several unions launched a union-based anti-Chinese effort that signaled the emergence of a consolidated trade-union movement in San Francisco. Once again, workers organized around their opposition to the Chinese. This time they sought the implementation of a clause in the new state constitution which prohibited corporations from employing Chinese workers. Once again the unemployed were recruited to march from factory to factory to urge the expulsion of the Chinese. But when the legislature enacted an implementing statute, the workers won only a nominal victory, for the corporations successfully appealed to the courts that the statute was unconstitutional.[61]

Although Kearneyism had galvanized San Francisco's working class and had provided an impetus for trade unions to mobilize, Kearney's reluctance to share power and thereby integrate trade unionists fully in the Workingmen's party leadership forced union workers to organize on their own. Riding the crest of the Workingmen's movement and united by their pent-up frustration with Kearney's domination of the anti-Chinese campaign, trade unionists led by Frank Roney formed the Representative Assembly of Trades and Labor Unions in 1878. These same trade unionists (printers, shoemakers, cigar makers, building and construction workers, shipyard and metalworkers, and seamen), now federated, had staged

[59]Reprinted in the *Daily Alta California,* September 12, 1882, p. 1. See also ibid., March 4, 1882, p. 1, and March 10, 1882, p. 1, for more analogies.

[60]Quoted in ibid., April 19, 1882, Editorial, p. 2.

[61]Within a year of ratification, three-fourths of the anti-Chinese provisions in the state constitution had been declared unconstitutional. Elmer Sandmeyer, "California Anti-Chinese Legislation and the Federal Courts: A Study in Federal Relations," *Pacific Historical Review,* 5 (1936), 189–211.

the abortive revolt against Kearney when he and Roney had locked horns over the question of union leadership in politics.

At several points in his autobiography, Roney (president of the Trades Assembly) insists that he never much cared for the anti-Chinese focus of the Workingmen's party,[62] but anti-Chinese nativism nonetheless provided the glue for much of the organization-building effort of the Trades Assembly in the 1880s. Ironically, few of the unions that owed their revival to the Trades Assembly were directly threatened by the Chinese competition. While the Chinese had taken over cigar making, no competitive conflict existed in such industries serving local markets as the building, metal, and maritime trades. General service industries outside Chinatown did not typically employ Chinese, so competition in the service sector (except, perhaps, for laundries) was also marginal. Yet opposition to the lurking Chinese presence continued to be the central political concern of the trade-union movement.[63]

Late in 1881 the Trades Assembly commissioned a statistical study of the Chinese position in industry. Roney called for the study, he later claimed, because data had been so sorely lacking during the agitation of the 1870s:

> Denunciation was of no value. Neither did results follow by charging the Chinese with being filthy, for the Chinese as a people are far more cleanly in all respects than many of those who were hostile to them. As president of the Trades Assembly, I appointed Henry Marsden and Charles F. Burgman to investigate the Chinese from a purely industrial standpoint. . . .[64]

The Committee on Chinese Statistics of the Trades Assembly produced a report that, while relatively restrained in racial and cultural commentary, was strident in its view of the labor market impact of the Chinese.

> The trades that have suffered the most are the cigarmakers, tailors, boot and shoemakers. . . . We find them employed in the manufacture of boots and shoes, barrels, boxes, brushes, brooms, blankets, bricks, blinds, clothing, canned goods, cigars and cigar boxes, cloth, cordage, furniture, flannels, gloves, harness, jute bagging, knitting, leather, matches, paper, ropes, soap, straw boards, sashes, saddles, shirts and underclothing of all kinds, slippers, twine, tinware, willow-ware, wine and whips. . . . We find them employed

[62]E.g., Roney, 287.
[63]Saxton, 167.
[64]Roney, 358.

in breweries, chemical works, flourmills, lumber and planing mills, distill-eries, smelting works, powder factories, vineyards, woolen mills, tanneries, on railroads, and as laborers in almost every department of industry.[65]

The report went on to document the adverse effect of Chinese labor on wages, particularly in the shoe and clothing industries: "In 1870, the price paid per dozen pairs was $18; . . . in 1878, $6 to $7. . . . Usual wages of Chinese, when competent, from $20 to $30 per month; white men (in the shoe industry) from $9 to $13 per week . . . and wages of white tailors average $15 per week." As a whole, however, the survey data showed that Trades Assembly unionists were affected only margin-ally by Chinese competition in the labor market, with the important excep-tions of cigar making, shoemaking, and the sewing trades. Still, anti-Chinese sentiment was a powerful impulse among San Francisco trade unionists.

The anti-Chinese activities of the Trades Assembly were productive: by 1882, forty-nine unions had been organized in San Francisco, all but two of which were affiliated with the city federation. Thirty-one of them had been established only after the Kearney agitation had mobilized workers in the city. Twenty-six unions were anchored in older trades—building and construction, maritime and metalworks. The remainder developed in crafts that had been organized at one time or another—printing, tailoring, carpentry, for example—and in a handful of newer service trades.[66]

In 1881 and 1882 the Trades Assembly was especially vigorous in its pursuit of anti-Chinese objectives but, unlike the Kearney agitation, it expressed its agitation against the Chinese through traditional trade-union channels. Until controversy over passage of the Chinese Exclusion Act erupted in the spring of 1882, moreover, the Trades Assembly respected its constitutional prohibition against direct involvement with politics. Trade-union economic action tended to be the vehicle through which anti-Chinese goals were pursued. Early on, for example, the assembly adopted the white labor label, arguing that union labor was the only guarantee of white labor. But along with the white label and the boycotts the label made possible, the Trades Assembly also began to develop lobbying strategies and networks—sending lobbyists and petitions to Congress, pressuring candidates, and establishing legislative committees to press for restrictions on immigration.

---

[65]Quoted in *Daily Alta California*, January 8, 1882, p. 1; Saxton, 169.
[66]Saxton, 160.

The Trades Assembly also appealed to union solidarities beyond San Francisco, sending representatives to the founding convention of the American Federation of Labor[67] to rally eastern workers behind anti-Chinese legislation. That such appeals were heard became clear in 1882 during the national debate over the Chinese Exclusion Bill. Three thousand workers in Philadelphia demonstrated in favor of the measure during the congressional phase of debate and passed a resolution petitioning the House of Representatives to "remove a menace to the welfare of American workingmen."[68] And when President Chester Arthur vetoed the bill, eastern workers, especially in Pittsburgh and Philadelphia, attended mass protest meetings and adopted resolutions condemning the veto and demanding an end to Chinese immigration.[69]

In San Francisco, the Trades Assembly responded to President Arthurs' veto by redoubling its efforts to win immigration controls. More explicitly political action was required because the focal point of union agitation was the reluctance of the Republican Administration to concede a restrictive immigration policy.[70] Within a few days of the presidential veto the Trades Assembly called a convention for the purpose of reaffirming labor's united front against the Chinese.[71] At its opening session the Anti-Chinese Convention devoted attention to the legislative struggle in Washington. It dispatched instructions to California senator John F. Miller, author of the vetoed bill, setting the terms for acceptable compromise legislation, and it heard Frank Roney's impassioned denunciation of Arthur's veto:

> Although . . . ours [is] a representative government, President Arthur, elected by the people, vetoed the Chinese bill in opposition to the voice of the nation, and at the insistance of the Chinese Minister at Washington. No

[67]Actually, to the founding of the Federation of Organized Trades and Labor Unions, the immediate predecessor of the American Federation of Labor.

[68]Quoted in *Daily Alta California*, March 18, 1882, p. 1.

[69]Ibid., April 15, 27, 1882. The most notable eastern labor protest occurred in Philadelphia, where six to eight thousand allegedly gathered to express indignation at the presidential action. The gathering was presided over by unionists, including the president of the State Labor Council.

[70]Republicans in California were embarrassed by the veto; Californians generally were enraged. In Santa Cruz, for example, when news of the veto was received, the flag was hung at halfmast, upside down. President Arthur was burned in effigy as funeral marches were played. Republicans were said to head the movement, which filled the main street of the town. See *Daily Alta California*, April 5, 1882, p. 1.

[71]Perhaps to guard against Kearney opportunism, the assembly "particularly requested that no organization . . . send as delegates any politician, demagogue, crank or hobbyist, as such persons would undoubtedly create inharmony and defeat the object which it is our earnest desire to attain." *Daily Alta California*, April 10, 1882, p. 1.

Republic could exist for any length of time if any such arbitrary power, constitutional though it may be, could be exercised by any one man.[72]

Later the convention established the League of Deliverance and named Roney as its chair. Though the League was clearly an arm of San Francisco unionism, virtually anyone willing to take an oath neither to buy from, sell to, or employ Chinese could become a member.[73] Even merchants could expect conditional membership as long as they indicated their willingness to discontinue the sale of Chinese-made goods within a specified time. The League's objective was to abolish Chinese employment and residence in the United States through boycotts against Chinese-made goods, other forms of direct action, and legislation. Some of the League's boycotts were successful in persuading employers to replace their Chinese workers. As the San Francisco *Morning Call* reported in late July 1882, "The effect of this depression in the Chinese factories is . . . encouraging revival of business where Chinese are not employed. Members of the White Shoe-makers' League say that they are running full time. About thirty of our large factories have discharged them [the Chinese] and are now employing white labor exclusively." The league replicated other tactics of Kearneyites as well, as when it conducted vigilante marches on Chinese communities. This anti-Chinese resolve was abruptly coopted, however, when President Arthur signed a revised Chinese exclusion bill into law on May 6, 1882.

The League continued its efforts for a time, even securing a pledge from the national trade-union federation to organize League branches in the East for the purpose of extending the boycott.[74] Still the League disintegrated soon after Chinese exclusion was achieved: though it felt that further federal action was necessary, with respect to reentry rights for resident Chinese, for instance, the League could not sustain the atmosphere of crisis once the Exclusion Act went into effect.[75] The Trades Assembly eventually disappeared for the same reason, though not without

[72]Quoted in ibid., April 25, 1882, p. 1.

[73]The oath further secured a promise not to "hold social intercourse with any person who in any manner employs, sells to or buys from, or rents or leases to, or has any dealings with the Chinese." Ibid., April 27, 1882, p. 1.

[74]Ibid., May 22, 1882, p. 1. The extent of Eastern interest in the boycotts is suggested by the efforts of eastern cigar manufacturers to capitalize on it. At least one Chicago company took out ads in local papers: "Anti-Chinese Voters . . . Use Only Our Celebrated VETO Smoking Tobacco, the Purest and Best in the Market . . . Manufactured Where CHINESE LABOR is Unknown. . .": ibid., May 22, 1882.

[75]Eaves, 41.

efforts to keep the Chinese issue alive. Chiefly the Trades Assembly complained that the Exclusion Act did not go far enough: that it contained too many loopholes and was far too generous with respect to reentry into the United States after return migration to China. Beyond this, the Trades Assembly protested the short life of the statute (ten years) and the fact that it restricted the immigration only of Chinese *workers,* not of all Chinese *persons.* With this objection, of course, trade-union anti-Chinese nativism—previously rationalized on (dubious) economic grounds—surrendered completely to race logic. At issue now were the Act's reentry provisions, which allowed Chinese workers residing in the United States to come and go at no penalty and to take their earnings with them, and its loopholes through which Chinese wives and children could move, flooding the Pacific Coast with generations of American Chinese.

Although Trades Assembly members and other anti-Chinese nativists were plainly dissatisfied with the statute, they were unable to exploit that dissatisfaction to sustain the mobilization of workers. Congress had, after all, acted to remove the much-loathed source of unfair labor competition. As the restrictions began to be felt in 1883, agitation quietly subsided and the Trades Assembly withered away. Further, the ebbing of that controversy permitted the limitations and jealousies of craft unionism to surface explicitly: should semi- and unskilled workers be organized, for example, and what kind of relationship, if any, should unions have with the Knights of Labor. The fear Henry George had expressed in 1880 proved real: labor had been first distracted and later immobilized by its obsession with the Chinese issue. Indeed, not only had potentially radical segments of labor been stymied, as George had predicted, but the career of San Francisco trade unionism, too, seemed to depend on the salience of the Chinese issue.

Still the quiet produced by the Chinese Exclusion Act was only temporary. As the Chinese themselves began to strike and to unionize, anti-Chinese nativism was resurrected among both workers and those small manufacturers and entrepreneurs most seriously threatened by Chinese labor organization. One direct result was that some white trade unions became stronger: the national Cigar Makers' International Union, for example, formerly eclipsed by the local White Cigar Makers' Association, made its presence in San Francisco permanent as Chinese workers themselves began to organize in 1884. The cigar makers' union engaged in anti-union activities against the Chinese, exempting the firm against which the Chinese declared a strike in 1885 from boycotts of Chinese-made goods, sending agents to the East to recruit white cigar makers, and accepting (now much improved) Chinese wage rates for its own members.[76] A less direct result was that resurgent anti-Chinese nativism—particularly as it reached a crescendo during the mid-1880s in reaction to the incomplete achievements of the Chinese Exclusion Act and in anticipation of the struggle to extend the act in 1892—was complemented by the militant national labor struggles of the mid-decade. The synergism of these two struggles reinvigorated the union movement in San Francisco. A more durable organizational structure would emerge in 1886, in the form of the San Francisco Federated Trades Council.[77] By 1900 San Francisco was a closed-shop town.

If anti-Chinese nativism was a cornerstone of the union movement in California, it was equally a building block of national trade-union politics. In its early years the AFL tried to promote racial inclusiveness with regard to blacks,[78] and it did not articulate a coherent opposition to the new European immigration until the latter 1880s. At its founding convention in 1881, however, the AFL enlisted in the anti-Chinese crusade. In his testimony before the Senate committee investigating labor-capital relations in 1883, Samuel Gompers spoke stridently and certainly against the Chinese.[79] The AFL campaigned for Chinese (and later Japanese) exclusion in openly racist terms, denouncing "Mongolians" for bringing "nothing but filth, vice and disease" and for degrading "our people on the Pacific Coast to such a degree that could it be published in detail the American people would in their just and righteous anger sweep them from the face of the earth."[80] A few years later the AFL would publish a pamphlet written by Gompers and Herman Guttstadt, whose title conveniently summarizes federation attitudes: *Meat vs. Rice: American Manhood vs. Asiatic Coolieism: Which Shall Survive?*

As the AFL perfected its racial arguments against the Chinese, its formal racial liberalism toward blacks gave way to racial prejudice. Not

[76]Walter Fong, "Chinese Labor Unions," *Chautauquan,* June–July 1896, 399–402.

[77]The council was renamed the San Francisco Labor Council in 1892, after the building trades seceded.

[78]Until the late 1890s the AFL denied charters to unions whose constitutions explicitly denied membership to blacks. Probably the most famous controversy arising from this policy involved the National Machinists' Association, whose union constitution drew the color line. Though the AFL (notably Gompers) helped organize a separate union that did not include a color bar in its constitution, it (and Gompers) acquiesced in a compromise that transferred the point of discrimination from constitution to individual admission decision. Bernard Mandel, "Samuel Gompers and Negro Workers, 1866–1914," *Journal of Negro History,* 40 (1955), 34–60.

[79]U.S. Senate, Committee on Education and Labor, *Relations between Capital and Labor,* Hearings, vol. 1 (1885), 280–82.

[80]AFL *Proceedings* (1893), 73.

only did the AFL submit to the practical necessity of Jim Crow within its ranks, but it also began to reason that blacks were racially unsuited for union membership. As Gompers would be saying before the end of the century, "those peculiarities of temperament such as patriotism, sympathy, etc., . . . are peculiar to most of the Caucasian race, and . . . also make an organization of the character and complexity of the modern trade union possible."[81]

Race analogies and race theory brought race logic into the core of trade unionism; meanwhile the labor-market anxieties that gelled around Chinese immigration placed immigration-centered labor-market remedies alongside race logic at the core of the AFL's political agenda. There race and labor-market issues interacted, ultimately rationalizing race-principled union opposition to the unrestricted immigration of other groups of workers who, like blacks, were not "union material" and who, like the Chinese, posed a hazard to the economic and cultural integrity of the Republic. As Gompers insisted in 1905, "the caucasians," by whom he seems to have meant old labor, "are not going to let their standard of living be destroyed by negroes, Chinamen, Japs, *or any others.*"[82] This interaction of race, labor market, and immigration would form the cornerstone of the exclusionary unionism practiced by the AFL, and it would produce the AFL's first foray into national politics.

Race and the Development of Labor Politics

In the mid-1880s union labor began to set about consolidating itself as the organizational representation of the working class. This move brought it into collision with capital, in the courts and in the workplace, and with rival representatives, chiefly the Knights of Labor. But it also brought union labor into collision with a rapidly expanding stratum of workers whose cheap labor and green hands were reminiscent of the Chinese. This collision between old labor and new immigrants pushed union labor into the national political arena, because the national government controlled

[81]*American Federationist,* 5 (1898), 269–71.

[82]Samuel Gompers, "Talks on Labor," *American Federationist,* September 1905, pp. 636–37, my emphasis. Alexander Saxton argues that "the phrase 'any others,' tacked on seemingly as an afterthought to the main sentence, actually contained a major significance. It referred to the so-called new immigration from southern and eastern Europe." Saxton, "Race and the House of Labor," in Gary B. Nash and Richard Weiss, eds., *The Great Fear: Race in the Mind of America* (1970), 115.

immigration policy. As the earlier collision with the Chinese had shown, moreover, immigration policy was not invulnerable to pressure from "respectable" labor.

Of course there were differences between the Chinese and the new European immigrants. For one thing, southern and eastern Europeans came in much greater numbers than did the Chinese, and they rapidly came to occupy dramatic proportions of the industrial labor force. For another, new European immigrants enjoyed the privilege of suffrage as the Chinese had not; they were seen if not as a force then at least as an important presence in electoral politics. Rather than broaden and diversify the American labor movement, however, the economic and political presence of these new European immigrants only hardened the nativist resolve of union labor. Exclusionist craft unionism was the organizational manifestation of this resolve, while narrow interest politics became its political expression.

Nativism was intimately tied to the development of unionism and labor politics: it cemented craft rigidity, limited the privilege of organization to a minority of workers, and was the first issue to link the economic interest of workers to their collective effectiveness in the political process. Nativism was an instrumental focus around which workers could be mobilized, whether through extra-institutional insurgency (viz., in the Workingmen's party) or through union organization. The experience of insurgent nativism demonstrated the potency of race and immigration issues; but the subordination of unions to insurgent nativism also underscored the urgent need for unions to coopt those issues. Once captured by unions, nativism was a reliable glue that such trade-union leaders as Roney and Gompers could use to secure old labor's monopoly of organization within the working class. Nativism activated the broad status solidarities of old labor, helping bridge geographic and jurisdictional separation. Further, nativism both coincided with organizational issues and transposed them: chiefly the question of the craft structure. But most important, nativism furnished job-conscious unionism with political purpose.

That nativism was a crucial ingredient in expanding trade unionism is adumbrated in Frank Roney's recollections. His initial response to anti-Chinese invective was unsympathetic:

> The restrictions, which many were at that time advocating, were, I thought, brutal and such as no self-respecting civilized people would dream of imposing upon the members of any race within their midst. The only objection to them that I felt had any validity was that they were cheap workers. . . . If the

energy and intelligence of the white man had been directed against herding and toward the creating of a picturesque Oriental section like Chinatown, they would have benefited themselves and also the Chinaman.[83]

But Roney did not miss the opportunity provided by the Kearney insurgency to mobilize workers, nor did he miss the necessity of redirecting that insurgency into union channels. Noting that "those who were most vociferously applauded [at the sand-lot rallies] pointed to the Chinaman as the true source of all the trouble," Roney made himself a leader of the anti-Chinese movement:

> It was essentially an anti-Chinese party as was indicated by its motto, "The Chinese must go." However, I never warmed to that feature of the agitation. I realized that the cry was superficial, but agreed to sail under the flag so emblazoned in order that I might in time have other and real subjects considered by the people, which I deemed to be of far greater importance to their permanent well-being.[84]

Out of the Kearney hysteria Roney called into being San Francisco's first federation of trade unions, the Trades Assembly. As its leader, Roney committed the Assembly to fighting the Chinese—through boycotts and through the vigilance of its auxiliary pressure group, the League of Deliverance. In this connection Roney further remarks upon the importance of anti-Chinese activities in developing and perfecting the tactics of trade-union economic action: those activities popularized the union label and taught unionists how best to use it (especially how best to circumvent employer and dealer fraud), for example, and they gave rise, by Roney's account, to the most effective union boycotts.[85]

Two of the elementary weapons of trade unionism—the boycott and the union label—were thus inspired to their modern use by the Chinese presence in San Francisco. Unlike strikes, which typically pitted workers in particular shops or trades against particular employers, the boycott and the union bug generalized economic action by providing fellow unionists with a supporting role in the struggles of aggrieved workers. The fact that San Francisco became a closed-shop town, and one of the strongest trade-union centers in the nation by the turn of the century, suggests the impor-

[83]Roney, 266–67.
[84]Ibid., 269, 287.
[85]Ibid., especially 369.

tance of anti-Chinese nativism as an instrument of mobilization as well as of building union organization.

Even more important, however, the Chinese problem was the first issue that forced trade unionism to abdicate its political neutrality outside city politics, because national intervention was essential to its solution. Nativism thus compelled bread-and-butter unionists to modify their pledge of voluntarism. Though voluntarist in principle, Roney's Trades Assembly was deeply and organically engaged in politics because its struggle to rid California of the Chinese required it to be so. Similarly the AFL abandoned principled voluntarism when nativst principles required its political advocacy of immigration restriction. What is more, anti-Chinese nativism among white union labor nationalized affinities to the Democratic party and, voluntarist instructions against partisanship notwithstanding, generated informal union-party ties. Although it would be ten years before union-party identities gelled, the anti-Chinese campaign revealed continuities within the Democratic tradition which reinforced ethnic partisanship with union interest and which provided a bridge between the Jacksonian message and the Bryanite vision.

Focused initially against the Chinese, but later generalized as a response to southern and eastern European immigrants, nativism further politicized old labor as *union* labor. This politicization developed along boundaries within the working class, boundaries drawn by changes in the economic and organizational position of old labor as well as by changes in its demographic position in society. This joining of organizational, labor-market, and race anxieties represented an explosive political mixture, its elements threatening the bonds of traditional partisanship which dominated Gilded Age politics. In this regard the response of the ruling parties was decisive in containing labor politics within traditional institutions. Tangible party responses to anti-Chinese pressures (e.g., the California state legislature's Memorial to Congress in 1878,[86] state restrictions on Chinese employment, and the federal Chinese Exclusion Act) demonstrated to nativist labor the permeability of the traditional party system, at least with respect to discrete policy demands. Because the party system was permeable on the Chinese issue, moreover, and because Chinese exclusion became a question of national policy, political pragmatism dictated that nativist labor work within existing structures to secure relief. Party—especially Democratic—rhetoric suggested party willingness to

[86]California, State Senate, *Chinese Immigration: Its Social, Moral and Political Effect*, Report of the Special Committee on Chinese Immigration (1878); *Daily Alta California*, April 15, 22, 1876.

restrict immigration; there was, after all, the large matter of the labor vote to consider, particularly after it had shown its clout by sweeping Workingmen into office in California local elections. Further, the Democratic party's speedy appropriation of union nativism and its ultimate delivery of Chinese exclusion pushed labor nativists toward an appreciation of positive state intervention, if on a limited scale. As union labor recognized these lessons, so the party system recognized that union labor was an interest to be reckoned with in the competition between parties.

Party responses to labor pressure helped direct labor politics into traditional, class-neutral channels. In an era of workplace militancy and political insurgency, the solvent for class dialogue would prove to be race. The Chinese issue and, of course, the moral death of Reconstruction Republicanism mediated the swift rehabilitation of race in national political dialogue. Ever-diffident racial liberalism stepped aside for more confident passions and interests. Although Republicans certainly contributed to the success of anti-Chinese nativism, it was the Democratic party that chiefly benefited from it. Class-neutral labor politics would not long sustain the pretense of partisan neutrality.

Race-thinking sharpened union nativism while relaxing voluntarism and distorting the political significance of the independent and class-charged industrial struggles of old labor. This interaction of race and union interest brought the AFL within the orbit of the Democratic party. A brief review of party and state responses to anti-Chinese pressure will remind us how this happened.

The Civil War brought with it important political changes, not the least of which was some degree of federalization of political authority.[87] The war itself, emancipation, the Reconstruction Amendments, and the Civil Rights Act federalized the race question. Alongside these shifts in the locus of autonomy and authority, immigration policy moved into the federal jurisdiction in response to wartime labor shortages. While the Immigration Acts of 1864 did not collide directly with local immigration policies (e.g., revenue-generating taxes), they placed federal authority on the side of an "open door." These wartime innovations would prove evanescent, and the return of the South to national politics would bring a general return to localism on race and economic questions,[88] but the status

[87]Barrington Moore, Jr., makes this point in *Social Origins of Dictatorship and Democracy: Lord and Peasant in the Making of the Modern World* (1966), 149–55.

[88]Stephen Skowronek, *Building a New American State* (1982), 30. Skowronek deals here with the failure of Civil War institutional arrangements to redefine the relationship between state and society. This point is central to his argument regarding the "state of courts and parties" during the late nineteenth century.

quo ante was never completely achieved. Immigration (and the labor-market policy it represented) remained squarely in the federal arena, for example: in 1876 the Supreme Court entrenched federal authority over immigration when it held that congressional commerce powers supersede the states' police powers in the regulation of immigration.[89]

By the time of the Workingmen's movement in 1877, it was clear that any limitation on Chinese immigration would have to be imposed by the Congress. Equally clearly, the futures of the Democratic and Republican parties in California were in good measure mortgaged to anti-Chinese nativism. Votes mattered, the Chinese had none, white labor did, and what is more San Francisco contained a decisive proportion of the state's electorate. Responding to electoral realities, both the Democratic and the Republican parties in California offered themselves as vehicles through which appeals to Congress could be made. California politicians had several ways to argue their case to the nation. In an era marked by a return to localism, especially on matters of race, local autonomy was one. Strictly economic labor-market reasoning was another, but it ran the political risk of directly arousing labor-capital controversy. A third line of argument emphasized race protection. This was the argument actually presented to the nation, though it subsumed the labor-market question. Thus California politicians stressed the racial and cultural attributes of the Chinese and warned Congress of the evil consequences of continued Chinese intermingling with the white race. In 1877 the Democratic state legislature published a three-hundred-page report that was distributed to members of Congress, newspapers, and public officials across the country. In part it read:

> Impregnable to all the influences of Anglo-Saxon life, they remain the same stolid Asiatics that have floated on the rivers and slaved in the fields of China for thirty centuries of time. . . . We thus find one sixth of our entire population composed of Chinese coolies . . . by the unalterable structure of their intellectual being, voluntary slaves.

Forecasting race war and class insurgency, the report continued: "Is it not possible that free labor, unable to compete with these foreign serfs . . . may unite in all the horrors of riot and insurrection, and defying

---

[89]Benjamin Klebaner, "State and Local Immigration Regulation in the United States before 1882," *International Review of Social History*, 3 (1958), 269–95; Sandmeyer, "California Anti-Chinese Legislation," 197.

the civil power, extirpate with fire and sword those who rob them of their bread, yet yield no tribute to the State?''[90]

In policy terms the first objective of the appeal to Congress was to win abrogation of the Burlingame Treaty, which, in advancing commercial interests, stood in the way of treating the Chinese as an undesirable race. This objective became the overriding priority in 1879 when Republican President Hayes vetoed the Passenger Bill, claiming it violated American treaty obligations. Despite the passion and depth of anti-Chinese conviction in California, however, treaty abrogation (and Chinese exclusion) was not easily secured. Though numerically a minority, pro-Chinese advocates were a powerful lobby within the Republican coalition: abolitionist clergymen, diplomats and industrialists, and railroad and shipping interests. These advocates had important friends in Congress, including Republican Senators George F. Hoar of Massachusetts and Oliver Morton of Indiana. During the Senate debate in 1882 Senator Hoar would appeal to the principles of the Declaration of Independence to argue against comprehensive Chinese exclusion, while during the congressional investigation of Chinese immigration that he chaired, Senator Morton presented the view

> that they [the Chinese] have injuriously interfered with the white people of California . . . may well be doubted. The great fact is, that there is to-day and always has been, a scarcity of labor on the Pacific Coast. There is work for all who are there, both white and Mongolian, and the State would undoubtedly develop much more rapidly were there more and cheaper labor. . . . There is work and remunerative work for all who choose to perform it.[91]

These sentiments would not ultimately prevail in the Chinese debate, but they ran to the core of Republican arguments that held open the doors to eastern and southern European immigration until the 1920s.

Despite moral and economic arguments by Republicans against Chinese exclusion, Democratic and Workingmen's pressures pushed the Republican party onto the anti-Chinese band wagon in 1880. Eighteen-eighty was a presidential year, and both parties needed to carry California to win. The national electoral controversy of 1876–77 suggested the importance of California in Republican (and Democratic) national futures.[92] Within

---

[90]*Chinese Immigration: Its Social, Moral and Political Effect* (1878), quoted in Coolidge, 83.
[91]Senator Oliver Morton, 1877, reprinted in Coolidge, 96.
[92]The California presidential vote in 1876 had been 49.1 percent Democratic. Walter Dean Burnham, *Presidential Ballots, 1836–1892* (1955), 293, 896.

California Reconstruction elections had shown Republicans that anti-Chinese nativism could be manipulated to harness the volatile California electorate. The Democrats, whose platform had denounced "the undue influx of Chinese and Mongolians" in 1867, had seized control of the state in that year. Remarkably, in the very heyday of Reconstruction, the new Democratic governor had explained his party's victory thus:

> I will simply say that in this result we protest against corruption and extravagance in our State of affairs—against populating this fair State with a race of Asiatics—against sharing with inferior races the Government of the country—against the military despotism which now exists in the South under the late acts of Congress; and this protest of ours, echoing the voice of Connecticut and Kentucky, will be re-echoed in thunder tones by the great central states until the Southern States are emancipated from negro domination, and restored to their proper places as equals and sisters in the great Federal family.[93]

California Democrats consolidated their hold on the state in 1876, in the election that returned the race question to the states.[94]

In 1877 Senator Morton's Committee on Chinese Immigration issued its report, recommending renegotiation of the Burlingame Treaty. (Senator Morton died before the findings were reported, and his views were presented posthumously in a minority report.) Republican President Hayes undertook this project, and by 1880 a new treaty had been completed. The new treaty (the Angell Treaty) substantially modified Burlingame, and specifically it recognized the right of the United States to regulate, limit, or suspend Chinese immigration. The treaty did not, however, permit comprehensive restrictions on Chinese immigration; it allowed only the suspension of the immigration of Chinese laborers, and this only for specified, "reasonable" periods of time.[95] Merchants, teachers, tourists, and workers already in residence were allowed under the treaty to come and go freely, and they were accorded the rights, privileges, and immunities of citizens of any most favored nation. The new treaty, while it fell short of settling the Chinese question, was the best Republicans could hope for, given the deep anti-exclusion convictions of capitalists and

---

[93]Henry Haight, quoted in Saxton, *Indispensable Enemy*, 91. To the oft-noted irony that San Francisco's Haight Street was home to America's "love generation" must be added the irony that the street bears the name of this politician of race-hate.

[94]On the Hayes-Tilden compromise see C. Vann Woodward, *Reunion and Reaction* (1956).

[95]Coolidge, 161.

abolitionists within the party. While the Angell Treaty gave the U.S. government the power to curtail Chinese labor migration to some extent, it also gave some protection to American commercial and industrial interests. Still, it opened the way to consideration of legislation to exclude new Chinese. Thus the chief messages broadcast by the new treaty were that the state was not impermeable to pressures from below and that such pressures could exact political exchanges on the electoral market.

The first restriction bill of 1882—passed to implement the Angell Treaty—ordered a twenty-year suspension of the immigration of Chinese workers, skilled and unskilled, and required the personal registration of all resident Chinese. President Arthur—the new Republican president—vetoed the bill on the grounds that twenty years was not a "reasonable" period, that the inclusion of the category "skilled labor" violated the Angell Treaty, and that the registration requirements were "vexatious discriminations" and "hostile to the spirit of our institutions." In his veto message Arthur went on to praise the Chinese:

> No one can say the country has not profited by their work. They were largely instrumental in constructing the railways which connect the Atlantic and Pacific Slope. The states of the Pacific are full of evidence of their industry and enterprise, profitable to capitalists and to laborers of Caucasian origin, which would have lain dormant but for them. The time has now come when it is supposed that they are not needed, and when it is thought by Congress and by those most acquainted with the subject, that it is best to try to get along without them. There may, however, be other sections of the country where this species of labor may be advantageously employed, without interfering with laborers of our own race. It may be part of wisdom, as of good faith, to fix the length of the experimental period with reference to this fact.[96]

The president's veto followed a rancorous debate in Congress in which the question of race ran headlong into the issue of the labor market. Against the views of the recently deceased Senator Morton and against the reasoning summarized in the president's veto message, Democrats, in particular, paraded unsavory racial attributes of the Chinese. Democrats and Republicans scored the Chinese for undermining the homogeneity and tempting the virtue necessary for a healthy republic. One senator wondered whether New England Republicans would be so moralistic if the issue were the immigration of Africans into their states. Arguing the moral

[96]Quoted in *Daily Alta California*, April 6, 1882, p. 1.

right of the nation to make "distinctions as to the foreigners we admit," another senator maintained that "nations and races as constituted by the Creator get on better with separate institutions than they would if amalgamating together, unless their characteristics are such as to admit of assimilation."[97]

Though the first restriction bill passed easily, congressional opposition to it was sharply partisan, particularly in the House of Representatives. Seventy-four percent of all House Democrats voted for passage as against less than 40 percent of all House Republicans, while Republicans accounted for 94 percent of the negative votes. In the Senate 72 percent of the bill's supporters were Democrats and 93 percent of the bill's opponents were Republicans.[98]

The presidential veto confirmed Chinese exclusion as a Democratic issue. The New York *Tribune* described Democrats in the House as "hugging themselves with joy over the President's veto." "We can get on the stump now and show the laboring men of the country that we have stood as a bulwark against the influx of a horde of Asiatics, but that the Republican Administration has denied the voice of the American people, as uttered by their votes."[99] Democratic congressional consensus and bipartisan California pressures helped develop a revised bill that, while conceding the registration and time-period issue to President Arthur, retained strong language prohibiting immigration of Chinese laborers (skilled and unskilled) and that denied citizenship rights to the Chinese under federal law.[100] The new law was signed by the president in May 1882. Two years later Democrats in Congress restored the registration provision, *sotto voce*, by requiring that reentering Chinese present a registration certificate. During the 1884 presidential contest Democrats contrasted the amended act to the 1882 original to show that Republican anti-Chinese policy required Democratic backbone.

Virtually the entire section on the protection of labor in the Democratic

[97]Ibid., March 4, 1882, p. 1; March 8, 1882, p. 1; March 9, 1882, p. 1; March 10, 1882, p. 1.

[98]U.S. Bureau of the Census, "Political Party Affiliations in Congress and the Presidency," ser. Y, 204–10, *Historical Statistics of the United States*, pt. II (1975), 1083. Of the bloc of senators recorded "absent" (43 percent of the Senate) partisanship was fairly evenly divided. Though overwhelmingly Republican, opposition to the restriction measure in both houses averaged only a third of the votes cast.

[99]*Daily Alta California*, April 8, 1882, p. 1.

[100]On final passage of the Chinese Exclusion Act in the House of Representatives the "yeas" were 52 percent Democratic and 44 percent Republican. Seventy-eight percent of House Democrats voted for passage, as compared to 60 percent of House Republicans. Ninety-one percent of the negative vote was Republican. The bill passed overwhelmingly, however, with only 16 percent of the House recorded in opposition.

bottom of a racial typology that differentiated Teutonic peoples from the rest of Europe.[107]

Incipient racial typologizing, though at the time still ad hoc, was evinced by leading congressional speakers. Race analogies between the Chinese and new immigrants supported this racial typologizing. While the Irish, Germans, English, and Scots were repeatedly hailed as "the best class of immigrant," southern and eastern Europeans were denounced as "coolies, serfs, and slaves." One senator averred, "To the warm-hearted and intelligent Celt, to the industrious and economical German, to the self-reliant Scandanavian, let the doors of the Republic be thrown wide open,"[108] while another urged closing the doors to those "people who have never conceived the idea of independent manhood."[109]

Poverty among new immigrants was presented as a racial attribute, just as dietary habits and living conditions had been for the Chinese. The consequences of the new immigrant presence were defined as "essentially parallel to that which induced Congress to prohibit the importation of the Chinese." Terence Powderly testified that "The diet of these men was water and mush with a small quantity of meat on Sunday. These men are brought into competition with skilled as well as unskilled labor, and it is fast becoming as bad as the competition of the Chinese in the West."[110] And in appealing for House passage of his bill, Representative Foran decried the "large numbers of degraded, ignorant, brutal Italians and Hungarian laborers" for imperiling the racial heights of the republic:

They know nothing of our institutions, our customs, or of the habits and characteristics of our people. . . . They are brought here precisely in the same manner that the Chinese were brought here . . . very many of them have no conception of freedom. . . . They seldom sleep in beds. . . . They do not know to purchase any of the luxuries which tend to elevate and enlighten people. . . . Being low in the scale of intelligence, they are . . . willing slaves. . . . The fact that American workingmen are vastly superior to these aliens in intelligence, skill, moral and social culture will no doubt be admitted. . . . No matter how high a moral standard a community may attain, the introduction into that community of any considerable number of persons of a lower moral tone will cause a general moral deterioration just as sure as night follows day. The intermarriage of a lower with a higher type

[107]I return to this matter in Chapter 4.
[108]*Congressional Record*, 48th Cong., 2d sess. (February 17, 1885), 1780.
[109]Ibid. (February 13, 1885), 1634.
[110]Reprinted in ibid. (June 19, 1884), 5360.

certainly does not improve the latter any more than does the breeding of cattle by blooded and common stock improve the blooded stock generally. . . . Let us lift our beloved America . . . so that she may move onward toward the shining heights which the hopes of her nativity foretold.[111]

The problem identified by the Foran Act was that of immigration induced by contract. But like the Chinese Exclusion Act, the Foran Act offered a solution that provided for qualitative restrictions on immigration which were justified on racial grounds. Although the problem of the new immigration was, in the mid-1880s, still narrowly framed in terms of recruited migrants, the problem would be posed more generally, as an immigration issue, within the next few years. As it became clear that contract labor was not the source of most southern, central, and eastern European immigration, and as the new immigration began to gather momentum during the 1880s and '90s, a new immigration controversy arose. At its center were race and labor market, inseparably intertwined. By the mid-1890s race-principled proposals to restrict immigration would hover over national politics.

The Chinese issue established the bounds for the larger debate over immigration. On the one side developed pro-capitalist arguments based not on the "rights of humanity" averred by Senator Hoar, William Garrison, and Henry Ward Beecher but on the labor-market interests of advancing industrialism as articulated by Senator Morton and President Arthur. During the 1890s Republican elites would dull the edge of this instrumental defense of open immigration by celebrating immigrant achievements in the great American "melting pot." On the other side developed pro-union arguments based on race and animated by the electoral strength of old labor.

The Chinese issue also foreshadowed the complexity of the immigration question, particularly with respect to what it signified for different groups and the alignments it produced in politics. This complexity would be particularly troublesome for Republicans, whose heterogeneity on other issues was replicated in the Chinese debate. Some Republicans were sympathetic to the racial perspectives of old labor and Democrats. This was true of James G. Blaine, for example. Though his presidential candidacy was tainted by his association with anti-Irish nativist appeals against "rum, romanism and rebellion," he unequivocally opposed Chinese immigration on racial grounds—thundering his opposition in the

[111]Ibid. (June 19, 1884), 5349–52.

Senate and staging anti-Chinese parades during his presidential campaign—and insisted upon distinguishing white immigrants (including the
Irish) "who assimilate at once with [their] own blood on this soil" from
the Chinese who "to-day approaches no nearer to our civilization than he
did when the Golden Gate first received him."[112]

Anti-Catholic nativists meanwhile would continue to collide with old
labor on matters of social and cultural intervention and conformity. For
anti-Catholic nativists the Republican party would remain home, and they
would endow the party with a strong streak of the older nativism. The
development of antiradical nativism, with its categorical opposition to
European labor migration, further complicated matters. Like anti-Catholic
nativists, antiradical nativists stressed political conformity, but they were
less concerned with ethnoreligious diversity than with the connection
between immigrants such as Kearney, Roney, and Gompers and working-
class insurgency and organization. Finally, out of and alongside Republican anti-Catholic and anti-radical nativism would develop a Republican form of racial nativism, for instance that espoused by Henry
Cabot Lodge. But the Republican party also hosted weighty *antinativist*
constituencies—most important among them, by the 1890s, industrialists
whose position against unions was strengthened by the steady supply of
new-immigrant labor. A Republican nativist consensus would be impossible to develop, but Republican protection of immigration would also be
slow to materialize.

The Democratic path to union nativism would be slightly less rocky
than the pro-immigration path that dominant forces in the Republican
party ultimately followed. The historic Democratic defense of old-stock
immigrants against Whig, Know-Nothing, and Republican anti-Catholic
nativism made nativism as such a problematic principle for Democrats to
embrace. The equally historic Democratic defense of race thinking, however, mediated this difficulty. The race implications of Chinese immigration, which Democrats were quick to stress, allowed Democrats to differ-

[112]James G. Blaine, *Political Discussions* (1887), 216–46. Blaine had been explicitly critical
of pro-Chinese views within his own party throughout the debates on restricting Chinese immigration. In a letter to the editor of the *New York Tribune*, Blaine had echoed labor and Democratic
sentiments in 1879: "When Mr. Garrison says the immigration of Englishmen, Irishmen,
Scotchmen, Frenchmen, Germans, and Scandinavians must be put on the same footing as the
Chinese coolies, he confounds all distinctions, and of course, without intending it, libels almost
the entire white race. . . . In the Chinaman the white laborer finds only another form of servile
competition. . . . Mr. Garrison would not feel obliged to receive into his family a person that
would physically contaminate or morally corrupt his children. As with a family so with a
nation: . . . the same duty to exclude that which is corrupting and dangerous to the Republic!"
(238–40).

entiate between defense of the ethnoreligious and political habits of *immigrants* and opposition to the race and labor-market effects of *immigration*. This differentiation allowed the Democratic party to remain a shelter from anti-Catholic and antiradical nativism while accommodating union nativism. But before the Democratic party could turn its ethnic shelter into a home for union nativism, it would first have to suffer internal and electoral upheaval.

By the turn of the century, contradictions within the parties with respect to immigration would be largely resolved. The Republican position would express procapitalist, pro-immigration interests, while the Democratic position would reflect nativist union sympathies. Also by the turn of the century, the organizational and labor-market anxieties of old labor would have hardened its race logic. The union-building and job-conscious concerns of union labor would be quite wittingly funneled through the sieve of racial nativism. Racial protection of society and labor market would be the first bond in the forging of a union-Democratic tie.

CHAPTER 4

Union, Class, and Party
in the System of 1896

To a considerable extent, . . . both the expansion of industry and
Republican political dominance rested on the immigrant.
—Samuel Lubell, 1951

[The effect of the 1896 realignment] apparently was to reduce the
degree of coincidence of class affiliation and partisan inclinations.
—V. O. Key, 1955

The lessons of Kearneyism for organizing trade-union labor were
chiefly political. It became clear across the decade between the outbreak
of anti-Chinese nativism in San Francisco and passage of the first federal
Chinese exclusion statute that trade union hostility toward particular
groups of immigrants compelled trade-union interest in securing political
influence in the state. Beyond this, the experience of the Workingmen's
party—especially the struggle between trade unionists and politicians for
control of the party apparatus—taught trade-union organizers that political
action by labor outside the party system did not necessarily guarantee
labor's independence from politicians, nor did it necessarily enhance
trade-union autonomy either in politics or over the labor movement.[1] But
the established parties' eventual responsiveness to the only issue as yet to

---

[1] Ideological and organizational rivalry between trade unions and the Knights of Labor was an
important aspect of labor movement politics throughout much of the Gilded Age. Because the
Knights' strength varied substantially from year to year, and because the organization was
moribund by the early 1890s, a discussion of trade union–Knights antagonism is beyond the
scope of this book. Most labor histories of the period can serve as useful references on the matter.
Gerald Grob, *Workers and Utopia* (1969), gives a full view of the different alternatives offered by
the Knights and the AFL. Leon Fink, *Workingmen's Democracy* (1983), looks at the Knights in
politics.

113

politicize labor nationally demonstrated that old labor could secure political leverage to forward its organizational and labor-market interests within the party system, chiefly by attaching policy expectations to the labor vote.

These lessons, along with those drawn from the United Labor party experience in New York in the mid-eighties, to some extent certified the ruling party structure as a medium for political change. They worked to direct trade-union politics into existing channels wherein combinations of groups and classes competed for policy outcomes and political privilege. Just as the New Deal would "let labor in" and thereby validate state pluralism, so Gilded Age nativism allowed the parties to invite labor into their coalition pluralism. As a result the party system was insulated against the transformation of mass democracy into class politics.

Still it was not until the 1896 election redistributed both electoral power and electoral allegiances that trade-union labor actively embraced the party system and its niche within it. Before 1896 party loyalties tended to be so deeply anchored in Civil War scars and cleavages that trade-union partisanship would have been at once counterintuitive and organizationally self-destructive. In the trade-union movement of the Gilded Age, the dominant constituencies were the first-generation Irish and their children, on the one hand, and first- and second-generation Germans, on the other. Trade-union leaders, theoreticians, and strategists were likewise drawn chiefly from these two groups: Strasser (cigar makers), McGuire (carpenters) and O'Connell (machinists), for example.[2] The Gilded Age unified these two groups within trade unionism, but the Civil War had aligned them each separately within the two parties. Offended by Know-Nothingism and Whiggery, and unmoved by abolitionism, the Irish reasserted their loyalty to Jacksonian Democracy by embracing its heir, while many Germans adopted the standard of Republicanism.[3]

[2]David Montgomery, "The Irish and the American Labor Movement," in David Doyle and Owen Edwards, eds., *Ireland and America, 1776–1976: The American Identity and the Irish Connection* (1980), 205–18, argues that by the turn of the century, Irish influence in the trade-union movement far outweighed Irish numerical strength. By the first decade of the twentieth century, when new immigrants were coming to comprise two-thirds of the work force in mining and manufacture, Irish-Americans occupied more than 50 of 110 union presidencies in the AFL.

[3]See James L. Sundquist, *The Dynamics of the Party System* (1973); Eric Foner, *Free Soil, Free Labor, Free Men* (1970); David Montgomery, *Beyond Equality* (1967). These partisan tensions survived even when many German unionists joined the rest of labor in Bryan's Democracy. In 1896 a separate German Democracy was organized in New York City, for example. Tammany disclaimed connection. When the German Democracy invited Governor John Peter Altgeld to speak on Bryan's behalf, Tammany insisted it had "nothing to do with it." *New York Times*, October 14, 1896, p. 8.

The party loyalties that emerged from the Civil War were, as so many have demonstrated, unshakeable for nearly a generation, even as the national parties moved closer together on most questions and as classes moved farther apart. As critical election theory has explained, a new disjuncture between politics and morality, or between polity and economy, would have to surface before an idiomorphic transformation of partisanship could be generated.[4] Until then trade unionism would justify its antipartisan practice in national politics by the disunity it imagined partisanship would bring to the movement. Meanwhile local partisanships could flourish unencumbered, in patterns that conformed with the autonomy of the craft and of the union local.

But neither local partisan autonomy nor a national antipartisan position precluded the discovery and articulation of political interest beyond the local level. Indeed, even before the Supreme Court nationalized the problem of injunctions during the 1890s, trade unionism had discerned a national political interest that pushed it, incrementally, into the national political arena. Beginning with the Chinese, each increment of new immigration prodded organizing labor to defend its position by seeking a national nativist policy, first against Chinese labor and then, successively, against contract labor, pauper labor, and ethnic labor.

The gradual politicization of trade unionism over the course of the Gilded Age prepared unionism to respond politically to the rupture in the party system which surfaced in 1896. Trade unionism, still only ten years strong, responded politically by making itself an agent of the partisan realignment precipitated by the contest between McKinley and Bryan. How did this happen? What role did nativism play in shaping trade-union partisanship, and what consequences did this partisanship have, not only for labor politics in the Progressive decades but for the transformation of American democracy as well?

The analysis in this and succeeding chapters suggests that 1896 was a crucial juncture in the development of the American polity because it let old labor into the party system *as labor*. Before 1896, workers had, to be sure, been part of the party system, but they had participated neither as workers nor as trade unionists. Early suffrage had given workers a place in the electorate, but their place was tied neither to their interest as members of a class nor to their interests as members of a labor movement. Indeed the

---

[4]V. O. Key, "A Theory of Critical Elections," *Journal of Politics* (1955), 17ff.; Sundquist, *Dynamics of the Party System;* Paul Kleppner, *Cross of Culture* (1970); Richard Jensen, *The Winning of the Midwest* (1971); Walter Dean Burnham, *Critical Elections and the Mainsprings of American Politics* (1970); and Samuel McSeveney, *The Politics of Depression* (1972).

liberal premises of mid-nineteenth-century mass democracy placed the individual citizen in a direct (though abstract) relation with the state. Parties organized this relationship, but partisanship was neither the key to policy nor the method of aggregating the programmatic interests of individuals.[5] Individual citizens combined to pursue their interests in politics, but there was a fluidity to faction, with individuals joining and separating as their interests intensified, abated, and changed. Hence American democratic assumptions recognized neither the permanence of certain economic or positional interests nor the permanence of the political formations— whether groups or classes—to which those interests were attached.

The presidential contest of 1896 changed things, however, by bringing unionists within one party on the basis of their group identity and by giving trade unions a voice as an organized group interest within the national Democratic coalition. Yet coherent trade-union partisanship had its costs; in particular, the party of capital rose to power on an industrial working-class base. As a result of this electoral arrangement the trade-union movement removed itself further from labor-based political majorities, while the party of capital enjoyed political ascendancy without having to pay a price for it.[6]

On the Democratic side of the realignment, moreover, democratic participation shifted in focus from the relationship between state and citizen mediated through parties and affirmed through elections to the relationship between group and state mediated through party coalitions. I argue, therefore, that the decision of 1896 began the reconstitution of American democracy wherein the participation of groups and the competition among them would come to substitute for the requirement of mass participation. Not surprisingly, the political rights and access of individuals were devalued as democratic premises changed: the democratic rights of some, especially of new-immigrant industrial workers, were retracted in both substantive and procedural terms while the democratic influence of others, especially of trade unions, was expanded through the celebration of political equality among groups. The numerical potential of anticapitalist majorities was thus defused both where voters congregated (in parties and elections) and where trade unions traveled (in parties and

[5]Cf. Theodore J. Lowi, "Party, Policy and Constitution in America," in William Nisbet Chambers and Walter Dean Burnham, eds., *The American Party Systems* (1975), 238–77.

[6]See Peter Gourevitch, "International Trade, Domestic Coalitions and Liberty: Comparative Responses to the Crisis of 1873–1896," in Thomas Ferguson and Joel Rogers, eds., *The Political Economy* (1984), 290–96, for a comparative discussion of the terms of industrial-sector political hegemony.

eventually in the state). At the same time, capital extended its influence in the state through its claim to democratic majorities. Legislative majorities would now complement judicial discipline, while majoritarian processes would legitimate the procapitalist bias of a Court-dominated state. The electoral choices of old labor and new immigrants were, as we shall see, essential to this reconstruction of the American political universe.

The American Federation of Labor refrained from lending official support to William Jennings Bryan's candidacy but state federations did not, and individual AFL leaders contributed their considerable personal energies to the campaign against William McKinley. The electoral realignment that such efforts produced would lay the groundwork for the AFL's formal entry into coalitional partisan politics during the Progressive Era. For what the realignment accomplished was the relocation of *blocs* within the electorate: into the Democratic camp went many old-stock, trade-union voters while new-immigrant workers veered to the other side. The partisanship of trade unions thus became less problematic; not only did trade-union voters now lean in the same direction, but the national Democratic party no longer had to cater to two antagonistic groups of workers. The Democratic party became more coherent, and coherent trade-union partisanship became possible, once the electoral outcome disentangled incompatible working-class constituencies.

Now new-immigrant industrial workers formed Republican electorates and now the dominant constituencies of both parties differed regarding unionism and ethnic pluralism, illuminating the political and the *partisan* interests of trade unionism. The case for translating the partisanship of individual trade-union voters into the organizational partisanship of trade unions could finally be made. Equally important, the movement of industrial workers into the high tariff, sound money, anti-union coalition gave union labor the field to itself in the Democratic party.

Rather than producing the alignment of party and class which Bryan's campaign rhetoric had predicted, therefore, the election of 1896 opened the way to an alignment of party and union. This tie followed from rearrangements inside the Democratic party which made it not only a low-tariff, free-silver coalition but a *pro-union* coalition as well. Injunction and immigration planks in the Democratic platform worked to strengthen affinities between union and party. Union-party affinities, in turn, helped produce a nativist alignment in the electorate. The party system thus proved its capacity to accommodate labor's group interest, and in so doing showed its relevance to at least one set of divisions produced by industrialism. Party constituencies on the Democratic side and party electoral

117

strategy on the Republican side divided working-class partisanship along a new axis, between union constituencies and nonunion voters.

Trade-Union Nativism Politicized

The election of 1896 culminated a decade of "irrepressible" economic conflict.[7] The militant labor movement that developed during two severe depressions exposed a fraying American consensus. Electoral volatility after 1885 in the industrial Northeast and industrializing Midwest betrayed instability within the polity, while the agrarian revolt in the South and Southwest raised the specter of class politics. But the decade did not climax with either the consolidation of class-based political institutions or a class alignment within the established party system. One reason was that the expansion of the working class through the new immigration created clear boundaries within the class, boundaries that reflected the ethnic, occupational, and organizational position of different groups of workers. Native and old-stock workers mobilized, both occupationally and organizationally, to defend those boundaries. By 1896 the divide between old labor and new immigrants had led old labor toward political action. But because union labor's political action expressed hostility to immigration, unionism could not offer a vehicle for class alignments in politics. And because nativism limited its rationale for purposive political action at the national level, union labor was easily coopted and integrated by the parties in power. As a result the party that accommodated both trade-union and agrarian interests in 1896 had no organic connection to the movements of either group. The party that looked like a class *party* was in fact merely the vehicle of a class *fragment* aligned against industrial workers.

Indeed the mass desertion of the Democratic party by new immigrant industrial workers in 1896[8] revealed how deeply immigration had divided the working class. The failure of the labor movement to deliver the "toiling masses" for Bryan bared a profound fissure within his electoral base. Further, the rejection of Bryan's "avowed class party"[9] by new immigrant workers demonstrated that nativism was obscuring a class basis for electoral choice. Finally, the pivotal role of immigrant workers in restor-

---

[7]Sundquist, 131. See also Lawrence Goodwyn, *The Populist Moment* (1978).

[8]Stanley L. Jones, *The Presidential Election of 1896* (1964), 243; Samuel Lubell, *The Future of American Politics* (1951, 1965), 50.

[9]See Sundquist, *Dynamics of the Party System.*

ing the Republican party to national dominance showed the political impotence of a labor movement cleft by nativism.

Immigration accelerated during the 1880s, increasing the impetus to nativism within trade-union ranks. The demographic changes that jolted America in the latter part of the Gilded Age hit settled workers hardest. Of the newer immigrant groups, the earliest arrivals were, disproportionately, unskilled males of working age whose very presence yielded an explanation for disruptions in the old consensus as well as for the difficult birth of trade unionism. Between 1880 and 1890 immigration swelled to nearly six million and so transformed the work force that by the latter year, 33 percent of workers in manufacture and 50 percent in coal mining were foreign born.[10] In many industrial ghettos in the Northeast, nearly three-fourths of the working population were immigrants. The conjuncture of surging immigration, depression, urban congestion, and labor unrest[11] heightened the salience of the immigration problem for settled workers and eventually elicited support from social reformers and intellectuals for trade-union nativism. By the end of the turbulent eighties, men as remotely connected as Samuel Gompers and the progressive economist Edward Bemis agreed that restrictions on immigration topped the agenda for social reform.[12]

Until 1896, however, the electoral behavior of workers concealed the depth of these problems, obscured the internal fragmentation of the working class, and blurred the nativist cleavage. A large share of the eligible working-class vote—whether native, old stock, or new immigrant, and whether organized or unorganized—had supported the Democratic party, mostly for reasons unrelated to economic position. In Democratic cities, old labor and new immigrants were recruited as Democratic voters, whether through patronage (old labor) or welfare (new immigrants). Across urban and industrial America more widely, workers could identify the Democratic party as the party of "personal liberty," in stark contrast to the pietistic and patrician moralism typical of Republicanism in the Midwest and North. For an increasingly Catholic working class, Democratic protection of social, cultural, and religious preferences and practices provided an important partisan appeal. Democrats had, among other

[10]William Z. Ripley, "Race Factors in Labor Unions," *Atlantic Monthly,* 93 (1904), 300. For an incisive discussion of this period, see Melvyn Dubofsky, *Industrialism and the American Worker* (1975), chaps. 1 and 2.

[11]See Harry Jerome, *Migration and Business Cycles* (1926); Jacob Riis, *How the Other Half Lives* (1890); and John Higham, *Strangers in the Land* (1977), 54.

[12]See Arthur Mann, "Gompers and the Irony of Racism," *Antioch Review,* 13 (June 1953), 211; Higham, 101.

things, traditionally opposed prohibition, defended parochial schools and instruction in native languages, and shielded Irish and German Catholics from the political nativism of anti-Catholic crusaders.[13]

The Democratic defense of personal liberty protected newcomers without discriminating among them. The party hosted overlapping ethnoreligious constituencies, but these same constituencies were internally segmented along organizational, labor-market, and racial lines. The Democratic defense against anti-Catholic nativism helped consolidate electorates who were the very targets of the racial nativism increasingly espoused by old labor. The GOP, meanwhile, was generally associated with a strident cultural and political nativism (Know-Nothingism, prohibition, and monoculturalism) directed against much of old labor as well as against new immigrants. Thus the Republican party was an implausible ally for nativists from the (increasingly Catholic) working class. Catholic old-stock workers, now nativists themselves, had, after all, been the victims of Republican nativism for a generation. Moreover, Republican anti-Catholic nativism survived well into the Gilded Age. It figured in the 1876 presidential contest, when Republicans attacked the church, associated the Democrats with papacy, and alleged that Democratic voters were under Vatican control. Also in 1876 House Republican leader James G. Blaine introduced a constitutional amendment to prohibit any public support for parochial schools while explicitly permitting the Protestant practice of Bible reading in any school or institution. In 1880 the Republican campaign charged that Democrats would destroy public schools, and the party platform called for the constitutional amendment sponsored by Blaine. And in 1884, in the first presidential contest lost by Republicans since the Civil War, Protestant ministers and Republican politicians sharpened their anti-Catholic attacks, calling the Democratic party the party of "rum, romanism, and rebellion."

Though all nativists shared the exclusionist ambition to return to an idealized homogeneous, consensual order, trade-union nativists—moved by labor-market and organizational anxieties—differed from their Republican counterparts—moved by cultural anxieties—on *who* should be excluded and on what grounds. Until nativisms and nativist remedies could be distinguished one from another, trade-union nativism and worker partisanship would remain unintegrated.

Neither party, clearly, could easily serve as a vehicle for the new nativism, part of whose constituency sat beside new immigrants in the

---

[13]See Jensen, *Winning of the Midwest*, and Kleppner, *Cross of Culture*.

Democratic party and whose ideology was orthogonal to the traditional strain of political nativism left over from the Civil War period. During the 1880s and '90s, however, both parties developed nativist rhetoric in response to Gilded Age demographic change, and both postured less and less distinguishably in support of some form of limited restriction—notwithstanding pro-immigration, capitalist constituencies in the Republican party and anti-nativist, Catholic constituencies in the Democratic party. This was, perhaps, a crucial sign of the permeability of the party system, for despite the fuzziness of party nativism with respect to the categorical exclusion of groups other than the Chinese, both parties bowed to pressures to legislate against "undesirable" individuals: convicts, lunatics, and slavish recruits. But neither party was willing to legislate any unilateral restriction on the new immigration. For quite different reasons, neither party had a method for such restriction available to it, because as yet, protest against immigration had not been translated into systematic racial criticism of particular new-immigrant groups. Further, as nativism's only *group* target, other than the Chinese, had for years been a *religious* target, and as new immigrants were invariably non-Protestant, trade-union nativists in particular were wary lest restriction by group became a means to resurrect religious criteria for participation in American political and economic life.

Hence neither party during the eighties and early nineties was able to aggregate, accommodate, and defuse the unfocused anxiety of the new nativism. As long as nativism remained politically undifferentiated from anti-Catholicism, the Democratic party could not easily embrace it. And as long as its own anti-Catholicism went unexorcised, the Republican party was an unlikely political home for the trade-union nativists of the Gilded Age. Moreover, *both* parties were composed of rival constituencies: trade-union and agrarian nativists vied with new immigrants in the Democratic party, while in the GOP the nativist heirs of Know-Nothingism were challenged by industrialists for whom unregulated immigration was the human side of laissez-faire. The compromise within the Democratic party took the form of a partisan nativism limited in its object to groups and persons irrelevant to electoral success: the Chinese, criminals, and the feeble. A similar compromise in the Republican party was expressed as nativism limited to the cultural arena, directed not against immigration but against the life-style associated with ritualistic religion.[14]

[14]Jensen, *Winning of the Midwest;* Kleppner, *Cross of Culture;* and Gerald K. Marsden, "Patriotic Societies and American Labor: The American Protective Association in Wisconsin," *Wisconsin Magazine of History,* 41 (Summer 1948).

The Union-Party Tie

The new nativism lacked coherent expression through political institutions for much of the Gilded Age, even as antiforeign sentiment crystallized among organized workers during the period. But except for the campaign against the Chinese, even trade-union nativism remained unfocused until intellectuals and reformers defined the problem as the *racially* indiscriminate nature of federal immigration policy.[15] Early political demands from trade unionists, aside from Chinese exclusion, centered on regulating the entry of *individuals* judged unfit. The trade-union standard of fitness was based on the distinction between voluntary and induced immigration, and its objective was to bar the entry of immigrant workers on contract. This position drew its logic from the positive association of "voluntary" with northern and western European immigration and the negative association of "induced" immigration with Slavic and Italian recruits. Northern and western European immigrants, it was understood, freely chose to come to America because they valued liberty, equality, and the American way of life. New immigrants, it was believed, came at the behest and on the terms of capital. Because they appeared to have responded to the pull of wages rather than of liberal democracy, they were viewed as materially instrumental and politically unassimilable—and thus as despoilers of the American way of life.[16]

The call for a ban on contract labor was implicitly a call for racial exclusion, but no racial basis for exclusion had as yet been systematically and explicitly articulated. Until the 1890s, when nativism became anchored in racial theories, labor and its allies pursued roundabout solutions to the immigration problem. Most of their solutions, tailored as they were to treat economic symptoms, proved inadequate. The passage of a federal contract labor law in 1884, for example, failed to stem the influx of immigrants recruited to break unionism and cheapen labor costs. Capital found that it could recruit an ample supply of immigrant workers without

[15]See Francis Walker, "Immigration," *Yale Review*, 1 (1892), 125–45, "The Great Count of 1890," *Forum*, 11 (1891), 406–18, and his "Immigration and Degradation," *Forum*, 11 (1891), 634–44; Barbara Solomon, *Ancestors and Immigrants* (1956), 72.

[16]These assumptions were axiomatic in nativist thought and propaganda. Articles documenting the moral, mental, and social inferiority of new immigrant groups were commonplace in periodicals, and intellectuals (e.g., John Commons, Frederick Jackson Turner, Woodrow Wilson) gave scholarly weight to these views. See, especially, Edward Bemis, "Restriction of Immigration," *Andover Review*, March 1888, pp. 25–64; Francis Walker, "Restriction of Immigration," *North American Review*, June 1896, pp. 823–29; and Richmond Mayo-Smith, "Control of Immigration," *Political Science Quarterly*, 3 (June 1888), 197–225. The AFL position was more cautiously articulated by Henry White in "Immigration Restriction as a Necessity" and by E. E. Clark, Grand Chief, Order of Railway Conductors, in "Immigration," both in the *American Federationist*, 4 (1897), 137–38.

without having to sign them to contracts, and the new immigration took on a momentum of its own.

Having failed to stop the new immigration at its source, organized workers stepped up their efforts to restrict the access of new immigrants to employment. By the late 1880s workers in several states had won discriminatory legislation designed to curtail job opportunities for new immigrants. But these statutes were mostly symbolic: under laissez-faire capitalism they could limit immigrant opportunities only with respect to *public* employment. Thus New York and Pennsylvania could bar all aliens from employment on state and local public works, while Illinois could apply a similar statute against immigrants who failed to declare their aspirations to citizenship. In New Jersey the Newark Board of Works went one step further, resolving that private employers who contracted for public works should give preferential treatment to unemployed *citizens*. States and localities could not always withstand conservative judicial scrutiny, however, even where their own public employment was concerned: the New York State Supreme Court struck down such a statute in 1896, for example.[17] Nor could states and localities attack immigrant labor at its core, the private industries into which new-immigrant workers were streaming.[18]

Policies directed against contract workers and toward the restriction of immigrant employment did not achieve the job protection that labor nativists sought. As the eighties drew to a close, in consequence, labor organizations inclined to identify the immigrant menace by group and to advance policy proposals aimed at restricting immigration by group. Still, restriction by immigrant category did not sit well with rank-and-file trade unionists, many of whom were themselves foreign-born. Understandably the rank and file was concerned about the criteria for restriction: would religious homogeneity, for example, become the rationale for immigration control? Beyond this, first- and second-generation workers feared that restriction policies would not draw fast lines between types of immigration, thereby imprecating immigration per se and undercutting the hard-earned acceptance of old-stock immigrants though regulating the influx of the new. Hence even as late as 1897, after the racial typology of immigration had given an anchor to racial nativism, the AFL rank and file was reluctant to

---

[17]The issue was of such importance to New York City labor unions in 1896 that when unionists learned that Judge Titus, a candidate for the Court of Appeals on the Democratic ticket, had concurred in the decision, the Central Labor Union adopted a motion to encourage all labor organizations to boycott his name on the ballot.

[18]McSeveney, 35; Higham, 46.

endorse the literacy test—only implicitly a racial criterion—as a way to control immigration.[19]

By the early 1890s most trade unionists were convinced of the need to restrict immigration by type, though uncertain about how to achieve it. Indeed, once persuaded that a new immigration policy could reflect the new nativism, several trade unions—including the citywide federation in New York—went on record in support of proposals for specific restrictions.[20] By the mid-nineties the immigration issue had been politicized along the lines of this new principle for restriction, enabling nativist trade unionism to provide a basis for trade-union political action on a national scale.

The political focus of trade unionism after 1890 followed upon the clear identification of new sources of immigration by three Boston economists. Because the economists married their discovery to a call to restrict only the new immigration, they made trade-union nativism intellectually and politically defensible. Because discovery of new sources established a racial principle for restriction, moreover, old-stock immigrants in trade unions—Irish, Germans, and British—could be confident that restrictive policy would favorably distinguish old labor from the mass of peasants who had become the new immigrant proletariat.

During the early period of working-class nativism the intellectuals who later appealed for restriction had accepted free immigration as necessary for industrial development.[21] To the extent that they shared nativist assumptions, they also shared the antebellum nativist focus on restricting *citizenship*—and thus on limiting the political power of the foreign-born—rather than on restricting *immigration*. But as census data began to corroborate the anxieties expressed by *both* cultural and trade-union nativism, scholarship began to reflect both anxieties. Eventually nativist scholarship formulated a policy antidote for the immigration problem that spoke to cultural fears while allaying trade-union fears of anti-Catholicism and embracing the trade-union analysis. Francis Walker, census chief in 1870 and an MIT economist, was the first of the Boston economists to break with older nativist prescriptions. In doing so, he repudiated his own earlier conviction that Irish Catholicism was inimical to the American way, thus helping distance the new nativism from religious argument. Although it took him twenty years to devise a scheme for restriction, Walker began in the early 1870s to sketch his concerns.

[19]See the AFL Convention *Proceedings* (1896), and *American Federationist*, 4 (1897).
[20]Higham, 71, 346 n. 9.
[21]Solomon, 71.

He first voiced his alarm about immigration when, through his work on the 1870 census, he discovered a decline in the birth rate of the native stock. Walker's discovery led him to two conclusions: first, that the foreign-born, increasingly Catholic, were more prolific than native Americans and hence less moral; second, that immigration, now the only factor accounting for aggregate population increases, was obscuring the stark decline in the birth rate. Walker hereafter attached a social significance to immigration which eclipsed his regard for its economic value. Implicit in his new approach was the belief that the displacement of the native stock by first- and second-generation ethnics posed a danger to the health of the polity.[22] When the 1880 census confirmed his fears of a sustained decline in the native birth rate, Walker shifted his attention to the relationship between immigrant fecundity and the new sources of immigration. He also noted the shift toward immigration from eastern, central, and southern Europe, bringing these concerns together in a racial criticism of new immigrant groups. When the 1890 census revealed that more than five million immigrants had arrived during the previous decade, Walker launched a blistering public attack against the new immigrant stream:

> Only a short time ago, the immigrants from southern Italy, Hungary, Austria and Russia together made up hardly more than one per cent of our immigration. Today the proportion has risen to something like forty per cent, and threatens soon to become fifty or sixty per cent or even more. The entrance into our political, social, and industrial life of such masses of peasantry, degraded below our utmost conceptions, is a matter which no intelligent patriot can look upon without gravest apprehension and alarm. These people have no history behind them which is of a nature to give encouragement. They have none of the inherited instincts and tendencies which made it comparatively easy to deal with the immigration of olden time. They are beaten men from beaten races; representing the worst failure in the struggle for existence.[23]

In articles appearing in the *North American Review, Forum,* and the *Yale Review,* Walker drew upon the Teutonic typology developed by students of Anglo-Saxon Studies at Harvard University in the 1870s to differentiate, "scientifically," the old immigrants from the new. Democracy, according to Teutonic theory, developed in the Teutonic forests and

[22]See Solomon, *Ancestors and Immigrants,* and Higham, *Strangers in the Land,* for thorough discussions of Walker's views.
[23]Walker, "Restriction of Immigration," 828. See also his "The Great Count of 1890."

was imparted to modern society by the lineal descendants of the people who presided at its birth. Northern and western Europeans were the Teutonic race and thus were capable of "democratic character"; peasants from the recesses of Europe were not. The theory allowed Walker to characterize the new immigrants as racially unfit to participate in American life because their inability to assimilate—to reason, to become civilized, to appreciate liberty—had been racially preordained. Thus he wrote:

> Their habits of life . . . are of the most revolting kind. Read the description given by Mr. Riis of the police driving from the garbage dumps the miserable beings who try to burrow in those depths of unutterable filth and slime in order that they may eat and sleep there! Was it in cement like this that the foundations of our republic were laid? What effects must be produced upon our social standards, and upon the ambitions and aspirations of our people, by a contact so foul and loathesome? . . . Centuries are against them, as centuries were on the side of those who formerly came to us. They have none of the ideas and aptitudes which fit men to take up readily and easily the problem of self-care and self-government, such as belong to those who are descended from the tribes that met under the oak trees of old Germany to make laws and choose chieftains.[24]

Underscoring his point, Walker retracted his earlier harsh condemnation of the Irish invasion. Observing that the republic had withstood the strain of religious and cultural (as opposed to racial) heterogeneity, Walker focused his indictment on neither immigration per se nor cultural idiosyncracies. Instead, his focus was the immigration of specified, racially inferior groups. For Walker, the question was not even one of

> preventing the wards of our almshouses, our insane asylums, and our jails from being stuffed to repletion by new arrivals from Europe; but of protecting the American rate of wages, the American standard of living, and the quality of American citizenship from degradation through the tumultuous access of vast throngs of ignorant and brutalized peasantry from the countries of eastern and southern Europe.[25]

Toward the end of the eighties, two of Walker's colleagues in the American Economic Association enlisted in his effort to design a policy

---

[24]Walker, "The Great Count of 1890." See also Riis, *How the Other Half Lives.*
[25]Walker, "Restriction of Immigration."

that would restrict the entry of this segment of humanity. In a series of lectures in 1887 and in a pair of articles in the *Andover Review* in 1888, Edward Bemis offered a landmark proposal, soon to become the chief legislative objective of nativists for thirty years: the literacy test. Arguing that restrictions against the immigration of criminals, paupers, lunatics, and anarchists were inadequate—and foreshadowing Southern rationales for analogous restrictions on black citizenship—Bemis advocated that "no man over the age of sixteen who cannot read and write in his own language" be admitted. By this simple provision, he argued, "all the most undesirable classes of all nations would be excluded." While the "Swedes, Germans, English, Scotch and most of the Irish would not be left out to any great extent," the test would reduce the volume of new immigration by at least 50 percent.[26] Clearly the undisguised purpose of the literacy test was to bar entry of a specific class of immigrant: the illiterate poor who constituted the new immigration.

The third theorist of the new nativism was slower to embrace restrictions than either Walker or Bemis. Through most of the 1880s, Richmond Mayo-Smith defended immigration as an economic necessity. As late as 1887 he was dismissing trade unionists' appeals for even the limited restriction of pauper labor as "demagogy."[27] But by the turn of the decade Mayo-Smith's regard for the economic advantages of immigration to capitalists had been displaced by his own concern for the racial integrity of the American republic. From 1888 onward he wrote prolifically in support of proposals for selective, racial controls on immigration.[28] He made his chief contributions to the new nativism in the early nineties, when he embellished upon Walker's Teutonic schema for restriction and when he helped found the Boston-based Immigration Restriction League.

Nativist intellectuals, by providing a formula for selective restriction, helped solidify a political agenda for trade-union nativism. Equally important, the Teutonic analysis of immigration—garnished with self-reprimanding praises of the Irish by their erstwhile critics—dispelled the fear lingering among old-stock Catholic workers that political nativism necessarily meant anti-Catholic bigotry.

The logic of new nativist theory gave systematic expression to the

[26]Edward Bemis, "The Restriction of Immigration," 263, and "The Distribution of our Immigrants," *Andover Review*, June 1888, pp. 587–96.
[27]Solomon, 78.
[28]Richmond Mayo-Smith, "Control of Immigration," and *Emigration and Immigration* (1890).

anxieties that underlay nativism within the trade-union movement. The nativism that had framed the group consciousness of organizing workers and distorted their economic critique of the industrial order could now become fully political. But once politicized by nativism, trade unionism set itself not only against new immigrants but also against the mounting industrial working class. Political trade-union nativism was openly racist: as it sought redress from the competition of unskilled immigrant workers, it also formalized the vague ethnic stereotypes that contaminated relations with those workers. Now political, trade-union nativism expunged the fiction that it was directed against immigrants solely as *economic* rivals—now its objective was overtly *racial* protection. Political trade-union nativism accordingly set in motion a political polarization of the working class along Teutonic lines. This political polarization was abetted by, and coincided with, an organizational polarization of the class: in an exclusionist unionism, working-class institutions (unions) served a restricted clientele (old labor), while nativist trade-union politics separated the electoral path of old labor from that of the new.[29]

The Bryan-McKinley contest of 1896 gave electoral expression to the nativist cleavage within the working class. Rather than produce an alignment of all nativists in one party against immigrants and their sympathizers (capital and some of the clergy) in the other, however, the election yielded a realignment that, with respect to nativism, was specific to the working class. In the long run the specificity of this nativist realignment would decide the political future of the labor movement. Electoral and institutional separation from the working class pushed the only organized segment of the class into coalition with classes above—to pursue union-conscious reform of labor policy, and to develop a race-conscious immigration policy.

Republican nativists generally remained Republican in '96. Some Prohibitionists switched allegiance to form a curious partnership with Irish

[29]In 1896 some unionists in Brooklyn and New York City worked to make the political struggle for immigration restriction an integral component of unionism. They organized the Protective Labor Union with the intention to extend the organization nationally through introduction "into the regular labor organizations." Their objective was to reach a position of organized strength in order to "approach Congressional nominees of both parties and urge their support for the restriction of immigration." Specifically, they demanded passage of the Lodge-Corliss Bill to restrict immigration by literacy test; additional legislation limiting the volume of immigration to 50,000 per year; and the establishment of an immigration board consisting of representatives of unions, which would have the power to distribute immigrants to localities not already overcrowded with workers, to prevent immigrants from taking the jobs of strikers and from accepting less than the current rate of wages, and to deport immigrants still unemployed after sixty days in the United States. See "Protective Labor Unions," *New York Times,* October 1, 1896, p. 12.

Catholics in the Democratic party.[30] But most members of the moribund American Protective Association stuck with the GOP, even in the face of McKinley's open courtship of Catholic voters. In addition the intellectual, reform, and patrician partisans of Teutonism tended to support McKinley. Clearly, nativism was for Republicans and for the middle class only one of a cluster of issues. Alone it could not compel support for the party of free silver, commodity price inflation, and organized labor.

Within the Democratic party, however, nativism pulled the electoral coalition apart and determined the new alignment of working-class votes. The labor plank in the party's platform made nativism a central principle of organized labor when it declared that "the most efficient way of protecting American labor is to prevent the importation of foreign pauper labor," which is to say, European new-immigrant peasants.[31] But while Bryan Democrats seized the standard of Populist and trade-union nativism, McKinley wooed and won new-immigrant voters.[32] Because McKinley offered himself as the defender of "cultural pluralism,"[33] Bryan's "toiling masses" were polarized. Settled workers who sought protection for unions and against immigration now faced their immigrant nemesis across party lines.

The Parties Realign

Although trade-union nativism was one of the factors shaping voter realignment in 1896, it was the economic and political crisis of the decade that triggered the realignment of America's political parties. The depression of 1893 and the Populist challenge heightened tensions among Democrats. Not only did the Democratic party, in control of the White House, preside over the depression, but the agrarian protest suggested profound discontent within the Democratic coalition. Associated with the "gold bug" wing of the party, Grover Cleveland did nothing to shore up the agrarian wing on questions of money and credit. Moreover, he alienated Democratic unionists when his administration appealed to the federal courts to discipline strikers and used federal troops during the Pullman

[30]Most of the prohibitionists who voted Democratic in 1896 had drifted out of the GOP and into the Populist Party after 1891.

[31]William Jennings Bryan, *The First Battle* (1896), 408.

[32]Jones, *Presidential Election of 1896*. Ignatius Donnelly was one of the most vigorous Populist nativists: see his *Caesar's Column* (1894) and *The Golden Bottle* (1892).

[33]Jensen, *Winning of the Midwest*, passim.

strike. By 1896 Cleveland's party looked like a procapitalist, anti-union party, notwithstanding the countervailing constituencies within it. Ultimately this forced a challenge to Cleveland's leadership within the party. What resulted was the capture of the Democratic party by agrarian Democrats and by urban Democrats sympathetic to organized labor, sharpening the differences between the Democratic and Republican parties. In 1896 electoral competition appeared to be a contest between parties that represented conflicting economic interests: farmers and workers, on the one hand, against industrial and finance capital, on the other.[34]

Unrelenting double-digit unemployment, the ravages of the crop-lien system, the temporary but precipitous decline in real wages, the mounting number of strikes, rising interest rates, the increase in farm foreclosures, and severe price deflation, all collaborated to polarize debtor and creditor interests within the Democratic party during the 1890s.[35] Cleveland's unswerving opposition to the monetization of silver focused discontent among agrarian Democrats who attributed their economic woes to the currency famine.[36] His inattention to problems of joblessness and poverty alienated workers who were otherwise unmoved by the controversy over silver coinage.[37] But what completed the rupture of Cleveland's Democracy was the president's use of federal troops and injunctions against Pullman strikers in 1894.[38] Cleveland had already frustrated unionists when he refused to enforce the anti-Chinese Geary Act even after the Supreme Court upheld the act in 1893. The use of federal weapons against strikers in 1894, a year that involved nearly 750,000 workers in strikes and that counted three million unemployed during the winter alone, frustrated unionists further.[39] The president's mustering of federal power in defense of the railroads during the Pullman strike was thus taken as studied contempt of organized labor. Not surprisingly, organized labor was thrown into angry coalition with agrarian silverites, while powerful

[34]For a thorough discussion of the economic effects of the depression see Charles Hoffman, "The Depression of the Nineties," *Journal of Economic History*, 16 (June 1956), 137–64.

[35]Kleppner, 141; Paul Douglas, *Real Wages* (1930); Sundquist, 30, 114; and Norman Pollack, *The Populist Response to Industrial America* (1962); C. Vann Woodward, in *The Orgins of the New South* (1971) provides an instructive discussion of the economic problems of farmers in the South and Southwest.

[36]The Sherman Silver Purchase Act was repealed in the autumn of 1893.

[37]J. Rogers Hollingsworth, *The Whirligig of Politics* (1963), 29.

[38]Matthew Josephson, *The Politicos* (1966), 568ff.; Philip Foner, *History of the Labor Movement in the United States*, vol. 2 (1955), 261–79; Nathan Fine, *Labor and Farmer Parties in the United States, 1828–1928* (1961), 80–81; and Sundquist, 134.

[39]John Commons et al., *History of Labor*, vol. 2 (1935), 501; Josephson, 560.

friends of labor within the party—Tammany Hall and Governor John Altgeld of Illinois—were mobilized against the old Democracy.

Heavy Democratic losses in the depression elections preceding 1896 exposed the vulnerability of the party in power. The party's continued alignment on the side of free trade, especially its support for the Wilson-Gorman tariff in 1892, exacerbated that vulnerability, because it was seen in many quarters to ensure a worsening of the depression.[40] In local elections in 1893 Republicans hammered hard on the depression issue, chiefly by associating their commitment to tariff protection with their commitment to a healthy economy. In Pennsylvania, Republicans campaigned on the tariff to win their largest margin of victory since 1872. In New Jersey, they elected majorities in both houses of the state legislature; in Massachusetts, they recaptured the governorship. In Ohio, William McKinley won his gubernatorial contest with more votes than any candidate in state history. In New York, where the election was complicated by a long-standing Cleveland-Tammany split, Republicans won all contested state offices to produce majorities at Albany and at the state constitutional convention.[41]

The anti-Democratic tide persisted in the 1894 federal elections. The GOP continued to press economic issues; the Democrats responded with non sequitur lambasts against Republican anti-Catholicism. In twenty-four states no Democrats were elected to the U.S. House; in six, Democrats elected only one; and in all New England, only one Democrat survived the congressional election. The most damaging losses were in northeastern cities and other centers of industrial unemployment. The election left the Democracy in a shambles: a House of Representatives that had been 62

[40]In a full-page spread describing the negative consequences issuing from the free-trade legislation of the Democratic Party, the *San Francisco Chronicle* argued: "Four years of Cleveland has been enough for the prunegrowers, and they regard Bryan as a free trade office seeker, who, in the event of success, would continue the work of impoverishing the country by advancing the interests of foreign producers rather than of Americans. . . . McKinley and protection means prosperity, while Bryan and tariff reform means low prices, cheapness, and bankruptcy." See "The Case of McKinley and Protection Versus Bryan and Bankruptcy," *San Francisco Chronicle*, September 1, 1896, p. 8. In a separate piece, "Labor and Wages in Milwaukee" (September 6, 1896, p. 34), the *Chronicle* went on to document the consequences of Democratic tariff policy for industry. Quoting a Milwaukee millowner, the *Chronicle* reported: "We were just getting a good foothold in a thousand or more small industries under the McKinley Law, when this foolish free trade legislation upset the whole business and threw a hundred thousand skilled mechanics out of work, and for what? . . . The advent of the tariff raiders in 1893 cost Milwaukee $27,000,000.00 in round figures in the decrease in the value of the product of her manufactures."
[41]McSeveney, 41.

percent Democratic after 1892 became 69 percent Republican, and the Democrats were reduced to a scant one dozen seats from the North and the West—only six from outside New York City.[42] Though Republican resurgence and Democratic decline in 1893 and '94 measured a growing discontent, however, neither signaled a permanent realignment of the electorate because neither represented a sharpening of differences between the parties. For the dealignment of the depression elections to become a realignment, at least one party had to break with the centrist bloc that moderated stands on the issues. Third-party pressures arising from Populism combined with the Pullman strike to provide the Democratic party with an incentive for such a break. When the break occurred, a farmer-labor alliance that had failed to come together in the People's Party materialized as the Democratic coalition.

For union labor, the role of the Democratic Administration in breaking the Pullman strike was decisive in pulling it into alliance with agrarian Democrats. That strike, broken by federal injunctions and troops, revealed union labor's special vulnerability to unfriendly state power. What is more, it made the stance toward unionism of *national* government a central union concern. The injunction issue thus joined the immigration issue to deepen union labor's interest in specifically national political outcomes.

What was significant about the Pullman strike was that it engaged coercive and punitive state power on the side of an employer notorious for feudal labor practices. The strike involved a national secondary boycott; consequently, federal intervention was of considerable scale. The strike marked a turning point in the development of the labor injunction, moreover, culminating two years of judicial rulings that had expanded judicial authority in industrial disputes and extending the scope of activities prohibited by injunctions. The Pullman strike gave the labor injunction national prominence and, by locating its use in the federal jurisdiction, made it a national weapon in the conflict between labor and capital.[43]

The story of the Pullman strike has been ably told elsewhere. Of relevance here is that as the secondary boycott spread among railway workers who refused to handle Pullman cars (at one point 150,000 workers were involved), President Cleveland's attorney general, Richard Olney, asked the U.S. District Court in Chicago to enjoin the strikers. Significantly, he cited the Sherman Anti-Trust Act as legal justification for an injunction—

---

[42]Hollingsworth, 28ff.; Sundquist, 135.
[43]See Arnold Paul, *Conservative Crisis and the Rule of Law* (1976), chap. 7.

the first appeal to federal power by a Democratic administration against labor.[44] In addition, Olney construed the Interstate Commerce Act, a law designed to regulate railroad corporations, so as to provide further support for the legal denial of the workers' right to combine. The sweep of the injunction allowed the federal government to secure indictments against strike leaders in Chicago and elsewhere for defying the courts, hindering interstate commerce, obstructing the mails, and conspiracy. The following year the Supreme Court lent its weight to the labor injunction, when it ruled, in *In Re Debs,*

> The entire strength of the nation may be used to enforce in any part of the land the full and free exercise of all national powers and the security of all rights entrusted by the Constitution to its care. The strong arm of the national government may be put forth to brush away all obstructions to the freedom of interstate commerce or the transportation of the mails. If the emergency arises, the army of the Nation, and all its militia, are at the service of the Nation to compel obedience to its laws.[45]

Once the injunction had been issued, Cleveland ordered federal troops to Chicago to enforce it, the Democratic party's traditional deference to local autonomy notwithstanding. He did so without consulting Governor Altgeld who, though sympathetic to labor, had not hesitated in the past to dispatch state troops to calm labor disorder. Altgeld's ire was only thinly veiled when he wired the president in protest:

> Sir: I am advised that you have ordered federal troops to go into service of the state of Illinois. Surely the facts have not been correctly presented to you in this case . . . for it is entirely unnecessary, and as it seems to me, unjustifiable. . . . I will say that the state of Illinois is not only able to take care of itself, but it stands ready to furnish the Federal government any assistance it may need elsewhere. Our military force is ample.

Altgeld further protested that "local self-government is a fundamental principle of our Constitution."[46]

Cleveland's action during the Pullman strike accomplished several things. It raised the labor question within the Democratic party. It linked

[44]Sherman Antitrust was first used against labor during a general strike in New Orleans in 1892.

[45]*In Re Debs,* 158 U.S. 564; 15 S.CT. 900 (1895).

[46]Quoted in Josephson, 584, and Ray Ginger, *Atgeld's America* (1973), 160. See also Foner, 2: 267–68.

his currency policy to a more general sympathy for capital. It permanently alienated one of the two most powerful Democratic state leaders—Governor Altgeld.[47] And it placed the central government—not simply judges—squarely in opposition to unionism. Presidential enforcement of judicial injunctions furthermore tied electoral outcomes to the future of unionism.

The immediate consequence of the Pullman episode was that a significant force within the Democratic party, Governor Altgeld, joined with Democratic silverites to denounce Cleveland and his allies in the ruling coalition. Altgeld—who became an important link between organized labor and the party—brought with him industrial Democrats now willing to rally to the free silver banner against Cleveland's Gold Democracy.[48] When the Democrats convened in 1896 to nominate their presidential choice, this internecine rift produced complete repudiation of the old Democracy. With the exception of its low-tariff provision, the platform—written by Altgeld—rejected every position associated with the Cleveland wing of the party. It called for the free coinage of silver at sixteen to one and for strict control of monopolies through a fortified Interstate Commerce Commission. It rebuked Cleveland for his use of troops in the Pullman strike and denounced "government by injunction." And it urged the restriction of European "pauper" immigration. Bryan's nomination and the "people's" platform betokened the triumph of agrarian and labor interests, completing the movement to wrest control of the party from the Gold Democrats.[49]

Because it impelled many Gold Democrats—that is, Eastern party leaders connected to capital—to bolt, Bryan's nomination allowed the party to distinguish itself sharply from the GOP. In its platform and rhetoric the new Democratic party appealed to farmers and unions directly, thereby clearly aligning itself with the economic interests of those who depended on credit, wages, and political protection of unions for survival. In these respects the new Democracy presented a stark contrast to the GOP, for the Republicans offered wage and price protection through gold and the high tariff, were antagonistic to unions, and promised cultural pluralism through absorption of new immigrant groups. Ironically, though the two parties differed on the tariff issue, both represented protectionist constitu-

---

[47]When Cleveland worked to subvert the prolabor gubernatorial candidacy of David Hill in New York later in the year, he alienated the other most powerful state leader. Jones, 47–48.

[48]Much of organized labor preferred Altgeld as the presidential nominee, but unfortunately he was foreign-born.

[49]For an account of Altgeld's role at the convention and in the Bryan campaign see Josephson, chap. 19, Bryan, 408–14, and Foner, 2: 333.

encies. But the protectionism of each reflected the opposing perspectives of capital and union labor: essential for capital was protection from *foreign goods* (hence the tariff), while essential for union labor was protection from *foreign workers* (hence immigration restriction). Both denounced "cheap foreign labor" as an economic evil, but by this capital meant the labor that produced cheap goods abroad while union labor meant the labor of new immigrants in American industry.

The electorate thus had a clear choice between presidential alternatives. Under the leadership of William McKinley, and more especially Marcus Hanna, the GOP became both unambivalently and uncontestedly the party of capital. The Democratic party, however, did not become the party in opposition to capital. If anything it became the party in opposition to industrialism.[50] As such, it joined unions and the South in opposition to state expansion;[51] and it joined unions and farmers in opposition to corporate liberalism and its financial and industrial policies. The Democratic party paid a heavy electoral price for the joining of these constituencies. In the industrial sector the Democratic electorate contracted dramatically even as the party gained the electoral support of union labor. For the Republicans, the changes in the Democratic coalition provided an opportunity, on the basis of common interests in industrialism, to court new voters and spurned Democrats. Republican leaders were prepared for this opportunity.

The Democratic hold on Catholic voters, particularly the Irish, had begun to alarm Republicans during the late 1880s. Accordingly, they had muffled their advocacy of prohibition in several northeastern and midwestern states; but it was not enough. The dramatic GOP defeat in 1890 underscored the need to prevent further pietist-liturgical conflicts from denying Republicans access to immigrant votes.[52] McKinley and his Re-

---

[50]During the campaign Theodore Roosevelt lambasted the Democrats for precisely this opposition: "Mr. Bryan and his supporters preach not merely class hatred, but sectional hatred. They strive to make you people of the mighty West believe that we your brothers in blood and feeling, whose homes are in the East, are alien in interest to you. Mr. Bryan speaks of the East as 'the enemy's country.' We of the East glory in the West. We appeal to all the citizens of this land alike as Americans to stand together, jealous of the honor of your country. . . ." Quoted in "Mr. Roosevelt in Chicago," *New York Times*, October 16, 1896, p. 7.

[51]In addition to opposing the expansion and concentration of judicial power, as symbolized in the labor injunction, the Democratic party also opposed proposals for civil service reform. In lieu of a merit system and collateral establishment of a permanent bureaucracy, the party proposed a "fixed term idea," which the National Civil Service Reform League equated with the institutionalization of the "spoils system." See "Bids for Spoils System," *New York Times*, October 16, 1896, p. 9.

[52]Jensen, 155.

publican mentors, Hanna among them, were the major force behind Republican efforts to recast the party's anti-Catholic image. In this, McKinley was less concerned to woo old victims of Republican nativism—the Irish—than to win the electoral allegiance of new immigrants.

The 1891 gubernatorial race in Ohio had given McKinley his first opportunity to build an electoral coalition with immigrant votes—a complete break from traditional Republican postures toward ethnocultural diversity. In his Ohio gubernatorial campaign sixteen years earlier, Republican Rutherford B. Hayes had effectively appealed to anti-Catholic anxieties, smearing Democrats as servants of the church. McKinley, by contrast, brought Republican electoral reasoning into alignment with the needs of advancing capitalism. Pursuing an argument tested in his congressional campaigns between 1876 and 1888, McKinley ventured that if wages could be protected by the tariff, the cultural antagonisms that were inflamed by job competition could be minimized.[53] By contrast McKinley's Democratic opponent in 1891 raved against the "imported Huns, Italians and Bohemians, usurping the places of American freemen"; he further pledged to put a "prohibitive tariff . . . on all aliens who came here without intending to become American citizens."[54] McKinley's victory by a plurality of eighty thousand—the only major contest in which the GOP recovered from the electoral disaster of the previous year—demonstrated the efficacy of a tariff-centered campaign that stressed immigration for industrial development and harmony in cultural diversity. Because the Democratic incumbent's dalliance with nativism helped lose the election for him, moreover, McKinley's victory gave new importance to the potential voting power of immigrant industrial workers.

The Republican party had served as the vehicle for pietistic nativism for more than forty years when McKinley became its presidential nominee. The success of McKinley Republicanism in 1891, however, put pietistic nativism in competition with its opposite—cultural pluralism—inside the Republican party. A trend developed to relax positions on Prohibition, the "puritan" Sabbath, and the use of foreign languages in parochial schools, particularly in states like New York, where a decline in Republican registration in rural areas was attributed to the naturalization of more than forty

[53]Ibid., 156, 18; Kleppner, 349.
[54]Quoted in Jensen, 155.

thousand aliens since 1888.[55] Nationally the GOP jockeyed for further immigrant support when it approved a convention platform calling for Irish home rule and denouncing the persecution of Jews in Russia.[56] These appeals to immigrant voters *as immigrants* would congeal in the Republican defense of cultural pluralism, the centerpiece of Republican electoral strategy in 1896. The strategy would work for new immigrants, but not for old labor.

The severity of the depression came as a shock to new immigrants and warmed them to Republican courtship; the last-hired-first-fired principle worked with a vengeance in new-immigrant communities. But the economic issue alone did not propel new-immigrant voters into the Republican fold, nor alone does it explain the clean political separation between old labor and new immigrants. One question raised by this separation, after all, is why old labor, given McKinley's cultural appeals and economic promises and given the Democratic alternative of free trade and domestic inflation, did not join the high-tariff coalition. One answer is that the Democratic party already provided old labor a shield against cultural bigotry. Equally important, the pro-union sympathies of the Democratic party, as expressed most concretely over the injunction question, overrode the appeal of the Republican formula for economic recovery. In this connection the clear anti-union bias of the Republican party, especially in the aftermath of the Pullman strike, undercut the political appeal of Republican economic argument and gave political priority to the organizational concerns of union labor. For union labor, in fact, the *real* symbol of Republicanism in the campaign was Mark Hanna, who was widely regarded and repeatedly denounced as a union buster.[57]

Another question raised by the political separation of old labor and new

---

[55]McSeveney, 29; actually, the naturalization figures are an inadequate measure of the immigrants' political voice, since suffrage was not determined by citizenship in many states. Even in the 1890s immigrants frequently could be legally enfranchised by a simple declaration of their intention to seek citizenship. Where citizenship was the rule for suffrage, political parties often secured voting rights for immigrants through fraud.

[56]Ibid., 258.

[57]When Bryan told unionists in Chicago that "one of the duties of the Government is to put rings in the noses of hogs," he was answered with laughter and cries of "Hanna is already fat!" See "Labor Unions All Right," *New York Times*, September 8, 1896, p. 2. Shouts of "Hanna, Hanna!" were repeated at various labor gatherings throughout the campaign; and various labor organizations, including the Cleveland Central Labor Union, the Clothing Cutters, and the Marble Cutters, appealed to fellow unionists to denounce "the labor crusher, Mark Hanna." "Mr. Hanna's Labor Record," *New York Times*, September 7, 1896; "They Shouted for Bryan," ibid., September 14, 1896; "Refuses to Endorse Bryan," ibid., September 21, 1896; "Wage Earners in Debate," ibid., September 23, 1896.

immigrants is why new immigrants flocked into the Republican electorate. Employers certainly gave them incentive to do so when they promised the return of business confidence—and of jobs—upon McKinley's election.[58] The Democratic party, moreover, with its protectionist position against foreign *people*, offered no alternative to Republican protection against foreign *goods*. Republican electoral strategy, finally, was deliberately fashioned to pull new-immigrant industrial workers into its presidential electorate.

If the decisive factor in the election of 1896 was the action taken by the industrial worker,[59] it was because McKinley Republicanism was able to attract immigrant voters more or less as a bloc. McKinley's cultural appeal worked for two reasons. First, the labor component of Bryan's coalition was dominated by organized labor, by now estranged from new-immigrant industrial workers both in its organizational logic and in its political purpose. Second, because of the importance of organized labor to Bryan's Democracy, the labor issues that the party embraced were of little relevance to the mostly unorganized new-immigrant workers. Republicans promised a way out of the *economic* crisis for *workers;* the Democrats promised relief from the *legal* crisis for *unions.* The Republican candidate praised new-immigrant workers for their economic contributions; the Democratic candidate lumped them with the money trust as part of the

---

[58]An employer in Milwaukee, for example, declared that "The moment we are certain of McKinley's election we shall start up again. . . . There are millions of dollars ready to go into rigging up the old mills, extending plants, building new shops, and putting things in shape for a period of good times. The 20,000 men now out of work in this city will at once be employed." Quoted in "Labor and Wages in Milwaukee," *San Francisco Chronicle,* September 6, 1896, p. 34. A few days before the election, the head of a Baltimore banking house promised that "$16 million was simply waiting McKinley's election for its investment in industrial enterprises in Maryland." Quoted in "Started by McKinley," *New York Times,* November 6, 1896, p. 1.

In the financial pages of the *New York Times,* articles argued that "If McKinley is elected by a large majority—and this latter is necessary—I believe there will be a rapid and complete restoration of confidence in America and American securities" and that although "at present there is a tendency in Wall Street to sell stocks in the expectation of a sharp reaction, I think it is the time to buy and not to sell." See "How Foreign Capital Feels," *New York Times,* October 1, 1896, p. 10, and "This Is a Time to Buy," ibid, October 3, 1896, p. 10. One response of Bryan and his allies to these claims was to cite a message from Bismarck to Governor Culberson of Texas in support of Democratic bimetallism. Andrew Dickson White wrote a scathing response to this intervention by Bismarck, which was printed on the front page of the *New York Times,* October 3, 1896, p. 1, under the headline "The Selfish Iron Prince."

[59]Cf. Jones, 243; Lubell, *Future of American Politics.* A complicating factor in the election was the problem of intimidation and fraud. See Josephson's *The Politicos* on this; for a different view, see Jensen, *Winning of the Midwest,* and Walter Dean Burnham, "Theory and Voting Research," *American Political Science Review* (1974), 1002–58.

"enemy's country." Bryan celebrated unions while McKinley cultivated nonunion, new-immigrant constituencies.[60]

In addition, the depression had completed the racial polarization of the working class: the constricted labor market, the decline in real wages, and the availability of immigrant strikebreakers intensified conflicts between unskilled immigrants and organized workers. Heightened antagonism turned labor disputes in some northeastern cities into attacks on new-immigrant groups,[61] while the special burden of alien unemployment directed new nativists to assert the primacy of immigration control for economic relief and social reform.[62] To industrial workers thus alienated from the Democracy, McKinley's vision of a "melting pot" sustained by the benign protection of the tariff compelled support for the GOP.[63]

During the campaign, as Richard Jensen and others have shown, McKinley appealed to new immigrants not by inviting more immigration but by applauding the economic and cultural contributions of those already in the United States. He set himself apart from the Democrats on this issue not by opposing restriction but by welcoming new immigrants. As he said to voters in Pittsburgh:

This assemblage here thoroughly typifies the national idea of a great American commonwealth in that it represents the equality of all which lies at the basis of popular government. It emphasizes the American spirit. Here are workingmen

[60]In his Labor Day speech to the annual picnic of the Building Trades Council in Chicago, Bryan made an interesting analytic distinction between workers "pressed by poverty" and workers in labor organizations. The latter, for him, were part of the "great middle classes" from which "has come almost all the good that blesses the human race." Quoted in the New York Times, September 8, 1896, p. 2.

[61]McSeveney, 35.

[62]The New York State Supreme Court decision, in 1896, against the restriction of public employment to citizens heightened political sensitivities on this issue. Candidate stance on this issue became a test for support or boycott by union labor. See "Decision to Scratch Judge Titus," New York Times, October 19, 1896, p. 8.

[63]The spokesman for the United Italian Republican Clubs of Pittsburgh, Pennsylvania, addressed McKinley thus: "Major McKinley, I have been assigned the pleasing task of introducing to you this delegation of Italian-American members of the United Italian Republican Club of the city of Pittsburgh. These humble toilers are here to greet you as the gallant standard-bearer of the party which stands for the promotion of the best interests of all who labor for their daily bread, and they yield to nobody in their devotion to the traditions and principles of that glorious old party." To which McKinley replied: "I am especially gratified to be assured that our Italian fellow-citizens are enrolled this year in the ranks of the great Republican Party, and that they are enlisted in a patriotic effort to achieve a victory for themselves, for their labor, for their occupations, and for their country." Quoted in "Italians Visit Canton," New York Times, October 9, 1896, p. 3.

in every department of industry, professional men, newspapermen—*the native born and the naturalized citizen*—all equal in privilege and power before the law, all alike interested in the Government of the country, and all with equal voice in controlling and shaping the destiny of our great Republic. Here is a striking protest against the unworthy effort on the part of those who would divide our citizens into classes and a striking condemnation of such an un-American appeal to passion and prejudice. . . .[64]

McKinley accepted his party's formal position on restriction—the Republican platform, under the influence of Henry Cabot Lodge and other Boston nativists, had called for the literacy test.[65] But his association with the pro-immigration, pro-capital wing of the party muted the significance of Republican nativism in the campaign. When it did arise, he argued the Republican position within the context of cultural pluralism. McKinley offered not traditional Republican nativism (with its appeal to the racial integrity of the Republic) or trade-union nativism (with its appeal to the racial integrity of the labor market) but *protection* to all workers in American industry. Because he could link tariff protection to higher wages, he could, moreover, argue (*sotto voce*) that tariff protection would support and in fact stimulate *further* immigration: the country could make room for and, indeed, could stand to benefit from more new-immigrant families as long as economic policies protecting wages were in effect.[66] Balancing the economic costs of immigration for wage earners against the economic benefits for capital, McKinley shed the rigid monoculturalism that had characterized Republican pietistic nativism.

From the point of view of organized workers, of course, McKinley's logic was unsupportable, for it failed to deal with the racial and organizational anxiety of the trade-union movement. Beyond the campaign rhetoric McKinley's record on the Chinese question revealed not only that he was unsympathetic on the race issue but that he was blind to its connection to labor's interests as well. Thus as one count of its indictment against McKinley's record, the Democratic party charged

that notwithstanding all of Mr. McKinley's vaunted partiality for the laboring man, he voted against excluding the most degraded class of competitors that the laborer has had and who have been brought here by companies under

[64]"McKinley to Workingmen," *San Francisco Chronicle,* September 6, 1896, p. 18, my emphases.
[65]Republican National Convention, *Official Proceedings* (1896), 84.
[66]Jensen, 260.

contract. . . . Pretending to be the friend of labor, he voted to table the bill providing for even a limited exclusion of the Chinese.[67]

Though offensive to organized labor, McKinley's stance on the immigration question bore electoral fruit. The mastermind behind his cultural appeal was Hanna, an industrialist loathed at the time by union labor and who had been grooming McKinley for the presidency since 1888.[68] Hanna's strategy was to educate workers in large urban areas and industrial communities into Republicanism. Direct appeals to the harmony among industrial-sector interests were complemented by a vigorous propaganda effort. In what has been characterized as the first modern presidential campaign, Hanna orchestrated and helped finance the production and distribution of some 120 million copies of 275 campaign pamphlets directed toward new immigrant workers. These materials, published in new-immigrant languages, inundated working-class areas. Clearly they were a concrete application of McKinley's rhetorical incorporation of naturalized Americans, but they also made Republican arguments for tariff protection and the Republican plan for economic recovery accessible, and comprehensible, to new-immigrant voters.[69] Democrats did not counter with a polyglot pamphleteering of their own. Indeed, Bryan largely ignored industrial centers other than Chicago, leaving the mobilization of voters to local parties whose relationship to the new Democracy was often problematic.[70]

---

[67]*Democratic Campaign Book, 1896,* 171, 177. This statement refers to McKinley's negative vote on the fifteen-passenger bill that was vetoed by President Hayes.

[68]See Herbert Croly, *Marcus Alonzo Hanna* (1912).

[69]It should be noted that Republican electioneering included less savory and less substantive tactics. The *New York Times,* for example, reprinted a piece from the *Chicago Tribune* alleging the following:

> An Italian, who was unable to read or write in any language, and whose vocabulary was restricted to one word, appeared to be naturalized:
> "What is your name?" asked His Honor.
> "McKinley," replied the Italian.
> Judge Burke smiled, while another Italian furnished the desired information.
> "Can you read or write the English language?" asked the Court.
> "McKinley," answered the Italian.
> "If you can neither read nor write, how do you expect to vote?" persisted the Court, while everyone laughed.
> "McKinley," replied the Italian, with a decisive shake of his head.
> He was given his papers.

Editorial, *New York Times,* September 30, 1896.

[70]*New York World,* September 12, 1896; Hollingsworth, 90; Jones, 346; Josephson, 699; and Croly, *Marcus Alonzo Hanna.*

Hanna's public relations effort had the symbolic effect of making McKinley's cultural pluralism creed credible; but substantively it related the Democratic plan for economic reform to impending economic collapse. Republican electioneering among industrial workers accordingly stressed the dire consequences of Bryan's free-trade, free-silver policy for wage earners. Free trade, they argued, would lower the wage standards of American workers as cheap foreign goods weakened the competitive position of domestic products. The monetization of silver, they warned, would force a decline in purchasing power as commodity prices spiraled upward.[71]

The effect of the Republican blitz was to underscore differences between the parties on four fronts: currency reform, industrial policy, injunctions, and nativism. On all fronts the Republican electoral method complemented the Republican economic argument, at least for industrial workers. The Democratic method and the Democratic argument, by contrast, offered nothing to workers who were not included in unions and who were the subject of the nativist critique of industrialism. The conflicting interests of capital and workers were thus obscured by a political verdict that decisively split unions from nonunion voters. The election of 1896 repudiated Bryan's economic rationale for the new party system.

The Union-Party Tie

The rupture in the Democratic party created for old labor an opening to the middle. Bryan's personal electoral strategy focused chiefly on the agrarian Midwest, leaving urban and industrial America to what remained of the national party, to local parties, and to unions. Appeals for votes in these areas often centered on union concerns: immigration restriction, the judiciary, labor injunctions. Bryan and his surrogates did little to counter McKinley's work among new-immigrant voters, even in Democratic cities. Local Democratic machines for the most part did not make major investments in Bryan's candidacy, and while unions did, they were not inclined to mobilize the new immigrants they deliberately excluded from their movement and wanted excluded from the American labor market. Hence union labor's role in the campaign produced only a union-party tie, not a party-class alignment.

[71]Hollingsworth, 92; S. K. Stevens, "The Election of 1896 in Pennsylvania," *Pennsylvania History*, 4 (April 1937), 76; and H. H. Kohlsaat, *From McKinley to Harding* (1923), 52.

Even this union-party tie did not develop automatically. Working against the enthusaism unleashed by labor's incorporation in the Democratic platform was the tradition of union ambivalence toward politics. Unhappy endings to union experiments in politics, particularly third-party politics, seemed to validate the voluntarist doctrine espoused by Samuel Gompers. The collapse of the United Labor party after Henry George's defeat in the 1886 New York City mayoral contest hardened voluntarist views, notwithstanding labor's gains in the aftermath of George's creditable second-place finish.[72] Part of the strength of the voluntarist conviction can also be attributed to trade-union successes in bargaining with both parties and individual candidates for favorable legislation on the few problems for which they had sought corrective state intervention: Chinese exclusion, for example, and the prohibition of contract labor.

Trade-union experiences in both third-party and two-party politics during the 1880s brought the AFL to reject Populist invitations for farmer-labor cooperation through the People's party. While some labor organizations lent support to the new party (the International Wire Workers, the United Mine Workers of Ohio, the Knights of Labor, and several midwestern city federations), the trade-union mainstream withheld participation. Even though the Omaha Platform adopted planks relevant to labor interests—calling, for example, for restrictions on "undesirable" immigrant labor, shorter hours, the right to strike, and abolition of the Pinkertons[73]—greater union participation was not forthcoming. And despite a creditable electoral performance in 1892—one million Populist voters elected seven members of Congress, three U.S. senators, and three governors—the national trade-union leadership resisted appeals to join in coalition.

The resilience of trade-union voluntarism during the early 1890s had much to do with both the course of the agrarian challenge and its prospects for pulling labor into coalition. As an antipolitical doctrine, voluntarism did not easily accommodate the political critique advanced by many populists and thus did not admit of the political action prescribed by that critique. The economic crisis in agriculture had no parallel in industry

[72]Following this election many labor laws in New York were relaxed and some even fashioned vaguely to protect labor. A board of mediation and arbitration was created to adjust labor disputes. Regulations were mandated for tenement housing, for the employment of women and children, and for hours of labor on street, surface, and elevated railroads. Most important, the Penal Code was amended to prohibit employers from enforcing yellow dog contracts. Peter Speek, *The Single Tax and the Labor Movement* (October 1917), 44, 88–89.

[73]Fine, 79; James Peterson, "The Trade Unions and the Populist Party," *Science and Society*, 8 (Spring 1944), 147.

until the depression of 1893, no doubt further obscuring trade-union incentives to articulate political opposition to the economic order. What is
more, the economic interests of farmers did not necessarily match the
economic interests of workers. Domestic inflation through the monetization of silver offered no obvious benefit to wage earners, though it would
improve the economic position of agrarian debtors.[74] On the tariff question, moreover, workers were divided among themselves; in the early
1880s, in fact, pro- and antitariff forces inside the AFL had come into
heated and disorderly conflict.[75] Finally, before 1894, when injunctions,
prosecutions, and the militarization of labor disputes changed union labor's relationship to the state, the trade-union movement lacked a clear
national political purpose—other than immigration restriction, which was
no more a Populist issue than a Republican or a Democratic one. These
factors made some sense of Samuel Gomper's insistence that third-party
action would fragment and undermine union labor.

Although the trade-union leadership was absolute in its voluntarism,
union voluntarism was by no means absolute across the country. At the
local level, at least in areas of Populist strength, organized workers actively supported Populist efforts to build a political agrarian-labor movement. Locally organized labor also became especially friendly toward the
Populists once the party had proved its commitment to labor during the
Pullman boycott. Thus in California, for example, the People's party
made substantial gains in working-class wards in San Francisco in 1894:
one of two Populist state assemblymen was elected from the city.[76] Elsewhere three hundred labor candidates entered local races in 1894, many of
them in open defiance of Gompers's ban on such political action.[77]

Rank-and-file political enthusiasm within the national trade-union
movement contributed to Gompers's temporary ouster as AFL president in
1894–95.[78] But the presidency returned to Gompers a year later—in time,
ironically, for Gompers to put the AFL presidency to work for William

[74]Irving Bernstein, "Samuel Gompers and the Irony of Free Silver, 1896," *Mississippi Valley Historical Review*, 29 (December 1942), 394–400.
[75]Samuel Gompers, *Seventy Years of Life and Labor*, ed. Nick Salvatore (1984), 70–71.
[76]Michael Rogin and John Shover, *Political Change in California* (1970), 18. San Francisco also elected a Populist mayor, Adolph Sutro.
[77]Pollack, 64.
[78]Ibid.; Gompers, *Seventy Years*, ed. Salvatore, xxiv, 107–9. Gompers was replaced by John McBride, president of the United Mine Workers. In 1896 McBride was "given a seat in the inner Popocratic circle . . . ostensibly to organize a labor bureau in connection with Popocratic head-quarters for the distribution of literary antidotes to the sound money literature which has been sent to every workshop by the enemy." See "Chairman Jones Summons McBride," *New York Times*, September 16, 1896, p. 2.

Jennings Bryan. Gompers had admonished his membership to political neutrality before the party nominating conventions,[79] but Bryan's nomination clearly changed the political ballgame. The Democratic platform and Bryan himself provided incentives to union labor to move inside a major party for the first time. For the first time a party and its presidential candidate pledged support for the *organizational* viability of unions.[80]

That the organizational concerns of union labor had become a Democratic priority was made clear in Bryan's speech at Tammany Hall:

> In my opinion there is no issue presented . . . more important and vital than the question they have raised of protecting the power and duty of the National Courts and National Executive. The defense of the Constitution and of the liberty of the Supreme Court of the United States, and of the President's power to send troops of the United States into any State without the call or consent of the Governor is an important and leading issue in the campaign. . . .[81]

And that the desirability of labor organization had become a central Democratic principle was driven home by Bryan in Chicago:

> Now, my friends, among all the agencies which for the past few years have been at work improving the condition and protecting the rights of this country, I believe that the labor organizations stand first. It has brought the laboring men together where they could compare their views, where they could unite in strength, where they could combine their influences and organization, and we have the laboring organizations to thank for many blessings they have secured for you. . . . The labor organizations have done as much good for society as any of the other organizations have done or will do.[82]

Although Gompers continued to resist official, formal AFL endorsement for Bryan, and although some unions did not find the decision to move into the campaign *as unions* an easy one, the majority of AFL

[79]In a general circular issued at AFL affiliates, Gompers warned of the dangers of partisanship and argued that "whatever labor secured now or in the past was due to the efforts of the workers themselves in their own organizations—trade unions on trade union lines, on trade union action." Quoted in Foner, 2: 337.

[80]"Cheap Money and Wages," *Review of Reviews*, 14 (September 1896), 262–63: "New York trades unionism has not been drawn toward Mr. Bryan and the Chicago platform through any great eagerness for free silver. . . . Mr. Gompers and the men of his way of thinking would be ready to admit that it is chiefly because of the other planks in the platform that they are supporting Mr. Bryan. . . . It is that part of the Chicago platform which we may term its Altgeldism and Debsism that has won the allegiance of Eastern labor leaders."

[81]"Mr. Bryan's Address," *New York Times*, September 30, 1896, p. 2.

[82]Quoted in "Labor Unions All Right," *New York Times*, September 8, 1896, p. 2.

affiliates rallied to the new Democracy. City and state federations, too, added their enthusiastic support for Bryan, even in the "sound money" East. Gompers himself joined a crowded field of labor leaders, including Eugene Debs, to stump vigorously for the Democratic ticket. By early autumn Hanna's agents were reporting from Chicago that "the labor organizations are against us to a man. Impossible to teach them. They are more interested in the question of federal jurisdiction over strikes than the money question."[83] So despite the official organizational abstention of the AFL in 1896, the federation membership and most of its leaders swung to Bryan.

Organized labor played an important part in mobilizing electoral support for Bryan in the industrial East. The exit of Gold Democrats from the party upon Bryan's nomination threw the reliability of the party's electoral apparatus into doubt. So certain was Bryan that his electoral position in the East was hopeless, in fact, that except for two major visits to New York City, he directed his electoral energies toward the West, South, and agrarian Midwest.[84] The rupture in the national party encouraged unions to turn labor discipline to electoral account. Similarly the incomplete commitment to Bryan of Democratic urban machines in the East increased the value of labor's political role.[85] Although Tammany, for example, endorsed Bryan shortly after the convention and sponsored his visits to New York City, it did not marshal all its electoral weapons on Bryan's behalf.[86] Tammany was, in fact, not solid in its support for Bryan, though it officially embraced his candidacy and platform.[87] Indeed, at the state level Tammany cooperated with the National Democrats—the rump party organized by the repudiated Cleveland Democrats.[88] Uncertain of Tam-

[83]*New York World,* September 12, 1896; Bernstein, 400; and Foner, 2: 341.

[84]*New York Tribune* and *New York World,* October 18, 1896; Hollingsworth, 87.

[85]Much of the traditionally Democratic press, including the *New York Times,* was hostile to the Bryan candidacy. In New York City the only umambivalent voice for Bryan (other than unions) was William Randolph Hearst's *New York Journal.* See W. A. Swanberg, *Citizen Hearst* (1961), 99–104.

[86]One campaign observer remarked on the occasion of Bryan's August visit to Madison Square Garden: "If the eminent politicians of the Democratic Party were absent from the Bryan meeting, it is true on the other hand that the leaders of trades unionism and organized labor were present on that occasion." See "Where Stand the Eastern Wage-Earners?" *Review of Reviews,* 14 (September 1896), 260.

[87]One of the Tammany officers read the following statement during Bryan's visit to Tammany Hall: "The Democracy of New York City, in a mass meeting assembled at Tammany Hall, to the Democracy of the Nation sends greetings and assures the friends of popular government throughout the land that in the contest now being waged for the vindication of the rights of the people, the Democrats of the metropolis are united and enthusiastic in support of the principles and policies declared at and by the National Democratic Convention in Chicago." Quoted in "The Platform Read," *New York Times,* September 30, 1896, p. 2.

[88]McSeveney, 169–72.

many's ability to discipline voters (and its own cadres) at the polling booth in this election—their uncertainties compounded by internal dissent as well as by the introduction of the Australian ballot in 1895 and the secret ballot in 1890—local party leaders cultivated union labor to capitalize on its organizational discipline.[89] To this end, Tammany named an official of the Central Labor Union (and a German-American)—Jacob Bausch—to its local slate as candidate for coroner. Upon doing this, Tammany also promised to name union men to its assembly slates.[90] The gesture toward union labor was greeted with appreciation and with the pledge that "the Democracy would have the solid support of organized labor" in the campaign.[91] Staunch voluntarists may have been uneasy with Tammany's move, but union labor was nevertheless led to distinguish between "good politics" and plain politics and to push forward in the direction of "good politics."[92] The at least partial incorporation of union labor as a political arm of the local Democratic machinery had an impact that is suggested by the rough equivalence of Bryan and Bausch votes in the November election, even though the two candidates were at opposite ends of the ticket and even though 1896 results indicate a marked increase in ticket splitting throughout New York state.[93]

The significance of union labor to the campaign did not go unnoticed by Bryan. On September 24, 1896, labor organizations across metropolitan New York combined to sponsor Bryan's visit to Brooklyn. At least eight thousand enthusiastic unionists turned out for the event, of which the San Francisco *Chronicle* said:

There has perhaps never been such a demonstration for William J. Bryan in the East as that given to-night in Brooklyn by the combined labor interests. It

---

[89]That the "real purpose" of union labor's incorporation in the campaign was to trade on union discipline was suggested by the *New York Times,* September 16, 1896, p. 2. See also "Tammany Hall Warfare," ibid., October 14, 1896, p. 8. The *Times,* it should be noted, was suspicious of labor's political activities throughout the campaign, as it was a pro-Cleveland paper.

[90]*New York Times,* October 2, 1896, p. 3; October 3, 1896, p. 1; October 5, 1896, p. 5. The *Times* went on to assert that "the bid made by Tammany Hall to the Central Labor Union, in offering it the only office on its ticket, the nomination of Jacob E. Bausch for Coroner, is generally regarded by the workingmen as an adminission of weakness of Tammany Hall" ("Tammany's Bid to Labor," October 11, 1896, p. 7). Tammany's "weakness," however, did not lead it to incorporate unions fully in its slatemaking. Shortly after Bausch was named to the ticket, Tammany rejected the Central Labor Union's nominees to the Assembly slate.

[91]"Tammany Hall Warfare," *New York Times,* October 14, 1896, p. 8.

[92]"Rushes into Politics," ibid., October 5, 1896, p. 5; "Bausch Will Not Withdraw," ibid., October 8, 1896, p. 8; "Decision to Scratch Judge Titus," ibid., October 19, 1896, p. 8.

[93]"The City Vote," ibid., November 5, 1896, p. 4. Richard McCormick documents an increase in ticket splitting in New York in his *From Realignment to Reform* (1981), 118.

has been a mooted question whether the labor people of the East would respond to a call for a mass meeting in favor of Bryan, but the demonstration at the Clermont rink tonight is the answer.[94]

Several days later, when Bryan spoke to a crowd of more than four thousand at Tammany Hall, the presence of union labor was clear: the New York state organizer for the AFL and various union representatives gave unions an official presence, and union members were prominent in the audience. Bryan's understanding of the pivotal electoral role of union labor was reflected in his speech, which before turning to the "paramount issue of the campaign," the money question, stressed *union* concerns: courts and presidents, injunctions and arbitration.[95]

The System of 1896

The role of organized labor in the campaign was crucial in several respects. The AFL did not bring Bryan victory, but it did enable Bryan to do relatively well in the more urban, unionized sections of the East, at least in comparison to much of his eastern rural vote. In Massachusetts, Bryan polled 32.6 percent of the urban vote (36.7 percent in Boston) and only 21.2 percent of the rural vote. Similarly in New York state, Bryan polled 41.6 percent and 35.8 percent respectively.[96]

The AFL's place in the Bryan coalition also helped the national Democratic party maintain a presence in urban America despite the lop-sided Republicanism of the national electoral regime. But because the constituency of organized labor was limited by its nativism, labor's role in the campaign produced only a union-party tie, not a party-class alignment in the electorate. Indeed the working class divided so sharply in 1896 that while unions moved inside the Democratic coalition, solidifying the party's labor base, industrial workers appeared to deliver industrial America to the party of capital. In New York City, for example, Bryan fared best in Tammany strongholds—typically inhabited by organized Irish workers—

---

[94]"Bryan Talks in Brooklyn—Laboring Men Meet," *San Francisco Chronicle*, September 24, 1896, p. 2.

[95]"At the Labor Stand," *New York Times*, September 30, 1896, p. 2; "Mr. Bryan's Address," ibid., September 30, 1896, p. 2.

[96]William Diamond, "Urban and Rural Voting in 1896," *American Historical Review*, 46 (January 1941), 287–88.

while Democratic defections were notable in east European Jewish and other new immigrant districts.[97]

The characterization of the 1896 realignment advanced by Walter Dean Burnham and others is generally appropriate in its emphasis on divisions between industrial and agrarian America. Within industrial America, however, significant cross-cutting cleavages also gained political expression. That unions did not follow industrial workers into the Republican party suggests that, within the working class at least, a realignment was taking shape based on internal divisions. The starkly different responses of union labor and industrial workers to Bryan and McKinley corresponded to the split between old labor and new immigrants.

Clearly unionism and union nativism played important roles in the creation of the system of 1896. The proposition is corroborated by the pro-Bryan activities of union labor. The affinity between union labor and the Democratic party as exhibited by its campaign efforts—most tellingly by chief voluntarist Samuel Gompers—when weighed against the voting decision of industrial workers, indicated discontinuities between union politics and working-class political behavior. The significance of unionism and nativism can also be inferred at the electoral level. Across the industrial Northeast, defections from the Democrats in 1896 over 1892 were massive: Democratic vote shares declined by 17.5 percent in New York City, 15.7 percent in Philadelphia, and 12.7 percent in Allegheny County (Pittsburgh).[98] These defections occurred even though trade unions, which claimed to represent the whole class, contributed a political arm to the Democratic party in urban and industrial America. Over the next several presidential elections, however, Democrats would recuperate some of their losses where unions were stronger, and particularly where unions and strong local Democratic parties sustained local alternatives to the Republicans' national hegemony. In the metropolitan counties of Massachusetts and New York, for example, Democratic defections in 1896 did not eliminate the Democrats from subsequent competition in national elections. There ethnic identities strongly correlated with unionism (name-

[97]In his discussion of the 1886 mayoral campaign in New York City, Martin Shefter notes that more recent immigrants—Italians, for example—voted for the Democratic (rather than the United Labor party) candidate. In later elections, Shefter notes, these same first-generation groups proved least inclined to support Tammany consistently. Shefter, "The Electoral Foundations of the Political Machine, 1884–97," in Joel Silbey et al., eds., *The History of American Electoral Behavior* (1978), 277.

[98]Edgar Robinson, *The Presidential Vote, 1896–1932* (1947); Walter Dean Burnham, *Presidential Ballots, 1836–1892* (1955).

ly Irishness)[99] were mobilized in local politics, aiding Democratic resilience. The net Democratic loss when viewed over the period 1892–
1904 contracts to 2.3 percent in Boston, 10 percent in New York County,
and 4.4 per cent in Richmond County (Staten Island), while the Democrats even gained, marginally, in Queens County. In these three New
York counties the average Democratic vote in presidential elections between 1896 and 1908 was a competitive 47 percent or better.[100]

In the coal and steel counties of Pennsylvania, by contrast, Republican
gains tended to *expand* after 1896. In the absence of real organization—
union or party—to contest Republican rule, Republicanism became
monolithic. The net Democratic losses between 1892 and 1904 expanded
to 22.5 percent in Schuylkill County (coal) and 21.1 percent in Allegheny
County (steel). In most of these areas the new-immigrant presence doubled between 1890 and 1900, and new immigrants formed an increasing
proportion of the foreign-born population, an ever larger share of the
potential electorate, and the preponderance of the nonunionized work
force.

Variations in the strength and durability of the Republican shift were
due not simply to the Hanna-McKinley strategy toward new-immigrant
voters but also to the absence of mobilizing alternatives. Where organized
alternatives existed, new-immigrant industrial workers were frequently
locked out of them (unions) or demobilized within them (urban machines).[101] In industrial Pennsylvania not even these limited alternatives
were available. Interparty competition had begun to decay in the early
1890s, and unionism was in disarray. Employers had deliberately—
and effectively—brought in new immigrants to undermine unionization;
meanwhile unions had separated themselves from new industrial workers
both by their method of organization and by their exclusionist politics. As
a result, unionism was weak and in some industries nonexistent. The steel
union had been nearly obliterated by the Homestead strike in 1892 (the
remnants clung to a narrow jurisdiction), and the anthracite union had
been rooted out utterly in the mid-1870s. Under these conditions the
industrial electorate had few institutions of its own through which
to filter electoral choices. Nor were competitive party organizations

[99]William V. Shannon, *The Irish Americans: A Political and Social Portrait* (1974), 140–41.
First- and second-generation Irish accounted for roughly half of the population in Boston and a
third in New York City and Brooklyn. U.S. Census Bureau, Eleventh Census, *Population of the
United States* (1890), pt. 1, 670–71, 710.

[100]Robinson, *Presidential Vote, 1896–1932.*

[101]Steven Erie discusses the strategy of urban machines toward new immigrants in "Two
Faces of Ethnic Power," *Polity,* 13 (Winter 1980), 262–74.

available against which to test electoral choice—either in company towns or in such Republican machine cities as Philadelphia and Pittsburgh.

Where unionism was stronger, unionists were often hostile to new immigrants and unions inhospitable to their organization. The unions wanted to consolidate their constituencies and to fight segmentation of the labor market; they looked to organize old labor, not to expand the union universe. Hence even where unions were vigorous, as in New York City, they did not act as mediating institutions for new immigrants in politics. Organization-centered appeals against the procapitalist Court and against unregulated labor markets did not address the concerns of disorganized industrial workers, did not speak in their languages, and very often voiced an antagonism toward new immigrants themselves. Injunction and antitrust relief were essential and essentially *union* demands, while calls to restrict immigration sharpened the separation between unions and working class. Union appeals and union mobilization thus represented group interests that were different from—and in political opposition to—the interests of the broader wage-earning constituency. As a consequence, although unions labored for Bryan in New York, for example, they were unable to defend the city against Republican inroads in 1896. Nor did local Democratic machines in Irish-dominated cities provide much of a defense, for they matched old labor in their exclusionism.[102]

The beginnings of a union-Democratic party tie and of new-immigrant Republicanism thus emerged from the decision of 1896. But an equally important development was the solidification of electoral incoherence within the industrial working class. This was reflected in sustained Republicanism among new-immigrant voters, in the decomposition of the wage-earning electorate in many urban and industrial areas, and in the "disappearance" of some industrial voters. Connected to the decline of interparty competition under the system of 1896 was the dissolution for industrial workers of any substantive linkage between party and voter.

Republican industrial workers helped entrench the electoral dominance of the party of capital; they thereby facilitated the ascendancy of capitalism and the demobilization of democracy during the first quarter of the twentieth century. Very little in the way of policy or patronage incentives explains their electoral decision. The Republican party did not offer anything in exchange for new immigrant votes: social insurance was not discussed, for example, nor was any improvement of working conditions

---

[102]Ibid.; see also Steven Erie, "The Lost Hurrah: Irish-Americans and the Dilemma of Machine Politics," ms., chap. 3.

promised. Moreover, the Republican platform placed the party squarely in opposition to working-class organization. Over the longer term, Republican reform initiatives during the Progressive Era to cleanse and defuse majoritarian politics would even limit the political rights and political access of new-immigrant industrial voters. Still, in 1896 Republican leaders promised a "full dinner pail" for everybody through the protective tariff and sound money, where Bryan promised only protection of the organizational rights and the autonomy of trade unions. More important, the Republican nominee celebrated immigrant contributions to American economic development. He stood in open defiance of both Democratic and traditional Republican rhetoric on the matter of immigration and in stark contrast to the pietism and nativism of the Bryanite coalition.

New-immigrant Republicanism in the presidential contest did not, however, produce a coherent partisanship across the several layers of federalism. In the cities, wage-earning Republicans helped return Republicans to state and national office, but in cities not controlled by Republicans, began to evidence disjunctures in their partisanship. For new-immigrant voters, at least for those in Democratic cities, the logic of patronage democracy worked to separate their national from their local electoral affinities. For unionists, by contrast, the union-party tie blurred the separation between workplace organization (unions) and political mobilization (patronage parties) and thereby enhanced the linkage between party and union voter. In New York City, for example, Tammany brought unions into the orbit of machine politics in 1896 *as unions;* nationally the Democratic party would bring the AFL into the state under Woodrow Wilson beginning in 1913.[103]

New York City exemplifies the concrete development of the problem. Irish mobilization within patronage democracy in Democratic cities like New York made for much stronger party linkages among Irish voters than among new immigrants. The political strategy of Democratic urban machines with respect to the Irish, as Steven Erie argues, was rather different from their strategy toward later immigrant arrivals.[104] This difference was to some extent the result of timing, in that the Irish were early constituents

---

[103]Continuity and coherence in union partisanship were most significant at the presidential level. At the congressional level, depending on the local political environment, unions often pursued a candidate-centered strategy. Thus in the Progressive Era the AFL endorsed Albert Johnson of Washington in his bid for Congress. Though a Republican, he was tough on immigration. Even at the congressional level, however, unions still tended to support Democrats. Thus the AFL played an important role in helping create a Democratic majority in the House at the time of the revolt against Speaker Cannon.

[104]Erie, "Two Faces of Ethnic Power."

of the machine-building enterprise—61 percent of the Tammany Society's officeholders in 1892 were Irish—and thus provided a natural constituency for machine consolidation. The Irish were incorporated in such a way that politics served as a route to mobility, through mobilization, the distribution of jobs, and policy decisions that affected unions; new immigrants, however, were merely organized into the electorate, through the distribution of services and occasional nods of symbolic recognition. The Irish, furthermore, were mobilized into unions while new immigrants generally were not. Thus for the Irish, political references were available, either through unions or through the local party.

Although new-immigrant voters were important constituents of patronage democracy, their links to the machine reflected dependency rather than integration and were based on low-cost, in-kind welfarism rather than on the more costly redistribution of political power. The disposition of local regimes toward new immigrants was, to be sure, by no means invariable. Where the Irish clearly dominated city politics, as in New York for example, the Democratic strategy tended to be containment, which offered symbolic and welfarist accommodation in lieu of incorporation or electoral activation. Where factionalism impaired Irish dominance and Democratic strength was contained by interparty competition, as in Chicago, local Democratic factions were more inclusionist in their electoral appeals, eventually naming new immigrants to slates and helping them overcome hurdles to voter participation.[105]

Whatever the differences in relationships between new immigrants and particular urban machines, two general trends can be discerned. First, dramatic expansions of potential electorates due to the new immigration were associated with contractions, rather than expansions, of actual electorates. Stricter requirements for naturalization and voter registration, along with such procedural reforms as the separation of election cycles, depressed voter participation. Especially where local regimes were relatively stable, of course, local political brokers—themselves the targets of reform—had little incentive to introduce political uncertainty by mobilizing the mass of new immigrants, and thus did little to counteract the consequences of reform. Republican and reform strategies to impede the mobilization of new immigrants by local Democratic machines were accordingly reinforced by the reluctance of established local Democratic coalitions, predominantly Irish, to share power with newer arrivals. The effect in New York City was striking: the adult male population tripled

[105]See Erie, ''The Lost Hurrah.''

between 1892 and 1912, but the voting population only doubled.[106] In New York City and Chicago, absolute numbers of voters in presidential elections between 1900 and 1912 did not increase substantially—even though adult male populations expanded as immigration crested after 1897—indicating that the electoral system had effectively sealed itself off from the entry of any significant numbers of new voters.[107] Participation rates declined as new-immigrant wage earners were recruited into the "party of nonvoters."

The system of 1896 saw a second, related development: the party linkages of those new immigrants who did vote at the local level did not necessarily translate into linkages with the national party coalitions to which urban political machines loosely belonged. Nor did new-immigrant electoral decisions at the local or national level necessarily represent substantive or consistent preferences: a vote for a local Tammany candidate one year and for Theodore Roosevelt the next was a perfectly plausible voting sequence for a new-immigrant New Yorker. Such discontinuities developed because new immigrants lacked mobilizing and reference institutions—other than ethnic associations. Local political machines serviced them; reformers and bosses demobilized them; unions marginalized them; and Hanna-McKinley polyglot Republicanism curried their support for the Republican national ticket. Hence, in New York City after 1896, while Tammany, unions, and the Irish created a coherent political constellation that helped the Democrats become competitive again in national elections, though not at pre-1896 levels, the several indicators of party *decomposition* also increased: split-ticket voting, drop-off, roll-off, and partisan swing.[108]

In the coal and steel counties of Pennsylvania, where the Republican regime was not confounded by separate local regimes, the principal indicator of electoral incoherence and its associated decay in party-voter linkages was the sharp decline in voter participation. There the "hole" in the labor movement dug by trade unions—crafted, to be sure, by ground-

---

[106]Erie reports in "The Lost Hurrah" that the adult male population tripled to 1.4 million while the voting population doubled to 594,000. The participation rate in New York City declined, between 1892 and 1912, from 64 percent to 41 percent of adult males.

[107]The adult male populations of New York City and Chicago increased by nearly 40 percent between 1900 and 1910. The number of voters increased by only 0.3 percent in New York and by 7.3 percent in Chicago between the presidential elections of 1900 and 1912. Turnout as a percentage of the adult male population declined by 16 percent in both cities during this period. See U.S. Bureau of the Census, Twelfth and Thirteenth Censuses, *Population of the United States* (1900, 1910); Robinson, *Presidential Vote, 1892–1932.*

[108]Walter Dean Burnham, "The Changing Shape of the American Political Universe," in his *Current Crisis in American Politics* (1982), 41.

breaking employers—coincided with the development of a "hole" in the electorate which would comprise what Burnham calls the "party of non-[or peripheral] voters." In the absence of political alternatives, potential voters either exited or did not enter the electoral system. Industrial Pennsylvania remained strongly Republican until 1928–32, but one-party inertia, procedural reform, and the contradiction between Republican electoral and governing coalitions led to the "disappearance" of some industrial voters and the demobilization of others.[109]

That new-immigrant industrial workers were part of the Republican electoral coalition from 1896 to 1928–32 exposes the extent to which nativist unionism had split the working class. Ironically the electoral asymmetry between union labor and nonunion voters conferred nearly a generation of undisputed power upon the party least sympathetic to the claims of labor. What is more, Republican hegemony sharply separated *electoral* coalitions from *governing* coalitions. Though the GOP now encompassed new-immigrant workers as a crucial voting bloc in national politics, it was clearly dominated by capital. Although internally divided between statist and antistatist approaches to the political economy, party policy nonetheless was decidedly procapitalist on most issues that mattered to workers. Furthermore, while the electoral power of the Republican party rested on the votes of industrial workers, it simultaneously depended on the demobilization of those voters. Republican workers were not an organized voice within the party, and they were thus excluded from group competition within the capitalist coalition. Republican elites built barriers to broader electoral participation by industrial workers, moreover, when they elevated the threshold for the exercise of political rights as part of the agenda for reform.

The retreat from mass democracy did not challenge assumptions of political equality. The requirement of democratic participation was fulfilled by the disorganized electoral participation of those industrial workers who did vote and by the organized and coherent group participation of union labor. But the electoral separation of the class and the electoral decomposition of the industrial electorate resulted, at least on the Republican side of the system of 1896, in accelerated decay for the relationship between elections and policy, between voter and party, and between citizen and state.

On the Democratic side the union-party tie would strengthen links

---

[109]Ibid. Burnham's data show a 15 percent drop in mean presidential election turnout in the coal and steel counties between the 1876–96 period and the 1900–1916 period (36–37).

between party and policy. Moreover, the incoherence of the industrial electorate would enhance the AFL's claims to be a representative voice for labor; indeed, the AFL was labor's *only* political voice. This would privilege trade unionism in politics, and the AFL would use that privilege to cultivate the asymmetries of organization and mobilization between the separated constituencies of the working class. The AFL would further use its privilege to fight those political interventions which threatened to put the state in a direct relationship with disorganized industrial workers—innovations in social welfare—and which thereby threatened to substitute the state for unions as the instrument of working-class amelioration. But the AFL's privileged political position did not transform the party of union labor into America's labor party. Nor did it move unionism much closer to winning its central political demands.

Not until the GOP split the immigrant vote with Theodore Roosevelt in 1912, making electoral room for a Democratic victory, would the AFL be in a position to press its interests to the state. Then it did so successfully, winning labor policies that formalized its position in the national political arena: the Clayton Act, a labor department, and participation in Woodrow Wilson's wartime corporatism. But these gains for labor under Wilson, it should be noted, were of immediate relevance only to the Democratic labor constituency that emerged from 1896: native and old-stock union labor.

Indeed, during the very years it was "in government" under Woodrow Wilson, the AFL used its organizational voice and political access to pursue its most vehement antistatism—chiefly in the form of unbending opposition to social legislation. Union labor used its electoral clout during the critical period of state expansion in the United States to help the nation choose against public-sector regulation of industrial relations and to impede social reform. But as it did so, it pressed from within the ruling coalition for state protection of union activities, legislative relief from court injunctions, and control of immigration. It took, in effect, its organization-conscious goals and strategy into the party system to help create an urban-rural antistatist coalition through which it could secure union interests.

Workers, divided one from another, voted away the electoral power needed to sustain political leverage and to achieve political independence. The clean break between antagonistic wage-earning constituencies in partisan politics left the AFL, unchallenged by any organized rival, to engage in interest politics. Now that new-immigrant industrial workers were Republican, peripheral, or incoherent voters—or were not voting at all—

organized labor could advance its political concerns through partisan activity, and the national Democratic party would support its political claims. The dog that did not bark in the late nineteenth century would not bark thereafter; it had died in the electoral upheaval.

The election of 1896 did not produce the party-class alignment suggested by Bryan's campaign rhetoric. Rather, it made political sense of the jealousies that kept industrial workers for the most part outside the labor movement. Furthermore, the party system accommodated old labor's group interest and accordingly removed any incentive that trade unions might have had to develop independent political alternatives. Disorganized at work and disempowered in politics, those who needed such alternatives under the system of 1896—new-immigrant urban and industrial workers—were in a weak position to build them.

The election and its aftermath reconstituted the liberal settlement in modern America, by separating old labor's group interest from class interest in capitalism's most brutal moment and by marginalizing the electoral potential of the nonunionized, ethnic working class. This accommodation was costly for old labor, for it would be slow to reap concrete rewards from its interest-group choice—neither it nor the Democratic party would be able to forge electoral majorities for nearly a generation. The price for industrial workers would be heavy, as well: continued disorganization, and a reluctance on the part of the American state to send political and social innovations in their direction.

PART III

The AFL and the Rise of the Democratic State

CHAPTER 5

Building a Labor Establishment, 1900–1916

Combinations of capital and combinations of labor are the great factors of industrialism. Their interests are all bound up together, reciprocal if not identical. They should work hand in hand, and adjust their quarrels in joint conference without outside interference.

—John Mitchell, 1902

The decision of 1896 reconstituted old parties on the basis of new cleavages in the electorate. In 1896 workers reaffirmed pluralistic politics and the two-party consensus through their electoral behavior: the clean electoral split within the working class seemed to indicate that, even under the strains of industrialism, the organizational interests of old labor had overwhelmed the political interests of the working class as a whole. As a result the decision of 1896 reproduced a central anomaly of American politics: a competitive party system without institutionalized, programmatic opposition.

It remained for the beneficiaries of Republican ascendancy to institutionalize this system of 1896. For the Republican party, electoral dominance depended on the votes of new-immigrant industrial workers who formed an unorganized, motley presence within the McKinley coalition. For the corporate interests represented in the Republican party, both control of the workplace and influence over political interventions in the economy depended upon the continued economic and political disorganization of the industrial working class. Union labor helped satisfy the requirements of workplace discipline and working-class disorganization, both in its methods of organization and in its alignment in politics. But even so, unionism expanded and labor disputes increased in number after 1897: discipline and disorganization were incomplete.[1]

Important Republican and business elites accordingly crafted new strategies for dealing with the "labor problem"—now the central issue of the day. At the core of these strategies lay a style of industrial relations less confrontational than what had been typical during the Gilded Age, at least among the corporate liberal business leaders who came together in the National Civic Federation. In practice this less confrontational style gave rise to an incipient liberal corporatist labor policy lodged in the private sector.[2] Limited unionism, explicitly recognized, was made an essential partner in this arrangement.

The escalation in labor disruptions and the expansion in union membership encouraged business leaders to promote union-employer cooperation in order to rationalize production and maximize efficiency. The AFL was the linchpin of such cooperation. Where AFL unions existed, the AFL could be called upon to manage labor conflict; equally important, the AFL was unlikely to sacrifice its organization to the volatility of industrial unionism. Thus Marcus Hanna argued a pragmatic defense of organized labor: "where the concerns and interests of labor are entrusted to able and honest leadership, it is much easier for those who represent the employers to come into close contact with the laborer, and, by dealing with fewer persons, to accomplish results quicker and better."[3]

---

[1]Strike frequency increased dramatically beginning in 1897. By 1901 the annual number of strikes had nearly tripled 1896 figures, approaching 3,000. The numbers of workers directly involved increased as well, from 183,813 in 1896 to 308,267 in 1899. So, too, did the number of establishments affected: from 5,462 in 1896 to more than 20,000 in 1903. Union membership increased even more swiftly, from 447,000 in 1897 to two million in 1903. See U.S. Bureau of Labor Labor, *Twenty-First Annual Report, 1906: Strikes and Lockouts* (1907), 15.

[2]Gerhard Lehmbruch discusses liberal corporatism thus: "The decision-making process in some liberal corporatist systems is characterized by the existence of two levels of bargaining (more or less distinct from each other). First, bargaining occurs among the 'autonomous groups.' . . . Then bargaining shifts to exchanges between the government and the 'cartel' of organized groups. . . . [The] essential feature [of liberal corporatism] is the large measure of constitutional autonomy of the groups involved, hence the voluntary nature of the institutionalized integration of conflicting social groups. Among the developmental conditions for liberal corporatism are . . . the replacement of classical liberal-competitive capitalism with 'organized capitalism' (Hilferding) and a growing 'politicization' of the market, by the transformation of competitive economies through the social power of oligopolistic firms and organized interest representatives. . . . Consensus-building here largely takes place on the level of the top elite, the leadership of the central interest associations, and depends upon their having a considerable freedom of action." Lehmbruch, "Consociational Democracy, Class Conflict, and the New Corporatism," and "Liberal Corporatism and Party Government," in Philippe Schmitter and Lehmbruch, eds., *Trends toward Corporatist Intermediation* (1979), 54, 170.

[3]Marcus A. Hanna, "Industrial Conciliation and Arbitration," American Academy of Political and Social Sciences *Annals,* 20 (July 1902), 25.

Beyond this, organized capital saw in organized labor something of a mirror image. Like the trusts, organized labor was an organic product of industrialism.[4] Herbert Croly would give full expression to the common heritage:

> The large corporations and the unions occupy in certain respects a similar relation to the American political system. Their advocates both believe in associated action for themselves and in competition for their adversaries. . . . In spite of many setbacks, the unionizing of industrial labor has been attended with almost as much success as the consolidating of industrial power and wealth; and now that the labor unions have earned the allegiance of their members by certain considerable and indispensable services, they find themselves placed, in the eyes of the law, in precisely the same situation as combinations of corporate wealth. Both of these attempts at industrial organization are condemned by the Sherman Anti-Trust Law and by certain similar state legislation as conspiracies against the freedom of trade and industry.[5]

The defense of industrial efficiency against political efforts to decentralize economic power further enriched the corporatist logic espoused by Croly, Hanna, and others. For, as Croly continued,

> just as there can be no effective competition between the huge corporation controlling machinery of production which cannot be duplicated by the small manufacturer in the same line, so there can be no effective competition between the individual laborer and the really efficient labor unions. . . . A democratic government has little or less reason to interfere on behalf of the non-union laborer than it has to interfere in favor of the small producer.[6]

Business-labor harmony was in practice elusive, to be sure, and the fruits of business-labor cooperation were correspondingly ambiguous, incomplete, and, at bottom, anti-union. In the absence of a strong union in his industries, for example, J. P. Morgan could afford to preach mediation and to concur in the appraisal of the AFL as responsible and respectable while in practice refusing to brook unionization or to tolerate any union presence in his mills and mines.[7] Moreover, business and union labor

[4]Ibid., 23–24.
[5]Herbert Croly, *The Promise of American Life* (1909, 1965), 130, 386.
[6]Ibid., 386–87.
[7]Morgan controlled the steel industry outright after the steel merger at the turn of the century. Because of the pivotal role of the House of Morgan in coordinating the coal-carrying railroads, he was also the dominant force in anthracite.

strongly disagreed on the knotty matter of labor-market policy. But with respect to industrial relations, organized labor and organized capital shared common concerns to discipline worker militancy and to resist new-immigrant, industrial *unions*.[8] These concerns led the most powerful segment of capital first to validate AFL unionism and then, in Hanna's words, to "make it the ally of the capitalist, rather than a foe with which to grapple."[9] Conversely, these concerns led the only organized segment of labor to enlist capital in *its* struggle to superintend unionism. What is more, they required that employers recognize the AFL, if not in the workplace then at least at the conference table. Samuel Gompers understood this implication. "The National Civic Federation," he wrote, "without a well-organized, thoroughly alert trade union movement, would be absolutely futile, and perhaps its very existence unnecessary."[10]

Ironically, then, the agent in the consolidation of corporate-Republican dominance in the Progressive Era was the most organized, most politically coherent, most Democratic fragment of the working class: the American Federation of Labor. In 1896 the AFL had gambled on the Democratic party in its struggle to secure a measure of legal relief from and political leverage within the "state of courts and parties." Under the electoral system of 1896—and under the state of Court and Party that developed from it—the AFL now gambled on the National Civic Federation to defend itself against the rule of unfriendly law and procapitalist party, and to establish the representational and institutional credibility of "responsible" unionism. Outside the law, the AFL had moved inside the party system in 1896. Now it moved inside an apparatus of industrial relations that promised the AFL no pain of legal penalty while assuaging the pain of political defeat.

[8]By the turn of the century "one union in a trade" was becoming a burning issue for the AFL. The blurring of craft divisions, jurisdictional battles, and the difficulties of coordinating separate jurisdictions within one trade against employers gave urgency to this issue, especially among the machinists and iron molders. AFL leaders, however, were quick to reject industrial unionism when a resolution supporting the concept was first introduced at the 1903 AFL convention, largely on institutional grounds. Speaking to the convention, Samuel Gompers argued that "industrial unionism is perversive of the history of the labor movement, runs counter to the best conceptions of the toilers' interest now, and is sure to lead to the confusion which precedes dissolution and disruption. . . . It is time for our fellow unionists to stem the tide of expansion madness lest either by their indifference or encouragement, their organizations will be drawn into the vortex that will engulf them to their possible dismemberment and destruction." AFL *Proceedings* (1903), 18–19.

[9]Marcus Hanna, *Mark Hanna, His Book* (1904), 32.

[10]Samuel Gompers, "The Trade Agreement Enthusiastically Endorsed: President Gompers' Address," NCF *Review*, May 15, 1905, pp. 6–7.

The AFL, though Democratic in its political action, cooperated with Republican business leaders in its economic action after 1900. Having gambled on the wrong party in 1896, it was perhaps wise to do so. The Republican monolith in national politics, combined with what was becoming a procapitalist judicial leviathan, closed off labor's political opportunities. Relief from injunctions was unlikely to emanate from a Republican Congress and a Republican White House, and without such relief the courts enjoyed full discretionary authority to constrict union labor's activities in the workplace.[11] Relief from immigration was similarly unlikely, and without this relief the AFL saw itself embattled from below, from workers it would not reach and from industrial unionism it would not tolerate.

Three harsh political realities corroborated union labor's vulnerability. First, any action that the state undertook with respect to labor was unlikely to be friendly toward it, at least as long as Republicans were in control. Prospects for overturning Republican majorities—and more important for creating prolabor majorities—were dim because of the electoral division of the working class under the system of 1896. Dimmer still were labor's prospects for overturning antilabor judicial majorities. Under these circumstances it made sense for union labor to build alliances in the economic arena and to accept the privileges extended by industrialists anxious to contract a labor peace.

Second, the year 1900 marked the beginning of the largest decennial surge in the new immigration, a large percentage of it involving working-age males. Most of the new immigrants who arrived between 1900 and 1909 moved into industry, where they became more than half of the labor force.[12] Because most of these new-immigrant workers moved into unskilled and semiskilled work, however, they were unreachable by the craft principles of the AFL. Moreover, trade-union rules and membership criteria combined job-based tests, such as "competency" exams and proof of craft skills, with nativist tests for determining the admissibility of new immigrants into unions. These tests worked as union analogues to the literacy test proposal that had been stymied in public policy. They included citizenship and naturalization requirements, initiation fees that

---

[11]The number of injunctions issued against unions climbed steadily, from 28 in the 1880s to 122 in the 1890s, then to 328 between 1900 and 1910. Edwin Witte, *The Government in Labor Disputes* (1932), 84.

[12]*Report of the Immigration Commission*, I (1911), 37; Niles Chamberlain, *Immigrants and Their Children* (1927), 62, 64.

low-wage industrial workers could not afford (sometimes as high as $500), and proof of membership in a home-country union.[13] Whether unreachable by default (craft principles) or by design (nativist membership criteria), these new workers presented the AFL with serious political problems, chiefly concerning how to hold the labor market in check and how to sustain its own institutional position. Well-equipped to keep new immigrants out of its own unions, the AFL had few weapons to prevent these workers from independently organizing in the workplace. Designation by capital as labor's bargaining agent would, however, enhance the AFL's claims to jurisdiction over union and nonunion worker alike.

A third problem confronting the AFL was the challenge to its authority mounted within the labor movement itself. This challenge came not only from industrial unionists and socialists but from within the AFL rank and file. Between 1897 and 1900 more than one-third of strikes were not authorized by unions.[14] This tested AFL control over working-class economic action and indicated the dimensions of the threat to AFL hegemony from below.

The AFL, isolated from the governing coalition above, stressed economic action and professed antistatism with increasing vehemence after 1896. But opposed to workers below, both in the labor market and in the labor movement, the AFL had no sure jurisdiction over economic action. Voluntarist, nativist, and organizational concerns thus converged in a strategy to install the AFL as arbiter of labor's interests. This strategy entailed relinquishing confrontational methods where employers were willing to cooperate. It also entailed cooperation between business and labor to hold the working class in check.

These concerns began to bring union leaders into the orbit of business at the start of the twentieth century. In 1900 the AFL, joining with the aristocracy of business (J. P. Morgan, Andrew Carnegie, August Belmont, and Marcus Hanna among them) and with representatives of the "public" (John Commons, Seth Low, Grover Cleveland, and others) in the National Civic Federation, pledged itself to industrial peace through trade agreements and conciliation with employers. Accepting the premise that labor and capital shared "reciprocal interests," the AFL used its participation to make conservative unionism respectable among its erst-

[13]Philip Foner, *History of the Labor Movement in the United States,* vol. 3 (1955), 258; Robert Wiebe, *Businessmen and Reform* (1962), 158; and Richard Hofstadter, *Age of Reform* (1955), 179 n. 5.
[14]David Montgomery, *Workers' Control in America* (1979), Table 1, p. 20.

while foes.[15] To this end it demoted the strike to a weapon of last resort;[16] worked to prevent sympathy strikes, the ultimate weapon of labor solidarity; and made conciliation and the "inviolability of contract" the first principles of unionism. These actions enhanced the AFL's credibility and promoted the view that labor's legitimate demands and methods could always be reconciled with those of capital.[17]

From within the National Civic Federation, AFL leaders (including John Mitchell, president of the United Mine Workers, and Samuel Gompers, president of the AFL and vice-president of the NCF until his death in 1924) pursued their organizational goals. Chief among those goals was to centralize authority within trade unionism and thereby to discipline trade-union ranks, to obstruct rival unionization and thereby to consolidate the AFL hold on the labor movement, to diffuse working-class majorities and thereby to preempt a wider labor-based politics, and finally, to participate in industrial self-regulation and thereby to defend by example against political interventions in industrial relations.[18] Part of the AFL's political project during the Progressive decades, then, was played out in the economic arena. There the AFL differentiated its brand of unionism from episodic, militant, and largely new-immigrant mobilization in the workplace, and it set itself in opposition to anticapitalist forces that tried syndicalist and socialist alternatives. There, too, the AFL worked to promote "industrial government" as an alternative to collision with capital in procapitalist political institutions.

Developing a Labor Policy

The National Civic Federation, from its founding until its decline in the 1920s, defined its principal role as the arbiter of labor disputes. But NCF activities involved far more than preventing and mediating strikes. The NCF ranked the "labor problem" as the first among social problems of

[15]See Ralph Easley, "What Organized Labor Has Learned," McClure's, 19 (October 1902), 483–92.
[16]See John Mitchell, "The Coal Strike," McClure's (December 1902), 220; Easley, 492.
[17]Herbert Croly, Marcus Alonzo Hanna (1912), 404. As Croly described Hanna, "his whole attitude towards labor and his program of conciliation are, indeed, the product of an innocent faith that his country was radically different economically and socially from Europe, and that no fundamental antagonism of economic interest existed among different classes of Americans. All they had to do was to deal fairly and feel kindly one towards another" (409).
[18]This view coincides with that developed by Bruno Ramirez in his excellent When Workers Fight: The Politics of Industrial Relations in the Progressive Era, 1898–1916 (1978).

the time; it used a three-tiered strategy to resolve it. On one tier, Civic Federationists built an institutional apparatus designed to prevent labor disruptions altogether and to mediate those which did occur. Here the NCF committed itself to preempting and defusing the confrontations between labor and capital which had militarized labor-capital relations and destabilized production. On a second tier, it fashioned corporate social policies aimed at holding worker militancy in check. Here the NCF was eager to attach worker welfare to business benevolence as an alternative to worker self-help and mutual aid through unions.[19] On a third tier, NCF employers pursued reform through legislation. Here NCF employers worked to socialize some of the welfare risks and burdens arising from the welfare work of individual corporations and to regularize those risks and burdens across state lines. In these various ways the NCF tried to contain the organization and discipline the behavior of the working class.[20] In the opinion of Eugene Debs, "the Civic Federation has been organized for the one purpose of prolonging the age-long sleep of the working class. Their supreme purpose is to keep [us] from waking up."[21]

During its first half-decade the NCF, under the stewardship of Marcus Hanna, emphasized the development of a labor policy that would pull the AFL into the preservation of industrial stability.[22] Appealing to the "sanctity of contract" and to the reciprocal concerns to be served through "conciliation" or mediation, the NCF, and labor leaders within it, sought to legitimate the AFL's partnership with capital by tying labor peace to labor organization. Asserting union labor's "common sense and fair dealing," Gompers defended the NCF's "social partnership":

> We have our combinations of capital, our organizations and federations of labor. These are now working on parallel lines and have evolved the National

[19]Stuart Brandes, *American Welfare Capitalism* (1976), 32; Peter Roberts, *Anthracite Coal Communities* (1904), 26.

[20]For detailed treatments of these matters, see Marguerite Green, *The National Civic Federation and the American Labor Movement* (1956); Gordon Maurice Jensen, "The National Civic Federation in an Age of Social Change and Social Reform," diss., Princeton University, 1956; James Weinstein, *The Corporate Ideal in the Liberal State, 1900–1918* (1968); and Ramirez, *When Workers Fight*.

[21]Eugene Debs, "Industrial Unionism," address at Grand Central Palace, New York, December 1905.

[22]Ever critical of AFL participation in the NCF, Eugene Debs wrote, "when at last it became apparent to the shrewder and more far-seeing members of the capitalist family that the union movement had come to stay, they forthwith changed their tactics, discarding their frowns and masking their features with the most artful smiles as they extended their greeting and pronounced their blessing upon this latest and greatest benefaction to the human race. . . . In fewer words, seeing that they could not head it off, they decided to take it by the hand and guide it into harmless channels." Eugene Debs, "Unionism and Socialism," in *Appeal to Reason* (1904), reprinted in Debs, *Writings and Speeches*, ed. Arthur Schlesinger, Jr. (1948), 102–3.

Civic Federation. Through the efforts of men noted for their ability, their straightforwardness, noted for the interest they take in public affairs, an effort is being made to bring about the greatest possible success industrially and commercially for our country with the least possible friction.[23]

Arguing further that "there is no hope that the workers can protect their interests or promote their welfare . . . unless they advocate conciliation," the AFL helped put NCF labor policy into practice. It thereby distanced itself from more volatile segments of the working class.[24]

The NCF pulled the AFL into its labor policy to some extent as an antidote to the polarizing effects of worker, employer, and judicial militancy. This would be a symbolically charged tactical alternative to the vigilant open-shop crusade that the National Association of Manufacturers launched in 1903. The extreme and publicly anti-union posture of NAM employers, mostly small manufacturers and independent industrialists, threatened to sharpen class tensions at a high point in union mobilization. Moreover, the NAM enlisted the courts in its campaign against unions, and the collisions between business and labor in the courts threatened to *politicize* unionism at a crest of worker militancy.[25] No less anti-union than the NAM in practice, NCF employers were nevertheless reluctant to assail unionism in principle. The National Civic Federation thus objected to the wholesale use of injunctions and the wholesale application of anti-trust laws to unions, because such measures turned labor-capital disagreement into conflict and politicized labor.[26] Most NCF employers may have maintained open shops, but if the NCF frontally resisted labor's right to organize—as the NAM and the courts did through injunctions—it would subvert the very premise upon which it was based: that *organized* labor and *organized* capital should and could cooperate because they shared "reciprocal" interests.[27] John Mitchell saw it in these terms: "if, while itself securing the advantage of combination it declares labor shall not have the same advantage, capital loses its cause."[28]

[23]Samuel Gompers, "The Limitations of Conciliation and Arbitration," American Academy of Political and Social Sciences *Annals*, 20 (1902), 33.

[24]Ibid., 31.

[25]Mary Beard, *A Short History of the Labor Movement* (1968), 109; Weinstein, 16–17. John Frey, president of the iron molders, wrote in his *Labor Injunction* (n.d.): "Possibly the most menacing feature in connection with the issuing of the labor injunction is, therefore, the sinister part played by the courts of equity in creating and supporting class distinctions" (57).

[26]Weinstein, *Corporate Ideal*.

[27]The NCF did not officially recognize the right of union membership until 1908—and when it did, it also recognized the obverse right of workers *not* to join a union.

[28]Mitchell, 220.

Still another pressure was pushing the NCF to develop a union-based labor policy: industrial peace could not be enforced until relations between unions (where they existed) and employers were made stable and contractually binding. AFL unions needed alternatives to confrontations with employers, such as procedures for negotiation and mediation. Guarantees were necessary to ensure that unions would obey negotiated agreements. And union recognition, at least in principle, was essential if the AFL was to shed its image as an outsider in labor relations. Recognition was equally necessary to distinguish conservative unionism from episodically militant unorganized labor and from renegade trade-union locals.

A central item on the NCF agenda, therefore, was to develop mechanisms for securing stable relations between organized labor and industrial employers. The first national conference of the NCF established an Industrial Department commissioned "to obviate and prevent strikes and lockouts, [and] to aid in renewing industrial relations where a rupture has occurred."[29] Though controlled by capital under the leadership of Marcus Hanna, the Industrial Department attracted considerable union participation. Among its charter members were Samuel Gompers and John Mitchell. Other union participants included the heads of the iron, steel, and tin workers, the longshoremen, the machinists, the boot and shoe workers, and the textile and garmentworkers. Of the industries concerned, steel, coal, and textiles were likely sites for unionization along industrial lines.

Early on, the Industrial Department formed a Conciliation Committee, composed of representatives of business and labor, to intervene in industrial disputes. The committee's priority was direct intervention in strikes, but the suppression of sympathy strikes became an equally essential objective. Sympathy strikes increased in frequency after 1899. They expressed solidarity across the boundaries of craft unionism and, beyond this, occurred outside the contractual relations between unions and employers which underpinned the NCF schema. Some of the NCF's most ardent conciliation efforts were designed to prevent such secondary union actions.

A first test of the conciliation process and of business-labor cooperation occurred in 1901, when the Amalgamated Association of Iron, Steel and Tin Workers struck to defend its organizational position and to coordinate

[29]"By-Laws of the Industrial Department of the NCF," quoted in Ramirez, 69, and Green, 500.

activities against the newly merged U.S. Steel Corporation.[30] If the purpose of conciliation was to mediate the differences between Morgan and the union, it failed. The union, still weakened by the Homestead strike of 1892, and its craft structure still impenetrable to the semiskilled and unskilled ethnic workers in the industry,[31] was decisively defeated. Between 1901 and 1909 what remained of the union was rooted out entirely. Business-labor cooperation, by contrast, proved successful. Not only did Gompers and Mitchell mediate between the steel corporation and the union but within the AFL itself they acted to defuse strike militancy. Gompers refused the Amalgamated's request to make the steel strike the "central fight for unionism," and both Mitchell and Gompers distanced themselves from the Amalgamated's call for a sympathy strike.[32]

Gompers and Mitchell thus affirmed the central premises of the NCF arrangement. Their decision not to make the strike a crusade for unionism, despite intense pressures from the Amalgamated, demonstrated to employers the reliability of conservative unionists. AFL efforts to forestall a sympathy strike and the silence of the mineworkers' union on the matter despite countervailing internal pressures proved that labor elites, at least, understood the "sanctity of contract." The AFL affirmed the NCF scheme, though at considerable cost to the organizational interests and autonomy of an affiliate. But the AFL's moderation during the strike brightened its own institutional prospects. Its interventions to subdue the militancy of the Amalgamated signaled a trend not only toward more conservative economic action but also toward the centralization within the union movement of authority over economic action. In addition, the AFL showed business leaders willing to see that the union movement contained elites upon whom they could depend.[33]

[30]The Amalgamated had decided at its 1900 convention that "should one mill in a combine or trust have difficulty, all mills in said combine or trust shall cease work until such grievance is settled"; Charles Gulick, *The Labor Policy of the U.S. Steel Corporation* (1924), 96. The corporation insisted on the independence of each of its plants in dealing with labor problems and declared its opposition to any extension of unionism. See John Garraty, "U.S. Steel vs. Labor: The Early Years," *Labor History*, I (Winter 1960), 10–11; Garraty, *Right Hand Man: The Life of George W. Perkins* (1957); and Ida Tarbell, *The Life of Elbert Gary* (1925), chap. 4.

[31]Garraty, "U.S. Steel vs. Labor," 8, 23; Gulick, 95–96. Union membership never recovered its 1891 high of 25,000. In 1900 there were 168,000 workers in the industry, 40 percent of whom were foreign-born. The leadership of the Amalgamated had highly ambivalent attitudes toward immigrants.

[32]Samuel Gompers, "The Steel Strike: Mr. Shaffer, His Accusations, Their Refutation," *American Federationist*, 11 (1901), 415–31; Green, 28–31; and Foner, 83.

[33]Ramirez quotes from Mitchell's correspondence: "Our connection with the negotiations has

Troubles in anthracite coal again tested the NCF entente. From the beginnings of labor unrest in 1900 to the historic anthracite coal strike of 1902, the NCF contributed conciliation and mediation services to try to find a peaceable resolution. Its efforts were helped by the fact that the leader of the United Mine Workers, John Mitchell, was a labor voice within the NCF.

The UMW was new to anthracite coal in 1900; indeed, anthracite miners had been disorganized since 1880, largely as a result of industry efforts to weaken the position of militant Irish and British miners. These efforts included the purge of the Molly Maguires, blacklisting, and the recruitment of new immigrant workers.[34] The costs of disorganization were considerable: miners did not receive a single wage increase for twenty years (annual earnings ranged from $210 to $616, depending on skill), while the number of working days declined to one hundred ninety per year as a consequence of limits on production coordinated by industry owners. The wages of many mineworkers depended on output. Production limits reduced wages absolutely, and the absence of standardized weighing procedures allowed coal operators discretion to dock workers for impurities and to vary the size of the "ton."[35]

Anthracite mineworkers thus had many reasons to organize, but they were not quick to respond when the UMW moved into eastern Pennsylvania in 1899.[36] One hindrance to organization was the Draconian discipline enforced by employers, both at work and in the company towns where mineworkers lived.[37] Equally important was the sharp separation, by skill and ethnicity, of new-immigrant mineworkers from the English-speaking veteran labor organizers.[38] This separation gave rise to both occupational and organizational antagonism, as new-immigrant mine laborers found

---

done much to strengthen our organization and I believe that the influence of the steel corporation can be used to help us should we need it. At least Mr. Schwab [president of U.S. Steel] said to me in confidence that any time I wished to discuss labor matters with him he would receive me and give careful consideration to all I said. He also said for myself personally, he desired to have the privilege of talking to me on any labor troubles that might arise" (57–58).

[34]Peter Roberts, *The Anthracite Coal Industry* (1901), 103–4; Arthur Suffern, *Conciliation and Arbitration in the Coal Industry* (1915), 203–13.

[35]Robert J. Cornell, *The Anthracite Coal Strike of 1902* (1957), 38, 40ff.

[36]The UMW had been established in 1890, with an organizational focus on bituminous mining. The union grew spectacularly after 1897, when it could claim only 10,000 members nationwide. Still, by the turn of the century 300,000 mine workers, half of whom were in anthracite, remained outside the union.

[37]Roberts, *Anthracite Coal Communities*, passim.

[38]Elsie Gluck, *John Mitchell, Miner: Labor's Bargain with the Gilded Age* (1929), 68ff.; Peter Roberts, "The Anthracite Coal Situation," *Yale Review*, 11 (1902–3), 34; and Frank Julian Warne, *The Slav Invasion and the Mine Workers* (1904).

themselves dependent upon skilled miners—who resented them as strike-breakers as well as for their low living standards—for occupational mobility and sometimes even for pay.[39] Demographic trends toward new-immigrant majorities in the anthracite labor force created real problems for union organizers. Within the anthracite sector itself, it was essential for union leverage against coal employers that new immigrants participate in the union; and across the coal industry, it was essential for union strength in the bituminous regions to organize in anthracite.

Yet, remarkably, when old-stock miners struck in 1900, new-immigrant workers joined them in overwhelming numbers. Of the 143,000 anthracite workers, between 80,000 and 100,000 did not report to work on the first day of the strike. By the end of the first week, 125,000 workers were idle. By the tenth day only 15 of the Reading's 39 collieries were operating, and by the third week all 39 were shut down.

What occasioned the strike was the operators' refusal to negotiate with the UMW. Although John Mitchell rejected the anthracite workers' request for permission to strike—"I am as opposed to strikes as I am to war," he would write later[40]—the miners went ahead anyway. The demands they presented, to notoriously stubborn employers, were union recognition; a union wage scale; payment by a standardized ton; union oversight of weighing; reduction of hours from ten to eight a day; and an end to company control of the social lives of workers.

The decision of the anthracite miners to strike in despite of Mitchell alarmed Marcus Hanna, particularly since the strike came in the midst of McKinley's reelection campaign. Conditions in anthracite and the specific grievances of the miners suggested that McKinley's 1896 promise of a "full dinner pail" had not been fulfilled.[41] The independent action of the miners and the intransigence of the coal-carrying railroads that dominated the industry, meanwhile, placed the business-labor entente in the NCF in jeopardy.

Hanna accordingly lent his energies to conciliation and enlisted John Mitchell to defuse the union side of the conflict. Mitchell complied. He insisted to strikers that the issue of union recognition should not stand in the way of a settlement while he bargained with employers to win some concessions on the strikers' wage demands.[42] Conciliation yielded a

[39]Roberts, "Anthracite Coal Situation"; Victor Greene, *Slavic Community on Strike* (1968), 79–80.
[40]Mitchell, 219.
[41]Foner, 86ff.
[42]Gluck, 82; Cornell, 44–47.

short-term settlement in which the operators acquiesced, among other things, to a 10 percent wage increase. As the expiration date of the pact approached, Mitchell positioned himself to exert greater authority over union activities. Early in 1901 he mobilized conservative miners behind a convention resolution that empowered him, in conjunction with the union's executive committee, to arrange and accept terms of a new settlement. Mitchell then worked with Hanna, who appealed to J. P. Morgan to facilitate a new agreement (the House of Morgan had extensive ties in the anthracite industry). Again the NCF's mediation services proved effective: operators agreed to maintain the wage agreement of 1900 and to consider, if Mitchell could discipline the rank and file, adopting a written contract the following year.[43]

But these agreements served only to postpone the confrontation between miners and employers. In the spring of 1902 the operators rejected the wage, union recognition, and contract demands of the miners. The union, again opposed by Mitchell, authorized a strike. The strike tested Mitchell's leadership within the union and his effectiveness in the NCF, and it challenged the capabilities of NCF's Conciliation Committee. More challenging than the strike itself, however, was the sympathy strike threatened, over Mitchell's vehement opposition, by the bituminous miners.

The Conciliation Committee, with Mitchell's blessing, conducted a six-week missionary effort in the soft-coal fields to persuade miners not to violate their contracts. Gompers offered to send twenty organizers into the bituminous fields, to "preach the inviolability of contract"[44] and to warn miners that a sympathy strike would provoke the AFL to expel the UMW.[45] Hanna, too, worked to mobilize support against the sympathy strike. Mitchell lobbied conservative convention delegates and ultimately lined up the UMW convention behind sanctity of contract. The convention then voted to demonstrate support for the anthracite strikers by setting up a strike fund. The NCF, joined by reformers and the press, applauded the UMW for its restraint and hailed its rejection of the sympathy strike as a "high water mark for organized labor."[46]

NCF mediation efforts were less successful in the anthracite strike itself. Not only did the strike drag on through summer and autumn, but the coal operators militarized the conflict when they activated the Coal and Iron Police and one thousand secret detectives. The governor of Pennsyl-

---

[43]Greene, 88.

[44]Easley, 489.

[45]Ibid.; Cornell, 103.

[46]Easley, 489–90; Lincoln Steffens, "A Labor Leader of Today: John Mitchell and What He Stands For," *McClure's*, 19 (August 1902), 356.

vania added the state's militia to this attempt to coerce rather than concili-
ate an end to the strike, dispatching nine thousand Pennsylvania "Cos-
sacks" to the region. As the strike dragged on into winter, forcing
factories to shut down for lack of fuel, it became a serious political issue.
The ruthlessness of employers, the inroads made by socialist organizers
under these volatile circumstances, and the consequences of interrupted
production generated popular demands for national political intervention.
From some quarters were heard demands that the mines be nationalized.
From within the NCF were heard appeals to Morgan to help the mediation
effort. Morgan's refusal to intervene, however, exposed a central flaw in
the NCF arrangement: its success depended upon the voluntary cooperation of its members.

Seeing the impasse, Theodore Roosevelt, then president, brought the
state into the conciliation process. He moved cautiously, by his own
account uncertain as to presidential authority in the matter, and avoided
interventions against one side or the other.[47] Roosevelt's caution turned
the strike into a watershed for relations between the state and labor: the
presidency intervened, not the Court; mediation was the method, not
injunctions; and negotiators were dispatched, not troops.

At the start Roosevelt attempted to mediate informally through the
office of the presidency. He directed the head of the Labor Bureau,
Carroll Wright, to investigate the dispute and dispatched Secretary of
State Elihu Root to confer with Morgan. He then conferred personally
with UMW officials, including Mitchell, and the coal operators. Unable
to resolve matters informally, Roosevelt proposed a presidential commission to arbitrate the dispute.

Both parties to the conflict at first resisted Roosevelt's proposal. Arbitration by the state represented, both for the industry and for the union, a
loss of autonomy. In addition, anthracite employers resisted any arbitration that involved representatives from the UMW.[48] Roosevelt finessed
the problem, however, by acceding to the employers' condition while
promising Mitchell some form of labor representation on the commission.[49] Mitchell accepted Roosevelt's compromise, agreeing to appear

[47]Theodore Roosevelt, *An Autobiography* (1914), 480–81. Robert Wiebe highlights the role of
Hanna-Roosevelt rivalries in the development of a mediation arrangement in "The Anthracite
Strike of 1902: A Record of Confusion," *Mississippi Valley Historical Review,* 49 (1961–2),
229–51.

[48]Employers would not accept the UMW as a bargaining agent in anthracite coal because its
membership included bituminous coal miners.

[49]Labor representation on the commission was achieved somewhat underhandedly, and even
then only symbolically. Roosevelt satisfied labor's demand for representation by appointing the
head of the conservative Brotherhood of Railway Conductors under the category "eminent
sociologist." Roosevelt, 483.

before the commission as the representative of the anthracite mineworkers rather than as president of the UMW. With Morgan pressuring the coal-carrying railroads and Mitchell leading the strikers to accept governmental mediation, both sides agreed to go to arbitration.

Roosevelt's commission developed a settlement that separated the issue of working conditions from the question of union recognition. The commission awarded workers a 10 percent wage increase (the union had been asking for 20 percent) and a nine-hour day (the union wanted eight), and it recommended replacing the private Coal and Iron Police with publicly supported and publicly accountable constabularies.[50] But it also condemned the principle of the union shop, insisting that the "right and privilege of being a non-union man are sanctioned in law and morals" and that "the contention that a majority of the employees in an industry, by voluntarily associating themselves, in a union, acquire authority over those who do not so associate themselves is untenable."[51] Moreover, while admitting that "the question of the recognition of the union and of dealing with the mine workers through their union, was considered by both operators and miners to be one of the most important involved in the controversy which culminated in the strike," the commission declined jurisdiction over it.[52] At the same time that it did so, however, it tied any eventual recognition of a union in anthracite to conditions that would dismember the UMW.[53]

The commission endorsed unionism in principle, to be sure, and allowed for a union in anthracite one day. It even echoed NCF assumptions about responsible unionism:

[50]The commission concluded that "the fact that deputies are, to all intents and purposes the employees of one of the parties, usually works injury to the cause in which they are engaged. . . . Their presence is an irritant, and many of the disturbances in the coal regions during the late strike grew out of their presence." Anthracite Coal Strike Commission *Report* (1903), 83–84.

[51]Ibid., 64–65. Distinguishing between majority rule in political government and majority tyranny in union government, the commission argued that "the fallacy of such argument lies in the use of the analogy of State government, under which the minority acquiesces in the rule of the majority; but government is the result of organic law, within the scope of which no other government can assume authority to control the minority. In all acts of government the minority takes part, and when it is defeated the government becomes the agency of all, not simply of the majority. . . . [The] trade union is a voluntary social organization, and . . . is subordinate to the laws of the land. . . . Yet it at times seeks to set itself up as a separate and distinct governing agency and to control those who have refused to join its ranks and to consent to its government, and to deny to them the personal liberties which are guaranteed to every citizen by the constitution and laws of the land. . . . Abraham Lincoln said, 'No man is good enough to govern another man without that other's consent.' "

[52]Ibid., 61.

[53]Ibid., 66–67; Appendix H, 227.

Experience shows that the more full the recognition given to a trades union, the more businesslike and responsible it becomes. Through dealing with business men in business matters, its more intelligent, conservative, and responsible members come to the front and gain general control and direction of its affairs. If the energy of the employer is directed to discouragement and repression of the union, he need not be surprised if the more radically inclined members are the ones most frequently heard.[54]

But even as it presented these views, the commission put the UMW on probation in anthracite and made any recognition of the union contingent upon union satisfaction of the employers' criteria. The chief criterion was that any union among anthracite workers had to be "governed by the anthracite mine workers and free from control or dictation of bituminous mine workers." In essence, the commission had accepted the arguments of the coal-carrying railroads against recognition of an industrywide union.[55] Furthermore, in declining to award a trade agreement as part of the strike settlement, the commission set forth the conditions under which a trade agreement might be undertaken: an open shop; organizational separation of bituminous and anthracite miners; two-thirds majorities to call strikes; and a union constitution that would require officers to exhaust avenues of negotiation before considering a strike and would empower union officers to discipline locals and members.[56] On the organizational issue, in effect, the union was awarded the status quo ante.[57]

NCF business and labor leaders touted the commission's report as a victory for miners greater than could have been anticipated. Union recognition was implied because the report did not explicitly recommend against it, John Commons argued; he hailed the report as a complete victory for the UMW.[58] And in his public pronouncements Mitchell credited the NCF with the strike's resolution; he proclaimed that the strike settlement vindicated the NCF's efforts at conciliation.

The anthracite strike was a proving ground for labor leaders in the NCF. They acquitted themselves as well, particularly in averting a sympathy strike. But in both steel and anthracite, it is important to note, NCF labor leaders consolidated the labor establishment at the expense of strong unionism in industry. Steel and coal opened back doors into trade union-

[54]Ibid., 63.
[55]Ibid., 227, 60.
[56]Ibid., 227–29.
[57]Ramirez, 42–45, provides a good discussion of the commission's recommendations.
[58]John R. Commons, "The Anthracite Coal Strike Award," NCF *Monthly Review*, April 1903, p. 15.

ism for new-immigrant industrial workers. In coal mining, in particular, union survival necessitated union surrender to organizational flexibility. But in anthracite, when new immigrants endured a long and bitter union struggle against considerable odds, union leaders were concerned more with demonstrating their professionalism, conservatism, and trustworthiness to NCF colleagues than with joining in the union struggle. Gompers and Mitchell chose conciliation over struggle, contractual stability over solidarity, and *group* recognition in the NCF over *union* recognition in particular industries. They enhanced the institutional position of the AFL, but part of the price they had to pay was a decline in union mobilization that began in 1904 and an unraveling of AFL jurisdiction in volatile industries.

The successful conciliation of the anthracite strike—widely regarded as the most serious industrial dispute since the Pullman strike—transformed the Conciliation Committee into a permanent department, institutionalizing NCF mediation activities. Some conciliation efforts would sap union efforts to standardize control over industrial sectors, as had happened in anthracite, but Gompers and Mitchell continued to participate in, and defend, these endeavors. By 1905 the NCF could boast of considerable success: it had either mediated or prevented labor strife in about three-fourths of the five hundred disputes in which it had become involved.[59]

The conciliation effort, however, invariably produced resolutions that did not establish the principles of union recognition and collective bargaining. Thus it did not automatically serve the broader NCF aim of legitimating conservative trade unionism as a partner in industrial relations. To be sure, AFL cooperation in averting strikes and negotiating settlements greatly improved the public image of at least the AFL leadership (Lincoln Steffens, for example, championed John Mitchell for winning the respect of both the miners and the business community).[60] Still, many strikes involved AFL affiliates—including, in the anthracite strike, the UMW—in dramatic confrontations with employers. The conciliation effort in itself could not dispel the impression that labor organizations per se, including the AFL, were necessarily inimical to industrial peace and efficiency.

Consequently Civic Federationists identified the trade agreement as the backbone of its labor policy. Designed to guard against industrial disturbances, the trade agreement formalized a contractual relationship between

[59]Jensen, 124–25.
[60]Steffens, 355.

union workers and their employers. The contract, in Ralph Easley's words "as sacred as any business contract," was "determined by mutual concessions in conferences with employers rather than by a demand submitted by the union as an ultimatum."[61] If the trade agreement represented contractual relations between unions and employers, it nevertheless did not require unions to submit to the rule of law governing most contractual relations of the time. The trade agreement was a voluntary relationship that did not depend on public coercion to work. Ironically, because the legal status of unions was so problematic at the turn of the century— individual workers had certain rights (contract), union members had certain duties (civil and criminal liability), but unions had neither—unions were not entities against which trade agreements could easily be enforced, except by persuasion of the sanctity of contract. This validated the NCF premise of industrial self-government. In the vision of the NCF the trade agreement was the essence of "mutual government" in industry by business and labor, because it represented a mutual and voluntary adjustment of interests and grievances by both actors in industry.[62] Equally important, the trade agreement provided a mechanism to further trade-union discipline. Where trade agreements were in effect, they imposed contractual responsibilities upon unionists not to strike, either directly or in sympathy. The AFL was ready to appeal to those contractual responsibilities as in the steel and coal strikes, to extract union obedience to its conservative leadership.

During the early years of the NCF the trade agreement was generally regarded as the centerpiece of the plan for industrial harmony. The Trade Agreements Department, chaired by mineworkers' president John Mitchell, successfully encouraged agreements between many of the federation's constituent employer groups and unions. By 1905 the NCF could boast a direct role in many of the fifty trade agreements then in effect, among them pacts in bituminous coal mining, the New York clothing trades, and iron molding.[63]

Obviously, trade agreements were practicable only in those trades and industries where workers were organized and employers recognized their organization. Indeed, the NCF argued, "a successful trade agreement

[61]Easley, 492.

[62]Jensen, 116; Frank Julian Warne, "The Trade Agreement in the Coal Industry," American Academy of Political and Social Sciences *Annals,* 36 (September 1910), 86–95; Samuel Gompers, *Labor and the Employer* (1920), 30, 48, 242.

[63]John Mitchell and Francis L. Robbins, "Report of the Department of Trade Agreements," NCF *Monthly Review,* January 1905, pp. 13–14.

system *presupposes* organization on both sides—a union of workmen and a union of employers."[64] But this did not mean that the NCF set out to extend union organization across all of industry—far from it. The trade agreement became the instrument of choice to regulate established unions, to prevent them from interrupting production and acting in solidarity with other unions, and to focus union concerns on the specifics of particular contracts. Through trade agreements and the collective bargaining that preceded them, the NCF did much to defuse conflict between labor and capital. Capital, however, was clearly not of one piece: NCF and NAM employers differed sharply about labor policy. Nor was "labor" of one piece: a labor establishment willing to incorporate business principles contrasted with an industrial work force that was largely unorganized but nonetheless intermittently militant and disruptive. Yet once NCF labor policy made these distinctions clear, group alignments rather than class alignments—group competition and bargaining rather than class confrontation—became the fulcrum of industrial politics. As Gompers explained it in 1916:

> All the predatory forces that menace the welfare of wage-earners do not come from employers. There exists among the workers and in the labor movement an element which is either misguided or is so depraved that it is willing to lead workers into unnecessary suffering and useless misery. . . . There are those who go among workers, whose present wrongs are great enough to appeal to the compassion of any human being, and lead these workers into strikes and then urge them to employ the methods of revolution, to refuse to enter into agreements with employers, or to accept any improvements because the full rights to which they are entitled are not granted at once. . . . The industrial contracts between workers and employers are the milestones of industrial progress. They clinch each forward movement in a tangible form and become a new basis for future demands and movements for greater progress.[65]

The trade agreements system, limited in practice to employers and unions enrolled in the NCF, demonstrated the compatibility between conservative trade unionism and business. For the trade agreement to work as an instrument of industrial harmony, unions had to be willing to compromise—even on the issue of union recognition—and to abide by the contractual obligations formalized in the agreements. The trade agreements

[64]"Joint Trade Agreements," NCF *Monthly Review,* April 1903, p. 12.
[65]Gompers, *Labor and the Employer,* 30.

system acted to reduce interruptions of production and to secure AFL intervention against disruptive and renegade union action. In effect, trade agreements obligated the AFL to act against labor and in defense of contract. Thus the AFL opposed the transit workers' union in its strike against August Belmont's IRT in 1904, for example, despite Belmont's use of strikebreakers, reasoning that the strike was illegitimate because the union's three-year contract was still in force.

Because it affirmed a theoretically equal partnership between organized labor and organized capital, the trade agreement became the linchpin of NCF corporatism. Because it implied mutual accommodation between partners in industry, moreover, the trade agreement system erected still another institutional barrier to solidarity within the labor movement. It delegitimated both direct and sympathy strikes except under expired contracts, removing the central weapon of collective action by workers and separating the labor establishment from the struggles of unionizing workers. Where expired contracts made legitimate strikes possible, the labor establishment could invoke the principle of conciliation to ensure that the strike would be used only "as a weapon of last resort."[66]

The twin pillars of the NCF labor policy—mediation and contract—promoted conservative trade unionism, giving it the tools with which to improve its public image as well as to exert internal union discipline. Yet neither mediation nor contract worked to forestall sporadic strikes and protests among industrial workers, chiefly because the AFL had no practical jurisdiction over them. Indeed, as industrial worker militancy began to surge around 1909, the NCF's labor policy proved ill-equipped to deal with it. Most important, the AFL was unable and unavailable to mediate the labor side of these conflicts.[67] Many strikes occurred beyond the pale of AFL unions. But even where the AFL had some organizational pres-

[66]See Croly's discussion of "good" vs. "bad" unions for an elaboration of the corporatist processes that might make the strike such a last-gasp instrument; *Promise of American Life*, 390ff.

[67]These points became clear at McKees Rocks, Pennsylvania, in 1909, when five thousand industrial workers rose up against U.S. Steel. See Louis Duchez, "The Strikes in Pennsylvania," *International Socialist Review*, 10 (September 1909), 193–203; Duchez, "Victory at McKees Rocks," ibid., 10 (October 1909), 290; and Paul Kellog, "The McKees Rocks Strike," *Survey*, 12 (October 1909), 665. Kellog calls the strike a "revolution in the labor movement." Strikes in the textile industry (e.g., in Lawrence and in New York City) further exposed the institutional limitations of the NCF and especially of the AFL. See Melvyn Dubofsky, *When Workers Organize: New York City in the Progressive Era* (1968); Dubofsky, "Organized Labor and the Immigrant in New York City, 1900–1918," *Labor History*, 2 (Spring 1961), 187–88; Mary K. O'Sullivan, "The Labor War at Lawrence," *Survey*, 28 (April 6, 1912), 73; and Gail Falk "Women and Unions: A Historical View," *Women's Rights Law Reporter*, Spring 1973, pp. 54–65.

ence—for example, in the Lawrence textile industry—it sometimes withheld institutional support from striking workers.[68] The AFL's isolation from and opposition to industrial worker militancy proved the federation's conservatism and discipline, but at the same time it pointed out the limitations of the NCF's mediation program.

Challenges to AFL Autonomy: Bringing in the State

Unable to achieve industrial peace through its trade-union policies alone, the National Civic Federation began in 1905 to develop "welfare work." Exclusively an employers' project (membership in the NCF's Welfare Department was off limits to labor), welfare work amounted to an effort to construct a "benevolent feudalism" in industry. Many welfare schemes did in fact yield benefits for workers—technical education, schools, low-cost housing, recreational facilities, health care, insurance, and pensions. But in most cases the price workers paid was prolonged disorganization and, with that, powerlessness in their relations with employers. For, by design, welfare work fostered workers' loyalty toward their employer patrons. As one steel official admitted to a congressional committee, U.S. Steel's benefits and stock-purchase schemes were calculated to bring workers to identify with the corporation and thus to preempt interest in unions.[69] Indeed, for most participating employers (an NCF survey documented 2,500 in 1914), welfare work—at least in theory—was a means of securing workers' consent to the terms of their employment short of recognizing unions and negotiating contracts with them.[70]

Welfare work supplemented NCF mediation and trade agreement policies by helping to stabilize industry; but it also offered a clear substitute for union-oriented NCF labor policies. In some companies, for example,

[68]Following Gomper's lead, the three AFL affiliates in Lawrence (the Central Labor Union, the Boston Women's Trade Union League, and the Textile Workers of America) all refused to support the Lawrence strikers even symbolically in 1912. See O'Sullivan, "Labor War at Lawrence"; Falk, "Women and Unions." Gompers later boasted that this "responsible" union behavior had enabled AFL unions to form seven new locals in Lawrence alone. Quoted in Weinstein, 14; Paul Brissenden, *The I.W.W.* (1957), 284–94.

[69]U.S. House, Committee on the Investigation of the U.S. Steel Corporation, *Hearings* (1912), 1569–75.

[70]"How the Welfare Department Was Organized," NCF *Review*, June 1904, p. 13; John A. Fitch, *The Steel Workers* (1910), 213; David Brody, *Steelworkers in America: The Nonunion Era* (1960), 179; Tarbell, 162–63, 171–73.

the provision of housing was conditional upon not joining a union, and leases often contained eviction clauses for workers who joined strikes.[71] Stock-purchase and pension plans typically contained subtle strictures against enrollment in unions. These plans reached mainly better-paid and better-skilled workers, who could afford to buy into them. For workers in steel and other industries, moreover, employees were not automatically eligible for stock-ownership plans; rather, eligibility was determined on a case-by-case basis, with each worker required to secure from his supervisor written acknowledgment of his continuing "interest in the welfare and progress of the Corporation."[72] As one worker complained not too long after the plans were adopted, "no stockbroker wants to try to organize a union when the terms of the agreement state that only those who show a proper interest in the affairs of the company will receive a bonus."[73]

The AFL's stance toward such patently anti-union policies was one of acquiescence, at least for as long as welfare work was pursued exclusively in the private sector. Gompers occasionally criticized corporate welfare work, but until World War I he and other AFL leaders accepted their exclusion from the NCF's Welfare Department.[74] One union leader even wrote a pamphlet for the Welfare Department expressing the view that welfare work supplemented the activities of unions.[75] To some extent the AFL could afford to be complaisant on this matter, for welfare work principally affected industries outside the AFL's jurisdiction.

Although the NCF's welfare policies were effective in certain key industries, they, too, were incomplete answers to the "labor problem." For one thing, welfarism was costly: risks and expenses were borne by individual employers. For another, welfare work neither prevented industrial workers' militancy absolutely (indeed, worker resentment against compulsory dependence on company stores and company housing sometimes fueled disruptions as in McKees Rocks) nor blocked socialist mobilization in politics. Nor did it put an end to social policy initiatives within the individual states. Accordingly NCF planners turned to politics to press for interventions that would supplement welfare work and be more manageable than the uncoordinated policies of the individual states. Recogniz-

---

[71]Brandes, 48–49.

[72]Garraty, "U.S. Steel vs. Labor," 18–19.

[73]Garraty, *Right Hand Man*, 111, quoting from the Survey.

[74]See Ramirez, 155; Brandes, 22–23; Green, 268–70.

[75]J. W. Sullivan, *The Trade Unions' Attitude toward Welfare Work* (1907), discussed in Ramirez, *When Workers Fight*.

ing many aspects of the "labor problem" as national in scope and unlikely to be redressed equitably on a voluntary, industry-by-industry basis,
NCF leaders sought to reinforce and regularize their efforts with uniform
state laws socializing employer risk, with protective labor legislation, and
with an invigorated labor-market policy tied to expanded immigration.
Each of these objectives brought NCF employers into conflict with the
AFL. NCF employers, though never as statist as some of the reformers
associated with them (Croly, Roosevelt, Kelley, and even Commons),
were clearly at odds with NCF labor leaders in their pragmatic pursuit of
state social policy.

Most of the NCF proposals for social reform—including accident insurance and the regulation of child labor—were addressed to the individual
states. Here NCF employers joined with progressive reformers to argue
for policies that would complement industry's private welfare schemes
and regularize diverse interventions. The business of social reform, however, was rather more problematic than NCF labor policy had been. NCF
employers could muster less agreement on the need and desirability of
state action than they had on the purpose and principles of labor policy.
Equally complicating, federalism made uniformity among the states' labor
policies difficult to achieve.[76] Judicial superintendence of social and economic interventions by government—cemented in the *Lochner* decision of
1905[77]—rendered labor policies by the states difficult to sustain.

In 1909, with an eye to developing public policy remedies for the
disabilities and dependencies of old age, sickness, and accidents, the NCF
established its Industrial Insurance Commission, with George Perkins as
chair.[78] And in 1910, in an effort to promote a regularity of policy
between states, the NCF brought forty-six governors together in a national
conference addressed by President Taft, established twenty-three state
councils to monitor the states' labor legislation on a permanent basis, and
drafted model proposals, most notably one for workmen's compensa-

---

[76]The president of the New York Life Insurance Company, for example, complained that
"business is faced by the reactionary effect of having within our own country to deal with forty-
six different frontiers, and is being paralyzed by the fact that the individual States are attempting
to supervise affairs that comprehend and relate to all the States. In other words, under the plea
that States' rights must be preserved, the States are invading the national domain and are
enormously retarding national development. The possibilities of social betterment . . . lie in a
wise joinder of the function of insurance in its various activities. . . . Interstate insurance must be
placed under federal control." Darwin P. Kingsley, "Life Insurance and the Moral Obligation of
Employers toward Their Workingmen," NCF *Review*, March 1, 1910, p. 25.

[77]*Lochner v. New York*, 198 U.S. 45 (1905).

[78]"Industrial Insurance Commission," NCF *Review*, March 1909, p. 13.

tion.[79] In this connection the NCF also maintained a department on compensation for industrial accidents, which formulated the federation's workmen's compensation plan in 1911.[80] The problem posed by the courts remained a knotty one, however, since judicial interventions to restrict economic regulation and to promote laissez-faire were meted out in a climate of judicial invincibility. In fact a New York state law embodying compulsory accident insurance principles similar to those proposed by the NCF was rejected by the state court of appeals shortly before the NCF unveiled its plan. Nevertheless, judicial willingness to allow regulation of certain groups of workers (e.g., women) made room for some movement in the direction of social reform.[81]

Alongside the structural impediments to social reform imposed by federalism and judicial superintendence of minimalist government stood organized labor's opposition to the NCF reform agenda. The AFL took many of its cues from NCF industrial policies, it is true, but it resisted, by and large, the proposals in social policy which were developed from the NCF experience. Here AFL and reform interests collided. The NCF employers and reform elites, who tried to "navigate between class politics and plutocracy," generally conceded some need for the state as a compass. The labor establishment, on the other hand, opposed most forms of social or economic intervention that took responsibility (and credit) away from unions: for example, wage guarantees, job security, comprehensive workmen's compensation, and unemployment insurance.[82] The only exceptions to the AFL's steadfast adherence to voluntarism developed beyond the scope of narrow union-management relations. Thus the AFL was not reluctant to press for government action on the immigration and injunction questions, it demanded legal status for unions, and it supported woman's suffrage, child labor regulation, and factory inspection. But the AFL would not embrace a bourgeois or corporate welfarism and would not formulate a broader social democratic collectivism of its own.

State action, however benevolent, was from the perspective of the AFL intrinsically suspect. A generation of judicial hostility toward organizing labor had culminated in 1907 and 1908 in the *Buck's Stove* injunction and subsequent criminal prosecution of the AFL leadership, and in the Court's

[79]Discussed in Weinstein, *Corporate Ideal,* 31ff.

[80]August Belmont, "Department on Compensation for Industrial Accidents and Their Prevention," NCF *Review,* July 1, 1911, pp. 21–22.

[81]E.g., *Muller v. Oregon,* 208 U.S. 412 (1908).

[82]Daniel Nelson, *Unemployment Insurance* (1969), chap. 4.

application of antitrust liability to union activity in its Danbury Hatters decision. That experience convinced the labor establishment that the state—especially a Court-dominated state—would intervene only to labor's disadvantage. Labor's view of the state as an adversary persisted, even as countervailing institutions (Congress and the Presidency) began to assert themselves against the Court, and as labor's friends in the NCF worked to secure certain exemptions for unions from the Sherman Act.[83] Throughout the Progressive decades AFL suspicion of government animated its opposition to policies favorable to workers. Though less coercive than the outright suppression of strikes and unions delivered by Court injunctions, friendly state policies, such as social insurance, were seen as hostile incursions by government into arenas properly controlled by unions. The AFL regarded proposals for workmen's compensation, health and unemployment insurance, pensions, and the minimum wage as designed to forge direct links between worker and state—pitting state against union in competition for workers' loyalty.

Interestingly the AFL quietly acceded to corporate welfare work until World War I while it objected loudly and early to the welfare state suggested by social reformers. The socialization of uncertainty (workmen's compensation, unemployment insurance) and social regulation (wages and hours laws for men)[84] were seen as incursions against a bread-and-butter unionism only beginning to consolidate itself. Furthermore, state intervention to resolve the "labor problem" might make immigration an even more difficult political problem: ties forged to workers by government would be ties forged to new-immigrant industrial workers as well as to trade unionists. If welfare work earned immigrant loyalty to employers, then it was likely that social insurance and the regulation of working conditions would induce immigrant loyalty to the state. But the analogy stopped there. Under democratic conditions, bringing the state directly into the lives of industrial workers could foreseeably elicit an affirmative political investment from them, not the passive loyalty intended by wel-

---

[83]After conferring with President Roosevelt in 1908, the NCF won the president's endorsement of the Hepburn Amendments to the Sherman Act. Although the amendments were chiefly intended to liberalize antitrust policy in favor of large corporations, they included a loose exemption for responsible unions. Under heavy pressure from the NAM and its litigation ally, the American Anti-Boycott Association, however, Congress rejected the proposals. This left standing the tight judicial proscriptions against union activities that the NAM and the Anti-Boycott Association had won in the Danbury Hatters' opinion. *Loewe v. Lawlor*, 208 U.S. 74 (1908).

[84]The AFL supported the minimum wage for women, in part because it was "protective" but mostly because it would reduce the wage-cutting consequences of the entry of women into the labor market.

fare capitalism.[85] Just as union benefits were conceived as incentives for union membership, so social policy might act as an incentive to mobilize workers in politics.

Unions and employers disagreed about social intervention. Many business leaders saw state social policies as interference, with the laws of the market and with the autonomy of business. Elbert Gary, for example, insisted that unemployment was a business problem, to "be met by business statesmanship through the normal channels of business and economic organization."[86] Others saw great virtue in interventions at the level of the individual states, however, and argued against national solutions chiefly on grounds of impractibility.[87] Still others viewed federal action as an essential relief from highly variable action by the individual states and as a necessary antidote to the anti-union practices of employers who could not afford comprehensive welfare schemes. From the AFL's point of view, by contrast, social policies assaulted union autonomy, robbing unions of their functions and substituting statism for unionism. NCF employer instrumentalism thus allowed for some state mediation of industrial relations, where AFL instrumentalism could not brook mediation of any kind. This steady union antistatism was driven home by Samuel Gompers in his editorial response to the *Lochner* decision. While he attacked the Court for faulty jurisprudence, he did not defend the statute regulating the hours of bakers. Rather, he seized the occasion of the Court's ruling to vindicate voluntarism: because bakers were organized, he argued, they were able to conclude their own arrangements for wages and hours through economic action.[88]

The AFL's position on unemployment insurance and workmen's compensation typified its general reaction to labor legislation formulated to benefit workers as a class. Although less rigid on the question of work-

[85]Elbert Gary summarized the salubrious effects of welfare work in 1915: "It is by reason of this attitude that employers to-day are receiving better service and better results from labor than ever before. . . . Each now has greater confidence in the other's integrity of motive, and in consequence many of the old difficulties, which were principally the result of a failure to understand each other's problems, have been eliminated. . . . Unrest would, I believe, disappear if the masses of the people were convinced that everything reasonable was being done by those more fortunate than themselves to promote the common comfort and well-being." Gary, "Unemployment and Business," *Harper's Magazine*, 131 (June 1915), 72.

[86]Ibid., 71.

[87]Andrew Carnegie, for example, admired the Massachusetts savings bank insurance plan but thought proposals for a national pension system unwieldy because of the size of the country. Carnegie, "For Peace between Capital and Labor," NCF *Review*, March 1909, p. 3.

[88]Samuel Gompers, "Bakers Lose at Law, But Win in Fact," *American Federationist*, 12 (1905), 361–64.

men's compensation, the AFL, through Gompers and his successors, opposed social insurance in principle and unemployment insurance in particular until the 1930s. In part AFL opposition to unemployment insurance can be explained by the fact that the craft unions were fairly well insulated from unemployment until 1928–29.[89] But beyond this, the anti-state AFL doctrine of self-help ("self-help is the best help," admonished Gompers),[90] coupled with organizational self-interest, rendered the AFL's opposition dogmatic. Thus Gompers, though without minimizing the menace of joblessness,[91] stood fast in his attack on the reform proposals and the philanthropy of their proponents. At the 1915 AFL convention, for example, Gompers charged that the reformers were "professional representatives of social welfare," who aimed to do "things for workers . . . that will prevent their doing things for themselves."[92] A year later, when the House Committee on Labor considered Socialist Representative Meyer London's social insurance commission bill, Gompers represented labor to the committee by denouncing social insurance and its connections to socialism.[93] Clarifying his position a few months later, Gompers argued that workers would pay a heavy price under the social insurance schemes, because they would be forced to surrender their freedom to charity or to socialism. As he would tell an AFL convention on the eve of his death: "I want to urge devotion to the fundamental of human liberty. . . . No lasting gain has ever come from compulsion. If we seek to force, we but tear apart that which united is invincible."[94] In place of state action, Gompers proposed union responsibility.[95] As he saw it, labor-market policies, once conceded by the state, and trade-union policies, once conceded by employers, would go far toward resolving the

[89]Nelson, 76. Interestingly, when immigration was at issue, the AFL complained of unemployment among its own. In 1908 Gompers told the chief of the Division of Information of the Immigration Bureau (the agency in charge of distributing immigrants away from congested cities and industries) that 25 percent of the nation's cigar makers were unemployed and that there was no need for immigrant distribution into the cigar industry. *Annual Report of the Commissioner General of Immigration* (1909), 232–33. As vice-president of the AFL, John Mitchell told the Immigration Commission that the Division of Information should publicize unemployment statistics rather than wage statistics and indications of job opportunities by reason of strikes.

[90]Samuel Gompers, "Self-Help Is the Best Help," *American Federationist*, 22 (1915), 113–15.

[91]Bernard Mandel, *Samuel Gompers* (1963), 121.

[92]AFL, 35th Convention, *Proceedings* (1915), 144.

[93]U.S. House, Committee to Study Social Insurance and Unemployment, *Hearings*, 64th Cong., 1st Sess. (1918), 175–78, 124–25.

[94]AFL, 44th Convention, *Proceedings* (1924), 5.

[95]Mandel, 490; Samuel Gompers, "Voluntary Social Insurance vs. Compulsory," *American Federationist*, 23 (1916), 464.

problem of unemployment. Chief among these policies were immigration restriction, the call for the shorter workday, and the rejection of wage scales based on productivity. Immigration restriction would relieve congestion in the labor supply. The shorter workday would automatically spread employment, because individual workers would produce less. Severing the connection between productivity and pay would lead to higher wages, especially as workers would need more money to finance their leisure. Moreover, once productivity ceased to determine wages, the grueling pace of labor would be eased and worker output reduced, thereby spreading available work.[96]

In the absence of employer concessions on production, and as an alternative to social insurance, Gompers proposed union relief. He used as his model the unemployment relief fund established by the cigar makers' union in 1889 and still in effect during the social insurance debate. Most unions were unable to shoulder the burden of caring for their own unemployed, but the idea that they rather than the state could provide relief was an important component of Gompers's unemployment scheme. By making unions the cornerstone of self-help, the plan invigorated AFL voluntarism. Further, by claiming union responsibility, the AFL answered demonstrations of business responsibility through corporate unemployment funds and the equalization of employment throughout the year.[97] By tying relief to union membership, union responsibility validated the need for unions, offered incentive to workers to join, and gave unions the key to resolving the unemployment problem. Finally, by substituting autonomous unions for wily employers—most of whom needed government incentives to meet their responsibilities—as the insurer of uncertainty in the labor market, the plan circumvented the state.

[96]See Jean T. McKelvey, *AFL Attitudes toward Production, 1900–1932*, Cornell Studies in Industrial and Labor Relations, 2 (1952), chap. 1; Nelson, 66.

[97]Louis Brandeis, as a lawyer and member of the Massachusetts NCF, developed seminal proposals for business responsibility early in the century. Working with employers in a Boston shoe company and in the New York garment industry, Brandeis formulated plans for year-round employment. Elbert Gary later endorsed this idea, arguing the need to alleviate seasonal idleness. In 1911 Brandeis, who continued to view employers, rather than unions, as the key to the unemployment problem, proposed the establishment of company unemployment funds, which "would . . . have not only the advantage of providing an incentive to make the employment regular, but . . . would also provide something like a benefit or insurance fund for current payments during the idle period." Quoted in Nelson, 29. See also Alpheus T. Mason, *Brandeis— A Free Man's Life* (1946), 143–46. For Brandeis, as for Gary, A. Lincoln Filene, and others, the issue was not unemployment compensation but unemployment prevention. To their minds, unemployment prevention gave employers the central role in resolving the unemployment problem, primarily through business efficiency and stabilized labor demands. Unemployment insurance, in this view, was to provide incentive to employers to keep people steadily employed.

The workmen's compensation issue was rather more complicated for union labor. Accidents were more frequent in American factories and mines than in European industry.[98] Yet guarantees for compensation to the American worker, in contrast to workers in Europe, were virtually nonexistent. Still, the AFL resisted compulsory public compensation for disabled or injured workers—again chiefly because it would weaken the claim that voluntary, politically neutral, workers' organizations were the best way to advance the interests of labor. The harshness of this position (for unions could not afford compensation plans of their own) was mitigated by the fact that injured workers could turn to tort litigation. Indeed, AFL leaders long maintained that compensation secured through courts, where jury sympathy for injured or disabled workers leavened judicial hostility toward unions, would produce cash awards more generous than those from insurance schedules standardized by law. The AFL's preferred remedy on this issue—and one that brought it into political conflict with capital—was to strengthen the claims of individual workers before juries through employer liability laws that cut through the traditional common-law defenses of employers.[99]

In contrast, much of the NCF business community endorsed the concept of accident insurance. In addition, 95 percent of the NAM's 25,000 constituent employers were supporting automatic compensation for industrial accidents by 1910. Although some of the larger trusts (e.g., International Harvester and U.S. Steel, both managed by Morgan's partner, George Perkins) instituted voluntary compensation programs that they integrated into their welfare work, many businesses could not afford on their own to guarantee relief benefits to their disabled workers.[100] But leaving compensation to juries, especially when employer common-law defenses were coming under assault, was not an adequate alternative to employer-financed compensation plans. Litigation was expensive and engendered "ill-feeling between workmen and employers,"[101] while jury

[98]See Werner Sombart, *Why Is There No Socialism in the United States?* (1976), 5; James Weinstein, "Big Business and the Origins of Workmen's Compensation," *Labor History*, 8 (Spring 1967), 157. Accident rates on American railroads were thrice those in Austria, for example. Looking at fatalities, the Anthracite Coal Strike Commission concluded that "accident death rates in the United States do not make a favorable showing for this country" (*Report*, 28). Fatality rates in Pennsylvania coal mines were twice those in Britain, France, and Austria in 1900; fatality rates on American railroads were more than twice those in Britain in 1901.

[99]Weinstein, *Corporate Ideal*, 41ff., and "Big Business," 157–58; Robert Asher, "Failure and Fulfillment: Agitation for Employers' Liability Legislation and the Origins of Workmen's Compensation," *Labor History*, 24 (1983), 198–222.

[100]Weinstein, "Big Business," 161–62.

[101]Belmont, "Department on Compensation."

remedies were unpredictable, expensive when favorable to workers, and highly variable among the states, depending on the status of common-law defenses and liability reform statutes.

Workmen's compensation laws by contrast, would convert compensatory relief into a calculable cost. Under the NCF scheme, employers would bear the burden of compensation but would be exempted from liability for damages. Further, if compensation were defined by law, the cost of relief could be integrated into the welfare work of corporations of all sizes. Instead of fighting workers in court, to escape prohibitive jury settlements and to forestall legal precedents that might establish employer liability, employers could use a compensation statute to demonstrate the self-reforming "benevolence" of capital toward labor and the quality of "business statesmanship." Legislated workmen's compensation would not deflect the thrust of corporate welfare work; indeed, by standardizing employer responsibility, it would strengthen it.

Several factors induced an AFL change of heart around 1909 so that, thereafter, the federation supported some form of accident insurance—though stricter employer liability laws remained its preferred remedy. First, industrial accidents were serious problems in certain industries, especially in mining. "Tomorrow not less than twenty men must die," John Mitchell said, while "the slow death that comes from working in a vitiated atmosphere . . . swells beyond computation the outnumbered victims of a restless progress."[102] Second, workers injured or disabled at work were victims of the workplace, and though unions could work to secure better working conditions, they could not prevent accidents or extract compensation from reluctant employers. Further, the admonition of self-help was inappropriate in this case, and the prospect of union relief implausible. Third, the AFL was faced with a fait accompli in many of the large corporations: voluntary compensation had become part of welfare work. Fourth, AFL agitation for employer liability laws had been unproductive. Fifth, with so much of the business community supporting automatic and therefore calculable compensation, the real focus of debate had shifted. At issue now were how extensive accident insurance should be and whether such insurance should be arranged and administered by the government or by employers and their insurance companies.[103] Radicalized workers, socialists, and some liberal reformers tended to favor compensation through government; businessmen, on the other hand, pre-

[102]John Mitchell, "Prevention of Industrial Accidents," NCF *Review,* March 1, 1910, p. 25.
[103]Weinstein, "Big Business," 166ff.

ferred a policy that would at once minimize state intervention in the particulars of compensation and enhance "business statesmanship." Accordingly, NCF employers argued for a system of compulsory private insurance: compensation mandated by government but delivered by employers.

The AFL, finding any form of political compulsion a threat to trade-union autonomy, at first fought the proposal: like unemployment insurance, workmen's compensation would pit the state and capital against trade unions in the contest for workers' loyalty. But when compulsory private insurance schemes were limited to hazardous industries—where the AFL presence was minimal—AFL leaders were persuaded to go along.[104]

Clearly, welfare policies tested the union-employer entente within the NCF, chiefly because the AFL's view of the state as well as its corollary concern to protect bread-and-butter unionism collided with the political confidence of employers and business interest in minimizing the need for unions. In some respects the divergence of opinion on political questions between the labor establishment and NCF employers imperiled the "harmony of interests" fashioned in labor-management relations. Indeed, these questions, ripened by reform elites, exposed the incompatibility of business autonomy and union autonomy.

For NCF employers, business autonomy required worker demobilization. In part, demobilization could be achieved by promoting the AFL as the voice of labor; and in part, it could be furthered by demonstrating, with modest incentives from government, the commitment of employers to the welfare of their workers. Considerations of worker welfare did not turn NCF employers into the statist opponents of antistatist unions, however. But such considerations did encourage employers to trade business autonomy at the margins and union autonomy at the core for social policies that enhanced their efficiency and control in the workplace. Where NCF employers were willing to concede a central role for the state—not as vehicle or benefactor but as rationalizer and receiver—the AFL was willing to concede only a minimalist one.

For the AFL, union autonomy required freedom from the state as well as demobilization of those workers who would change the structure, function, and political purpose of unionism as the AFL knew it. Freedom from the state required steady opposition to political incursions into industry. Freedom from state and class could best be achieved by securing the

[104]Ibid.

economic and political position of the labor establishment, by restricting entry to that establishment, and by demonstrating that direct trade-union action could win for deserving workers what liberal reformers and radical agitators believed should be supported by the state.

Labor and NCF employers differed fundamentally over the purpose and desirability of state action. What the AFL feared most in social insurance was that reform plans would subvert trade unionism. However, two factors deflected the collision threatened by the contest of interests over social welfare. First, liberal reformers, several of whom were representatives of "the public" in the National Civic Federation, agreed with at least one item on organized labor's political agenda: legislation protective of special categories of workers. The AFL saw "protective" state intervention in the form of maximum hours and minimum wage legislation for women as a means of restricting unwelcome competition in the labor market and keeping women out of "men's" jobs.[105] To be sure, sometimes these laws were equally beneficial to men, for they fortified union demands for shorter working hours. But as Florence Kelley explained, typically "men who saw their own occupations threatened by unwelcome competitors, demanded restrictions upon the hours of work of those competitors for the purpose of rendering women less desirable as employees."[106]

Protective labor legislation put many social reformers on common ground with the AFL. Though these reformers—Kelley and the National Consumers' League that she headed, for example—favored legislation to protect all workers, they were forced by judicial intransigence to focus on women. The "women first" strategy, articulated in the politics surrounding *Muller v. Oregon* (1908) met the needs of trade unionism quite effectively. Common cause between labor and reformers on this issue helped obscure union recalcitrance on gender-neutral reform.

A second factor that muffled disagreement on social welfare issues was AFL voluntarism itself. As private-sector alliances with organized capital and liberal reformers matured, and as ties were forged to the state under Democratic auspices after 1912, the AFL became more fixed in its voluntarism. Though it turned to the Democratic state to demand labor policies, it did so in the spirit of direct trade-union action and of worker self-help. It

[105]Women in the printing trades in New York, for example, lost their jobs when a 1913 statute prescribing a 54-hour work week and forbidding nightwork for women was interpreted to cover newspaper offices.

[106]Florence Kelley, "Some Ethical Gains through Legislation," quoted in Ann Hill, "Protective Labor Legislation for Women: Its Origin and Effect," in Barbara Babcock et al., *Sex Discrimination and the Law* (1975), 35–36.

pressed for legal status for unions, injunction relief, and immigration restriction—all policies that would remove impediments to trade unionism.

What was important about AFL voluntarism was that it limited the scope of trade-union political action. For employers wedded to the idea of business solutions to social problems union voluntarism served the ends of business autonomy. And for reform elites, who deeply feared class politics, better that the only politically coherent segment of the working class argue a limited view of the state than that it mobilize, as in Britain or Germany, to vie for control over a more expansive state. Not only did AFL voluntarism demonstrate trade-union conservatism, defend business against unruly political interventions, and entrench normal politics, but it also reinforced the organizational segmentation and political quiescence of the working class. In so doing the AFL helped reinforce the political anomalies of the system of 1896. Demobilization of industrial workers in politics—the result of the system of 1896 itself, as well as of reform efforts to displace party and tighten electoral access—was reproduced in industry with the aid of the AFL's conservative leadership and organizational strategy. With neither political nor economic organizations available for mobilizing industrial workers and in the absence of universalistic appeals, mass democracy would not be ionized.

If the issue of political intervention strained cooperation between business and labor, the question of immigration openly challenged it. Union expansion in the first years of the twentieth century, followed by unmediated strikes such as the one at McKees Rocks, indicated the limit of NCF labor policies both for employers and for AFL leaders. But business and union responses to demographic and organizational volatility could not be reconciled. Beginning in 1904, business pressed for more open immigration policies, including federal assistance in the distribution of immigrants and repeal of the prohibition on contract labor.[107] By 1907, when the NAM abandoned its earlier support for immigration restriction, a class consensus was congealing in favor of increased immigration. On the upswing after 1900, immigration in fact increased at around this time to create labor-market conditions generally favorable to capital.[108]

---

[107]Wiebe, *Businessmen and Reform,* 182–86.

[108]Unemployment increased to an average 12.5 percent in the nonfarm labor force between 1908 and 1915, from an average 8.8 percent between 1900 and 1907; Ramirez, 133. W. Jett Lauck, who later worked with John L. Lewis, complained in 1912 of the connections between liberal immigration policy, the characteristics of the new immigrants, and corporate profits: "a study of the cost records of the United States Steel Corporation . . . found that the entire cost per

As capital defended policies favorable to immigration, the AFL began to harden its resolve toward immigration restriction. This signaled irreparable divisions between business and unions on the issue. In 1903 the labor press began to comment regularly on the significance of immigration, and in 1905 the AFL stepped up its campaign for the literacy test.[109] By 1910 Samuel Gompers was concluding:

> American labor has to bear the burden of competition with an immigration that in the last decade has brought to the population a net increase of at least five million laborers, the great majority ignorant of the English language and nearly all so poor on arrival that a month's idleness would have brought them face to face with starvation. To this class has been mostly due the undermining of American labor in certain industries . . . and much of the increase in whatever is permanent in the American Socialist vote.[110]

On the matter of immigration, AFL strategies to strengthen its position in industry ran headlong into employer strategies to build an open-shop society. Inside the NCF an immigration department was established in 1906 to investigate the issue, but only to abandon the effort in 1907 when the U.S. Immigration Commission began work. Within their particular industries NCF employers were unwilling to compromise with unions on the issue. Though friendly to AFL leaders in other contexts,[111] Andrew Carnegie, for example, was adamant in his defense of immigration: "taking the cost, the value of a man, a woman or child . . . as low as you put the slave, and that was an average of $1000, you are getting 400,000 a year and that means $400,000,000 cash value. . . . And every man who comes here is a consumer and ninety per cent of all his earnings go to employ other labor of some kind."[112]

More to the point, immigration was a major element in the "labor program" of many large corporations that participated in the NCF. Newly

---

ton of producing Minnesota and Michigan iron ore and delivering it to the lower lake ports was $2.88. Of this amount only 35 cents per ton, or 12 percent of the aggregate outlay, was for labor at the mines. The expense of producing a ton of coke in the Connellsville, Pennsylvania, region was ascertained to be $3.69, out of which only 25 cents was expended for productive labor." Lauck, "A Real Myth," *Atlantic Monthly*, September 1912, pp. 391–92.

[109]A. T. Lane, "American Trade Unions, Mass Immigration, and the Literacy Test: 1900–1917," *Labor History*, 25 (Winter 1984), 5–25.

[110]Samuel Gompers, "Mr. Hunter's Dilemma Proven," *American Federationist*, 17 (1910), 486.

[111]Carnegie helped pay for Gompers's defense in *Bucks Stove and Range*, for example.

[112]"The National Conference on Immigration," NCF *Review*, January–February 1906, pp. 1, 2, 5.

arrived immigrants were cheap and docile;[113] settled new immigrants could be kept docile either through welfare incentives or through living arrangements and residential patterns that emphasized communal identities and corresponded to ethnic and job segregation at work. Quite apart from the strategies of capital, for many new immigrants (perhaps as much as one-third of all who came) anything other than docility in the work place would have been counterintuitive. The expectation or hope of return to the homeland to some degree fostered instrumentalism: fostered work without protest, and in some cases over the protest of others.[114] Those who migrated permanently felt an incentive to fit in, to find a place in the American dream, and to pursue and enjoy improved material standards. In both cases, though there were important exceptions, the dynamics of labor migration did not translate into an early assessment of employers as adversaries or of capital as concentrated economic power against which collective worker power should be mobilized.

Hence many industries—most notoriously anthracite coal and steel—preferred new immigrant workers and supported unrestricted immigration. An ad in a Pittsburgh paper during a 1910 tin mill strike expressed this preference: "Wanted: 60 tin house men, tinners, catchers, and helpers to work in open shops; Syrians, Poles and Rumanians preferred."[115] Many of the larger industries maintained rigid segregation between nationality groups as well. John Commons recounted, after a visit to a Chicago employment office in 1904,

> I saw, seated on benches around the office, a sturdy group of blond-haired Nordics. I asked the employment agent, "How comes it you are employing

[113]The magnitude of the wage gap between San Francisco Chinese and Italians in Italy suggests the magnitude of the wage gap between new immigrants and old labor: (in lira) San Francisco Chinese shoe cobblers, 7.25, Italy Italian shoe cobblers, 2.50; San Francisco Chinese cigar makers, 5.75, Italy Italian cigar makers, 3.00; San Francisco Chinese leather workers, 6.25, Italy Italian leather workers, 2.75. See Francisco Cordasco and Eugene Bucchioni, *The Italians* (1974), 133. Of new immigrant docility, W. Jett Lauck wrote: "The southern and eastern European also, because of his intractability, necessitous condition, and low standards, has been inclined, as a rule, to acquiesce in the demand on the part of the employers for extra work or longer hours. . . . Where older employees have found unsafe or unsanitary working conditions prevailing, and have protested, the recent immigrant wage-earners, usually through ignorance of mining or other working methods, have manifested a willingness to accept the alleged unsatisfactory working conditions." Lauck, "The Vanishing American Wage-Earner," *Atlantic Monthly,* November 1912, p. 694.

[114]For a discussion of return migration see Gerald Rosenblum, *Immigrant Workers* (1973).

[115]Quoted in Gulick, 129. See also David Brody's discussion of immigration as an important source of labor "stability" and of the steel industry's encouragement of the migration of blacks and Mexicans after the immigration restriction act of the 1920s dried up the "free-flow supply of unskilled labor." Brody, 265–67.

only Swedes?'' He answered, ''Well, you see, it is only for this week. Last week we employed Slovaks. We change it about among different nationalities and languages. It prevents them from getting together. We have the thing systematized.''[116]

For union friends and union leaders, the continued free flow of labor into the country was unacceptable. Not only did the new immigration interact with new machines to displace old labor in many industries (a conclusion reached by the Immigration Commission, to Gompers's pleasure), but it destroyed the bargaining power of unions. The decline in union membership after 1904 confirmed this view and stoked the AFL's resolve to secure immigration restriction. As W. Jett Lauck put it,

> The labor unions of the original employees, which should have been among the greatest factors in assimilating industrially the recent immigrant, and in educating him to American standards, in some industries . . . have been completely inundated, and wholly or partially destroyed by the sudden and overwhelming influx of southern and eastern Europeans.[117]

> The bargaining strength of the employer, on the other hand, has been improved, and ''protection of the American wage-earner'' [through tariffs] in the face of an unrestricted alien labor supply of a low grade has had the effect of adding to the profits of the manufacturer, mine-operator, and wholesale merchant. . . .[118]

The only solution to the disruption in union organization and the erosion of union bargaining power was a change in immigration policy.

The clear impasse between the AFL and NCF employers with respect to labor-market policy deepened the AFL's political commitments. In 1906 the AFL began to hone its organization to demonstrate the power of the labor vote. Demanding restrictions on the use of injunctions and on immigration, the AFL moved deep into the Democratic coalition, thereby transferring its collision with business over immigration into electoral politics and the state.

---

[116]Don Lescohier and Elizabeth Brandeis, *History of the Labor Movement in the United States, 1896–1932*, ed. John Commons (1935), xxv.
[117]Lauck, ''Vanishing American Wage Earner,'' 695.
[118]Lauck, ''A Real Myth,'' 393.

Challenges to AFL Autonomy: Pressures from Below

NCF employers were unwilling to relinquish their defense of open immigration, but they eventually conceded several points of the AFL's critique. In the National Industrial Survey, convened by the NCF to promote the precepts of capitalism (individual liberty, private property, the inviolability of contract), an impressive group of business, union, and reform elites named immigration as a central problem of industrialism and identified it as a principal source of disorder in industry and society.[119] The survey charged that the new immigration, interacting with the trusts, had produced profound shifts in the distribution of wealth and thus had created conditions for class politics. Joining the sentiments of labor leaders and reformers on the middle ground of concern for the *political* consequences of immigration, the survey further accused the new immigration of "swelling the ranks of those prompt to put the worst construction on the motives of the more fortunate."[120]

The survey thus clearly identified immigration as a political problem. But it also created an identity between the "immigration problem" and the "labor problem," particularly among reformers who would enlist in the campaign to restrict immigration. What is more, this identity linked policy on both matters, since open immigration produced workers whose activities the AFL could neither mediate nor discipline. Between the recommendations of the U.S. Immigration Commission in 1911 and the conclusions of the National Industrial Survey in 1913, the AFL received real boosts to its nativist argument.

Class pressures from beneath the AFL help account for the survey's diagnosis of the immigration problem. Dramatic, unmediated strikes among industrial workers, syndicalist insurgency, and socialist tenacity at the polls seemed to imperil industrial and political stability. Though none of these developments managed to place class at the center of industrial or electoral politics, the fear that class divisions would "dissolve society" was a central one.

NCF practitioners had tried to safeguard against classwide mobilization by elaborating within industry political structures that emphasized social

---

[119]Green, 182–83; Weinstein, *Corporate Ideal*, 128. Participants included Gompers, George Perkins (U.S. Steel), Jeremiah Jenks (Cornell University), Edwin Seligman (Columbia University), and Charles Miller (*New York Times*). The four hundred sponsors signed on by 1914 included Jane Addams, Alton B. Parker, Roscoe Pound, Elihu Root, Frank P. Walsh, Booker T. Washington, Walter Weyl, and William Allen White.

[120]Quoted from the National Industrial Survey, press release, October 13, 1913, in Weinstein, *Corporate Ideal*, 125.

partnership between employers and unions. Promoting the mutual interaction and accommodation of elites on both sides of industry, the NCF framework provided a hopeful alternative to conflict between unions and repressively anti-union employers. This framework allowed for conflict to be contained within channels of representation and mediation. But it presupposed the organization of both capital and labor into "peak associations" that enjoyed real authority and jurisdiction over their memberships. On the employer side, clear tactical differences between the NCF and the NAM were partially obscured by the fact that major industrial sectors subscribed to the NCF. Within the NCF, employer truculence (for example, the anthracite-coal-carrying railroads' refusal to negotiate with the union) was partially remedied by a state that could be called upon to intervene. NCF member employers were hardly compliant, but they endorsed the social partnership in theory—and, when it went their way, in practice.

The labor side of the NCF framework was more compliant, but it was also the weak link in the social partnership. For the partnership to work, labor representation had to be based, at least in principle, on class. That is, ties between union elites and the working class had to be real enough to empower unions with jurisdiction over the struggles of workers. Unions had to be strong, and unionization, if not yet extensive, had to be potentially inclusive.[121] In the case of the AFL and its leaders, however, ties to the class were missing, and—with only 6 percent of the labor force enrolled in unions in 1905—the AFL represented only a narrow constituency. While the AFL worked to contain mobilization outside its constituency, it could not mediate when mobilization occurred. Struggles that should have been decided within organizations on each side of industry thus took place between them. Only where AFL unions were the central parties to industrial conflict could the NCF framework plausibly work. Militancy that erupted beneath the AFL could not be channeled toward compromise.[122]

[121]Thus Herbert Croly chastized the nonunion worker: "As a type the non-union laborer is a species of industrial derelict. . . . He is the laborer who . . . either from apathy, unintelligence, incompetence, or some immediately pressing need prefers his own individual interest to the joint interests of himself and his fellow laborers. . . . In fact . . . the non-union industrial laborer should, in the interest of a genuinely democratic organization of labor, be rejected; and he should be rejected as emphatically, if not as ruthlessly, as the gardener rejects the weeds in his garden for the benefit of the fruit- and flower-bearing plants." Croly, *Promise of American Life,* 387.

[122]Much of this discussion takes analytic cues from the literature on corporatism. See especially Leo Panitch, "Trade Unions and the Capitalist State," *New Left Review,* 125 (1981), 21–43; Lehmbruch, "Consociational Democracy," and B. Jessop, "Corporatism, Parliamentarism and Social Democracy," both in Schmitter and Lembruch, *Trends toward Corporatist Intermediation;* and Peter J. Katzenstein, *Corporatism and Change* (1984), Introduction and chap. 4.

The NCF framework both enhanced the power of the AFL and exaggerated it. It enhanced the AFL's power by helping install the AFL as the legitimate voice of labor. This elevated the AFL's political status, both among cooperating employers and among political elites, and thereby smoothed the AFL's integration into a politics premised on group representation, competition, and mediation. But it exaggerated the AFL's actual command over the labor side of industrial conflict. The social partnership crafted within the NCF was thus doomed to failure. As this failure became apparent, NCF employers turned to strategies for workplace demobilization which not only circumvented unions but were designed to undermine them.

The elusive rewards of business-union reciprocity in the NCF, particularly in averting political and industrial militancy, underscored the organizational vulnerability of the AFL. One response of union leaders to this vulnerability was to press for immigration controls.[123] But within the union movement itself, their response was rather more complicated. The doctrinal rigidity of AFL organizational principles and prejudices interacted uneasily with a strong streak of pragmatism. Thus while many AFL affiliates continued to exclude new-immigrant industrial workers from membership, others were forced to attempt broader organization in order to survive. The UMW did so in anthracite coal between 1900 and 1902, claiming jurisdiction over all jobs in the mines, naming ethnic leaders to district committees and carrying Slavic-language sections in its *Journal* (though often in issues that also contained nativist commentaries).[124] Other unions responded to changes in the organizational and occupational position of their crafts by expanding jurisdictions. And the AFL itself relaxed its strict adherence to craft principles in 1911 when it adopted a policy of "craft-leadership."

Meanwhile the movement of radicals into the "hole" in the labor movement presented the AFL with hard challenges that neither NCF corporatism nor "flexible" union exclusionism could answer. Indeed, both the AFL's participation in the NCF and its exclusionism seemed to heighten pressures from syndicalists and socialists as well as from certain groups of excluded workers. Socialists lambasted AFL leaders for their complicity in a social partnership they viewed as hurtful to the interests of workers. Eugene Debs summed up their criticism:

[123]A. A. Graham, "The Unamericanization of America," *American Federationist,* 17 (1910), 302; Gompers, "Mr. Hunter's Dilemma Proven," 486.

[124]See Robert Asher, "Union Nativism and the Immigrant Response," *Labor History,* 23 (Summer 1982), 344–45.

It is not Gompers, who banquets with Belmont and Carnegie, and Mitchell, who is paid and pampered by the plutocrats, who are going to unite the workers in their struggle for emancipation. The Civic Federation, which was organized by the master class . . . in connivance with labor leaders, who are used as decoys to give that body the outward appearance of representing both capital and labor, is the staunch supporter of trade unions and the implacable foe of industrial unionism and socialism . . . and this in itself should be sufficient to convince every intelligent worker that the trade union under its present leadership is more beneficial to the capitalist class than it is to the workers, seeing that it is the means of keeping them disunited and pitted against each other.[125]

From within the AFL socialist unionists assailed the AFL leadership and worked to check its authority. At every AFL convention after 1901, socialist unionists introduced resolutions of no confidence in the NCF. At the 1911 convention they pressed three resolutions, two condemning the premises and purposes of NCF labor policy and one demanding that union leaders sever their ties to the NCF. Though the resolutions were defeated, the challenges they represented were serious ones. Most serious of all was the ultimatum presented to John Mitchell by socialists within the UMW, forcing him to choose beween the UMW and the NCF. Reluctantly he relinquished his chairmanship of the federation's Trade Agreements Department.

These pressures were reinforced where workers organized. The Industrial Workers of the World moved into the organizational vacuum left by the AFL in Lawrence, Massachusetts, and Paterson, New Jersey, for example. In New York City between 1907 and 1918 socialist, ethnic, and industrial unions developed as concrete alternatives to the largely craft, largely male, largely old-labor union establishment.[126]

The initial union response to the mobilization of new immigrants and industrial workers in New York was to fight it. Many new immigrants formed dual unions, most notably the United Hebrew Trades. The AFL countered with institutional sanctions, first advising its affiliates to enjoin their locals from affiliating with the UHT and then, in 1907, censuring the UHT for interfering with the progress of the AFL *by associating along*

---

[125]Eugene Debs, "Working Class Politics," *International Socialist Review,* 11 (November 1910).

[126]Unions excluding new immigrants, at least until 1910, included shoe workers, painters and decorators, plasterers, marble workers, hotel and restaurant workers, cigar makers, and the United Textile Workers. See Asher, "Union Nativism," 339–40 n. 30.

race lines.[127] Several years later, new-immigrant unions organized along occupational rather than ethnic lines were either denied admission or expelled from the AFL: the Amalgamated Clothing Workers of America and the Cloth Hat and Cap Makers were among the victims of this policy. But AFL boycotts of new-immigrant workers and their organizations did not resolve the problems that mobilization at the base was posing for the AFL. Admittedly, unrepresented workers tended to mobilize only under exceptional circumstances: where socialist organizers were strong, workers politicized, and ethnic and gender identities tightly interwoven with workplace identities and experience. Even so, what mobilization did occur among excluded workers chipped away at the AFL's claim of jurisdiction over the class.

This pressure from dual unions and ethnic labor movements led the AFL to temper its categorical opposition to new-immigrant unionism in New York City in 1912. The scandalous fire at the Triangle Shirtwaist Factory in 1911, which spurred organization among women in the needle trades, proved to be a turning point. The mobilization of women needle workers coincided with expansions in the UHT and the Italian Socialist Federation; meanwhile socialists were also working within established unions. The links between ethnic, gender-based, and left unionism in New York City threatened the AFL with a triangle of opposition in the hub of trade unionism.

The organization of workers, particularly garmentworkers, outside the AFL exposed the limit of the AFL's logic. In particular, it suggested that by excluding "undesirable" workers, the AFL was forcing an opening to the left. With radical elites and workers themselves ready to move into this opening, the AFL needed to rethink its exclusionary premises and perhaps even to forge ties to mobilized new immigrants. This it did, becoming an advocate of such reforms as protective labor legislation and factory inspection and absorbing, where necessary for organizational hegemony, new-immigrant workers into the AFL along "flexible" craft lines.

Indeed, after 1912 the AFL even began to assist some of the more stable, more homogeneous unions of new workers in the needle trades, as long as they accepted voluntarist principles and hewed the now flexible craft line. By 1914 Samuel Gompers had recognized the United Hebrew Trades as "theoretically bad but practically necessary," the painters and

---

[127]Dubofsky, "Organized Labor and the Immigrant," 188. My emphases.

decorators had begun to admit Jews, and the cigar makers had begun to take in new immigrants.

Clearly the AFL was coming to see that new-immigrant workers who were politically engaged and economically mobilized created special problems that required special solutions. Strategies and attitudes directed toward demobilized workers were inappropriate for those whose mobilization was sustained and coherent. Accordingly the AFL bent its organizational nativism to accommodate pockets of pressure from below.

The AFL coupled its relaxation of "internal protectionism" with heightened political appeals for labor-market protection and with sharpened political strategies for defending its embattled position. In this way the AFL diluted challenges to its dominance within the labor movement, where such challenges were likely to materialize, while strengthening its electoral resolve to secure political remedies for its organizational vulnerability. The failure of exclusionist unionism to govern the labor side of industry effectively forced it to begrudgingly accept ties to elements within the class beneath. But the success of exclusionist unionism in controlling labor politics allowed it to forge ties to the state in pursuit of its cause.

CHAPTER 6

The Decision of 1912

The AFL and the Democratic
Party in the Progressive Era

What happens in politics depends on the way in which people are
divided into factions, parties, groups, classes, etc.
—E. E. Schattschneider, 1960

The AFL forged an "opening to the middle" during the Progressive
Era through which it charted a political course between class and state. Its
course followed from its relationship with the Democratic party under the
system of 1896 and culminated in the accommodation struck between
union labor and the central government under Woodrow Wilson. This
smooth, early mobilization of trade unionism within the existing apparatus
of regime and party visited important consequences upon workers, politics, and the state. The AFL's movement into established political arrangements consolidated its power, legitimated its strategies, and gave to
conservative trade unionism preemptive control of labor's political space.
The organizational interests of a minority within the working class thus
became a central force in politics. As we shall see, the AFL's political
strategies and activities were important determinants of the patterns of
state intervention and interest representation that developed during the
Democratic decade. They were particularly important for the interposition
of national policy-making institutions as broker among interests in combat
in the courts and in the economy, and for the policy silence of national
government with respect to worker-oriented social welfare reform.

Its autonomy endangered from above and below, the AFL moved into
formal coalition with the Democratic party in 1912. This was not a sudden
decision. The AFL's association with the Democrats stretched back to

1896, when the party had adopted anti-injunction and anti-immigration planks in its platform. Industrial workers may have repudiated Bryan's party of the "toiling masses," but union labor worked to promote it. The electoral reorganization that congealed in that year's election strengthened the AFL-party tie. The Republican party became the home for an incoherent electorate of new-immigrant industrial workers in national politics, giving to union labor a relatively free run of the Democratic party outside urban machine politics.[1] Still, the union-party tie remained informal until William Howard Taft ascended to the White House and Joseph Cannon took control of the House of Representatives. Antilabor judicial innovations completed the triangle of governmental hostility to trade unionism.

AFL experimentation in industrial relations and in electoral strategy set the stage for the federation's emergence as the labor side of the Democratic party in 1912. Underlying this "class compromise" and electoral cooperation, of course, had been the exclusionist logic of the trade-union mainstream. AFL participation in the National Civic Federation hardened union labor's organizational isolation from the class, while its electoral strategy widened its political separation from the class.

Significantly, the AFL's experience in the National Civic Federation had centralized trade unionism and thereby enhanced its capacity to make centralized political choices in electoral politics. Moreover, that experience had distinguished the AFL from more stubborn labor militants and thereby enhanced its political stature. Through the NCF, the AFL helped formalize distinctions between class and group. It also worked to convert conflict into mediation and bargaining. In the end this course rendered trade unionism "legitimate," at least in the eyes of important political and reform elites—men like John Commons, Louis Brandeis, and Herbert Croly.

Business-labor cooperation through the National Civic Federation

[1] It should be emphasized that we are talking about national partisanship. Industrial, new immigrant workers generally returned Republicans to office at the state and national level after 1896. They were central to Republican dominance until 1928–32. Those who did not vote Republican were usually nonvoters at the national level rather than Democrats. However, in part because of separated election cycles, in part because of the nature of patronage politics, and in part because of the introduction of hurdles to voting, many Democratic cities stayed Democratic even though large percentages of their populations were foreign-born. W. D. Burnham notes that drop-off, roll-off, split-ticket voting, and partisan swing were quite high in New York City after 1896, at least by nineteenth-century standards. Thus while the Republicans dominated national politics, electoral erosion clearly set in under the system of 1896. See Burnham, "Changing Shape of the American Political Universe," in his Current Crisis in American Politics (1982), 41.

served both sides well. It put the best-organized, most narrowly political segment of the labor movement in the mainstream of the economy at a time when industrial unrest was threatening to unleash political conflict along class lines. It thus helped professionalize labor relations and contract a framework for labor peace. In these respects, cooperation secured the economic and political interest of large employers while serving the institutional needs of the emerging labor establishment. For NCF employers, cooperation with the AFL was essential to keep the working class demobilized. However symbolic, the elevation of trade unionism into partnership with capital sharpened the division between organized labor and working-class majorities, both in the workplace and in politics. Business-labor cooperation in the NCF, whether it put the AFL to work against mass unionism or simply provided the occasion for corporate innovators to devise alternatives to that unionism (e.g., "welfare work"), fostered business unionism and thereby promoted industrial stability.

The AFL, clearly, was well-served by this experiment in liberal corporatism. Premised on cooperation among elites in dominant interest associations, business-union partnership validated the AFL as the representative of labor interests. Partnership also gave the AFL important weapons with which to enforce disorganization among the labor-based majorities to which it had relinquished access, both electorally and at work, in the 1890s. Equally important, partnership with capital shielded the AFL from state interventions in the affairs of labor. It did so by placing labor relations squarely in the private arena and by regularizing those relations through conciliation processes and trade agreements. Although influential NCF enthusiasts, among them Theodore Roosevelt, would see a role for the state in this arrangement, the experiment in self-regulation of the private sector provided the AFL with a practical defense of its voluntarist critique of positive government. From the union labor point of view, liberal corporatism, American-style, was effected to preempt coercive interventions by the state. Finally, and as a result of this experiment, the self-designated "voice of labor" could present itself as the voice of reason in the cacophony of industrial conflict.

The AFL thus enjoyed certain institutional rewards from its participation in the NCF. These rewards were, however, largely negative in their impact on the struggle for trade-union autonomy. To be sure, rival unionism was blunted. But more positive boosts to trade unionism (union recognition, the union shop, collective bargaining) were not forthcoming. NCF employers themselves were at best ambivalent about, and more typically were hostile to, unionization in their own companies. In addition, employers from the National Association of Manufacturers were intransigent on this score and had the full weight of the courts behind them.

In politics the rewards for ''legitimate'' trade unionism were less ambiguous. Separated from radical and intractable elements within the labor movement by its participation in the NCF, the AFL achieved the political legitimacy necessary to express its electoral energies in political outcomes. Moreover, because the labor policies developed by the NCF promoted quiescence and incoherence among electorates inside the party of capital (new-immigrant industrial workers), no organized labor-based constituency had emerged to rival the AFL in either party. If anything, organizational quiescence among industrial workers combined with their electoral demobilization to increase AFL influence in electoral outcomes.[2] Meanwhile, the third-party alternative to the AFL's hold on politics and trade unionism was itself crippled by internal division, including nativist factionalism. The resulting uneasy relations between the Socialist party and labor's social base limited the party's electoral appeal among demobilized industrial voters.[3] This left the AFL as labor's only electorally significant voice when Democratic progressivism won control of the state under Woodrow Wilson.

The AFL decided to formalize its ties to the Democratic party in response to a series of specific setbacks to the private bargains struck inside the NCF. Immigration increased dramatically between 1900 and 1910, and 78 percent of migrants were from outside ''Teutonic'' Europe. Labor-market and organizational pressures mounted as a result, while ethnic fragmentation within the working class accelerated. Expanded immigration also improved employers' opportunities to use new workers against unions.[4] Employers were aided in their recruitment of new workers by the establishment of a division of information within the Immigration Bureau of the Department of Commerce in 1907. The division, charged with promoting the effective distribution of immigrants, disseminated information about wages and job prospects—including job prospects due to strikes. From the AFL's point of view, this activity put the state on the

---

[2]Burnham traces electoral demobilization to the ascendancy of capitalism over democracy which developed out of the decision of 1896. He links the decline of party linkages to the nature and substance of party competition. For a perspective that stresses the impact of procedures, see Jerrold G. Rusk, ''The Effect of the Australian Ballot Reform on Split Ticket Voting: 1876–1908,'' *American Political Science Review*, 64 (1970), 1220–38.

[3]Ira Kipnis discusses nativism among socialists in *The American Socialist Movement, 1897–1912* (1952), 277–79, 286–87, 423.

[4]Samuel Gompers, *Seventy Years of Life and Labor*, vol. 2 (1925), 155–59.

side of cheap labor and scabs while diverting public attention away from the evils of immigration.[5] More important, a class consensus in favor of immigration developed among employers around this time, rendering remedy by restriction a remote prospect as long as Republicans were in power. Indeed, Speaker Joseph Cannon blocked passage of a literacy test provision in the very bill that created the Immigration Bureau's Information Division.

Of further concern to the AFL was the development of an alternative unionism, through the Industrial Workers of the World. Although organization was not their strong suit, the Wobblies excelled, at least episodically, in new-immigrant industries and thus threatened to mobilize a broader labor constituency. The Wobblies' connections to Socialist party, until 1913, threatened meanwhile to introduce class politics into a depoliticized constituency. The central presence of the IWW in Lawrence in 1912 invigorated industrial unionists, even attracting the cooperation of such conservative, craft-union Socialists as Victor Berger.[6] The Lawrence experience suggested the extension of economic organization to workers structurally and ideologically excluded from the AFL, and it turned, though in the end only briefly, the much-debated interdependence between industrial unionism and socialist politics into a concrete possibility for the labor left. The IWW would prove to be an idiosyncratic alternative in industry, and the Socialist party ambivalent about whether to organize the working class industrially as well as politically. By their activities, nonetheless, they pressured the AFL to move beyond unproductive collisions with employers in the courts and in industry, and into the political arena.

In addition to these challenges to the AFL were the heavy blows delivered by courts and employers. The development of the labor injunction and the antitrust weapon impeded AFL organizing drives and diluted the strike threat. With strikes and boycotts circumscribed by the judiciary, the conciliation arrangement worked out inside the NCF lost its promise of a square deal for labor. J. P. Morgan, for example, could bust unions once the "last resort of labor" was made so vulnerable to the last word from the state. Under pressure from antilabor courts, anti-union NCF employers, and the NAM's open-shop offensive, the AFL had, in fact, lost 220,000 members between 1904 and 1906. By the latter year AFL enroll-

---

[5]Samuel Gompers, "Schemes to Distribute Immigrants," *American Federationist*, 18 (1911), 519–25.
[6]"Victory at Lawrence," *International Socialist Review*, 12 (April 1912), 679.

ment was well under two million. What is more, though the number of strikes remained fairly constant, the number of workers involved had declined sharply—as had the percentage of strike victories. Some 603,000 workers had gone out on strike annually between 1899 and 1904, and 45 percent of those strikes had been won. In 1905 strikes involved only half those workers, while by 1908 only one-third of the number participated in strikes—the lowest figure since 1888. The number of strike victories hit a low of 25 percent in 1907, increasing only slightly to 29 percent in 1908.[7]

Participation in the NCF may have enhanced the AFL's stature, but it certainly had not improved the climate for trade unionism. Hence the AFL, beginning with the congressional elections of 1906, began to devise an electoral complement to its "economic action."[8] Though union labor had been linked to the Democratic party since 1896, the AFL had maintained an official pretense of partisan neutrality. In this first formal electoral venture it offered congressional candidates in both parties the opportunity to win labor's endorsement. The AFL presented the candidates with seven policy demands: two dealt with immigration, the rest with injunction relief, an eight-hour law for federal workers, legal relief from involuntary servitude for seamen, and union exemption from antitrust liability.[9] Republicans were generally cool, if not hostile, to the AFL's agenda; the Democrats were by comparison supportive. The AFL-Democratic party affinity was accordingly maintained, and the AFL worked to defeat unfriendly Republicans and promote friendly Democrats. The electoral outcome was disappointing for Democrats and unionists; but the AFL nonetheless celebrated the defeat of a handful of Republicans, the election of six card-carrying trade unionists to Congress, and the demonstration of labor's intent, in Samuel Gompers's words, to hold "men in public affairs . . . responsible for their actions" and to participate directly "in the proceedings of the Federal Government."[10]

The Republican decision to nominate William Howard Taft in 1908, the

<hr />

[7]Philip Foner, *History of the American Labor Movement*, vol. 3 (1955), 32, 59.

[8]Gompers, *Seventy Years*, 2:242–44.

[9]Ibid., 162; Marc Karson, *American Labor Unions and Politics* (1958), 43. Gompers and John Mitchell conferred personally with President Roosevelt about tightening up the Chinese Exclusion Act.

[10]Gompers reviewed the AFL's political strategy and accomplishments for his membership in 1912, in Samuel Gompers, "Labor's Political Campaign: Its Causes, and Progress—Labor's Duty," *American Federationist*, 19 (1912), 801–14. See also John D. Buenker, *Urban Liberalism and Progressive Reform* (1973), 84. The *American Federationist*, 20 (1913), 594–611, also charts the development and practice of the AFL's political strategy.

platform committee's refusal to invite Gompers to defend the AFL's planks, and the convention's pledge that the "Republican Party will uphold at all times the authority and integrity of the courts"[11] pushed the AFL more deeply into the Democratic fold. By the time of the party nominating conventions in 1908, in fact, the AFL leadership had more or less decided that it would officially position itself inside the Democratic party. So apparent was the relationship between organized labor and the Democratic party that rumors floated around the convention that William Jennings Bryan might take on John Mitchell as his running mate.[12]

Taft's victory in 1908 and Speaker Cannon's continuing reign in Congress, coming at the crest of judicial hostility toward unions, heightened the AFL's political anxieties. The AFL saw in Taft not only a president unsympathetic to unions but one who brought to the office the prejudices of the conservative judiciary. As a promising young federal judge, Taft had written pioneer opinions expressing hostility to union activities and supporting the labor injunction under the Interstate Commerce Act of 1887.[13] For this he was dubbed "father of injunctions" by Samuel Gompers. As president, Taft did not abate his opposition to unionism. Indeed, his opportunity to make five Supreme Court appointments meant that his antilabor bias reverberated across institutions—presidential power both reinforced and extended judicial conservatism.[14] Given the AFL's longstanding urgent concern to secure union rights,[15] Taft's judicial reputation and presidential performance stoked union fears that his unfriendly administration would use existing laws, chiefly the Sherman Act, to dissolve unions.

In Congress, Cannon's elevation to the speakership in 1903 entrenched and expanded an autocracy in the House of Representatives which favored employers and opposed labor. Cannon, indeed, loomed "more powerful than the President," according to Herbert Fuller, on policy matters.[16]

[11]Quoted in Stephen Scheinberg, "Theodore Roosevelt and the AFL's Entry into Politics," *Labor History*, 3 (Spring 1962), 141.

[12]Gompers, *Seventy Years*, 2: 264.

[13]*Toledo, A.A. & N.M. Railway Company v. Penna. Co.*, 54 Fed. 730 (N.D. Ohio, 1893). See also *In Re Phelan*, 62 Fed. 803 (1894). Interestingly, it was Chief Justice Taft who delivered the opinion in *Coronado* (1922) which extended liability to unions as distinct (and suable) entities.

[14]One of Taft's appointees, Mahlon Pitney, later wrote the principal opinion that gutted the Clayton law in 1921.

[15]See, especially, Gompers's testimony in U.S. Senate, Committee on Education and Labor, *Relations between Capital and Labor*, Hearings, 49th Cong., 1st. sess., vol. 1 (1885), 374–79; U.S. House, Committee on the Judiciary, *Hearings on the Antitrust Legislation*, 62d Cong., 1st sess., vol. 2 (1911), 1757; 63d Cong., 2d sess., vol. 1 (1914), 16–28.

[16]Herbert Bruce Fuller, *The Speakers of the House* (1909), 269.

With committee assignments and the distribution of perquisites at his discretion, Cannon punished opponents and rewarded supporters on both sides of the aisle. Moreover, through the power of recognition and through control over the calendar and the Rules Committee, he could directly promote or suppress legislation.[17] As a result, labor issues rarely won a satisfactory hearing in Cannon's House. This fact was driven home when, notwithstanding nativist pressure generated inside his own party by unprecedented immigration, Cannon, through his grip on the rules Committee, single-handedly killed the literacy test proviso to the 1907 immigration bill.[18]

Conservative Republicanism ruled the Senate, as well. Because of the indirect selection of senators, however, the Senate was more or less impervious to direct labor—or other popular—pressures. Conservative control of the Senate was less secure in that it flowed from the personal power of Nelson Aldrich, but it would prove slightly more durable than the institutionally supported conservatism that ruled through Cannon.

By 1910, in part because of the electoral efforts of the AFL, Cannon's rule would prove to be considerably less than absolute. Its tie to the Democratic party still informal, the AFL helped return insurgent Republicans along with Democrats to Congress in 1908. This prepared the ground for the revolt against Speaker Cannon in 1909–10. The AFL pushed forward on the electoral front in 1910 and took credit for the purging of Republican conservatives, the expansion of the Labor Group in the House to fifteen, and the formation of a Democratic congressional majority.[19] Not only did control of the House pass to the Democrats, but "union card Congressman" William B. Wilson became chair of the House Committee on Labor. Champ Clark, heralded as "labor's intrepid friend," succeeded Cannon as speaker.[20]

Congressional intransigence could be remedied through elections, but judicial hostility was a knottier problem. This was a central dilemma for union labor because union-friendly federal and state legislation invited the Court to deal blows to unionism where union activity did not. In a decision characteristic of laissez-faire jurisprudence, the Court excised the special protection for railroad unions embodied in Section 10 of the Erdman Act. Striking down a congressional prohibition on yellow dog

[17]George Rothwell Brown, *The Leadership of Congress* (1922), 86; George W. Norris, *Fighting Liberal* (1945); and Champ Clark, *My Quarter Century in American Politics* (1920).
[18]See John Higham, *Strangers in the Land* (1977), 128–29.
[19]Gompers, 2: 224–55, 275; "Labor's Political Campaign."
[20]Gompers, *Seventy Years*, 2: 275.

contracts on the railroads, the Court argued, in *Adair v. U.S.* (1908), that the freedom of contract was an essential guarantee of the Fifth Amendment and that the relationship between unions and commerce was insufficient to justify congressional action favorable to unions under the commerce clause. Railroad employers, thus armed with the freedom to hire and fire, were free to winnow unions and unionists from the industry.

On the heels of *Adair* came the Danbury Hatters' decision, dealing a further blow to the rights and possibilities of organized labor. The Supreme Court ruled unanimously that the Sherman Act covered unions and their activities (in this instance a boycott) and remanded the case for trial; later the Court awarded treble damages to the hatters' employer, in a quarter-million-dollar judgment for which—in the absence of legal standing for unions—union members were liable.[21] Worse, prison sentences for Gompers, Frank Morrison, and John Mitchell (president, secretary, and vice-president of the AFL) were impending in the *Bucks Stove and Range* prosecution of the AFL leaders for the contempt of a lower court injunction against a union boycott.[22] Deprived of trial by jury under the equity procedures that determined the relationship between unions, employers, and the courts, antilabor judicial bias in *Bucks Stove* and other cases went essentially unchecked. These judicial assaults effectively ruled out the boycott, both as a labor weapon against employers and as an instrument of labor solidarity. All three decisions raised the possibility of judicial dissolution of unionism[23] and pointed to the need for legislative relief from the jurisdiction of the courts.

Under fire from the Court, and its victories in Congress still incomplete (the Republican-controlled Senate intercepted eighteen of twenty-seven labor bills reported from the Democratic House, including another literacy test proposal), the AFL turned its attention to the presidential contest in

---

[21]*Loewe v. Lawlor*, 208 U.S. 274 (1908); Lieberman, 56–70; Scheinberg, 141. The homes and savings of individual members of the Danbury Hatters Union were seized to pay the damages awarded to the employer: Florence C. Thorne, *Samuel Gompers: American Statesman* (1951), 128.

[22]James Van Cleave, president of the NAM, was also president of the Bucks Stove and Range Company. He secured a sweeping injunction that prohibited the AFL from discussing or publicizing the boycott. Proceedings were instituted against the AFL leadership for violating the injunction when they continued to promote the boycott (as well as to discuss the injunction). The case was seven years on appeal and remand between courts, where contempt convictions, prison sentences, and fines were alternately delivered and mitigated against the AFL leadership. When the Supreme Court rendered a final ruling in 1914, the statute of limitations for criminal procedures had expired, so none of the leaders went to jail.

[23]Dallas L. Jones, "The Enigma of the Clayton Act," *Industrial and Labor Relations Review*, 10 (January 1957), 202.

1912.[24] The split in the Republican party opened the possibility that labor could elect a friend to the White House. Meanwhile the split within progressivism created an opportunity for the AFL to align with reformers on its own terms.

The Democratic Moment

The race between Theodore Roosevelt and Woodrow Wilson was critical for labor politics and for the future of the American state. It provided the occasion for the AFL to formalize its ties to the Democratic party and to help make a national decision between the voluntarist state proposed by Wilson and the social statism associated with Roosevelt. Further, the Democratic outcome that the union-party tie helped produce elicited from the White House an unprecedented reciprocity toward labor. Though that reciprocity did not markedly enhance labor's legal and economic status, it significantly altered the AFL's political status.

The contest between Roosevelt and Wilson clarified the divisions within progressivism that validated the Democratic party as organized labor's political home. The most important division between the candidates lay in their attitudes toward concentrations of economic and political power. Wilson spoke of breaking up the trusts, Roosevelt spoke of regulating them;[25] Wilson admonished workers to self-reliance, Roosevelt proposed

[24]The defeated measures included the literacy test, even in the wake of the Dillingham Commission's negative conclusions about unregulated immigration and drastic recommendations for curbing it. The U.S. Immigration Commission, set up in 1907 by Congress and headed by Senator William P. Dillingham, published its *Report* in 1911. It recommended restrictions on the entry of unskilled workers, including the exclusion of those unaccompanied by wives or families. It also called for a literacy test, a quota plan, increases in the cash minimum required for entry at American ports, increases in the head tax, and a reduction in head taxes for immigrating men with families. A decade later Dillingham would head the Senate Immigration Committee, whose report on restriction proposals would distinguish explicitly between the old and the new immigration to support revival of the quota idea.

[25]See George Mowry, *The Era of Theodore Roosevelt and the Birth of Modern America, 1900–1912* (1958), 131–34, 200–206, 274–95; Elting E. Morison, ed., *The Letters of Theodore Roosevelt*, vol. 6 (1954), 1558–70. While in the absence of a regulatory mechanism (or prospect for one) Roosevelt opted for "judicious" use of the antitrust weapon, as president he had approved the merger of Tennessee Coal & Iron with U.S. Steel. Though Roosevelt liked to present himself as wielding his "big stick" against the trusts, he agreed with Croly that economic concentration was an organic necessity in a modern, efficient economy. Typically Roosevelt distinguished between "good" and "bad" trusts, often taking the existence of welfare programs as an indicator of a "good" trust. See Robert Ozanne, *A Century of Labor-Management Relations at McCormick and International Harvester* (1967), 80–81, and Henry F. Pringle, *Theodore Roosevelt* (1956), 300–302, 310–11. Roosevelt viewed large, interstate corporations as "sub-

that the state take responsibility for the social welfare.[26] Wilson argued for limited government and defended the autonomy of the several states on such matters as woman suffrage and child-labor legislation, while Roosevelt promoted the nationalization of political authority through such innovations as a modern standing army and social insurance. Both wanted to strengthen the presidency; but through the presidency Wilson wanted to strengthen political discipline and moral leadership while Roosevelt wanted to strengthen the state itself. Wilson wanted to be Gladstone; Roosevelt, Lloyd George.

The party platforms conformed to the visions of each candidate. The Democratic platform promoted a progressive antistatism in which unions played a central role; the Progressive platform proposed a social statism aimed at improving the condition of the working class as a whole. The Democratic party adopted most of the AFL's labor planks, including relief from injunctions and immigration, trial by jury in contempt proceedings, the right to organize into unions, and union exemption from antitrust liability. The party, however, maintained silence on social rights other than workman's compensation within the federal jurisdiction. The Progressive party, by contrast, was silent on the question of union rights. The Progressive platform thus did not go far enough on some fundamental union issues, while it loomed in opposition on others: it pledged, for example, to protect immigrants from exploitation and to promote immigrant education and assimilation; and it proposed sickness, unemployment, and old-age insurance, a minimum wage for women, the eight-hour day for continuous industries, occupational safety and health regulation, and federal mediation of labor disputes.[27]

Roosevelt's more expansive view of government's role in industrial society combined corporate liberalism with social statism. The AFL had

---

jects without a sovereign'' and therefore wanted to extend federal jurisdiction to them. But the problem for Roosevelt was not the trusts themselves but those trusts which abused their economic power. Thus regulation (including licensing and federal inspection) was his remedy rather than trust busting.

[26]Woodrow Wilson, *The New Freedom* (1913); E. David Cronin, ed., *The Political Thought of Woodrow Wilson* (1965); and Arthur Link, *Woodrow Wilson and the Progressive Era, 1900–1917* (1954). In contrast to Wilson, Roosevelt believed, for example, that the worker's ''protection in the place where he works should be guaranteed by the laws of the land. . . . The matter of compensation for injuries to employees is, perhaps, more immediately vital than any other. . . . In all dangerous trades the employer should be forced to bear the burden of the accident.'' Theodore Roosevelt, *The New Nationalism* (1910; 1961), 105, 107. See also ''President Roosevelt on Automatic Indemnity for Injury,'' NCF *Review,* July 1, 1911, p. 8.

[27]Kirk Porter, *National Platforms* (1924), 336, 383; Gompers, ''Labor's Political Campaign,'' 806.

no problem with Roosevelt's corporate liberalism—it had, after all, been drawn into deep and friendly association with corporate liberals through the National Civic Federation, in good measure because the NCF enterprise required acceptance, at least in principle, of existing union labor. Roosevelt embraced corporate liberal premises for industrial relations quite emphatically: "Where capital is organized, as it must be organized under modern industrial conditions, the only way to secure proper freedom . . . is to have labor organize also. . . . I believe in this practice of collective bargaining."[28] Nor did the AFL find corporate liberal premises for industrial structure problematic. Indeed, the AFL reciprocated corporate liberal views of unions by endorsing corporate liberal views of economic concentration: in the words of Gompers, "the trust system is the most perfect yet attained. . . .Organized labor has less difficulty in dealing with large firms and corporations . . . than with many individual employers or small corporations."[29] But just as economic concentration was not a central political issue for the AFL, so unionism was not a priority for corporate liberals. Corporate liberals, including Roosevelt, were less interested in promoting unionism than in seeing "radicalism prosper under conservative leadership."[30] Thus Roosevelt and his allies neither championed creation of a legal personality for unions nor defended union rights; nor did they advocate legislative restrictions on antilabor judicial intervention. The pragmatic compromises struck between corporate liberals and the AFL in the NCF thus did not yield bases for an AFL-Roosevelt alliance in politics.

Roosevelt's social statism was, moreover, quite problematic for the AFL. His advocacy of social welfare through political intervention, modeled on British and German innovations, collided with AFL concerns to establish trade-union autonomy because it offered "protections guaranteed by law" for protections secured by unions. This ensured that the Democratic party would continue to enjoy an affinity with organized labor, for the AFL, in 1912, was interested in union legislation not social legislation, in union rights not social security. Roosevelt's vision of national dominance ("it is idle," he insisted, "to ask us not to exercise the powers of government when only by that power. . . can we exalt the lowly and give heart to the humble and downtrodden")[31] was incompati-

[28]Roosevelt, *New Nationalism*, 99.

[29]Samuel Gompers to the Chicago Conference on Trusts, October 1907, quoted in Thorne, 127.

[30]NCF *Review*, July 1, 1911.

[31]Quoted in Eric Goldman, *Rendez-Vous with Destiny* (1955), 168.

ble with that of the AFL philosopher who, even in 1920, "still believed with Jefferson that that government is best which governs least."[32]

Wilson's position on many issues that mattered to labor did not, to be sure, accord with the AFL's own view. During the years immediately preceding 1912, in fact, Wilson had developed a reputation for hostility toward union labor. His commencement address at Princeton University in 1909 captured his precandidacy views:

> Labor is standardized by the trades unions, and this is the standard to which it is made to conform. . . . I need not point out how economically disastrous such a regulation of labor is. . . . It is so unprofitable to the employer that in some trades it will not be presently worth his while to attempt anything at all.[33]

But by 1912 Wilson had been reborn as a Democratic progressive who championed labor's right to organize and denounced the trusts for having "broken down the organization of labor."[34] Still, his diffident progressivism and untutored understanding of trade unionism were apparent during the campaign. Though he pledged his administration to protect labor's right to organize and stated his opposition to the unrestricted use of injunctions,[35] Wilson was reluctant to endorse comprehensive anti-injunction legislation and relief of organized labor from prosecution under antitrust laws—though both were promised in the Democratic platform—because he opposed "class" legislation. He refused to support child labor regulation or a minimum wage for women because he believed such policies would infringe upon economic freedom. He opposed a constitutional amendment for woman suffrage, arguing pragmatically that the issue was best left to the states and going on record philosophically as believing:

> the power to vote does not bring any material advantage to women, as has been proved by experience in those States where women have had the suffrage granted them. . . .[The] ballot privilege . . . has already become near-

[32]Samuel Gompers and Henry J. Allen, *Debate* (1920), 30.
[33]"Woodrow Wilson Hits Labor Unions," *New York Times*, June 14, 1909, p. 5. Wilson retreated from this harsh stance a year later, when New Jersey unionists assailed his reported hostility to labor. Arguing that his position had been misrepresented, Wilson explained: "I have criticized some of the things organized labor has done, but I have criticized them as a friend." "Wilson to Unions," ibid., September 2, 1910, p. 4.
[34]"Taft Meets Wilson for Pleasant Chat," ibid., September 27, 1912, pp. 1, 3.
[35]Woodrow Wilson, "The Old Order Changeth," in *The New Freedom* (1913), 19–29.

ly a dead-letter. . . . I am afraid, that were the power given them every-
where, it would not prove an unmixed blessing to the rest of the world.
Women . . . would, I am afraid, be apt to be led away by charm of manner
and speech.[36]

Finally, Wilson objected to the literacy test proposed for would-be immigrants, chiefly because he needed to overcome his published record of
racial nativism.[37]

Yet many of the AFL demands that Wilson would not personally embrace were part of the Democratic platform.[38] Others were already gaining ground before a Democratic Congress.[39] As for the nominee himself,
the language with which he expressed his reticence even on labor issues
echoed the AFL's antistatism. What is more, Wilson's mentor throughout
the campaign was Louis Brandeis, and Brandeis, though an attorney for
businessmen, was a critic of lopsided concentrations of business power in
industry, a proven friend of labor, and a foe of centralized state power.[40]

Although Brandeis and the AFL parted company on some issues (for
example, on scientific management, *ex parte* injunctions, union incorporation, and the closed shop), their friendship was strong enough to withstand such disagreements. Brandeis had demonstrated, both professionally
and politically, a profound commitment to unionism and union autonomy
as preconditions for correcting the imbalances of rights and political
power between workers and capital. Deep concern for workers figured
prominently in his campaign against the trusts, for example. Brandeis saw
in the anti-union activities of the trusts the sources of social unrest and
union violence, and assailed their very existence as antisocial: "The essence of the trust is a combination of the capitalist, by the capitalist, for
the capitalist," he wrote in 1911. Further, he contributed his considerable
skills to struggling unions, helping devise a settlement for the New York
garmentworkers' strike in 1910. That settlement not only included maximum hours, minimum wage, and regularity of employment guarantees

---

[36]"Women Expose Wilson's Animus: Speech in Bermuda Recalled," *San Francisco Examiner*, April 30, 1912, p. 7.

[37]"Italian Leader Scores Arrogance of Wilson," ibid., April 26, 1912, p. 9; Editorial, "More
Wilson Generalities," *San Francisco Chronicle*, October 5, 1912, p. 6.

[38]For a blow-by-blow account of the Republican and Democratic conventions, see William
Jennings Bryan, *A Tale of Two Conventions* (1912).

[39]E.g., the Clayton injunction limitation bill, the Industrial Relations Commission bill, the
literacy test, and the seamen's bill.

[40]Philippa Strum, *Louis D. Brandeis: Justice for the People* (1984), chaps. 7, 10, 11. See also
Thomas K. McCraw, "Rethinking the Trust Question," in McCraw, ed., *Regulation in Perspective* (1981).

but also eliminated worker liability for certain costs of production (electricity) and secured an innovative "affirmative action" plan for unionists through the preferential union shop.[41]

Finally, Brandeis took a position on the proper relationship between government and unions that conformed with the AFL's own view. He objected, for example, to universalistic and political remedies to problems soluble by and tailored to workers in their own institutions: "Do not pin too much faith in legislation," he wrote; "remedial institutions are apt to fall under the control of the enemy and to become instruments of oppression."[42] To improve the quality of workers' lives and to promote political equality, he stressed the development of industrial democracy—through affirmation of union rights and development of autonomous unions—rather than reliance on the coercive instruments of political democracy.[43] In keeping with this view, Brandeis would later defend the Clayton Act not by suggesting a need for government support and protection of unionism but by arguing that such laws "declare the right of industrial combatants to push their struggle to the limitations of the justification of self-interest."[44] The essence of the Wilson-Brandeis promise, then, was state *neutrality* in labor-capital relations and thus enhancement of trade-union autonomy. Such government impartiality would require legislative restraint of the judiciary, but in the name of sweeping away "special privilege" and class protection.

The progressive antistatism of Wilson and Brandeis provided for the AFL an attractive alternative to Taft's judicial antistatism, Eugene Debs's "working class republic," and Theodore Roosevelt's social statism. Throughout the campaign, competing conceptions of the American state were kept in the foreground, particularly in the battle between Roosevelt and Wilson. For Roosevelt, it was a "war . . . between those who believe in uplifting the people by the strengthening of government [and] those who believe that government to be best that governs least." Before an audience of ten thousand in New York City, Roosevelt characterized Wilson's view:

Mr. Wilson said the story of liberty is a history of the limitation of a governmental power, not the increase of it. . . . Mr. Wilson is absolutely in

[41]Brandeis supported union recognition but thought the closed shop coercive. Strum, 175–76.
[42]Quoted in Alpheus T. Mason, *Brandeis—A Free Man's Life* (1946), 585.
[43]See Brandeis to the Commission on Industrial Relations, Senate document 415, 64th cong., 1st sess. (1916), Serial 6936, 7657–81. With respect to social welfare, Brandeis develops the view that socially responsible business, rather than government initiative, is central to industrial democracy and social justice in his *Business—A Profession* (1914).
[44]*Duplex Printing Company v. Deering*, 254 U.S. 443 (1921).

error in his statement from the historical standpoint. So long as governmental power existed exclusively for the King and not at all for the people, then the history of liberty was a history of the limitation of governmental power. But now the governmental power rests in the people, and the King who enjoyed privileges are the Kings of the financial and industrial world, and what they clamor for is the limitation of governmental power, and what the people surely need is the extension of governmental power. . . . Now friends, you can adopt one philosophy or the other. You can adopt the philosophy of laissez-faire, of the limitation of governmental power, and turn the industrial life of this country into a chaotic scramble of selfish interests, each bent on plundering the others and all bent on oppressing the wage workers. This is exactly what Mr. Wilson's proposal means, and it can mean nothing else. Under such limitation of governmental power as he praises every railroad would be left unchecked, every great industrial concern can do as it chooses with its employees, and with the general public.[45]

Roosevelt's running mate, Hiram Johnson, carried on the attack, tying Wilson's antistatism to the embarrassment of American social backwardness in comparison to Western Europe:

You may think this programme and covenant of ours is unduly radical. Not so, my friends. Imperial Germany has to-day carried out this programme to the full; royal England has gone half the way, and under Lloyd George is now engaged in going the other half. The laggard of all the nations of front rank in caring for its human kind is this great, free, boasting nation of ours. And our object is to take our country which we love so dearly and to put it into the very van and leadership of all the nations of the world in caring for its men, its women, and its children.[46]

Beyond questions of state, Wilson also represented an alternative to Roosevelt's procapitalist, assimilationist view of immigration. Roosevelt did not embrace the exclusionist politics of either Republican nativists or the AFL, though his attitude toward non-Teutonic peoples (particularly Indians and blacks) was certainly not lacking in racialist assumptions. He saw immigration not as the source of economic and eugenic degeneration but chiefly as a political problem.[47] As a political problem, Roosevelt

[45]"Roosevelt Scorns Wilson's Philosophy," *New York Times*, September 15, 1912, p. 8. See also "Bull Moose Hits Back at Wilson," *San Francisco Chronicle*, September 4, 1912, p. 10.
[46]"Cheer Governor Johnson at Meeting Here," *New York Times*, October 6, 1912, p. 15.
[47]Theodore Roosevelt, *Writings* (1967), 241. In his first five annual messages, Roosevelt argued that character should be the principle criterion for immigrant admission. On these grounds he supported some form of test for moral and economic "fitness." See his *Works*, 15 (1926), 95–97, 245.

distinguished between its domestic and international implications. On the one hand, he was willing to believe that immigration created social problems that threatened the continuity and stability of the liberal political tradition. But on the other hand, he was also concerned that how the United States dealt with immigration would rebound diplomatically, militarily, and commercially. Thus though he agreed, as president, to tighten the Chinese Exclusion Act, he insisted that the Japanese—now that Japan was demonstrating military muscle—had to be treated more gingerly. In keeping with this view, he signed, in 1907, a Gentlemen's Agreement with Japan, in which the Japanese government agreed not to issue new passports to America-bound laborers while retaining the right to reissue passports to workers who had already been to the United States, as well as to their parents, wives, and children. The resulting influx of "picture brides" infuriated nativist Californians and their sympathizers—and reminded them of the thousands of Chinese "paper sons" who managed to gain entry despite the Chinese exclusion acts.[48]

Roosevelt had also angered nativist workers when he pressured for rescission of the San Francisco school segregation order of 1906,[49] and when he pronounced in favor of naturalization for Japanese immigrants. In addition, some of California labor still remembered vice-presidential candidate Hiram Johnson's role in the graft prosecution of Boss Reuf and Mayor Schmitz of the San Francisco Union Labor party. The memory compounded their hostility toward the Progressive ticket.[50]

Quite apart from his diplomatic maneuvers and policy pronouncements as president, Roosevelt's earlier writings displayed considerable faith in the ideal of the "melting pot." In his *Winning of the West*, he suggested that immigrant strains would fade away within one generation of life in the American "forest"—yielding to distinctively American characteristics that made all Americans, regardless of national origin, "same in speech, thought, and character."[51] In a piece on New York written in 1890, Roosevelt had treated the city's ethnic diversity with equanimity and denounced political nativism. He confessed that Americanization in urban New York could well take several generations (in contrast to the relatively

[48]"Democrats Hit Roosevelt Hard," *San Francisco Chronicle,* October 7, 1912, p. 2; "Hot Debate Will Mark Labor Meet," ibid., October 9, 1912, p. 3.

[49]The San Francisco city government had ordered Japanese and Korean pupils barred from public schools attended by whites. The Chinese were already segregated into the Oriental School.

[50]See Walton Bean, *Boss Reuf's San Francisco* (1952); John Shover, "The Progressives and the Working Class Vote in California," in Joel Silbey and Samuel McSeveney, eds., *Voters, Parties and Elections* (1972), 263.

[51]Theodore Roosevelt, *The Winning of the West* (1917), 89.

swift process in the less congested melting pot of the frontier) but he also
held that

> the only way to teach our foreign-born fellow-citizens how to govern them-
> selves is to give each the full rights possessed by other American cit-
> izens. . . . It has been my experience moreover in the legislature that when
> Hans or Paddy does turn out really well, there are very few native Americans
> who indeed do better.[52]

Roosevelt's faith in the American melting pot tempered his commitment to restrictions on immigration. Although he supported his friend
Henry Cabot Lodge's literacy test proposal and although he summoned
racial arguments to justify American imperialism ("fitness [for self-gov-
ernment] is not a God-given, natural right," Roosevelt wrote, "but comes
to a race only through the slow growth of centuries, and then only to those
races which possess an immense reserve fund of strength, common sense,
and morality"), he never subscribed to Lodge's theory of racial determin-
ism with respect to America's immigrants. Indeed, as he told an Italian
group in New York City, "our object is not to imitate one of the older
racial types, but to maintain a new American type and then to secure
loyalty to this type." In his public commentary he explained his endorsement of immigration regulations on political grounds, arguing that immigration swelled the ranks of the "hopelessly poor" and of American
radicalism. One solution to this political aspect of the immigration problem was, in Roosevelt's view, to reverse the diminishing birth rate among
native-stock Americans. Thus he campaigned against "willful ster-
ility"—birth control—and assigned its practitioners "contempt as hearty
as any visited upon the soldier who runs away in battle." What was
further needed, he maintained, was a policy to "dry up the pestilential
social conditions in our great cities, where anarchistic organizations have
their greatest possibility of growth."[53]

In this he shared a political concern with Lodge, who maintained that
"socialism was not so much a war of classes as it was a conflict of

---

[52]Theodore Roosevelt, "A Phase of State Legislation," *Works*, 13 (1926), 49. For a fictional
account of Roosevelt's friendly receptivity to a "Paddy" who turned out "really well," see
William DeAndrea, *The Lunatic Fringe* (1984), a detective novel featuring Roosevelt as New
York City police commissioner on the eve of the 1896 election.

[53]Herman Hagedorn, ed., *The Works of Theodore Roosevelt* (1926–27), 10: 248, 18: 402;
"Race Decadence," *Outlook*, April 8, 1911, p. 766; James Richardson, ed., *Messages and
Papers of the Presidents*, 14 (December 3, 1901), 6651–52.

races.''[54] But Roosevelt never drew the invidious racial distinctions between old and new immigrants which were the mainstay of Teutonic theory, holding, instead, that all European peoples were of the same "ancestral culture" and educable to American virtues and standards—in other words, "Americanizable."

Roosevelt's "cultural nationalism," though couched in different language, harked back to McKinley's cultural pluralism and hinted at differences that would matter greatly later: between the AFL's nativism, anchored in the politics of labor markets, and middle-class and Republican nativism, elaborated in reaction to labor militancy and in fear of labor radicalism. In 1912 the principal significance attaching to this difference was that neither Roosevelt nor the Republican old guard was moved by racial argument to close the doors to immigration unilaterally.

In 1912 the campaign debate focused on the issue of trust regulation—on the relationship between the federal government and large corporations. But much of the vote-getting effort fixed on winning the working class. To some extent it brought Wilson and Roosevelt into competition for the pro-union label,[55] but it also brought them into competition for the new-immigrant vote. Disruption in the GOP meant that ordinary partisanship would not decide the presidential contest. Whoever could attract significant blocs within the industrial electorate might well win the election. Taft, hoping to retain new-immigrant Republicans, pledged to veto the literacy test. Roosevelt, hoping to swing new immigrants out of the Republican column, visited anthracite Pennsylvania, reminded workers of his friendly intervention in the strike of 1902, and otherwise pledged to defend new immigrants against exploitation and to promote their political integration through education. Further, he appealed to new immigrants as workers, through promises of an eight-hour day in twenty-four-hour industries, social insurance, and health and safety regulation.[56]

Wilson's position was somewhat more complicated. His overriding appeal was to the union vote: when he spoke to labor issues, he spoke of unionism rather than of the social conditions of the working class. But he also followed Taft and Roosevelt in heaping praises on new-immigrant groups and promising to keep America's doors wide open. These praises chiefly appealed to new immigrants as immigrants, or as ethnic Ameri-

---

[54]Henry Cabot Lodge, *The Restriction of Immigration* (March 6, 1896), 15.

[55]"Wilson and Unionism Now Johnson Theme," *San Francisco Examiner*, October 8, 1912, p. 2; "T. R. Denies Wilson Is Friend of Workers," ibid., October 10, 1912, p. 4; and "Gov. Wilson Scores Roosevelt's Plans," *New York Times*, September 5, 1912, p. 1.

[56]"Roosevelt Scorns Wilson's Philosophy"; "T. R. Denies Wilson is Friend of Workers."

cans, rather than as workers or as potential constituents of the labor vote. Wilson's ethnic appeals and celebration of a Democratic open door were not readily persuasive, however, for they required him to repudiate his well-documented nativism completely, much as his assertion of friendship with union labor had required his retreat from printed remarks. His scholarly writings, indeed, had expressed considerable nativist anxiety over the consequences of immigration for American democracy. In 1889 he had warned:

immigrant minds cast in every mold of race—minds inheriting every basis of environment, warped by the diverse histories of a score of different nations . . . threatened . . . our Saxon habits in government. . . . Were the nation homogeneous, were it simply composed of later generations of the same stock by which our institutions were planted, few adjustments of the old machinery of politics would, perhaps, be necessary. . . . But every added element of variety, particularly every added element of foreign variety, complicates even the simpler questions for politics.[57]

And in 1894 Wilson complained:

our own temperate blood, schooled to self-possession and the measured conduct of self-government, is receiving a constant infusion and yearly experiencing a partial corruption of foreign blood. Our own equable habits have been crossed with the feverish humors of the restless old world. We are unquestionably facing an ever-increasing difficulty of self-command with ever-deteriorating materials, possibly with degenerating fibre.[58]

Only a decade before his presidential race, moreover, Wilson had argued in his *History of the American People* that

multitudes of men of the lowest classes from the south of Italy and men of the meaner sort out of Hungary and Poland, men out of the ranks where there was neither skill nor energy nor any initiative of quick intelligence . . . came in numbers . . . as if the countries . . . were disburdening themselves of the more sordid and hapless elements of their population.[59]

Yet though Wilson's writings provided rhetorical ballast for labor nativists, his nativism was from the trade-union perspective not without flaws. Wilson's was fundamentally a middle-class nativism; it dis-

[57]Woodrow Wilson, "Make Haste Slowly," *Selected Literary Papers*, vol. 1 (1925), 30–39.
[58]Wilson, *Selected Literary and Political Papers*, 107.
[59]Woodrow Wilson, *History of the American People*, vol. 5 (1902), 212–13.

tinguished between unenfranchised, faceless coolie labor and those immigrants to whom political equality had been extended through naturalization and who thereby introduced diversity and change into the political, economic, and cultural order. In singling out new immigrants, for example, as "men whose standards of life and work were such as American workmen had never dreamed of hitherto," Wilson had compared them *unfavorably* to the Chinese. Although he had reviled the Chinese in his *History,* calling them "the thrifty, skillful Orientals, who with their yellow skin and strange, debasing habits of life, seemed hardly fellow men at all, but evil spirits, rather,"[60] he went on to argue that "the Chinese were more to be desired, as workmen if not as citizens, than the most coarse crew that came crowding in every year at eastern ports."[61] With these remarks Wilson managed to offend both new-immigrant Europeans and their unionized antagonists.

During the campaign for the nomination the "stop Wilson" movement, and especially the anti-Wilson press, seized upon such statements to vilify his candidacy and to question his new liberalism.[62] So, too, did new-immigrant leaders, though clearly not from nativist sympathies:

> Professor Wilson's assertion that the Chinese are more desirable as workmen, if not as citizens, than the Italians, at once stamps him as a man in favor of coolie labor, as against the higher class of labor; and stamps him as a man unworthy of the respect of the honest, industrious workingmen of this country, regardless of creed or nationality. . . . I feel safe in saying if his election depends upon the Italian vote he will never know he was running.[63]

Richard Croker echoed this judgment, from Tammany's electoral perspective, when he warned fellow Democrats that "no man can be a good Democrat who, like Governor Wilson, has assailed practically every foreign born citizen in the United States, as he has in his books and speeches."[64]

Added to Wilson's troubles with party bosses and immigrants were his troubles with unionists. During the nomination campaign, unionists were partisans of Champ Clark, whom they identified as a genuine friend of

[60]Ibid., 185.
[61]Ibid., 213.
[62]Alexander L. George and Juliette L. George, *Woodrow Wilson and Colonel House* (1964), 100–101; Arthur Link, *Wilson: Road to the White House* (1947).
[63]"Italian Leader Scores Arrogance of Wilson."
[64]"Wilson Sure Loser, Richard Croker Says," *San Francisco Examiner,* April 4, 1912, p. 6.

labor. As Andrew Furuseth of the Coast Seamen's Union put it: "With reference to Wilson and Clark, there is no choice from a labor point of view. Clark is, by all odds, the best of the two; he has never flinched for one moment on the serious questions. Always against the injunction evil, the immigration evil, the Oriental immigration evil. . . ."[65] In California, where union labor joined women to effect a union gap alongside a threatened gender gap, Clark battered Wilson in the presidential primary, winning 71.5 percent of the Democratic vote.[66]

Though Wilson lost the California primary in part because his opponents played up his remarks about Chinese, however, his response to those assaults put him on firm ground for the general election—especially in comparison to Roosevelt. Wilson supporters extracted from him a clarification of his views on the Chinese during the primary. Drawing an analogy between the "Chinese question" and the "Negro question," Wilson wrote:

In the matter of Chinese and Japanese coolie immigration I stand for the National policy of exclusion. We cannot make a homogeneous population out of a people who do not blend with the Caucasian race. Their lower standard of living as laborers will crowd out the white agriculturalist and is, in other fields, a most serious industrial menace. The success of free democratic institutions demands of our people education, intelligence and patriotism, and the state should protect them against unjust and impossible competition. Remunerative labor is the basis of contentment. Democracy rests on the equality of citizens. Oriental coolieism will give us another race problem to solve and surely we have had our lesson.[67]

During the general election campaign this message was widely circulated and emphatically contrasted against Roosevelt's 1906 proposal to naturalize the Japanese. With Taft off the ballot, Wilson split Progressive California with Roosevelt, losing the state by fewer than two hundred votes and carrying the labor stronghold of San Francisco.[68]

[65]Quoted in "Clark Is Labor's Champion," ibid., May 4, 1912, p. 6.

[66]"Wilson Jeer at Women to Lose Him California," ibid., April 13, 1912, p. 6; Congressional Quarterly, *Presidential Elections since 1789* (1975), 84, 103.

[67]*San Francisco Daily News*, May 4, 1912. See also Roger Daniels, *The Politics of Prejudice* (1977), 55. It should be remembered that the Wilson administration formally brought Jim Crow to the federal bureaucracy in 1913. Many government offices and facilities in Washington were segregated, and the autonomy of the South on race matters was extended to the federal jurisdiction (e.g., post offices).

[68]Wilson and Roosevelt each received 41.8 percent of the statewide vote. Wilson won 48.4 percent of the San Francisco vote. Congressional Quarterly, *Presidential Elections*, 103; Edgar Robinson, *The Presidential Vote, 1896–1932* (1947), 148.

While Wilson promised to defend the Pacific Coast from the Chinese and Japanese to win nativist votes in California, he floated promises of an Atlantic open door to garner new-immigrant support in the East. With the help of the anti-Wilson press, however, new-immigrant clubs and periodicals had discovered his nativist scholarship—and protested loudly. Wilson replied vigorously even pledging to a Polish-American group that he would rewrite offensive passages in his *History*. He wrote to new-immigrant leaders in an attempt to remedy his nativist offenses. He addressed the editors of the foreign-language press, saying that "we are all Americans."[69] He told the editor of the Italian review *Il Carroccio* that in his *History* he had merely been "deploring the coming to this country of certain lawless elements which I has supposed all thoughtful Italians themselves deplored. . . . Certainly, the Italians I have known . . . have constituted one of the most interesting and admirable elements in our American life."[70]

Wilson's apologies proved sufficient neither to lose union labor nor to win new immigrants.[71] While Wilson in important respects "urbanized" the Democratic party, he did so by pulling union labor more fully into the Democratic coalition—around issues of race, state, and union—not by expanding that coalition to include the new-immigrant electorate—howsoever he tried to expunge his nativism. In fact, the electoral alignment that developed during the 1890s—relegating the Democratic party to minority status—was more or less maintained on the Democratic side in 1912. While Wilson carried many counties in urban and industrial New York, Massachusetts, and Pennsylvania, for example, he did not carry them with *new* Democratic votes. His 36.3 percent average vote earned him victories that his Democratic predecessors missed at the federal level because Roosevelt pulled roughly one-third of the Republican vote over to the Progressive banner. In some of the most heavily new immigrant counties, Roosevelt forced a better than 40 percent defection from the GOP. Though not enough to secure a Progressive victory nationally, it was enough to deprive the Republicans of many industrial counties in Pennsylvania and four districts in New York City.[72]

[69]"Wilson to Foreign Editors," *New York Times*, September 5, 1912, p. 2.
[70]Quoted in Edward N. Saveth, *American Historians and European Immigrants, 1875–1925* (1948), 143.
[71]Italians in Chicago repudiated Wilson, for example, where he trailed Roosevelt by 24,183 votes (and took 31.4 percent of the city-wide vote). Humbert S. Nelli, *The Italians in Chicago: A Study in Ethnic Mobility* (1970), 118.
[72]Roosevelt carried the major steel counties of western Pennsylvania, and Luzerne and Lack-

So Wilson, polling even fewer votes than Bryan had against Taft in 1908, defeated social statism. New-immigrant defections to the Progressives clearly played their part—a lesson not lost on Wilson when presented with legislation to restrict immigration. Shrinkage in the national electorate also helped. Between 1900 and 1912 participation rates dropped by an average of 16 percent in urban and industrial Pennsylvania, for example. Overall voter turnout was down sharply, to below 60 percent; and new immigrants, who appear to have been receptive to Roosevelt if they voted, were generally underrepresented in the electorate because of stricter naturalization laws, personal registration requirements, and other hurdles to electoral mobilization.[73]

Decomposition and demobilization on the Republican side of the system of 1896 created electoral space for the Democratic party in 1912. In a sense, the "hole" in the electorate that Walter Dean Burnham traces back to the system of 1896 was the basis for Woodrow Wilson's victory.[74] That "hole" would become the foundation for the Democratic state crafted under Wilson.

Equally important was the union-party tie, which controlled the political space occupied in other countries by labor and social democratic parties. That tie gave to the AFL a strategic presence in the Democratic campaign, a presence for which it would be rewarded when its party assumed power. The AFL wrote the labor plank for the party's platform,

---

awanna in the northeast—the heart of anthracite coal mining. Robinson, *Presidential Ballots;* Pennsylvania *Handbook,* 1912; and Higham, 190. While it is impossible to infer anything absolutely from these data, it does appear that many of the people (immigrants and urbanites) who Lubell, Degler, Burner, and others have argued gave McKinley his margin of victory in 1896 abandoned Republicanism in 1912 for Roosevelt's third-party incarnation of the McKinley-Roosevelt-Hanna era. The Republican share of the vote dropped in Allegheny County (Pittsburgh), for example, from 60.8 percent in 1908 to 18.8 percent in 1912. Similarly in Cook County, Illinois (Chicago), the GOP suffered a 38.1 percent decline in 1912 over 1908. And in Republican-controlled Philadelphia, it took a 32.6 percent decline.

[73]Although the population expanded rapidly in industrialized states after 1900, especially with the crest in immigration between 1900 and 1910, voter participation did not reflect that expansion. One factor involved was the introduction of personal registration systems, beginning around 1896. See Philip Converse, "Change in the American Electorate," in Angus Campbell and Converse, eds., *The Human Meaning of Social Change* (1972). Another factor was the tightening and federalizing of naturalization procedures in 1906, which included a federal bar on naturalization within thirty days of an election. See Chapter 4 for a general discussion of new immigrant electoral participation and mobilization under the system of 1896. Despite the massive expansion of adult male populations in urban and industrial areas between 1900 and 1910, turnout as a percentage of that population declined sharply.

[74]Burnham, "Changing Shape," and "Party Systems and the Political Process," both in Burnham, *Current Crisis.*

published weekly campaign newsletters, sponsored speakers, and sent its leaders on campaign tours.[75] Though the AFL represented only a fraction of the working class, splits within Republicanism—and among wage-earning Republicans—enhanced union labor's electoral role. The impact of the AFL's campaign activities in generating the plurality by which Wilson won was clear. San Francisco, a center for unionism ever since the agitation for Chinese exclusion, went for Wilson, helping him hold Roosevelt to the barest of pluralities in California. This was the best Democratic performance in the state in twenty years and particularly remarkable because California's Progressive governor, Hiram Johnson, was on the Roosevelt ticket. In New York City and Boston, two other union strongholds, Wilson hauled in what was for this election a solid 47 percent of the vote. The AFL, despite the precariousness of the Democratic victory, celebrated its role in delivering government to the Democrats.[76] The AFL had become the central labor force in politics.

The Socialist Alternative

The AFL's economic and political alliances during the Progressive era were built upon divisions in the work force. But more important, from its position in the political mainstream the AFL defended the barriers to a politically independent working class. Underlying the AFL's defense was the deep fragmentation of the working class. By the turn of the century, workers shared only their objective status as wage earners, but even as wage earners some had interests that were fundamentally antagonistic to the interests of the rest. As a result, opponents of the AFL's political strategy found it difficult to muster resistance.

Not even the Socialist movement could step into the breach left when the AFL married voluntarism to Democratic politics: for the Socialists themselves had considerable difficulty building solidarity from a split working class. Much of the Socialist party, indeed, shared the economic and racial prejudices of the conservative AFL. Even Eugene Debs had difficulty reconciling his industrial unionism with his suspicion of new immigrants. Scooping Woodrow Wilson with an unfavorable assessment

[75]See Avril E. Harris, "Organized Labor in Party Politics: 1906–1932," University of Iowa, 1937.

[76]*American Federationist*, 20 (1913), 594–611; Link, *Woodrow Wilson and the Progressive Era*, 24; and Karson, 73. Taft polled 3.5 million, Roosevelt 4 million, Debs 901,602, and Wilson 6 million.

of non-Teutonic European immigrants in comparison to the Chinese, Debs wrote in 1891 that "the Dago works for small pay and lives far more like a savage or wild beast, than the Chinese. [The Italian] fattens on garbage . . . and is able to underbid an American workingman. Italy has millions of them to spare and they are coming."[77] Though Debs's deep concern for the economic and political organization of the working class would greatly temper these sentiments, Socialists with roots in the AFL were adamant in their demands for restrictive immigration policies.

Socialist nativism constrained Socialist party organizational drives among industrial workers, depriving the movement of potential majorities to challenge conservative trade unionism. In 1908—when new immigrants constituted two-thirds of the work force—71 percent of the Socialist party membership was native-born, and another 18 percent were old-stock immigrants from northern and western Europe.[78] What is more, bickering on the immigration issue greatly embittered Socialists against one another, feeding the ideological rifts that retarded party cohesion.

Speaking from the socialist left, Eugene Debs and IWW leader Bill Haywood maintained that unskilled new workers formed the core of the American proletariat. The restriction question was a "fake issue" much as the tariff and free silver had been, invented by "civic federation unionists" to divert attention away from legitimate social issues. In his "Plea for Solidarity," Debs argued that

> the great mass of common, unskilled labor steadily augmented by the machine process, is the granite foundation of the working class, and of the whole social fabric; and to ignore or slight this proletarian mass, or fail to recognize its essentially fundamental character, is to build without foundation or rear a house of scantlings instead of a fortress of defense.[79]

Haywood, too, was quite critical of trade-union nativism:

> It is this attitude of the AFL that has been a potential force used against the submerged mass. Capitalism has used this force to keep the millions of unskilled and unorganized down to the lowest possible standard of living. There has been a pernicious spirit of patriotism cultivated among these

[77]Quoted in Nick Salvatore, *Eugene V. Debs: Citizen and Socialist* (1982), 104.

[78]Ira Kipnis, *The American Socialist Movement* (1952), 423; Stanley Aronowitz, *False Promises* (1974), 142.

[79]Eugene Debs, "A Plea for Solidarity," *International Socialist Review,* 14 (March 1914), 534–38.

American workmen, by which they have been consciously taught to despise the foreigner from all countries, and fight him.[80]

But speaking for "conservative" socialism, Morris Hillquit and Victor Berger embraced trade-union nativism—and successfully urged the 1908 and 1910 Socialist party conventions to oppose all immigration "stimulated by capitalists" on economic grounds and to denounce Asian immigration on racial grounds.[81] In Hillquit's view,

the majority of American socialists side with the trade unions in their demand for the exclusion of workingmen of such races and nations as have yet not been drawn into the sphere of modern production and who are incapable of assimilation with the workingmen of the country of their adoption and of joining the organization and struggles of their class.[82]

Echoing Hillquit, Berger argued in 1910 that socialism could thrive only if America were protected as a "white man's" country. He further warned that unless immigration was regulated, "this country is absolutely sure to become a black-and-yellow country within five generations."[83] And from the floor of the U.S. House in 1911, Berger denounced the "Slavonians, Italians, Greeks, Russians and Armenians" as "modern white coolies."[84]

Between 1908 and 1913 the Socialist party feuded internally over immigration policy. The debate provoked by the issue in socialist circles closely paralleled the debate raging over internationalism and industrial unionism. Generally, the lineup of factions more or less corresponded on the various issues. Internationalists, industrial unionists, and syndicalists—like Debs and Haywood—spoke of one working class and abjured strategies that would entrench or engender divisions within it. Nativists and trade unionists—like Hillquit and Berger—aimed to capture the mainstream labor movement by winning control of conservative unionism. The strategy estranged them from working-class majorities, for their concern was to subdue voluntarists within and thereby politicize trade unionism rather than to undo the craft structure or extend political power to the

[80]Bill Haywood, "An Appeal for Industrial Solidarity," *International Socialist Review*, 14 (March 1914), 545; Paul Brissenden, *The I.W.W.* (1957), 84, 208.

[81]Kipnis, 278–79; 286–87.

[82]Morris Hillquit, "Immigration in the United States," *International Socialist Review*, 8 (August 1907), 75.

[83]Quoted in Kipnis, 62.

[84]*Congressional Record*, 62d Cong., 1st. sess. (June 14, 1911), 2026–30.

working class as a whole.[85] Moreover, the trade-union Socialists who dominated the party membership brought with them the nativist consensus forged within the AFL. As a result, the Socialist party presented an alternative to the AFL with respect to the role of the state and independent "collective" labor politics but not on the two issues that isolated unions from working-class majorities: the craft structure and immigration restriction.

The immigration issue first emerged as a major indicator of ideological cleavage in the Socialist party in 1908. At the party's national convention a resolution was presented to restrict undesirable immigration. The issue was raised by socialist nativists disgruntled by the Stuttgart resolution on immigration passed by the International Socialist Congress of 1907, which contradicted and thus undercut the position of American socialists—at least as argued by the American National Executive Committee at the Congress. While the committee at Stuttgart had called on socialists to "combat with all the means at their command the willful importation of cheap foreign labor calculated to destroy labor organizations,"[86] the congress roundly condemned all efforts to restrict immigration on national or racial grounds.[87] Socialist nativists in America— particularly those who had burrowed within the AFL—regarded the Stuttgart outcome as a challenge to their autonomy. They pressured the American party to respond.

Among the many who championed nativism were Max Hayes, who challenged Gompers for the AFL presidency that year, and John Spargo, the leading party theoretician. Spargo defended the 1908 American resolution by arguing that "to deny the right of workers to protect themselves against injury to their interests caused by the competition of imported foreign laborers whose standards of living are materially lower than their own, is to set a bourgeois utopian ideal above the class struggle."[88]

The convention tabled the issue in 1908 but directed the 1910 convention to deal with the question of exclusion based on race. In addition, the convention established a standing committee on immigration and elected five nativists to serve on it. Some, including Victor Berger, were openly racist. Others, such as John Spargo, favored immigration restriction for

[85]Victor Berger, for example, fought efforts to bypass the AFL, whether through industrial unionism or through the IWW's syndicalism. At party conventions in 1908 and 1910 he led the opposition to resolutions favoring organization of unorganized, unskilled workers. Discussed in Salvatore, 201 and chap. 8.

[86]Quoted in Kipnis, 277.

[87]James Weinstein, *The Decline of Socialism in America* (New York, 1969), 65ff.

[88]Socialist Party National Convention *Proceedings* (1908), 105.

chiefly economic reasons.[89] For the next two years debate in the committee reflected the major splits in the party as a whole: on what grounds should the party justify advocacy of the nativist restriction of immigration? Debated rationales for nativism included racial protection, economic justice, and protection of the socialist movement from the deleterious presence of docile and unorganizable immigrants.

The committee disagreed with respect to the advisability of explicit racial protectionism, preventing it from reporting a comprehensive resolution on immigration to the 1910 convention. Instead, its resolution limited racial arguments to Asian immigration, declaring it ''a menace to the progress of the most aggressive, militant and intelligent elements of our working class population . . . which relegates the class war to the rear.''[90] From the floor of the convention Hillquit pressed a substitute that confronted the new immigration as well.

Briefly, Hillquit condemned the recruitment of unskilled immigrants by industry: by now ''recruitment'' and ''contract labor,'' having been rendered unnecessary by the momentum of immigration, were code words for the new immigration. But his substitute resolution also included compromise language meant to appease internationalists and Jews:

> The Socialist Party of the United States favors all legislative measures tending to prevent the immigration of strikebreakers and contract laborers, and the mass importation of workers from foreign countries, brought about by the employing classes for the purpose of weakening the organization of American labor, and of lowering the standard of life of American workers. . . . [But] the party is opposed to the exclusion of any immigrants on account of their race or nationality, and demands that the United States be at all times maintained as a free asylum for all men and women persecuted by the governments of their countries on account of their politics, religion, or race.[91]

The convention narrowly adopted the substitute (by 55 to 50). Some internationalists found the new language of qualified nativism palatable. Those loyal to Debs and opposed to the AFL generally did not, reading it as a call for the exclusion of Italians, Poles, Hungarians, and non-Jewish Russians. Hardcore nativists preferred stronger language, particularly

[89]See Charles Lienenweber, ''The American Socialist Party and New Immigrants,'' *Science and Society*, 32 (1968), 8.
[90]Socialist Party National Convention *Proceedings* (1910), 76.
[91]Ibid., 98. The Hillquit substitute took five days to debate.

with respect to Asians. But on the whole the convention finessed the issue: the resolution had different meanings for different people. Meyer London, who would be elected to Congress from New York's Lower East Side, voted for the substitute because it seemed to reject race as a basis for exclusion; Robert Hunter did so because it allowed the party "to do whatever is necessary to protect the class interests of the workers of America."[92] It may have pacified some, but the ambiguity of the 1910 resolution served to stir the coals of nativist debate within the party rather than to resolve the issue.

The same convention also authorized the establishment of foreign-language affiliates. But it did so on a Jim Crow basis: immigrant groups were invited to take on the party label, but as autonomous units and without voting privileges at national conventions.[93] Between 1910 and 1912, five foreign-language federations (representing, among others, Bohemians, Hungarians, Slavs, and Italians) affiliated, bringing nearly sixteen thousand nonvoting members under the party's banner. The new-immigrant locals tended to be rather unstable (membership turnover was high) and isolated from the mainstream of the party. Foreign-language locals rarely came into contact with English-speaking ones, and so were never integrated into the party apparatus or community. Their distance from American socialism was reflected in the fact that they apparently devoted much of their energy to supporting movements in the old country.[94]

Debs viewed the decisions of the 1910 convention, though they were softened by compromise, as "utterly unsocialistic, reactionary, and in truth outrageous."[95] Calling socialist nativists "subtle and sophisticated defenders of the civic federation unionism," Debs characterized the immigration resolution as pandering to the exclusionism of the AFL. In a letter to the *International Socialist Review,* Debs wrote:

> The plea that certain races are to be excluded because of tactical expediency would be entirely consistent in a bourgeois convention of self-seekers, but should have no place in a proletarian gathering under the auspices of an international movement that is calling on the oppressed and exploited workers of all the world to unite for their emancipation.[96]

He continued:

[92]Quoted in Weinstein, *Decline,* 66.
[93]Nathan Fine, *Farmer and Labor Parties in the United States* (1961), 325–26.
[94]Lienenweber, 20; Socialist Party National Convention *Proceedings* (1912), 80.
[95]Quoted in Salvatore, 245.
[96]Eugene Debs in the *International Socialist Review,* 11 (July 1910), 16–17.

233

Let those desert us who will because we refuse to shut the international door in the faces of their own brethren; we will be none the weaker but all the stronger for their going, for they evidently have no clear conception of the international solidarity, are wholly lacking in the revolutionary spirit, and have no proper place in the Socialist movement while they entertain such aristocratic notions of their own assumed superiority.

Little emerged in the way of rank-and-file opposition to socialist nativism, however. In fact, the party became more stridently nativist even as it worked to promote Debs's presidential candidacy. At the 1912 convention, nativists carried the day:

Race feeling is not so much a result of social as of biological evolution. . . . Class consciousness must be learned, but race consciousness is unborn and cannot be wholly unlearned. . . . Sentimental solidarity works wholly into the hands of the capitalist class and injures the revolutionary movement of the most advanced workers of this nation. . . . [97]

And in the year of Debs's unprecedented opportunity to drive a wedge into the party system, the 1912 Socialist *Campaign Book* carried an unmistakably nativist message:

Immigration presents for our serious consideration a formidable array of dangers. It is unnecessary to summarize the facts and the arguments which have been given. They are the two things which, of all that have been stated, seem the most important: the likelyhood of race annihilation and the possible degeneration of even the succeeding American type.

Nativism gelled as party doctrine in 1913, when the center-right secured control of the party. Long-simmering animosities toward the IWW erupted in 1912, cutting across other divisions and culminating in the expulsion of the IWW. Close to twenty-three thousand members left the party as a result—and with them, many of the internationalist defenders of the working-class melting pot. The purge of 1913 left the bulk of the party unsympathetic to the new immigrants who formed the bulk of the industrial work force and sapped the Debsian commitment to industrial unionism.

Oscar Handlin and others have suggested that the new immigration was, in the main, a wasteland for radicalism. But the profound strain of

[97]Socialist Party National Convention *Proceedings* (1912), 166ff.

the nativism in American socialism suggests that the obverse was equally true: that radicalism was a wasteland for new immigrants. American socialism offered new immigrants no serious organizational or political alternative, either to their ethnic isolation or to their "melting" into mainstream American pluralism, because at least on the matters of race and skill, it did not even offer an alternative to conservative trade unionism. Whether new immigrants might have responded to a different strain of socialism is moot. But undeniable is the fact that nativism locked most new immigrants out of the labor movement's mainstreams of both left and right. New immigrants would have to wait until the New Deal to find their place in American labor politics.

When the socialists bowed to trade-union nativism, the only labor-based party in national politics insulated itself from working-class majorities. Dominated by a membership of native-born and preferred-stock Americans, the Socialist party never made it its business to integrate new immigrants—and blacks, for that matter—into its own war against advancing capitalism. One result was that American socialists could never agree to organize industrial workers. Another—and Debs had warned of this—was that they had no broad and solid economic base from which to build the Socialist party into a central force in American politics. Yet another was that, even as Eugene Debs reached his zenith at the polls in 1912, he secured on average a share of the vote in the urban and industrial counties of New York, Pennsylvania, and Massachusetts only marginally greater than his share of the national popular vote.[98] Indeed, Debs did best far away from industrial constituencies, in areas where Populists had once been strong. Thus even in 1912 the AFL was essentially uncontested as the voice of labor in national politics.

[98]In Chicago, Debs received fewer Italian votes than Wilson, though he won a respectable 13 percent of the citywide vote; Nelli, 118. Debs did better in some Pennsylvania counties: in Allegheny and Westmoreland he took 15 percent of the vote. But on average in industrial Pennsylvania he controlled barely 7 percent of the vote. His national average was 6.2 percent. See Pennsylvania *Handbook* (1912).

CHAPTER 7

Forging Ties to the State, 1912–20

Q: And you would not support any kind of regulation, no matter how extreme might be the abuse?
A: Regulation by the state or—
Q: Yes, by the State.
A: No.
—Samuel Gompers to the Lockwood Commission, 1922

When the AFL entered the state under Wilson, it did so not to secure government protections for workers but to seek policies that would promote its own autonomy. The AFL's attitude toward the state followed from its politics of union preeminence. As it opposed wages and hours laws and social insurance, the AFL pressed from within the ruling coalition for relief from government interference: from injunctions and from antitrust liability. The only positive demands it made of government (where government was not the employer) had to do with securing relief from the visible hands of cheap labor: restrictions on immigration, "protections" for women, and regulation of child labor.[1] The AFL's political labors won it important recognitions and recommendations from government: a labor department; the relocation of the Immigration and Naturalization bureaus to the Labor Department; a promise of antitrust relief in the Clayton Act; a guarantee of jury trials for union members and leaders

[1] See legislative committee reports and presidential speeches in AFL Convention *Proceedings* and the *American Federationist*, 1906–16, especially Samuel Gompers, "Labor's Political Campaign: Its Causes and Progress—Labor's Duty," *American Federationist*, 19 (1912), 801–14. Stephen B. Wood notes that while the AFL was an intensely interested and helpful ally on child labor reform, it was not a principal actor in the struggle for child labor laws. Middle-class reformers took up the issue while the AFL was preoccupied with other political objectives. *Wood, Constitutional Politics in the Progressive Era* (1968), 32–38.

charged with criminal contempt; legislative restrictions on immigration; and incorporation, where appropriate, into the presidential advisory network.

It is perhaps ironic that the AFL elaborated its most vehement anti-statism—chiefly in the form of unbending opposition to social legislation—during the very years it was "in government" under Woodrow Wilson, and at the same time that it pressed from within the ruling coalition for state protections of union activities, legislative relief from court injunctions, and immigration reform. But the AFL's antistatist participation in the Democratic state was the practical application of its voluntarism.

When Samuel Gompers articulated voluntarism as the AFL's "pragmatic philosophy," he was responding to challenges to trade-union autonomy on several fronts. The overriding challenge, I have argued, was the expansion of the labor market through immigration. This expansion not only gave rise to ethnic and occupational differentiation and antagonism but to organizational jealousy as well. New immigrants had been used by employers to break unions, and new immigrants, if organized, would threaten old labor with a new, industrial unionism, so their increasing presence in industry heightened trade-union anxieties about organizational autonomy—even survival. Voluntarism, in its celebration of individual liberty and self-reliance, worked in this context to deny politics within the class and then to prevent the politicization of the class which might follow from political mediation of worker-employer relations.

Judicial intervention on the side of employers provided a further challenge to trade-union autonomy. Hostile federal rulings against striking and boycotting unions, beginning with the Pullman strike in 1894, had reduced the effectiveness of "economic action" and restricted the spread of the union shop. Various decisions lifted the labor question out of state legislatures and state courts more permeable to popular majorities and into the national arena under judicial surveillance.[2] What is more, these decisions entrenched a powerful and static jurisprudence in which unionism had no place. While laissez-faire constitutionalism brought unions within the orbit of restrictive laws, equity procedures, and Fourteenth Amendment interpretation, it denied unions legal rights and recognition. Unions were thus inside the law when it came to constraining activities but outside

---

[2]Arnold Paul, *Conservative Crisis and the Rule of Law* (1960), provides an illuminating discussion of the emergence of antilabor jurisprudence, especially in chaps. 6 and 7. See also Felix Frankfurter and Nathan Greene, *The Labor Injunction* (1930), and Elias Lieberman, *Unions before the Bar* (1950).

the law—without capacity to contract, for example—when it came to legal status and legal remedies.

Injunctions, fines, criminal contempt citations, and prison sentences were meted out seriatim by the federal judiciary beginning with *Debs* in 1894. The burden was onerous, on union leaders in particular, for though the courts actively intervened to obstruct union activity, they did so without granting legal personality to unions. Hence the members and leaders of unions were individually liable for union actions.[3] Moreover, many of the legal issues, and hence many of the remedies available to employers, were defined as matters of equity law, which foreclosed for unionists the possibility of exoneration by jury.[4] Beyond this, judicial application of the Sherman Anti-Trust Act against organized labor further hampered unionism by defining the activities through which unions sought to win recognition and autonomy in the workplace as activities in restraint of trade.

In its decisions against labor the Court altered existing political arrangements. The American constitutional scheme had decentralized power and politics, in part to bring government into proximity to the people and in part to impede the exercise of capricious or countermajoritarian coercive public authority by remote political actors. But in its interpretation of that constitutional scheme beginning in the 1890s, the Court began to nationalize many political questions and to centralize political power. It did so, however, to promote laissez-faire. Accordingly, the Court did not exercise its interpretative powers to allocate greater authority to national government. Rather, it developed a constitutionalism that located national power in the hands of the federal judiciary—power to oversee and intercept local policies and economic organization that interfered with rights the Court indentified as deserving national protection, namely, contract and property. Laissez-faire constitutionalism thus centered a weak state in a strong Court. This new jurisprudence weighed heavily upon unions, for in its defense of individual liberty it defined the associational claims and actions of individual workers as inimical to it.

Because laissez-faire constitutionalism gave the Court the central position in national government, the AFL defined the Court as the state. Because of the Court's unflinching hostility to labor, the AFL viewed the state as a crucial obstacle to trade unionism. And because the Court meted out harsh penalties to labor, the AFL viewed state action as unalterably

---

[3]E.g., *Loewe v. Lawlor,* 208 U.S. 274 (1908). The liability of unions as legal entities distinct from their members and leaders was not established until 1922, in *Coronado,* 259 U.S. 344. In this case the legal status of unions was established punitively rather than affirmatively.

[4]Frankfurter and Greene, chap. 1.

coercive. Labor's belief in the identity of Court and state fed into a labor politics that was suspicious of government and of the formalism associated with law. Accordingly, the Court not only pressed the AFL into politics (to secure relief through legislation from judicial interpretations) but also shaped its labor politics. The AFL rejected the possibility of friendly state interventions and, along with that, the possibility that labor-based political majorities in government could supervise such interventions. As Samuel Gompers would repeat:

> Several times the plain question has been put to me by members of the Senate Committee on Judiciary: "Mr. Gompers, what can we do to allay the causes of strikes that bring discomfort and financial suffering to all alike?" I have had to answer: "Nothing." . . . But it is difficult for lawyers to understand that the most important human justice comes through other agencies than the political. Economic justice will come through the organization of economic agencies, the increasing adjustment of economic relationships in accord with principles evolved through experience, the formulation of material scientific standards and the development of the principles and coordinating functions of management, based upon understanding of human welfare.[5]

The relationship between unions and the Court was an important component of the AFL's antistatist politics. As Gompers saw it, through the state and the law, workers could purchase only an "academic and theoretic liberty," and this at the cost of their practical, industrial rights. Still, the AFL's demands for political relief from the Court would help shift the balance among the branches, in particular the rise of the executive and the attendant expansions of government's administrative capacity. But the AFL's experiences under a Court-dominated state placed trade unionism squarely in opposition to efforts to broaden and centralize state authority.

In this connection, reformers, corporate liberals, and socialists posed yet another challenge to trade-union autonomy in their attempts to build a state friendlier to labor. The AFL regarded social insurance and wages and hours laws for men, for example, as hostile incursions by government, threatening to substitute a relationship between worker and state for the still tenuous relationship between worker and union. The AFL viewed legislation to socialize uncertainty, create social rights, and regulate the conditions of work as alternative, rather than complementary, to the bene-

[5]Samuel Gompers, *Seventy Years of Life and Labor*, vol. 2 (1925), 26.

fits allocated from union funds to union members and to the bargain struck in the wage contract. If important union functions were satisfied by government, the incentive to join and to remain loyal to unions would be correspondingly reduced. Policies friendly to workers were thus treated as impediments to trade-union autonomy, in the workplace and among wage earners. The organizational self-interest that underlay AFL opposition to social-welfare innovations was captured by one trade-union official:

> If you feed lions cooked meat, they are not going to roar. If you want the lions to roar you will have to hold raw meat under their noses, and then they will roar. The only way to get wage earners interested in the trade union movement and make it a driving force is to convince them that . . . it is only through strength, the fighting strength of that economic organization that you are going to get higher wages and shorter hours.[6]

The AFL, then, forged ties to the state at least in part to oppose reforms designed to ease the dislocations, hardships, and strife of capitalist industrialization. Its response to localized reforms was somewhat more flexible, but its opposition to national social reform was unambiguous. Even as the relationship between the AFL and the state changed under Woodrow Wilson, the AFL would not retreat from its limited view of that relationship.[7]

A final challenge to the AFL developed from socialist insurgency within the labor movement. The electoral rumblings of the Socialist party after 1900 and the dissidence of socialist-leaning unionists within the AFL jeopardized the AFL's claims to jurisdiction over the working class. More important, pressures from below threatened to plug the "hole" in the electorate as well as the "hole" in the labor movement upon which AFL autonomy depended. The successes of British Labour in electing candidates and winning trades disputes legislation to mitigate the effects of Taff Vale gave American socialists the weight of example as they mounted efforts to engage the AFL in class politics.[8]

---

[6]John Frey, quoted in Michael Rogin, "Voluntarism: The Political Functions of an Anti-Political Doctrine," in David Brody, ed., *The American Labor Movement* (1971), 114 n. 8.

[7]American unions were not unique in their suspicion of government, though union suspicion was unique in its duration, intensity, and political impact. See Chapter 1, n. 63.

[8]Henry Pelling, *Origins of the British Labour Party* (1965), chap. 10, Pelling, *A History of British Trade Unionism* (1976), 123–28, and Sidney and Beatrice Webb, *History of Trade Unionism,* rev. ed. (1920), 600, discuss the impact of Taff Vale on British labor. Jay Lovestone of the Workers' party of America describes the politicizing effect of injunctions in *The Government—Strikebreaker* (1923).

Against these efforts the AFL set voluntarism as its theoretical defense of "politics without class" and "corporatism without the state." But as it gave ideological celebration to individualism, liberty, and class neutrality, so the AFL discarded that aspect of voluntarism which cautioned political neutrality. In its place it developed ties to the Democratic party and the Democratic state. It thereby relied on associations with classes above to produce majorities friendly to trade-union interests. On the crucial and potentially politicizing antitrust question, for example, the AFL's friends in the National Civic Federation pushed for the removal of unions from the jurisdiction of the Sherman Act when they fought for the Hepburn Bill in 1908.[9] On the questions of immigration and "protective" labor legislation, which politicized the problem of entry into and competition within the labor market (and the labor movement), the AFL built alliances with liberal reformers, nativists, and Democrats to pressure the state for action. And on the pivotal issue of labor's legal status, the AFL used its electoral presence to argue, successfully, for compensatory political status.

The AFL's near-victories on these matters enhanced its political position, validated its political strategy, and sustained its continued regulation of the internal politics of the labor movement. The AFL answered corporate liberal, social statist, and socialist calls for political intervention in industrial capitalism, and its answer was voluntarism. But the persuasiveness of the voluntarist argument hinged on the capacity of union political strategy to produce political and institutional achievements. That requirement relaxed voluntarist dogma with respect to union participation in politics and produced a pragmatic political strategy keyed to the Democratic party's sympathy for trade-union autonomy. That strategy, though insufficient to win real relief from the Court and from the new immigration, brought the AFL into an accommodation with a friendly state and forged centers of labor privilege within it.

The AFL in Government

The victory of Wilsonian progressivism gave the AFL an opportunity to carve a historic place for itself in national politics and to press Jeffersonian principles against Rooseveltian social statism. Despite Wilson's reluctance to forward the "class" aims of organized labor, his presidency proved very friendly to the AFL. The AFL won unprecedented legislative

[9]Gabriel Kolko, *The Triumph of Conservatism* (1963), 134–38.

victories, particularly during Wilson's first term; secured the institutionalization of government concern for labor questions through the creation of a labor department; and won the appointment of labor allies to top
positions in government—William B. Wilson, ex-mineworker, UMW
official, and labor congressman, to the Labor Department, and Louis
Brandeis to the Supreme Court. The AFL enjoyed voice and access,
which it exercised to promote autonomous trade unionism.

What enabled the AFL to make good its promise of "direct participation . . . in the proceedings of the Federal Government"[10] was the clean
fit between AFL antistatism and Wilson's New Freedom. Wilson's defense of limited government was appealing to a labor establishment that
viewed centralized political authority as the real trust to be feared.[11] The
nostalgic localism in which much of Wilson's resistance to national social
policy was couched made sense to a trade unionism that idealized craft
autonomy, that had forged a modus vivendi in local politics, and whose
leader for a generation "would rather help in the inauguration of a revolution against compulsory insurance and regulation than submit."[12] As
Wilson had explained to workers in Buffalo during the campaign, in
language redolent of union antistatism,

> When you have the whole thing out . . . you will find that the programme of
> the new party legalizes monopolies and systematically subordinates work-
> ingmen to them and to plans made by the Government. . . . By what means,
> except open revolt, could we ever break the crust of our life again and
> become free men, breathing an air of our own, choosing and living lives that
> we wrought out for ourselves? Perhaps this new and all-conquering combina-
> tion between money and government would be benevolent to us, perhaps it
> would carry out the noble programme of social betterment, but who can
> assure us of that?[13]

[10]Gompers, "Labor's Political Campaign," 802.

[11]Gompers, *Seventy Years*, 2: 22–24. Gompers summarized his views on *economic* concentration to the Chicago Conference on Trusts in October 1907: "Our modern plan of production,
which . . . we call the trust system, is the most perfect yet attained. We do not, however, mean
to imply by this that the individuals who form trusts, who manipulate them, who profit by them,
are logically and inevitably right in many of the methods they employ or the lengths to which they
go. . . . [But] it is only fair to say that the greatest and most enlightened combinations of capital
in industry have not seriously questioned the right and, indeed, the advisability of organizations
among employees. There is economy of time and power and means of placing responsibility in
'collective bargaining' with employees which bring the best results for the benefit of all. Organized labor has less difficulty in dealing with large firms and corporations today than with many
individual employers or small firms." Quoted in Florence C. Thorne, *Samuel Gompers: American Statesman* (1957), 127.

[12]Gompers reacting to Congressman Meyer London's social insurance proposal, April 1916,
reprinted in Gompers, *Labor and the Employer* (1920), 149–51.

[13]Quoted in Goldman, *Rendez-vous with Destiny* (1952), 167.

The AFL's incorporation into the state under Wilson proceeded from its role in the campaign. Nineteen-twelve marked the Socialist party's strongest showing in a national election, but the party made little headway in most working-class constituencies. The industrial electorate generally split between Taft and Roosevelt, moreover, sustaining the AFL monopoly both as the only organized and coherent representation of the working class in national politics and as the labor constituency of the Democratic party. The coalition in which the AFL lodged itself was, interestingly, one dominated by the conservative and sparsely industrialized South. America's trade-union party was thus not only the party of privileged unionism but also the party of Jim Crow and states' rights. As such, it presided over innovation and reform while navigating among constituencies whose bases for coalition lay in their common antistatism and in the parallel interests of elite minorities to sustain immobility among potential majorities. One response of Wilson and his party to pressures from within the coalition—from the Southern elites and union labor—and to mounting counterpressures from business and reformers, was to enfold constituencies and interests into government and its processes rather than to decide between them. Connected was the tendency to create mechanisms rather than rules: a labor department, for example, but no labor policy; an administrative apparatus to regulate immigration but no effective immigration policy; legal weapons that unions could take into court but no clear affirmation of union rights. Yet the AFL welcomed these mechanisms. It preferred its interests to be brokered through democratic institutions, where the power of coherent votes could compete against the power of capital, rather than to collide with the interests of capital in courts invulnerable to democratic majorities and inaccessible to labor pressure.

The significance of the union-party tie became immediately apparent upon Wilson's inauguration. Delivering on his campaign covenant of friendship with union labor, Wilson appointed the AFL's choice, William B. Wilson, as the first Secretary of Labor.[14] Closely associated with the AFL, William Wilson made the Labor Department union labor's home:

Inasmuch . . . as it is ordinarily only through organization that the many in any class . . . can become articulate with reference to their common needs and aspirations, the Department is usually under a necessity of turning to the labor organizations that exist and such as may come into existence for

[14]John Lombardi, *Labor's Voice in the Cabinet* (1942, 1968), 75.

definite and trustworthy advice on the sentiments of the wage earning classes regarding their common welfare.[15]

The following year, the secretary reiterated his sympathies to the AFL convention:

I have never understood the trade union movement stood for anything else than justice to the workers. It never has desired to impose an injustice on anybody else. If securing justice to those who earn their bread in the sweat of their face constitutes partisanship, then count me as a partisan of labor.[16]

As secretary, Wilson worked to promote AFL goals. With the help of Assistant Secretary of Labor Louis B. Post—another well-credentialed, prolabor reformer—he redefined the activities of the Division of Information when it was transferred to the Labor Department in 1913. Insisting that the department would not "make itself a medium for conveying information of demands for wage earners where labor disputes are the cause of the demand," and that it would not work against American workers "by directing cheap alien labor to American labor markets already supplied . . . in excess" of job opportunities, Wilson transformed the division into the U.S. Employment Service. The refusal to supply workers to employers during strikes and lockouts sided the service squarely with the unions. And the service tied its information gathering and administration to public agencies (post offices and state and local labor bureaus), thereby insulating itself from direct employer participation.[17]

William Wilson forwarded union interests on other fronts as well. Empowered by Congress to "act as mediator . . . in labor disputes," he established within the department a division of conciliation based on principles of voluntary mediation. Importantly, the division signified government support for collective bargaining. Further, the department's efforts, although weakened by employer resistance, gave a political personality to unions similar to the industrial personality established by NCF labor policy: the collective bargaining assumed by mediation also assumed trade unionism. Reproducing the premises of NCF labor policy, moreover, federal conciliation anticipated the voluntary, mutual accommodation between unions and employers rather than formal (and coercive)

[15]Quoted in ibid., 92.
[16]AFL *Proceedings* (1914), 403.
[17]Discussed in Lombardi, 150–57.

intervention.[18] That the Wilson administration was generally sympathetic to mediation rather than intervention was indicated by the fact that indictments against union officials in two of the bitterest strikes of the day, the West Virginia and Colorado coal strikes of 1913–14, were entered without the approval of the attorney general.[19] And that President Wilson stood by his secretary was clear in 1914 when coal operators at Ludlow refused government conciliation of the Colorado coal strike on the grounds that any conciliators selected by the labor secretary would be "partisans of the men who have made necessary the presence of the federal troops in the strike district." President Wilson replied: "Allow me to protest with great earnestness against the implications of your letter that the Department of Labor 'as now manned' is likely to express in all its opinions a pronounced bias. I have never known a more careful and judicial mind than that of Secretary Wilson."[20] Indeed, that President Wilson acted as often as he did to adjust industrial disputes has been attributed chiefly to Secretary Wilson's influence.[21]

On legislative matters the secretary lobbied the AFL position, most notably for immigration restriction and injunction relief. Although unable to prevent presidential vetoes of two immigration bills (the second veto fell to an override), Wilson won the president's approval of a crucial anti-injunction rider to the Sundry Civil Appropriations Bill. The rider prohibited the use of Justice Department funds to prosecute unions for antitrust violations, at a minimum suggesting the willingness of Congress and the president to withhold their complicity from judicial application of the Sherman Act against unions—a complicity for which the previous Democratic president, Grover Cleveland, had been punished resoundingly at his own party convention. Secretary Wilson's pro-union advocacy, along with congressional and presidential policy rewards for the AFL's electoral contributions, opened for union labor its magic moment in government.

As the AFL worked to secure policy outcomes, it was aided by a rare moment of party government in American politics.[22] Using the disciplinary weapons of patronage and caucus to give programmatic coherence to

[18]The AFL opposed government-managed collective bargaining until the New Deal, for example. See Irving Bernstein, *The New Deal and Collective Bargaining Policy* (1950), chaps. 1, 2.
[19]Dallas Jones, "The Enigma of the Clayton Act," *Industrial and Labor Relations Review*, 10 (January 1957), 204.
[20]Ray Stannard Baker, *Woodrow Wilson, Life and Letters*, vol. 4 (1931), 392.
[21]See Edward Berman, *Labor Disputes and the President of the United States* (1924), 253; Lombardi, 356.
[22]Richard Bolling, *Power in the House* (1968), pt. 2. James Ceaser examines Wilson's version of party democracy in *Presidential Selection* (1979), chap. 4.

the Democratic state, the first Wilson administration generated symbols and policies that recognized union influence in party and state. Chief among them were the Seamen's Act, the Clayton Act, and child labor regulation. Importantly, party government served union labor from different directions. On some issues, presidential leadership clearly bludgeoned a reticent Congress into cooperation, but on others, the Clayton Act among them, internal party pressures subdued presidential and congressional conservatism.

Woodrow Wilson also convened the Commission on Industrial Relations early in his first term and offered Louis Brandeis the chair. When Brandeis declined, ambivalent about taking on a government position, Wilson gave the appointment to Frank Walsh, another reformer with solid credentials as labor's friend. Several years later, in its report and recommendations, the commission would greatly strengthen the political claims of organized labor. It exposed "industrial feudalism," defined the organization of labor as a right, and concluded that industrial feudalism was the rule whenever labor was prevented from organizing. Further, though the commission by no means spoke with one voice, it explicitly criticized in its report the antilabor interventions of the federal courts and called for legislation to protect labor's right to organize and to empower the Department of Labor to prosecute corporations for infringing on union rights.[23] The change in the government's tone toward labor even extended to federal troops. By some accounts, those sent in following the Ludlow Massacre in 1914 demonstrated an uncharacteristic concern for the workers' rights.

All in all, the AFL won some twenty-six measures under Wilson. The labor clauses of the Clayton Act were clearly the AFL's most heralded achievements under the first Wilson administration, despite Wilson's refusal to concede immunity from antitrust liability to organized labor. They were also the labor enactments most urgently required, for judicial rancor now reached beyond union activity: lower-court rulings in the *Hitchman* case had declared the United Mine Workers an illegal monopoly.[24]

The cooperative legislative efforts of Gompers and the AFL's friends in Congress exacted compromise from President Wilson and turned recalcitrant presidential silence on fundamental union issues into a half-step toward the Democratic promise of 1912.[25] Exempting unions from anti-

[23]U.S. Commission on Industrial Relations, *Final Report* (1916).
[24]*Hitchman Coal and Coke Co. v. Mitchell*, 202 Fed. 512 (1912); 214 Fed. 685 (1914).
[25]Jones, 207–18.

trust proscriptions, under certain circumstances, and narrowing the reach of the injunction remedy, under certain circumstances, the Clayton Act inched union labor toward its goal of autonomy from judicial interference. There were clear problems with the new law, not the least of which being that Woodrow Wilson prevented passage of strong and forthright labor clauses and thus left it to the judicial scrutiny of a Court dominated by Taft appointments (and later by Taft himself) to determine the meaning of a vague law "conceived in political timidity."[26] What that meaning would be, Taft foreshadowed in his presidential address to the American Bar Association in 1914: he argued that the Clayton Act merely affirmed existing law and predicted that the courts would reject any labor immunities and protections.[27] Still the act, though marred by ambiguous statutory language, interpretive controversy, and judicial predisposition, did arm labor with some statutory weapons for battle in court. It would ultimately fall to judicial interpretation,[28] but the Clayton Act amended equity procedures to allow for jury trials in cases of criminal contempt arising under it (thus answering a major union complaint arising from the *Bucks Stove and Range* case); circumscribed, though it did not bar, the use of injunctions in labor disputes; and exempted labor and farm organizations from antitrust liability when they "lawfully" acted to seek "legitimate" objectives.[29]

Though the Clayton Act would not withstand judicial assault, that assault lay in the future. Thus Gompers praised the Clayton Act upon

[26]Jones, passim; Stanley I. Kutler, "Labor, the Clayton Act, and the Supreme Court," *Labor History*, 3 (1962), 19–39.

[27]Kutler, 23–24. Taft argued in 1921 that it was obvious at the time of its enactment that the Clayton Act did not promise immunity to labor unions in unlawful conspiracies: "As long ago as 1914 . . . the president of the American Bar Association, in discussing this then new legislation pointed out that labor unions were going to be disappointed in their assumption that it enabled them lawfully to engage in a 'compound' boycott directed against and intended to injure the interstate trade of an employer." Taft, "Gompers and the Law," Philadelphia *Ledger*, January 12, 1921. See also Taft, "Labor Is Not a Commodity," *New Republic*, December 1, 1916, pp. 112–14.

[28]Frankfurter and Greene, 161–82, agree that the language of the act was so ambiguous as to leave interpretation fully to the courts. Between 1916 and 1920 lower courts applied Section 20 in thirteen cases in which opinions are reported. In ten of these the Clayton Act did not stand in the way of injunctions. Courts construed Clayton not to change preexisting law, to be inapplicable where strikes were to *unionize* (rather than to improve working conditions), to leave the boycott issue unresolved, and to be inoperative once employers had filled vacancies created by strikes (striking workers, once replaced, were not "employees" protected by the act). Eventually the Supreme Court joined the lower courts in gutting the act. As Frankfurter and Greene concluded, "the more things [were] legislatively changed, the more they remained the same judicially."

[29]Arthur Link, *Woodrow Wilson and the Progressive Era* (1954), 69; Frankfurter and Greene, 166. See the dissenting opinions in *Paine Lumber Co. v. Neal*, 244 U.S. 459 (1917).

passage as the "Industrial Magna Carta upon which the working people will rear their structure of individual freedom."[30] Incorporating language developed by Gompers and endorsed by the AFL years before, Section 6 of the act declared that "the labor of a human being is not a commodity or an article of commerce."[31] It further held that "nothing contained in the anti-trust laws shall be construed to forbid the existence and operation of labor organizations . . . nor shall such organizations, orders or associations, or the members thereof, be held or construed to be illegal combinations or conspiracies in restraint of trade."[32] Section 20 spelled out what activities labor organizations could indulge in legally, thus impeding arbitrary actions—specifically, injunctions—by the Court.

The AFL's policy achievements under Wilson were important components of the incipient broker state that developed under the pressure of two progressivisms. The New Deal would "save pluralism" by institutionalizing a much broader labor presence in the broker state, but the New Freedom legitimated pluralism, by dealing union labor into the Democratic state. Alongside a national regulatory apparatus extracted from the two progressivisms were created centers of labor privilege in national government.

As important as the AFL's statutory and institutional achievements, however, was its successful deflection of many friendly interventions around which a welfare state might have congealed. Typically the AFL feared that social interventions would make the state a surrogate for unions, whether in the economy or in politics. Public policies might supplant the union contract; political mobilization to influence or wield control over those policies might replace unionization; either some new movement or dependency might displace organization and autonomy; the wage-earning mass might depose the unionized elite as labor's representative before employers and presidents; and the AFL might lose its autonomy to speak for the whole class while acting principally in its own self-interest.

Thus the AFL resisted proposals for a minimum wage, maximum hours, and social insurance. In fact the AFL retreated from a central and historic trade-union demand: maximum-hours legislation for workers. The

[30]Samuel Gompers, "The Charter of Industrial Freedom," American Federationist, 21 (1914), 971–72. See also John S. Smith, "Organized Labor and Government in the Wilson Era," Labor History, 3 (1962), 273; Gompers, Seventy Years, 2, chap. 36, and "Labor's Influence in Congress," Literary Digest, 48 (June 13, 1914), 1423–24.
[31]AFL Proceedings (1908), President's Report.
[32]Frankfurter and Greene, 142.

trade-union movement in general, and the AFL in particular, had always opposed minimum wage legislation, except for women, on the theory that trade unions could secure optimal wages through direct action against employers. It had, however, fought for enforcement of federal hours legislation since its inception. But the AFL's struggle for protections for government workers did not feed into a similar struggle for all workers. Reasoning that it had no interest in securing protections for workers in the private sector other than through economic action—a logic at which Gompers had hinted in his commentary on *Lochner*[33]—the AFL had refused to support a more comprehensive eight-hour law that would govern conditions in industry. And in 1914 the AFL openly opposed it. This was not a policy departure for the federation; Gompers had hinted at voluntarist reasoning on the hours question as early as 1883:

> Q: Let me see if I understand your idea about this eight hour law. . . . You propose a rule of action by which shall be prohibited the exaction of more than eight hours of labor daily of any one man. Now, suppose the man wants to work more than eight hours, would you favor a law prohibiting it?

> Gompers: No, I would not favor such a law. I believe that the regulation of that would easily evolve out of the organized efforts of labor and the means that would be taken to agitate the question and educate the workers to understand that it would be to their benefit . . . to abstain from more than eight hours' work.

> Q: You think that would become the universal custom and rule?

> Gompers: Yes, sir.[34]

The AFL's position, given its enhanced political status under Wilson, effectively put an end to the hours question and derailed the "women first" strategy of social reformers. Even the *Bunting* decision in 1917,[35] extending hours protection to men, had little practical impact and failed to reopen consideration of laws on working hours.[36]

Only where government was the employer or women the workers was the AFL interested in political regulation of the terms of employment. In

[33]Samuel Gompers, "Bakers Lose at Law, But Win in Fact," *American Federationist,* 12 (1905), 361–64.

[34]U.S. Senate, Committee on Education and Labor, *Relations between Capital and Labor,* Hearings, vol. 1 (1885), 296–300.

[35]*Bunting v. Oregon,* 243 U.S. 426 (1917).

[36]Elizabeth Brandeis, "Hours Laws for Men," in Don Lescohier and Brandeis, *History of Labor in the United States, 1896–1932* (1935), 540–57.

the public sector, public policy—for example, the eight-hour day for federal workers—was the analogue to the union contract, the state the analogue to employers, and the labor lobby the analogue to unions. Accordingly, the AFL did not oppose government action on this score—indeed, it expected such action from a prolabor state. In the private sector, where the AFL regarded government intervention as emasculating to unionism and union manhood, the AFL at least tolerated and sometimes actively pursued special protections for women.[37] The special role of women as mothers, on the one hand, and the special position of women in the labor market, on the other, differentiated women from male workers and, in the AFL's view, justified state paternalism toward them. Hence the AFL defended hours legislation for women and welfare pensions for widowed mothers.[38]

State intrusion into the domain of male workers, by contrast, it generally would not tolerate. Samuel Gompers repeatedly editorialized throughout this period in opposition to social insurance; typical are these words, from 1917: "Social insurance cannot remove or prevent poverty. It does not get at the causes of social injustice. The only agency that does get at the cause of poverty is the organized labor movement."[39]

The AFL position on social insurance, while unambivalent, was not uncomplicated. Though the AFL greeted proposals for health and unemployment insurance with unwavering opposition,[40] it ultimately acquiesced to workmen's compensation in hazardous industries and gave mild support to noncontributory old-age pensions.[41] Gompers and others had initially resisted accident insurance, pushing instead for tougher employer liability laws to enhance prospects for verdicts by sympathetic juries.[42] By 1910, however, the AFL had withdrawn its opposition and

[37]Arguing that "it is the so-called competition of the unorganized and defenseless woman worker, the girl and the wife, that often tends to reduce the wages of the father and the husband," Gompers at one point advocated equal pay for women and defended the minimum wage for women as a step toward it. Samuel Gompers, "Should the Wife Help Support the Family?" *American Federationist*, 13 (1906), 36.

[38]Florence Kelley explained the AFL's support of protective labor legislation: "men who saw their own occupations threatened by unwelcome competitors, demanded restrictions upon the hours of work of those competitors for the purpose of rendering women less desirable as employees. Quoted in Ann Hill, "Protective Labor Legislation for Women," in Barbara Babcock et al., *Sex Discrimination and the Law* (1975), 35–36.

[39]*American Federationist*, 24 (1917), 47.

[40]E.g., ibid., 23 (1916), 270–71.

[41]See Harry Weiss, "Employers' Liability and Workmen's Compensation," in Lescohier and Brandeis, 564–610; AFL *Proceedings* (1908), 97.

[42]Robert Asher discusses labor struggles to win employer liability legislation in "Failure and Fulfillment: Agitation for Employers' Liability Legislation and the Origins of Workmen's Compensation in New York State, 1876–1910," *Labor History*, 24 (1983), 198–222.

250

was supporting state-level accident insurance policies. On workmen's compensation the AFL demonstrated political flexibility, as it did on certain other social policies that were not universalistic even within states, that had no equivalent enforceable by unions (e.g., factory inspection), and that did not rely on national government. But where social welfare innovations assumed or promoted dependency on central government, the AFL was adamant in its insistence on the mutual self-reliance of workers through their autonomous associations.

It was the national insurance schemes developed by reform elites and one or two socialist congressmen which provoked from Gompers his most impassioned celebrations of individual and associational autonomy. Not only did the AFL never identify social insurance as a central labor demand, it used its voice in government to defend trade unionism against the use of the state for wage earners, the unemployed, and the poor. Though the AFL did not represent an absolute consensus among unionists on many social welfare issues—the New York State Federation of Labor endorsed health insurance, for example—the AFL's opposition was the only politically recognized position.[43]

Only on the issue of old-age relief did the AFL admit of any role for the state in the affairs of male workers in private industry. In some measure, AFL views on this matter were conditioned by the central government's long-standing role in providing pension benefits to Civil War veterans. Thus Gompers had ventured in 1883:

> If the government will take men as soldiers to fight their battles, and, in consequence of injuries received, give them pensions, I think that a man who works from the earliest time that he can work is entitled to some consideration in his old age. How that is to be arranged is probably more than I should attempt to say. To whom the responsibility belongs I cannot say, but I think that it is right that such a man should be cared for, and that there is that responsibility somewhere.[44]

In 1908 Gompers conceded the need to deal with the problem of old-age dependency by political intervention,[45] and in 1909 the AFL convention

---

[43]Roy Lubove, *The Struggle for Social Security, 1900–1935* (1968), 85. Ann Shola Orloff and Theda Skocpol discuss local union support for social innovations in "Why Not Equal Protection? Explaining the Politics of Public Social Welfare in Britain and the United States, 1880s–1920s," paper presented to the American Sociological Association, 1983, pp. 43–46.

[44]*Relations between Capital and Labor*, Hearings, 289.

[45]AFL *Proceedings* (1908), 97.

endorsed a proposal introduced in Congress by future labor secretary William B. Wilson. AFL support for Wilson's proposal—to create an Old Age Home Guard of the U.S. Army—did not, however, signal a retreat from antistatism, for the plan itself hardly constituted an innovation in social welfare. Under the scheme, elderly American citizens would quite literally earn their "pay": in return for enlisting and reporting to the War Department once a year on the state of patriotism in their neighborhoods, they would receive $120 annually.[46] This sum was less than the average pension benefit in 1896 for Civil War veterans and not even one-fourth the average annual wage for an unskilled, new-immigrant Pennsylvania steel-worker in 1907.[47]

William Wilson's proposal, moreover—however primitive and meager as a social policy—did not call for an expansion of the state's role regarding old-age security. Significantly, it was connected symbolically to the Civil War pension system, which had treated dependency relief as something earned through service in the Union Army and had been distributive in its implications.[48] Nonetheless the Old Age Home Guard did not become a salient demand for the AFL, even after 1912 when Wilson's appointment to the new Department of Labor gave the AFL a berth in government. Nor did more universalistic old-age pension policies win even limited AFL acquiescence during the interlude of Democratic control.[49]

Health and unemployment insurance proposals aroused the AFL's most vehement opposition. Gompers attacked health insurance as paternalistic and "repugnant to free born citizens,"[50] while a member of the AFL's Legislative Committee charged that physical examinations would allow employers to dismiss "able-bodied, skilled workmen . . . at the recommendation of the company physicians who found in them the disease of unionism."[51] Further, Gompers condemned unemployment insurance as

[46]*Report* of the Commission on Old Age Pensions (1910), 339–44, cited in Orloff and Skocpol, 54.

[47]Heywood T. Sanders, "Paying for the Bloody Shirt," in Barry Rundquist, ed., *Political Benefits* (1980), 137. Stanley Aronowitz, *False Promises* (1973), 150, provides the wage rates that are the basis of this (merely illustrative) calculation.

[48]The program figured prominently in party competition, mostly as a Republican weapon. Considerable discretion was allowed to the Pension Bureau. Further, many of the most "needy" constituencies were defined out of the system: all post–Civil War immigrants (i.e., most industrial workers), most blacks, and most Southerners. Pensions reached not quite a million people in 1896.

[49]Daniel Nelson, *Unemployment Insurance* (1969), 67–68.

[50]*American Federationist*, 23 (1916), 270–71 and 347.

[51]Quoted in Lubove, 85.

an invitation to the state to "investigate into and regulate the lives, the conduct and the freedom of America's workers."[52] He sermonized, even as the AFL reaped favorable labor policies from the Democratic state:

> Whither are we drifting? There is a strange spirit abroad in these times. The whole people is hugging the delusion that law is a panacea. Whatever is ill . . . or the ideal, immediately follows the suggestion—enact a law. . . . If wages are low, a law or a commission is the remedy proposed. What can be the result of this tendency but the softening of the moral fibre of the people? When there is unwillingness to accept responsibility for one's life and for making the most of it then there is a loss of strong, red-blooded rugged independence and will power to grapple with the wrong of the world and to establish justice through the volition of those concerned.[53]

In Europe, working-class militancy, competition from labor parties, and trade-union pressures were eliciting protections, pensions, and compensation for old, sick, disabled, and jobless workers from governments; at the same time a social welfare vacuum developed in the United States. Though European labor did not typically formulate or promulgate social policies, it created the context and provided the constituencies for such policies. As a result, unions were frequently incorporated into the administration of the social policies that were substituted for union programs. Where labor posed a political threat—through parties, militancy, and mobilization—governments tended either to anticipate or to respond with social welfare schemes. There was no such threat in the United States, and no such policy until the New Deal.

In Britain, union expansion and the "worker's rebellion" combined with increasing union support for the Labour party to invite social welfare innovations from the Liberal government.[54] (The conversion of the miners from Liberalism in 1909 was particularly significant.) By 1912 a variety of public schemes had been launched: improved workmen's compensation (1906), old-age pensions (1908), sickness and unemployment insurance

---

[52]Quoted in Louis Reed, *The Labor Philosophy of Samuel Gompers* (1930), 116.

[53]Gompers in the *American Federationist*, 22 (1915), 113.

[54]See Paul Adelman, *The Rise of the Labour Party, 1880–1945* (1972), chap. 3; George Dangerfield, *The Strange Death of Liberal England* (1935, 1961), chap. 4; and Bentley Gilbert, *The Evolution of National Insurance in Great Britain* (1966), 211, 256–79. Union membership doubled in Britain between 1905 and 1913–14, from 11 percent of the labor force to 22 percent. In the United States between 1906 and 1916 union membership also doubled—but only to 10 percent of the labor force. See John D. Stephens, *The Transition from Capitalism to Socialism* (1979), 115.

(1911), and a minimum wage in the "sweated" trades and for miners (1909 and 1912). Labour's role in the development of these policies varied, to be sure. Labour improved the Workmen's Compensation Act of 1906, and the Trades Union Congress made old-age pensions its number-one platform plank in 1907, but British labor was generally skeptical of unemployment insurance. In some cases, labor demands lay behind Liberal policies, as in the Minimum Wage Act of 1912; in others, labor suspicions lay behind the way that policies were administered, as in the Board of Trade's decision to integrate unions into the administration of unemployment insurance.[55]

In the United States, AFL pressures inside the Democratic government, its claim to speak for the whole class, and its dogmatic opposition to social legislation concealed the context and the constituency for social reform. Unions and labor parties in Britain and Germany generally favored state involvement to offset the problems of dependency and risk. In the United States, by contrast, the AFL insisted that relief was inimical to red-blooded Americanism, and that, anyway, trade unionism, if granted autonomy and a tightened labor market (through restricted immigration) was the real solution to the "social question."[56]

The defeat for social statism that Woodrow Wilson's election signified was more than merely symbolic and electoral. With Wilson's rise to power and the AFL's emergence as the labor arm of the Democratic party, both workers and unions escaped the interventions of a Lloyd George. The voluntarist state would not open its treasury to compensate for the failures of industrial democracy, nor would it offset the price paid by millions of industrial workers for their exclusion from those institutions of industrial democracy, the unions. With the AFL entrenched as the central labor force in politics, the only price to be paid for the renewal of liberal democracy was the promotion of the AFL's autonomy from courts, immigration, and the state.

Despite its crucial presence in the Democratic state, the AFL did not win on everything. The AFL exercised its force, even if it was the central labor force in politics, from a subordinate political position. Woodrow Wilson's distaste for "class" legislation and his concern to secure business approval for his antitrust program overrode his ties to union labor and

[55]Gilbert, 256, 279–80. From the beginnings of the unemployment system in Britain, the Board of Trade drew unions in insured trades into its administration. Unions could elect to become an administrator for the government, and members could draw their benefits through union offices.
[56]Nelson, 4, 66.

produced an ambiguous anti-injunction statute, open to conflicting and eviscerating interpretations. Further, Wilson's electoral need to transcend his own nativist scholarship placed immigration relief beyond the AFL's grasp until 1917, when the Congress overrode Wilson's second veto of the literacy test. More important, government grew, and its activities expanded. At the national level, dispersed authority became more centralized as Wilson worked to create a presidency capable of programmatic leadership. So far did Wilson take the nation toward redeeming the Progressive promise of 1912 that an impressive roster of corporatist, regulatory, and welfare progressives associated with Roosevelt, including Herbert Croly, flocked to the Wilson camp in 1916.[57]

And there were direct assaults on trade-union autonomy as well. Wilson threatened state intrusion into workplace economic action when he advocated compulsory arbitration in industrial disputes.[58] Moreover, the AFL, under the pressure of impending war, was unable to forestall other state encroachments onto traditional trade-union turf: the Adamson Act, for example, established an eight-hour day for railroad workers. The railroad brotherhoods generally viewed the Adamson legislation as an acceptable way out of a deadlocked labor dispute, but Gompers was quite unhappy:

Government power grows by what it feeds on. Give an agency any political power and it at once tries to reach out after more. Its effectiveness depends upon increasing power. This has been demonstrated by the experience of the railroad workers in the enactment of the Adamson law. When Congress exercised the right to establish eight hours for regulating railroad men it also considered a complete program for regulating railroad workers which culminated in taking from them the right to strike and the conscription act providing for compulsory service.[59]

While national security and political considerations made room for policy disputes between the AFL and the Wilson administration, the union-party tie gave the AFL the voice and access with which to haggle and compromise. Particular disagreements did not diminish the broader significance of the Democratic regime: the willingness of state and party to broker labor claims. Congress and the president proved this by their incorporation of unions into governmental processes; they proved it in their enactment of measures friendly toward the AFL. Union labor was

[57]Link, 239–40 n. 42.
[58]Smith, 271–72.
[59]American Federationist, 24 (1917), 48; Gompers, Seventy Years, 2: 143–44.

even beginning to penetrate the Court, though real changes there would be slower to arrive: Wilson added a voice for unionism and a voice against judicial interference in legislative experiments when, after consultations with Gompers, among others, he appointed Louis Brandeis to the Supreme Court in 1916.

Its mission in government far from complete, the AFL hailed the accomplishments of the first Wilson administration and campaigned vigorously to help Wilson win his second term. Unionism was in fact more prosperous under Wilson: it had a cabinet-level department; William B. Wilson's appointment had set a precedent that future secretaries of labor be labor men (and for the next twenty years they were); and in the Clayton Act, unionism won a few defensive legal weapons where none had existed before. In this friendly climate, moreover, trade-union membership had nearly doubled over 1906 levels and was fast approaching four million. So the AFL redoubled its electoral efforts to return Wilson and the Democrats to office: Gompers and Andrew Furuseth even wrote the Democratic National Committee's campaign pamphlet, *Wilson and Labor*. Gompers himself worked so actively for Wilson's reelection that in his memoirs he unabashedly took credit for Wilson's success.[60]

The contraction of Democratic majorities in Congress and the war in Europe created a more uncertain political climate after 1916; nonetheless the second Wilson administration continued to promote the AFL. With America's entry into World War I, Wilson drew the AFL deeply into government service; meanwhile Congress delivered an omnibus immigration statute (over Wilson's veto), including a literacy test, as well as the more rigorously restrictive Asiatic Barred Zone Act.[61] During the war, Gompers was drafted onto the advisory committee of the Council of Defense; later he was made chair of the subcommittee on labor, which handled questions regarding wages, hours, and collective bargaining in war-related industries. The secretary of labor was designated War Labor Administrator, and in that capacity he continued to work closely with the AFL. When the conciliation services of the Labor Department were formalized in the War Labor Board, Frank Walsh and W. Jett Lauck were among its members. The board adopted a wartime labor code that satisfied union concerns for recognition and protection from arbitrary dismissal by

[60]Gompers, *Seventy Years*, 1: 548–49. The AFL has even been credited with carrying Ohio and California to give Wilson his narrow but winning margin of 600,000 votes. See Wilfred Binkley, *American Political Parties* (1964), 368–69.

[61]The act (passed in 1917) did not cover the Japanese, since the Gentlemen's Agreement concluded under Roosevelt was still in force. But it did prohibit the entry of most other Asians.

anti-union employers. Finally, trade unionists were designated the managers of labor relations in every government venture in war production, and the president of the United Mine Workers was given a seat on the Food and Fuel Administration.

The Elusive Fruits of Labor Politics

The AFL's political privilege was abruptly and bitterly interrupted in the aftermath of World War I. Resurgent trade-union economic action and an explosion of labor militancy stoked bourgeois anxieties about the place of labor in the political economy.[62] Despite its accommodationist stance toward state and party, organized labor was increasingly perceived as the conduit of class politics. Class-neutral nativism surrendered to class polarity as middle-class nativists joined anti-union employers to define labor organizations as intrinsically un-American.

In this climate the second Wilson administration betrayed its union allies, enjoining the 1919 coal strike under the antistrike provisions of the wartime Lever Act. This came as a particular blow to the AFL, which had acquiesced to the act only after the president had promised that it would not be used against labor, and which assumed that the act had become inoperative upon the signing of the Armistice.[63] In a few short years the AFL's ties to the state had clearly frayed. When the Democratic party betrayed its union partners in 1920, omitting an anti-injunction plank from its platform for the first time since 1896, the union-party tie loosened as well. Although the AFL formally endorsed the Democratic nominee, James Cox, many labor organizations deserted the Democrats. Some forty labor leaders went so far as favorably to contrast Republican Warren Harding's dubious labor record to that of the Democratic administration.[64]

The Democratic betrayal enhanced the centrality of the Court as political superintendent of industrial society. Outside the "class compromise" initiated under the prewar Democratic state, the Court dealt repeated blows to trade unionism. The Court's power to nullify made problematic any change by legislation while "the correction of judicial infelici-

[62]For accounts of the dramatic strike wave of 1919, see "The Revolution—1919," *Nation*, October 4, 1919, pp. 452ff.; Robert K. Murray, *Red Scare* (1955); Melvyn Dubofsky, *We Shall Be All* (1969); Dubofsky and Van Tine, *John L. Lewis* (1977); and William Luechtenberg, *The Perils of Prosperity, 1914–1932* (1958).

[63]Lombardi, 322; Leuchtenberg, 76.

[64]Robert H. Ziegler, *Republicans and Labor, 1919–1929* (1969), 34–46.

257

ties . . . by judicial recantation," as Thomas Reed Powell noted, would be impossible until the Court itself changed.[65] In 1915 it ruled in *Coppage* that a state law prohibiting yellow dog contracts violated the due-process guarantee of the Fourteenth Amendment.[66] The Supreme Court's ruling in *Hitchman Coal and Coke Co. v. Mitchell* in 1917 was particularly foreboding, an augur of the judicial assault on trade-union autonomy that was to come. In that case the Court judged the United Mine Workers an illegal combination under the Sherman Anti-Trust Act, held that the union violated the company's property rights when it tried to unionize mineworkers, affirmed the yellow dog contract then in force in the company, and upheld the use of injunctions to enforce judicial pronouncements. Between 1918 and 1922 the Court further eroded union protections under the Clayton Act; offered the Fourteenth Amendment shield to employers against state-level limitations on the labor injunction;[67] and, giving unions legal personhood for the first time, held unions to be legally liable associations in what Gompers denounced as "America's Taff Vale."[68]

At midpoint in the Democratic tenure, then, the Court began to intimate the gutting of Clayton Act protections for labor which would culminate in the *Duplex, American Steel Foundries,* and *Coronado* decisions of 1921 and 1922.[69] Emphasizing the requirement in the labor clauses of the Clayton Act that activities be "lawful" and "peaceful," the Court in *Duplex* held the secondary boycott to be outside the injunction protections of the Clayton Act. Applying the same logic in *American Steel Foundries,* the Court found picketing to be likewise outside the immunities provided in Clayton, because "persuasion or communication attempted in such a presence and under such conditions was anything but peaceable and lawful."[70] (Taft became chief justice shortly before this decision was ren-

[65]Thomas Reed Powell, *Vagaries and Varieties in Constitutional Interpretation* (1965), 14.
[66]*Coppage v. Kansas,* 236 U.S. 1 (1915).
[67]*Truax v. Corrigan,* 257 U.S. 312 (1921).
[68]Samuel Gompers, "Freedom's Legalistic Octopus," *American Federationist,* 29 (1922), 504–11. Viewing the analogy narrowly, and thus missing the point that it was the breakdown of the MacDonald-Gladstone agreement, and the assertion of political independence by British labor through a new parliamentary party in the aftermath of Taff Vale, that produced the Trades Disputes Act in 1906, Gompers drew the lesson that it was the American court that explained the backwardness of American labor law in contrast to English reforms. "America's Taff Vale" inspired ever more furious attacks from Gompers against court and state but no impulse to independent political effort.
[69]*Paine Lumber Company v. Neal,* 244 U.S. 459 (1917); *Duplex Co. v. Deering,* 254 U.S. 443, 465 (1921); *American Steel Foundries v. Tri-City Trades Council,* 257 U.S. 184 (1921); United Mineworkers v. Coronado Coal Company, 259 U.S. 344 (1922).
[70] 257 U.S. 184 (1921), 205.

dered.) And in *Coronado* the Court resolved the question of labor's legal status by pulling unions fully within its punitive framework of legal liability. These judicial maneuvers elicited from Gompers an ever more vigilant defense of unions against the state:

> There is a considerable movement toward the extension of legalistic machinery for the control of human labor power. There is a movement which has as its object and its fetish the erection of a vast machinery of state for the regulation of human activities. . . . As between those who believe that law . . . is for the protection of freedom and for the promotion of justice, and those who believe that every social activity . . . should be subjected to the control of law, there is undoubtedly a great contest. . . . It is but one of the paradoxes of history that those who profess a belief in the destruction of the present order of things should find themselves joined in the trend toward this legalistic super-state by those who lean backward in reaction toward yesterday.[71]

Finally, the Court nullified reform measures that had enjoyed AFL support, namely, protections for women and children.[72] The Court's ruling in 1922 against the child labor tax led Gompers to reaffirm the virtues of economic action: "The only reason children are at work in the textile industry—and that is where there is the greatest abuse of childhood—is because *the union is not yet strong enough to accomplish their liberation.*"[73] And when the Court invalidated the minimum wage for women in 1923,[74] Gompers reissued his call for union autonomy from the state, proposing, as the route to that autonomy, a constitutional amendment revoking the power of judicial review.[75]

When the Democratic state yielded to judicial and Republican control in 1921, the AFL entered a lean decade. Under the pressures of a renewed open-shop campaign, welfare capitalism, and vigorous antilabor jurisprudence, union membership, which had doubled under Wilson, receded to

---

[71]Samuel Gompers, "The Courts and Mr. Taft on Labor," *American Federationist,* 28 (1921), 223.

[72]*Hammer v. Dagenhart,* 247 U.S. 251 (1918), struck down a federal prohibition on the interstate sale of the products of companies in which children under the age of fourteen were employed; and *Bailey v. Drexel,* 259 U.S. 20 (1922), invalidated a federal tax on the profits of companies employing children.

[73]Samuel Gompers, "Let Us Save Our Children," *American Federationist,* 29 (1922), 413–14, my emphasis.

[74]*Adkins v. Children's Hospital,* 261 U.S. 525 (1923).

[75]Samuel Gompers, "Take Away Its Usurped Power," *American Federationist,* 30 (1923), 399–401.

pre-Wilson lows by 1923. By 1929 unions were viable in only a handful of industries, and the strike as an inducement to collective bargaining had fallen into almost total disuse. By that same year the Democratic affinities of union labor were barely detectable, and the AFL's political discipline had disappeared. In 1928, the year of Al Smith's unprecedented and portentous candidacy, the AFL declared itself neutral. But the AFL could not enforce even neutrality within its ranks: some trade-union officials and union groups strayed toward Republican Herbert Hoover.[76]

The only Republican policy received favorably by the AFL was the more stringent regulation of immigration provided in the National Origins Act. Republican responsibility for this legislation would combine with Republican Prohibition to make the Democratic party a real alternative for industrial workers beginning in 1928. Ironically, nativism would till the soil for a Democratic electoral harvest, in the darkness of economic depression, among old labor *and* new immigrants. But this electoral harvest was not reaped from the union-party tie: in 1932, in the election that resurrected the Democratic state—and anchored it in Democratic majorities—the AFL sat out the campaign. Indeed, in the moment of transition from the state of Court and Party—and in a moment that elsewhere saw a social democratic breakthrough—old labor was ill-prepared and poorly positioned to help reverse the "ascendancy of capitalism over democracy," in despite of electoral upheaval.

Common Democratic partisanship among workers after 1932 would not easily heal a fractured working class. Antagonistic union visions and jurisdictional interests continued to collide in the workplace, in fact with greater intensity once the Democratic state extended formal legal and political recognition to unionism. Within the Democratic coalition, *de facto* party-class affinities did not produce a coherent alignment of party and class. And so the Democratic party did not become America's equivalent of a labor party, even after 1932. Instead, disjoined work-class groups organized as discrete interests within the Democratic party, alongside farmers, reformers, some of business, and the South: they entered the party union by union (sometimes union against union), ethnic group by ethnic group, and, for the majority who still remained unorganized, worker by worker. Never significantly challenging the American political mainstream, union labor resumed its straight and narrow path within that mainstream, repairing union ties to the existing system of broker parties and institutionalizing ties to an expanded broker state.

[76]See J. David Greenstone, *Labor in American Politics* (1969, 1977), 29–38; Irving Bernstein, *The Lean Years* (1960).

Back to the Future

The overthrow of Speaker Joseph Cannon in 1910 launched a decade of considerable innovation and realignment in politics and among institutions. Federalism was transformed as policy makers set about building a national administrative apparatus to regulate economic power and broker organized interests. Accompanying the shift in the balance between national institutions and among levels of public authority was an erosion of nineteenth-century patterns of interest representation and electoral mobilization. Bureaucratization and participatory reforms proliferated in states and cities in an assault on patronage democracy, and competition between groups and sections filled the gap left by the decline in party competition under the system of 1896. The expansion of administrative arenas for the interpretation and implementation of policy meanwhile enhanced the role of organized minorities in determining policy outcomes. Associated with many of these changes was the rise of trade unionism—specifically, the American Federation of Labor—as the central labor force in national politics.

Although the Court remained an arena for class confrontation until the New Deal, electorally accountable institutions—Congress and the executive—provided the political stage for "class compromise" during Woodrow Wilson's administration. That strain of progressive reform which sought to remove "politics" from government resonated with a collateral concern to remove conflict from politics. On the one hand, this entailed elevating the state above the economy, chiefly through administrative expansion and regulatory reform. On the other, it meant recognizing new "estates"—in this case, union labor—and folding them into the interior processes of government, where antagonisms between estates could be organized into competition and compromise among interests. As the state extended its reach during this period, it carved the economy into separate spheres and parceled those spheres out to the most interested parties.[1]

[1] Cf. Theodore J. Lowi, *The End of Liberalism* (1969, 1979), chap. 4.

Trade unionism received opportunities and arenas alternative to collision with capital in the courts and in the workplace for bargaining over rights and remedies. Further, the stakes of party competition and, in particular, the stakes of its Democratic paritsanship were raised for the AFL. Its fortunes tied to those of the ruling coalition beginning in 1912, the AFL traded its organizational and electoral clout for public policies that would enhance labor's claims against employers and against the Court.

American union labor was "let in" to government for the first time during the Progressive Era, at a time that was in other countries a magic moment for labor-based politics and social welfare innovation. American labor's entrance validated pluralism—wherein electoral and governmental processes broker the claims of organized representations of interests—as class-neutral. From union labor's standpoint, labor-based or social democratic politics, already improbable because of the sharp political divide between union labor and labor's social base, became unnecessary, as well.

Union labor's political breakthrough institutionalized union labor's separation from the working class. It was conditioned by the requirements of organizational autonomy and by pressures arising from the coincident segmentation of the American work force along organizational, occupational, ethnic, and political lines. Union ties to party and state helped decide the patterns and habits of broker politics and helped subordinate social statism to voluntarism. Though union labor suffered economic and political demobilization during the 1920s, and though resurgent unionism was driven by industrial workers in the 1930s, the relationship between union, party, and state which characterized the New Deal arrangement was prefigured in the New Freedom.

The AFL, despite its antistatism, moved into Democratic politics to help build a state that would eventually be strong enough to broker labor's right to trade-union autonomy in labor-management relations. But union labor's role in politics and its relations to party and state were far more significant than what it actually got out of politics. The ascendancy, in 1912, of the party electorally marginalized under the system of 1896 produced a state to which union labor enjoyed privileged access. Though commanded by centralized elites and representative of at best a limited membership, union labor earned considerable political status as the only organized representation of the working class. That political status gave union labor a strategic role in both representation and intervention, that is, in both the electoral and the policy-making processes.

By contrast, its policy successes were often symbolic and sometimes evanescent. While a labor department was created and a labor man placed at its helm, labor law remained at the discretion of the Court; and while the Clayton Act seemed to provide union labor a defense against judicial bias, statutory ambiguity and interpretative controversy allowed the Court to decide the real meaning of the law. The antitrust exemption and injunction shield offered in the Clayton Act succumbed to judicial surveillance. Still the AFL's participation in formulating remedies signified that party and state could be receptive to labor interests and defined the remedies for a future experiment. Twenty years later, when a more expansive unionism would be reckoned a "countervailing power" essential to the New Deal coalition and to the Keynesian breakthrough, the arenas and policies developed for trade unionism under Wilson would be extended, refined, and strengthened.[2] A less timid state—and a subdued judiciary—would be more successful in joining union labor's political status to its legal rights. Out of this would emerge a more durable broker state.

The AFL's presence in the Democratic state not only helped launch the American broker state, it also helped defer formation of a welfare state. Wilson gave the AFL a platform from which to argue against policies that it believed would undermine trade unionism, and its argument was consistent with the decentralist and entrepreneurial spirit of Wilsonian progressivism. Further, the AFL's opposition to social legislation meant that the party in power did not have to respond to working-class militancy, or earn (or coopt) labor's electoral loyalty, through a range of social interventions which elsewhere launched welfare states.

The central role of trade-union autonomy in labor politics clearly took its toll on the timing of social welfare innovations in the United States, as well as on the nature and management of those innovations when they did arrive. The welfare state as it finally emerged in the United States was less corporatist, less extensive, and less worker-directed than in Europe; and American trade unions, having been at the margins of welfare-state formation—indeed, opposed to it—have also been at the margins of its expansion and administration.[3] Unions have shaped and managed worker welfare to some extent since the New Deal, but they have done so through

[2]Joseph Huthmacher, *Senator Robert Wagner and the Rise of Urban Liberalism* (1968), 76; John Kenneth Galbraith, *American Capitalism* (1962); Ellis Hawley, *The New Deal and the Problem of Monopoly* (1966), chap. 10; and James MacGregor Burns, *Roosevelt: The Lion and the Fox* (1956).

[3]Robert T. Kudrle and Theodore R. Marmor, "Development of Welfare States in North America," in Peter Flora and Arnold Heidenheimer, *The Development of Welfare States in Western Europe* (1981), 81–116; Bentley Gilbert, *The Evolution of National Insurance in Great Britain* (1966), 279–80.

Afterword

bargaining with employers for health, pension, and other benefits in the union contract.

The AFL's voice and access developed from its economic, organizational, and political position in the system of 1896. From its economic and organizational position, the AFL attempted a bilateral, liberal corporatist arrangement with an important segment of industrial capital in the National Civic Federation. From its political position, the AFL fastened its ties to the Democratic party and developed ties to the state when Congress and the White House passed to Democratic control in 1912. The only electorally coherent segment of the working class, the AFL extended its "monopoly of representation" into government under the Democratic regime. Democrats in government offered the informal, mediating services of the state to enhance the organizational, and political, position of union labor where the labor-capital social partnership could (or would) not.

Like unions in industrializing Europe, the AFL offered a system of mediation and regularized exchange, but it did so only between its members and employers and between its members and party and state.[4] Lacking a broad social base, the labor side of the NCF experiment was only half a partner, and lacking a broad social base, the labor side of the Democratic party was only a group interest. But on the basis of a coalition that explicitly included union labor and recognized the requirements of union autonomy, the Democratic state worked to union labor's positional advantage. If it often delivered only split-the-difference solutions to labor problems, the Democratic state nonetheless incorporated the AFL into problem solving; further, the Democratic state shielded the AFL from intrusive social remedies to class-bound dependencies, uncertainties, and inequalities.

But AFL-Democratic ties were riddled with contradictions. Most important, AFL-Democratic ties arose from union-party affinities, chiefly with respect to race, immigration, and the role of the state. The union-party tie expressed union dependence on a middle-class party, not party

[4]For discussions of unions, liberal corporatism, and parliamentary democracy see Peter Lange, George Ross, and Maurizio Vannicelli, *Unions, Change and Crisis: French and Italian Union Strategy and the Political Economy, 1945–1980* (1982), chap. 3; Charles S. Maier, "Fictitious Bonds . . . of Wealth and Law: On the Theory and Practice of Interest Representation," Charles Sabel, "The Internal Politics of Trade Unions," and Philippe C. Schmitter, "Interest Intermediation and Regime Governability in Contemporary Western Europe and North America," all in Suzanne Berger, ed., *Organizing Interests in Western Europe* (1981); Bob Jessop, "Corporatism, Parliamentarism and Social Democracy," in Schmitter and Gerhard Lehmbruch, eds., *Trends toward Corporatist Intermediation* (1979); and John Goldthorpe, ed., *Order and Conflict in Contemporary Capitalism* (1984).

dependence on a significant labor wing. From union labor's standpoint, the tie was a slack one. Indeed, when union labor became politically tainted with class mobilization after World War I, the Democratic party surrendered to the contradictions of union dependence on a middle-class party, and the Democratic state, in pursuit of middle-class normality, broke its promises to union allies. The union-party tie frayed, and union labor returned to its late nineteenth-century focus on militant economic action—until resurgent employer autonomy and judicial vigilance put an end even to that.

Across industrializing Europe, unions typically forged political alliances to pursue broad programs of social and political change. American union labor was no different in the fact of political alliance, but it was quite different in the nature of its alliance and in the substance of its programs. Union interests were elements of labor-based agendas in Britain, for example (viz., the Trades Disputes Act), while union political programs were essential to the birth of what Albert Dicey called the "collectivist era."[5] Working-class opposition, through unions and labor-based parties, posed challenges to states and to the principles of individualism and laissez-faire. In the United States, however, union labor championed individualism and laissez-faire in a defense against state and class. Unions in western Europe may have receded from explicitly labor-based politics, often moving into varying degrees of corporatist intermediation under the impact of social democratic Keynesianism, but union labor in the United States was never organically tied to radical or reformist labor-based politics to begin with. In America, union labor aimed, "above all, at the maintenance or change of the industrial *status quo*, not the inclusive social *status quo*."[6]

The fragility of the Democratic arrangement followed from the mobilization of union bias. Union labor forged ties to party and state to promote its position and maximize its interests within the industrial system in which it was embedded and over which it claimed jurisdiction. The AFL's positional interests developed at the intersection of its internal (organizational) and external (system) interests, and the AFL was guided by challenges to trade-union autonomy at that intersection: namely, the vast

[5]Albert Venn Dicey, *Law and Public Opinion in England* (1913). Many scholars do not find the term descriptively appropriate; but as between Britain and the United States, it highlights an important contrast.

[6]Ralf Dahrendorf makes this point with respect to unions in "post-industrial" Europe in *Class and Class Conflict in Industrial Society* (1959), 271. Perhaps Werner Sombart was right when he termed American labor not an exception but "the ghost of Europe's future." *Why is There No Socialism in the United States?* (1976).

expansion of the class through the new immigration, and the consolidation of coercive public authority against unionism in the Court-dominated state. The AFL's positional interests required continued AFL hegemony over class and autonomy from state. Its requirements included labor-market controls against cheap labor and scabs; an autonomous system of intermediation within industry which would reduce or eliminate judicial opportunities to disembowel unionism; a monopoly of representation in industry that would enforce AFL jurisdiction over the class; and a monopoly of benefits to sustain that jurisdiction. The requirements of autonomy lay behind the AFL's venture in liberal corporatism in the first decade of the twentieth century, and they lay behind its formal ties to party and state in the second.

But the requirements of hegemony set the AFL against the social base it claimed, even though the premises of liberal corporatism and the possibilities of representative democracy required the incorporation of that social base. Thus Progressive Era democracy along liberal corporatist lines could not yield workable settlements. Still, it provided a model for labor relations and union politics a generation later. Then the state made itself the formal referee of union rights, and then unions and employers resuscitated bilateral management of workers' social rights through welfare protections negotiated in the union contract.

The political choices made by union labor in the industrial period continue to affect American politics. Though exclusionist unionism died in the New Deal upheaval, union labor is still characterized by its low-density membership. Government has intervened to lift the bottom of the working class (through such measures as the minimum wage and social security) and to equalize the quality of workplace life (through such measures as occupational safety and health regulation), but the vast majority of workers, nearly 82 percent, remain outside the wage and benefit exchange between unions and employers. Meanwhile the incomplete and segmented structure of the American welfare state reflects union labor's historic preference for organization-centered and private-sector solutions to distributive problems.[7] And though the welfare state now enjoys union support, the political weakness of the segmented welfare state constituencies—women, children, the disabled, for example—and the corresponding vulnerability of social policy are arguably connected to old labor's historic resistance to universalistic or "collectivist" remedies.

[7]On the admixture of intervention and clienteles in the welfare state, see Michael K. Brown, "The Segmented Welfare State: The Political Origins and Consequences of U.S. Social Policy, 1938–1980," paper presented to the Western Political Science Association, 1985.

Although the union-party tie was secured in the New Deal, unions are alternately viewed as politically weak—they have been unable to secure organizational protections from the Democratic state since the New Deal[8]—and as obtrusively powerful "special interests." As union representation of working people's interests in politics has come under increasing criticism, so the union-party tie has suffered assault from within labor's own party. Union ties to a middle-class party may have generated policy reciprocities that enhanced union labor's institutional position, but union labor's very dependence on a middle-class party and its short organizational reach into labor's social base have contributed to its institutional vulnerability under Ronald Reagan and may contain the seeds of future political weakness. The current erosion in popular support for unions and the welfare state, and the stalemate within the Democratic social base, have been historically conditioned by the political divide between old labor and the working class during the industrial period. The politics of old labor has proved to be the ghost of America's future.

[8]No relief from 14b, no common situs picketing, no labor law reform.

Selected Bibliography

Government Documents

California, Constitutional Convention. *Debates and Proceedings,* vol. 2. Sacramento, 1881.

California. *Journal of the Assembly.* 3d sess. Sacramento, 1852.

California. *Journal of the Assembly.* 23d sess. Sacramento, 1880.

California Legislature. *Amendments to the Codes, 1877–78.* 22d sess. Sacramento, 1878.

California, State Senate, Special Committee on Chinese Immigration. *Chinese Immigration: Its Social, Moral and Political Effects.* Report to the California State Senate. Sacramento, 1878.

Pennsylvania. *Handbook.* Harrisburg, 1912.

U.S. Anthracite Coal Strike Commission. *Report to the President on the Anthracite Coal Strike of May–October, 1902.* Washington, D.C., 1903.

U.S. Bureau of the Census. Ninth Census (1870). *Population of the United States,* vol. 1. Washington, D. C., 1872.

———. Eleventh Census (1890). *Population of the United States,* vol. 1, pt. 1. Washington, D.C., 1895.

———. Twelfth Census (1900). *Population of the United States,* vol. 1, pt. 1. Washington, D.C., 1902.

———. Thirteenth Census (1910). *Population of the United States,* vol. 1, pt. 1. Washington, D.C., 1913.

———. *Immigrants and Their Children: 1920.* Washington, D.C., 1927.

———. "Political Party Affiliations in Congress and the Presidency." Series Y, 204–10. *Historical Statistics of the United States,* pt. II. Washington, D.C., 1975.

———. *Statistical Abstract of the United States: 1950.* Washington, D.C., 1950.

U.S. Bureau of Immigration and Naturalization. *Annual Report of the Commissioner General of Immigration.* Washington, D.C., 1909.

Selected Bibliography

U.S. Bureau of Labor. *Twenty-First Annual Report of the Commissioner of Labor, 1906: Strikes and Lockouts.* House Doc. 822. 56th Cong., 2d sess. Serial 5213. Washington, D.C., 1907.

U.S. Commission on Immigration. *Reports.* Presented by William P. Dillingham. 42 vols. Washington, D.C., 1911.

U.S. Commission on Industrial Relations. *Final Report and Testimony.* Senate Doc. 415. 64th Cong., 1st sess. Serial 6936. Washington, D.C., 1916.

U.S. Congress. *Congressional Record.* 47th, 48th, 49th, 62d, 63d, and 64th Congresses.

U.S. Congress. House. Committee on Immigration. *Biological Aspects of Immigration.* Hearings, April 16–17, 1920. 66th Cong., 3d sess. Washington, D.C., 1921.

U.S. Congress. House. Committee on the Investigation of the United States Steel Corporation. *Hearings.* 8 vols. 62d Cong., 1st sess. Washington, D.C., 1912.

U.S. Congress. House. Committee on the Judiciary. *Anti-Trust Legislation.* Hearings. 63d Cong., 2d sess. Vol. 1. Washington, D.C., 1914.

U.S. Congress. House. Committee on Labor. Commission to Study Social Insurance and Unemployment. *Hearings,* April 6 and 11, 1916. 64th Cong., 1st sess. Washington, D.C., 1916.

U.S. Congress. House. Select Committee on Existing Labor Troubles in Pennsylvania. *Labor Troubles in the Anthracite Region of Pennsylvania, 1887–1888.* House Rept. 4147. 50th Cong., 2d sess. Washington, D.C., 1889.

U.S. Congress. Senate. Committee on Education and Labor. *Relations between Capital and Labor.* Hearings, vol. 1. 49th Cong., 1st sess. Washington, D.C., 1885.

U.S. Congress. Senate. Committee on Interstate Commerce. *Anti-Trust Legislation.* Hearings, vol. 2. 62d Cong., 1st sess. Washington, D.C., 1912.

Proceedings and Publications of Organizations

American Federation of Labor. Convention *Proceedings.* Annual.
American Federationist.
National Civic Federation Review.
Socialist Party National Convention. *Proceedings.* Annual.

Articles and Papers

Asher, Robert. "Failure and Fulfillment: Agitation for Employers' Liability Legislation and the Origins of Workmen's Compensation in New York State, 1876–1910." *Labor History,* 24 (1983), 198–222.

——. "Union Nativism and the Immigrant Response." *Labor History,* 23 (1982), 325–48.

270

Barker, Charles A. "Henry George and the California Background of Progress and Poverty." California Historical Society *Quarterly*, 24 (June 1945).

Bechdolt, Jack. "San Francisco's Labor Problem." *Pacific Monthly*, 2 (1904), 107.

Belmont, August. "Department on Compensation for Industrial Accidents and Their Prevention." *National Civic Federation Review*, July 1, 1911, pp. 21–22.

Bemis, Edward. "The Distribution of Our Immigrants." *Andover Review*, 9 (1888), 587–96.

——. "Restriction of Immigration." *Andover Review*, 8 (1888), 250–64.

Bernstein, Irving. "Samual Gompers and the Irony of Free Silver, 1896." *Mississippi Valley Historical Review*, 29 (1942), 394–400.

Bonacich, Edna. "Capitalism and Race Relations in South Africa: A Split Labor Market Analysis." *Political Power and Social Theory*, 2 (1981), 239–77.

——. "A Theory of Ethnic Antagonism: The Split Labor Market." *American Sociological Review*, 37 (1972), 547–59.

Brandeis, Louis. "Workingmen's Insurance—The Road to Social Efficiency." In National Conference on Charities and Corrections. *Proceedings*, 1911.

Brody, David. "The Old Labor History and the New." *Labor History*, 20 (1979), 111–26.

Brown, Michael K. "The Segmented Welfare State: The Political Origins and Consequences of U.S. Social Policy, 1938–1980." Paper presented to the Western Political Science Association, 1985.

Burnham, Walter Dean. "The Changing Shape of the American Political Universe." *American Political Science Review*, 59 (1965), 7–28.

——. "Party Systems and the Political Process." In *American Party Systems*, ed. William Chambers and Walter Dean Burnham. New York, 1975.

——. "The System of 1896." In *The Evolution of American Electoral Systems*, ed. Paul Kleppner. Westport, Conn., 1981.

——. "Theory and Voting Research." *American Political Science Review*, 68 (1974), 1002–23.

Chandler, William E. "Methods of Restricting Immigration." *Forum*, 13 (1889), 128–42.

Cherney, William. "Working Class Politics." *International Socialist Review*, 11 (1910), 257–61.

Clark, E. E. "Immigration." *American Federationist*, 4 (1897), 137–38.

Commons, John R. "The Anthracite Coal Strike Award." *National Civic Federation Monthly Review*, April 1903, p. 15.

——. "Immigration and Labor Problems." In *The Making of America:* vol. 8, *Labor*, ed. Robert La Follette. Chicago, 1906.

——. "Karl Marx and Samuel Gompers." *Political Science Quarterly*, 41 (1926), 281–86.

——. "Race and Democracy." *Chautauquan*, 38 (1903), 33–42.

Converse, Philip. "Change in the American Electorate." In *The Human Meaning of Social Change,* ed. Angus Campbell and Converse. New York, 1972.

Cornwell, Elmer. "Bosses, Machines, and Ethnic Groups." American Academy of Political and Social Sciences *Annals,* 353 (1964), 27–39.

Dancis, Bruce. "Social Mobility and Class Consciousness: San Francisco's International Workingman's Association in the 1880s." *Journal of Social History,* 11 (1977), 75–98.

Davis, Mike. "Why the U.S. Working Class Is Different." *New Left Review,* no. 123 (1980), 3–44.

Debs, Eugene V. "A Letter on Immigration." *International Socialist Review,* 11 (1910), 16–17.

——. "A Plea for Solidarity." *International Socialist Review,* 14 (1914), 534–38.

Diamond, William. "Urban and Rural Voting in 1896." *American Historical Review,* 46 (1941), 281–305.

Dubofsky, Melvyn. "Organized Labor and the Immigrant in New York City, 1900–1918." *Labor History,* 2 (1961), 182–201.

——. "The Origins of Western Working Class Radicalism, 1890–1905." *Labor History,* 7 (1966), 131–54.

Duchez, Louis. "The Strikes in Pennsylvania." *International Socialist Review,* 10 (1909), 193–203.

——. "Victory at McKees Rocks." *International Socialist Review,* 10 (1909), 289–300.

Dye, Nancy Schrom. "Creating a Feminist Alliance: Sisterhood and Class Conflict in the New York Women's Trade Union League." *Feminist Studies,* 2 (1975), 24–38.

Easley, Ralph. "What Organized Labor Has Learned." *McClure's,* 19 (1902), 483–92.

Erie, Steven P. "The Organization of Irish-Americans into Urban Institutions: Building the Political Machine, 1840–1896." Paper presented to the American Political Science Association, 1983.

——"The Two Faces of Ethnic Power: Comparing the Irish and Black Experience." *Polity,* 13 (1980), 261–84.

Falk, Gail. "Women and Unions: A Historical View." *Women's Rights Law Reporter,* 1 (1973), 54–65.

Fitch, John. "Labor in the Steel Industry." American Academy of Political and Social Sciences *Annals,* 33 (1904), 307–15.

Fong, Walter. "Chinese Labor Unions." *Chautauquan,* 23 (1896), 399–402.

"For Peace between Capital and Labor." *National Civic Federation Review* (March 1909), 3.

Garraty, John. "U.S. Steel vs. Labor: The Early Years." *Labor History,* 1 (1960), 3–38.

Gary, Elbert H. "Unemployment and Business." *Harper's Magazine,* 131 (1915), 70–72.

George, Henry. "Chinese Immigration." In *Cyclopaedia of Social Science*, I (1881), 409–14.

——. "How to Help the Unemployed." *North American Review*, 158 (1894), 175–84.

——. "The Kearney Agitation in California." *Popular Science Monthly*, 17 (1880), 433–53.

——. "The Single Tax on Land Values." *Century*, 40 (1890), 394–403.

Gompers, Samuel. "America Must Not Be Overwhelmed." *American Federationist*, 31 (1924), 313–17.

——. "Bakers Lose at Law, But Win in Fact." *American Federationist*, 12 (1905), 361–64.

——. "The Charter of Industrial Freedom." *American Federationist*, 21 (1914), 957–74.

——. "The Courts and Mr. Taft on Labor." *American Federationist*, 28 (1921), 220.

——. "Freedom's Legalistic Octopus." *American Federationist*, 29 (1922), 504–11.

——. "Mr. Hunter's Dilemma Proven." *American Federationist*, 17 (1910), 484–91.

——. "Immigration—Up To Congress." *American Federationist*, 18 (1911), 17–22.

——. "Labor's Political Campaign: Its Causes and Progress—Labor's Political Duty." *American Federationist*, 19 (1912), 801–14.

——. "Labor vs. Its Barnacles." *American Federationist*, 23 (1916), 268–74.

——. "The Lesson of the Recent Strikes." *North American Review*, 159 (1894), 201–6.

——. "Let Us Save Our Children." *American Federationist*, 29 (1922), 413–14.

——. "The Limitations of Conciliation and Arbitration." American Academy of Political and Social Sciences *Annals*, 20 (1902), 29–34.

——. "Not Even Compulsory Benevolence Will Do." *American Federationist*, 24 (1917), 47–48.

——. "Organized Labor in the Campaign." *North American Review*, 155 (1892), 91–96.

——. "Organized Labor and the National Civic Federation." *American Federationist*, 18 (1911), 181–92.

——. "Schemes to Distribute Immigrants." *American Federationist*, 18 (1911), 519–25.

——. "Self-Help Is the Best Help." *American Federationist*, 22 (1915), 113–15.

——. "Should the Wife Help Support the Family?" *American Federationist*, 13 (1906), 36.

——. "The Steel Strike: Mr. Shaffer, His Accusations, Their Refutation." *American Federationist*, 7 (1901), 415–31.

——. "Take Away Its Usurped Power." *American Federationist*, 30 (1923), 399–401.

273

Selected Bibliography

——. "A Tale of Labor's Struggle and Its Conflict with Industrial and Political Corruption." *American Federationist,* 20 (1913), 585–611.

——. "Talks on Labor." *American Federationist,* 12 (1905), 636–38.

——. "The Trade Agreement Enthusiastically Endorsed: President Gompers' Address." *National Civic Federation Review,* May 15, 1905, pp. 6–7.

——. "Voluntary Social Insurance vs. Compulsory." *American Federationist,* 23 (1916), 333–57.

——. "Voluntary Social Insurance vs. Compulsory (Continued)." *American Federationist,* 23 (1916), 453–66.

Goren, Arthur. "A Portrait of Ethnic Politics: The Socialists in the 1908 and 1910 Congressional Elections on the East Side." In *Voters, Parties, and Elections,* ed. Joel Silbey and Samuel McSeveney. Lexington, Mass., 1972.

Gourevitch, Peter. "International Trade, Domestic Coalitions and Liberty: Comparative Responses to the Crisis of 1873–1896." In *The Political Economy: Readings in the Politics and Economics of American Public Policy,* ed. Thomas Ferguson and Joel Rogers. New York, 1984.

Graham, A. A. "The Unamericanization of America." *American Federationist,* 17 (1910), 302–6.

Gulick, Charles A., and Melvin K. Bers. "Insight and Illusion in Perlman's Theory of the Labor Movement." *Industrial and Labor Relations Review,* 6 (July 1953).

Hall, John. "The Knights of St. Crispin in Massachusetts, 1869–1878." *Journal of Economic History,* 18 (1957), 161–75.

Hanna, Marcus A. "Industrial Conciliation and Arbitration." American Academy of Political and Social Sciences *Annals,* 20 (1902), 21–26.

Hays, Samuel P. "History as Human Behavior." *Iowa Journal of History,* 58 (1960), 193–206.

——. "The Politics of Reform in Municipal Government in the Progressive Era." *Pacific Northwest Quarterly,* 45 (1964), 157–69.

Haywood, William. "An Appeal for Industrial Solidarity." *International Socialist Review,* 14 (1914), 534–38.

——. "Socialism the Hope of the Working Class." *International Socialist Review,* 12 (1912), 461–71.

Hessen, Robert. "The Bethlehem Steel Strike of 1910." *Labor History,* 15 (1974), 3–18.

Higham, John. "The American Party, 1886–1891." *Pacific Historical Review,* 19 (1950), 37–47.

——. "Immigration." In *The Comparative Approach to American History,* ed. C. Vann Woodward. New York, 1968.

——. "The Origins of Immigration Restriction." *Mississippi Valley Historical Review,* 39 (June 1952).

Hillquit, Morris. "Immigration in the United States." *International Socialist Review,* 8 (1907), 65–75.

Hittell, Theodore H. "Observations on the New Constitution." *Overland Monthly*, 1 (1883), 34–41.

Hoffman, Charles. "The Depression of the Nineties." *Journal of Economic History*, 16 (1956), 137–67.

"How the Welfare Department Was Organized." *National Civic Federation Review*, June 1904, p. 13.

Hughes, Everett C. "Queries Concerning Industry and Society Growing out of the Study of Ethnic Relations in Industry." *American Sociological Review*, 14 (1949), 211–20.

Hunter, Robert. "Immigration: The Annihilation of Our Native Stock." *Commons*, 9 (April 1904).

"Industrial Insurance Commission." *National Civic Federation Review*, March 1909, p. 13.

Jacoby, Robin Miller. "The Women's Trade Union League and American Feminism." *Feminist Studies*, 3 (1975), 126–39.

Jessop, Bob. "Corporatism, Parliamentarism, and Social Democracy." In *Trends toward Corporatist Intermediation*, ed. Philippe C. Schmitter and Gerhard Lehmbruch. Beverly Hills, 1979.

Johnson, Bruce. "Taking Care of Labor: The Police in American Politics." *Theory and Society*, 3 (1976), 89–117.

"Joint Trade Agreements." *National Civic Federation Monthly Review*, April 1903, pp. 12–14.

Jones, Dallas L. "The Enigma of the Clayton Act." *Industrial and Labor Relations Review*, 10 (January 1957), 200–221.

Kauer, Ralph. "The Workingmen's Party of California." *Pacific Historical Review*, 13 (1944), 278–91.

Kellog, Paul. "An Immigrant Labor Tariff." *Survey*, 25 (1911), 529–31.

Kessler-Harris, Alice. "Where Are the Organized Women Workers?" *Feminist Studies*, 3 (1975), 92–109.

Key, V. O. "A Theory of Critical Elections." *Journal of Politics*, 17 (1955), 3–18.

Kingsley, Darwin P. "Life Insurance and the Moral Obligation of Employers toward Their Workingmen." *National Civic Federation Review*, March 1, 1910, p. 25.

Klebaner, Benjamin. "State and Local Immigration Regulation in the United States before 1882." *International Review of Social History*, 3 (1958), 269–95.

Kutler, Stanely I. "Labor, the Clayton Act, and the Supreme Court." *Labor History*, 3 (1962), 19–38.

"Labor's Dangers and Tragedies Told." *National Civic Federation Review*, March 1, 1910, p. 27.

"Labor's Influence over Congress." *Literary Digest*, 48 (June 13, 1914), 1423–24.

Selected Bibliography

Lane, A. T. "American Trade Unions, Mass Immigration, and the Literacy Test." *Labor History*, 25 (1984), 5–25.

Laslett, John. "Reflections on the Failure of Socialism in the AFL." *Mississippi Valley Historical Review*, 50 (1964), 635–51.

——. "Socialism and the American Labor Movement: Some New Reflections." *Labor History*, 8 (1967), 136–55.

Lauck, W. Jett. "A Real Myth." *Atlantic Monthly*, September 1912, pp. 388–93.

——. "The Vanishing American Wage Earner." *Atlantic Monthly*, November 1912, pp. 691–96.

Lienenweber, Charles. "The American Socialist Party and New Immigrants." *Science and Society*, 32 (1968), 1–25.

Lipset, Seymour Martin. "Radicalism or Reform: The Sources of Working-Class Politics." *American Political Science Review*, 77 (1983), 1–19.

——. "Trade Unionism and the American Social Order." In *The American Labor Movement*, ed. David Brody. New York, 1971.

Lodge, Henry Cabot. "The Restriction of Immigration." *North American Review*, 152 (1891), 27–36.

Lowi, Theodore J. "Party, Policy, and Constitution in America." In *American Party Systems*, ed. William Chambers and Walter Dean Burnham. New York, 1975.

McCormick, Richard L. "Ethnocultural Perspectives on 19th Century Political Behavior: An Evaluation." *Political Science Quarterly*, 89 (1974), 351–77.

McSeveney, Samuel. "Ethnic Groups, Ethnic Conflicts, and Recent Quantitative Research in American Political History." *International Migration Review*, 7 (1973), 14–33.

Mandel, Bernard. "Gompers and Business Unionism, 1873–1890." *Business History Review*, 28 (1954), 265.

——. "Samuel Gompers and Negro Workers, 1866–1914." *Journal of Negro History*, 40 (1955), 34–60.

Mann, Arthur. "Gompers and the Irony of Racism." *Antioch Review*, 13 (1953), 203–14.

Manson, George J. "The 'Foreign Element' in New York City." *Harper's Weekly*, 34 (1890).

Marsden, Gerald K. "Patriotic Societies and American Labor: The American Protective Society in Wisconsin." *Wisconsin Magazine of History*, 41 (1958), 287–94.

Matthews, Fred H. "White Community and 'Yellow Peril.'" *Mississippi Valley Historical Review*, 50 (1964), 612–33.

Mayo-Smith, Richmond. "Control of Immigration, I." *Political Science Quarterly*, 3 (1888), 46–47.

——. "Control of Immigration, II." *Political Science Quarterly*, 3 (1888), 197–225.

Mitchell, John. "The Coal Strike." *McClure's*, 20 (1902), 219–24.

———. "Prevention of Industrial Accidents." *National Civic Federation Review*, March 1, 1910, p. 25.

Mitchell, John, and Francis L. Robbins. "Report of the Department of Trade Agreements." *National Civic Federation Monthly Review*, January 1905, pp. 13–14.

Montgomery, David. "The Irish and the American Labor Movement." In *Ireland and America, 1776–1976: The American Identity and the Irish Connection*, ed. David Doyle and Owen Edwards. Westport, Conn., 1980.

———. "The Shuttle and the Cross: Weavers and Artisans in the Kensington Riots of 1844." *Journal of Social History*, 5 (1972), 411–46.

Morgan, Appleton. "What Shall We Do with the Dago?" *Popular Science Monthly*, 38 (1890).

Nash, Gerald. "The Influence of Labor on State Policy." California Historical Society *Quarterly*, 42 (1963), 241–57.

"The National Conference on Immigration." *National Civic Federation Review*, 2 (January–February 1906), 1–20.

Noble, John Hawks. "The Present State of the Immigration Question." *Political Science Quarterly*, 7 (1892).

O'Donnell, Edward. "Women as Breadwinners: Error of the Age." *American Federationist*, 4 (1897), 186–87.

"Opening Guns in the Immigration Fight." *Literary Digest*, 77 (May 5, 1923), 9–11.

Orloff, Ann Shola, and Theda Skocpol. "Why Not Equal Protection? Explaining the Politics of Public Social Welfare in Britain and the United States, 1880s–1920s." Paper presented to the American Sociological Association, 1983.

O'Sullivan, Mary K. "The Labor War at Lawrence." *Survey*, 29 (1912), 72–75.

Ozanne, Robert. "Trends in American Labor History." *Labor History*, 21 (1980), 513–21.

Panitch, Leo. "Trade Unions and the Capitalist State." *New Left Review*, no. 125 (1981), 21–43.

Paulsen, George E. "The Gresham-Yang Treaty." *Pacific Historical Review*, 37 (1968), 281–99.

Perlman, Selig. "The Basic Philosophy of the American Labor Movement." American Academy of Political and Social Sciences *Annals*, 274 (1951), 57–63.

Pessen, Edward. "The Workingmen's Movement of the Jacksonian Era." *Mississippi Valley Historical Review*, 43 (1956), 428–43.

Peterson, James. "The Trade Unions and the Populist Party." *Science and Society*, 8 (1944), 143–60.

Phelan, James D. "Why the Chinese Should Be Excluded." *North American Review*, 178 (1901).

Pitt, Leonard. "The Beginnings of Nativism in California." *Pacific Historical Review*, 30 (1971), 23–38.

Plehn, Carl C. "Labor in California." *Yale Review*, 4 (1896), 409–25.

"President Roosevelt on Automatic Indemnity for Injury." *National Civic Federation Review*, July 1, 1911, p. 8.

"The Revolution—1919." *Nation*, October 4, 1919, p. 452.

Rezneck, Samuel. "Distress, Relief and Discontent in the United States during the Depression of 1873–1878." *Journal of Political Economy*, 58 (1950), 494–512.

Ripley, William Z. "Race Factors in Labor Unions." *Atlantic Monthly*, 93 (1904), 299–308.

Roberts, Peter. "The Anthracite Coal Situation." *Yale Review*, 11 (1902).

Rodman, Paul. "The Origins of the Chinese Issue in California." *Mississippi Valley Historical Review*, 25 (1938), 181–96.

Rogin, Michael. "Voluntarism: The Political Functions of an Anti-Political Doctrine." *Industrial and Labor Relations Review*, 15 (1962), 521–35.

Rood, Henry. "The Mine Laborers in Pennsylvania." *Forum*, 14 (1882–83), 110–22.

Rudolph, Frederick. "Chinamen in Yankeedom: Anti-Unionism in Massachusetts in 1870." *American Historical Review*, 53 (1947), 1–30.

Rusk, Jerrold G. "The Effect of the Australian Ballot Reform on Split-Ticket Voting: 1876–1908." *American Political Science Review*, 64 (1970), 1220–38.

Safford, John. "The Good That Trade Unions Do, I." *American Federationist*, 9 (1902), 357–58.

Sanders, Heywood T. "Paying for the Bloody Shirt." In *Political Benefits*, ed. Barry Rundquist. Lexington, Mass., 1980.

Sandmeyer, Elmer. "Anti-Chinese Legislation and the Federal Courts: A Study in Federal Relations." *Pacific Historical Review*, 5 (1936), 189–211.

Saxton, Alexander. "Race and the House of Labor." In *The Great Fear: Race in the Mind of America*, ed. Gary B. Nash and Richard Weiss. New York, 1970.

——. "San Francisco and the Populist and Progressive Insurgencies." *Pacific Historical Review*, 34 (1965), 421–38.

Scheinberg, Steven J. "Theodore Roosevelt and the AFL's Entry into Politics, 1906–1908." *Labor History*, 3 (1962), 131–48.

Schlesinger, Arthur M. "The Significance of Immigration in American History." *American Journal of Sociology*, 37 (1921), 71–85.

Shaler, Nathaniel. "European Peasants as Immigrants." *Atlantic Monthly*, 71 (1893), 646–55.

Sharron, Fred A. "A Post-Mortem on the Labor-Safety Valve Theory." *Agricultural History*, 19 (1945), 31–37.

Shefter, Martin. "The Electoral Foundations of the Political Machine: New York City, 1884–1897." In *The History of American Electoral Behavior*, ed. Joel Silbey, Allan Bogue, and William Flanigan. Princeton, 1978.

——. "Party, Bureaucracy and Political Change in the United States." In *Political Parties: Development and Decay*, ed. Louis Maisel and Joseph Cooper. Beverly Hills, 1978.

——. "Party and Patronage: Germany, England and Italy." *Politics and Society*, 7 (1977), 403–51.

——. "Trade Unions and Political Machines." In *Working Class Formation: Nineteenth Century Patterns in Western Europe and the United States*, ed. Ira Katznelson and Aristide Zolberg. Princeton, N.J., 1985.

Sherwin, H. "Observations on the Chinese Laborer." *Overland Monthly*, 7 (1886).

Shover, John. "The Progressives and the Working Class Vote in California." In *Voters, Parties and Elections*, ed. Joel Silbey and Samuel McSeveney. Lexington, Mass., 1972.

Smith, John S. "Organized Labor and Government in the Wilson Era, 1913–1921: Some Conclusions." *Labor History*, 3 (1962), 265–86.

Steffens, Lincoln. "A Labor Leader of Today: John Mitchell and What He Stands For." *McClure's*, 19 (1902), 354–56.

Stevens, S. K. "The Election of 1896 in Pennsylvania." *Pennsylvania History*, 4 (1937), 65–87.

Sturmthal, Adolph. "Comments on Selig Perlman's *A Theory of the Labor Movement*." *Industrial and Labor Relations Review*, 4 (1951), 483–96.

Tilly, Charles. "Collective Violence in European Perspective." In *The History of Violence in America*, ed. Ted Gurr. New York, 1969.

Urofsky, Melvin I. "Wilson, Brandeis and the Trust Issue, 1912–1914." *Mid-America*, 49 (1967), 3–28.

Valesh, Eva McDonald. "Women and Labor." *American Federationist*, 3 (1896), 221–23.

Walker, Francis. "The Great Count of 1890." *Forum*, 11 (1891), 406–18.

——. "Immigration." *Yale Review*, 1 (1892), 125–45.

——. "Immigration and Degradation." *Forum*, 11 (1891), 634–44.

——. "Mr. Bellamy and the New Nationalist Party." *Atlantic Monthly*, 65 (1890).

——. "Restriction of Immigration." *North American Review*, 67 (June 1896), 823–29.

Warne, Frank Julian. "The Real Cause of the Miners' Strike." *Outlook*, 71 (1902).

——. "The Trade Agreement in the Coal Industry." American Academy of Political and Social Sciences *Annals*, 36 (1910), 86–95.

Weinstein, James. "Big Business and the Origins of Workmen's Compensation." *Labor History*, 8 (1967), 156–74.

Weyl, Walter. "Immigration: The Industrial Situation." *University Settlement Studies Quarterly*, 1 (1905).

White, Henry. "Immigration Restriction as a Necessity." *American Federationist*, 4 (1897), 67–69.

Wiebe, Robert. "The Anthracite Strike of 1902: A Record of Confusion." *Mississippi Valley Historical Review*, 49 (1961–62), 229–51.

Witte, Edwin. "The Clayton Bill and Organized Labor." *Survey*, 32 (1914), 358.

——. "Labor Is Not a Commodity." *New Republic,* December 2, 1916, pp. 112–14.

Wittke, Carl. "Immigration Policy Prior to World War I." American Academy of Political and Social Sciences *Annals,* 262 (1949).

Woods, Robert A. "The Breadth and Depth of the Lawrence Outcome." *Survey,* 28 (1912), 67–68.

Woodward, C. Vann. "The Populist Heritage and the Intellectual." *American Scholar,* 29 (1959).

Autobiographies, Biographies, Reminiscences, and Collected Writings

Addams, Jane. *A Centennial Reader.* New York, 1960.

——. *The Second Twenty Years at Hull House.* New York, 1930.

——. *Twenty Years at Hull House.* New York, 1910.

Baker, Ray Stannard, ed. *Woodrow Wilson, Life and Letters.* 8 vols. Garden City, N.Y., 1927–29.

Baker, Ray Stannard, and William E. Dodd, eds. *The Public Papers of Woodrow Wilson.* 6 vols. New York, 1925–27.

Blaine, James G. *Political Discussions: Legislative, Diplomatic, and Popular.* Norwich, Conn., 1887.

Blum, John. *The Republican Roosevelt.* Cambridge, Mass., 1954.

——. *Woodrow Wilson and the Politics of Morality.* New York, 1956.

Bryan, William Jennings. *The First Battle.* Chicago, 1896.

Burns, James MacGregor. *Roosevelt: The Lion and the Fox.* New York, 1956.

Clark, Champ. *My Quarter Century in American Politics.* New York, 1920.

Croly, Herbert. *Marcus Alonzo Hanna: His Life and Work.* New York, 1912.

Debs, Eugene V. *Writings and Speeches of Eugene V. Debs.* Introduction by Arthur Schlesinger, Jr. New York, 1948.

Destler, Chester M. *Henry Demarest Lloyd and the Empire of Reform.* Philadelphia, 1963.

Dubofsky, Melvyn, and Warren Van Tine. *John L. Lewis.* New York, 1977.

Garraty, John A. *Right Hand Man: The Life of George W. Perkins.* New York, 1960.

Ginger, Ray. *Altgeld's America.* New York, 1973.

——. *The Bending Cross: A Biography of Eugene Victor Debs.* New Brunswick, N.J., 1949.

Gluck, Elsie. *John Mitchell, Miner: Labor's Bargain with the Gilded Age.* New York, 1929.

Gompers, Samuel. *Seventy Years of Life and Labor.* 2 vols. New York, 1919, 1925.

——. *Seventy Years of Life and Labor.* Ed. Nick Salvatore. Ithaca, 1984.

Josephson, Matthew, and Hannah Josephson. *Al Smith: Hero of the Cities*. Boston, 1969.

Kohlsaat, H. H. *From McKinley to Harding: Personal Recollections of Our Presidents*. New York, 1923.

La Follette, Robert M. *La Follette's Autobiography*. Madison, Wis., 1913.

Lang, J. T. *I Remember*. Sydney, Australia, 1956.

Mandel, Bernard. *Samuel Gompers: A Biography*. Yellow Springs, O., 1963.

Mason, Alpheus T. *Brandeis: A Free Man's Life*. New York, 1946.

Morison, Elting E., ed. *The Letters of Theodore Roosevelt*. Vol. 6. Cambridge, Mass., 1954.

Mowry, George E. *Theodore Roosevelt and the Progressive Movement*. Madison, Wis., 1946.

Norris, George W. *Fighting Liberal: The Autobiography of George W. Norris*. New York, 1945.

Norton, Charles E., ed. *Orations and Speeches of George William Curtis*. 3 vols. New York, 1894.

Powderly, Terence V. *Thirty Years of Labor*. Columbus, O., 1889.

Pringle, Henry F. *Theodore Roosevelt, A Biography*. New York, 1956.

Richardson, James D., ed. *A Compilation of the Messages and Papers of the Presidents, 1789–1902*. Vol. 9. New York, 1911.

Roney, Frank. *Frank Roney, Irish Rebel and California Labor Leader: An Autobiography*. Ed. Ira Cross. Berkeley, 1931.

Roosevelt, Theodore. *An Autobiography*. New York, 1914.

——. *The Works of Theodore Roosevelt*. 20 vols. New York, 1926.

——. *Writings*. Ed. William H. Harbaugh. Indianapolis, 1967.

Salvatore, Nick. *Eugene V. Debs: Citizen and Socialist*. Urbana, Ill., 1982.

Schlegel, Marvin. *Ruler of the Reading: The Life of Frank B. Gowen, 1836–1889*. Harrisburg, Pa., 1947.

Schurz, Carl. *The Intimate Letters of Carl Schurz*. Ed. Joseph Schafer. Madison, Wis., 1928.

Steffens, Lincoln. *Autobiography of Lincoln Steffens*. New York, 1931.

Strum, Phillippa. *Louis D. Brandeis: Justice for the People*. Cambridge, Mass., 1984.

Swanberg, W. A. *Citizen Hearst*. New York, 1961.

Tarbell, Ida M. *The Life of Elbert H. Gary: The Story of Steel*. New York, 1925.

Books, Dissertations, and Pamphlets

Adamic, Louis. *Dynamite: The Story of Class Violence in America*. (1931). Gloucester, Mass., 1963.

Addams, Jane. *Philanthropy and the Social Progress*. Boston, 1893.

Adelman, Paul. *The Rise of the Labour Party, 1880–1945*. London, 1972.

Selected Bibliography

Andersen, Kristi. *The Creation of a Democratic Majority, 1928–1936*. Chicago, 1979.

Aronowitz, Stanley. *False Promises: The Shaping of American Working Class Consciousness*. New York, 1974.

Babcock, Barbara, et al. *Sex Discrimination and the Law*. Boston, 1975.

Bancroft, Hubert Howe. *History of California*. 7 vols. San Francisco, 1887.

——. *Works*. 39 vols. San Francisco, 1887.

Banfield, Edward, and James Q. Wilson. *City Politics*. Chicago, 1963.

Bean, Walton. *Boss Reuf's San Francisco*. Berkeley, 1952.

Beard, Mary. *A Short History of the Labor Movement*. New York, 1968.

Bell, Daniel. *Marxian Socialism in the United States*. Princeton, 1967.

Bellamy, Edward. *Looking Backward, 2000–1887*. (1888.) New York, 1960.

Bendix, Reinhard. *Nation-Building and Citizenship*. Berkeley, 1977.

Benson, Lee. *The Concept of Jacksonian Democracy: New York as a Test Case*. Princeton, 1961.

Berger, Suzanne, ed. *Organizing Interests in Western Europe*. New York, 1983.

Berman, Edward. *Labor Disputes and the President of the United States*. New York, 1924.

Bernstein, Irving. *The Lean Years: A History of the American Worker, 1920–1933*. Boston, 1960.

——. *The New Deal and Collective Bargaining Policy*. Berkeley, 1950.

Billington, Raymond Allen. *The Protestant Crusade: 1800–1860*. Gloucester, Mass., 1963.

Bimba, Anthony. *The Molly Maguires*. New York, 1932.

Binkley, Wilfred. *American Political Parties*. New York, 1964.

——. *President and Congress*. New York, 1962.

Bogue, Donald J. *The Population of the United States*. Glencoe, Ill., 1959.

Bolling, Richard. *Power in the House*. New York, 1968.

Boone, Gladys. *The Women's Trade Union Leagues in Great Britain and the United States of America*. New York, 1942.

Bornstein, Stephen, David Held, and Joel Krieger, eds. *The State in Capitalist Europe: A Casebook*. London, 1984.

Boston, Ray. *British Chartists in America: 1839–1900*. Manchester, 1971.

Brandeis, Louis. *Business—A Profession*. Boston, 1914.

Brandes, Stuart. *American Welfare Capitalism*. Chicago, 1984.

Bridges, Amy. *A City in the Republic*. New York, 1984.

Brissenden, Paul. *The I.W.W.: A Study of American Syndicalism*. New York, 1957.

Brody, David, ed. *Labor in Crisis*. Philadelphia, 1965.

——. *Steelworkers in America: The Non-Union Era*. New York, 1960.

——. *The American Labor Movement*. New York, 1971.

Broehl, Wayne. *The Molly Maguires*. Cambridge, Mass., 1964.

Brown, George Rothwell. *The Leadership of Congress*. Indianapolis, 1922.

Bryan, William Jennings. *A Tale of Two Conventions*. New York, 1912.

Bryce, James. *The American Commonwealth*. 2 vols. New York, 1910.

——. *Modern Democracies*. Vol. 2. New York, 1921.

Buenker, John D. *Urban Liberalism and Progressive Reform*. New York, 1973.

Bullough, William. *The Blind Boss and His City: Christopher Augustine Buckley and Nineteenth Century San Francisco*. Berkeley, 1979.

Burnham, Walter Dean. *Critical Elections and the Mainsprings of American Politics*. New York, 1970.

——. *The Current Crisis in American Politics*. New York, 1983.

——. *Presidential Ballots, 1836–1892*. Baltimore, 1955.

Carleton, Frank Tracy. *The History and Problems of Organized Labor*. Boston, 1911.

——. *Labor Problems*. Boston, 1933.

Carnegie, Andrew. *Triumphant Democracy*. New York, 1887.

Carroll, Mollie Ray. *Labor and Politics*. Boston, 1923.

Ceaser, James. *Presidential Selection: Theory and Development*. Princeton, 1979.

Chamberlain, John. *Farewell to Reform*. Chicago, 1932.

Chambers, William Nisbet, and Walter Dean Burnham, eds. *The American Party Systems*. New York, 1975.

Cole, G. D. H. *British Working Class Politics, 1832–1914*. London, 1941.

Commons, John R. *The History of Labor in the United States*. 4 vols. New York, 1918–35.

——. *Labor and Administration*. New York, 1913.

——. *Races and Immigrants in America*. 2d ed. (1920.) New York, 1967.

Commons, John R., ed. *Trade Unionism and Labor Problems*. New York, 1921.

Congressional Quarterly. *Presidential Elections since 1879*. Washington, D. C., 1975.

Coolidge, Mary Roberts. *Chinese Immigration*. New York, 1909.

Cordasco, Francisco, and Eugene Bucchioni. *The Italians: Social Backgrounds of an American Group*. Clifton, N.J., 1974.

Cornell, Robert. *The Anthracite Coal Strike of 1902*. Washington, D.C., 1957.

Couvares, Francis G. *The Remaking of Pittsburgh: Class and Culture in an Industrializing City*. Albany, N.Y., 1984.

Croly, Herbert. *The Promise of American Life*. New York, 1965.

Cross, Ira. *History of the Labor Movement in California*. Berkeley, 1935.

Dahrendorf, Ralf. *Class and Class Conflict in Industrial Society*. Stanford, Calif., 1959.

Dangerfield, George. *The Strange Death of Liberal England*. New York, 1961.

Daniels, Roger. *The Politics of Prejudice: The Anti-Japanese Movement in California and the Struggle for Japanese Exclusion*. New York, 1968.

Davis, Winfield, J. *The History of Political Conventions in California, 1849–1892*. Sacramento, 1893.

Dawley, Alan. *Class and Community: The Industrial Revolution in Lynn.* Cambridge, Mass., 1976.

Democratic Campaign Handbook, 1896. 1896.

Democratic National Committee. *The Political Reformation of 1884: A Democratic Campaign Handbook.* New York, 1884.

Destler, Chester McArthur. *American Radicalism, 1865–1901.* New London, Conn., 1946.

Dicey, Albert Venn. *Law and Public Opinion in England.* London, 1913.

Donnelly, Ignatius. *Caesar's Column: A Story of the 20th Century.* Boston, 1894.

——. *The Golden Bottle; or, The Story of Ephraim Benezet of Kansas.* New York, 1892.

Douglas, Paul. *Real Wages in the United States.* New York, 1930.

Doyle, David, and Owen Edwards, eds. *Ireland and America, 1776–1976: The American Identity and the Irish Connection.* Westport, Conn., 1980.

Dubofsky, Melvyn. *Industrialism and the American Worker, 1865–1920.* Arlington Heights, Ill., 1975.

——. *We Shall Be All: A History of the I.W.W.* New York, 1969.

——. *When Workers Organize: New York City in the Progressive Era.* Amherst, Mass., 1968.

Duverger, Maurice. *Political Parties: Their Organization and Activity in the Modern State.* New York, 1960.

Dye, Nancy Schrom. *As Equals and as Sisters: Feminism, the Labor Movement, and the Women's Trade Union League of New York.* Columbia, Mo., 1980.

Eaves, Lucille. *A History of California Labor Legislation.* University of California Publications in Economics, vol. 2. Berkeley, August 23, 1910.

Engels, Friedrich. *The Conditions of the Working Class in England.* (1845.) Stanford, Calif., 1968.

Erickson, Charlotte. *American Industry and the European Immigrant, 1860–1885.* Cambridge, Mass., 1957.

Erie, Steven. "The Lost Hurrah: Irish-Americans and the Dilemma of Machine Politics." Manuscript. San Diego, Calif., 1985.

Fine, Nathan. *Labor and Farmer Parties in the United States, 1828–1928.* New York, 1961.

Fink, Leon. *Workingmen's Democracy: The Knights of Labor and American Politics.* Urbana, Ill., 1983.

Fitch, John. *The Steel Workers.* New York, 1910.

Flexner, Eleanor. *Century of Struggle: The Women's Rights Movement in the United States.* New York, 1974.

Flora, Peter, and Arnold Heidenheimer, eds. *The Development of Welfare States in Western Europe.* New Brunswick, N.J., 1981.

Foner, Eric. *Free Soil, Free Labor, Free Men: The Ideology of the Republican Party before the Civil War.* New York, 1970.

——. *Politics and Ideology in the Age of the Civil War.* New York, 1980.

Foner, Philip. *The Great Labor Uprising of 1877.* New York, 1977.

——. *The History of the Labor Movement in the United States*. 6 vols. New York, 1947–82.

Forcey, Charles. *The Crossroads of Liberalism: Croly, Weyl, Lippman and the Progressive Era, 1900–1925*. New York, 1961.

Frankfurter, Felix, and Nathan Greene. *The Labor Injunction*. New York, 1930.

Frederickson, George M. *White Supremacy: A Comparative Study in American and South African History*. New York, 1981.

Freeman, Gary. *Immigrant Labor and Racial Conflict in Industrial Societies: The French and British Experience, 1945–1975*. Princeton, 1979.

Frey, John. *The Labor Injunction: An Exposition of Government by Judicial Conscience and Its Menace*. (1923.)

Fuller, Herbert Bruce. *The Speakers of the House*. Boston, 1909.

Galbraith, John Kenneth. *American Capitalism*. Boston, 1962.

Galenson, Walter, ed. *Comparative Labor Movements*. New York, 1952.

Garis, Roy. *Immigration Restriction: A Study of the Opposition to and Regulation of Immigration into the United States*. New York, 1927.

George, Alexander, and Juliette L. George. *Woodrow Wilson and Colonel House: A Personality Study*. New York, 1964.

Ghent, W. J. *Our Benevolent Feudalism*. New York, 1902.

Gilbert, Bentley. *The Evolution of National Insurance in Great Britain: The Origins of the Welfare State*. London, 1966.

Glazer, Nathan, and Daniel Patrick Moynihan. *Beyond the Melting Pot*. New York, 1970.

Goldman, Eric. *Rendez-Vous with Destiny*. New York, 1952.

Goldthorpe, John H., ed. *Order and Conflict in Contemporary Capitalism*. New York, 1984.

Gompers, Samuel. *Labor and the Common Welfare*. New York, 1919.

——. *Labor and the Employer*. New York, 1920.

Gompers, Samuel, and Henry J. Allen. *Debate*. 1920.

Gompers, Samuel, and Herman Guttstadt. *Meat vs. Rice: American Manhood vs. Asiatic Coolieism: Which Shall Survive?* San Francisco, 1902.

Goodman, Wilbain T. "The Presidential Campaign of 1920." Diss., Ohio University, 1951.

Goodwyn, Lawrence. *The Populist Moment*. New York, 1978.

Gordon, David M., Richard Edwards, and Michael Reich. *Segmented Work, Divided Workers*. New York, 1982.

Gordon, Milton M. *Assimilation in American Life: The Role of Race, Religion and National Origins*. New York, 1964.

Gossett, Thomas R. *Race: The History of an Idea in America*. New York, 1965.

Gourevitch, Peter, et al. *Unions and Economic Crisis: Britain, West Germany, and Sweden*. London, 1984.

Grant, Madison. *The Passing of the Great Race; or, The Racial Basis of European History*. New York, 1916.

Green, Marguerite. *The National Civic Federation and the American Labor Movement*. Washington, D. C., 1956.

Greene, Victor. *The Slav Community on Strike: Immigrant Labor in Pennsylvania Anthracite*. Notre Dame, Ind., 1968.

Greenstone, J. David. *Labor in American Politics*. Chicago, 1977.

Grob, Gerald. *Workers and Utopia: A Study of Ideological Conflict in the American Labor Movement, 1865–1900*. New York, 1969.

Gross, James A. *The Making of the National Labor Relations Board: A Study in Economics, Politics, and the Law, 1933–1937*. Albany, N.Y., 1974.

Gulick, Charles A. *Labor Policy of the U.S. Steel Corporation*. New York, 1924.

Gutman, Herbert. *Work, Culture and Society in Industrializing America*. New York, 1976.

Haber, Samuel. *Efficiency and Uplift, 1890–1920*. Chicago, 1964.

Handlin, Oscar. *Boston's Immigrants, 1790–1880*. (1941.) New York, 1970.

——. *The Uprooted*. New York, 1951.

Harris, Avril E. "Organized Labor in Party Politics: 1906–1932." Diss., University of Iowa, 1937.

Hartz, Louis. *Economic Policy and Democratic Thought: Pennsylvania, 1776–1860*. Cambridge, Mass., 1948.

——. *The Founding of New Societies*. New York, 1964.

——. *The Liberal Tradition in America*. New York, 1955.

Hawley, Ellis. *The New Deal and the Problem of Monopoly*. Princeton, 1966.

Hays, Samuel. *The Response to Industrialism: 1885–1914*. Chicago, 1957.

Hechter, Michael. *Internal Colonialism: The Celtic Fringe in British National Development, 1536–1966*. Berkeley, 1977.

Henry, Alice. *Women and the Labor Movement*. New York, 1923.

Hicks, John D. *The Populist Revolt*. Omaha, 1961.

Higham, John. *Send These to Me: Jews and Other Immigrants in Urban America*. New York, 1975.

——. *Strangers in the Land*. New York, 1977.

Hobsbawm, Eric. *Labouring Men*. Garden City, N.Y., 1964.

——. *Workers: Worlds of Labor*. New York, 1984.

Hofstadter, Richard. *Age of Reform*. New York, 1955.

Hollingsworth, J. Rogers. *The Whirligig of Politics*. Chicago, 1963.

Holt, Michael. *The Political Crisis of the 1850s*. New York, 1978.

Horan, James. *The Pinkertons: The Detective Dynasty That Made History*. New York, 1967.

Horowitz, Ruth. *The Ideologies of Organized Labor*. New Brunswick, N.J., 1978.

Hugins, Walter. *Jacksonian Democracy and the American Working Class*. Stanford, Calif., 1960.

Hunter, Robert. *Poverty: Social Conscience in the Progressive Era*. Ed. Peter d'A. Jones. New York, 1965.

Hurwitz, H. L. *Theodore Roosevelt and New York State, 1880–1900.* New York, 1968.

Huthmacher, Joseph. *Senator Robert Wagner and the Rise of Urban Liberalism.* New York, 1968.

Jensen, Gordon Maurice. "The National Civic Federation in an Age of Social Change and Social Reform." Diss., Princeton University, May 1956.

Jensen, Richard J. *The Winning of the Midwest: Social and Political Conflict, 1888–1896.* Chicago, 1971.

Jerome, Harry. *Migration and Business Cycles.* New York, 1926.

Jones, Elliot. *The Anthracite Coal Combination in the United States.* Cambridge, Mass., 1914.

Jones, Maldwyn Allen. *American Immigration.* Chicago, 1960.

Jones, Stanley L. *The Presidential Election of 1896.* Madison, Wis., 1964.

Josephson, Matthew. *The Politicos, 1865–1896.* New York, 1966.

——. *The President Makers.* New York, 1966.

Karson, Marc. *American Labor Unions and Politics, 1900–1918.* Carbondale, Ill., 1958.

Katzenstein, Peter. *Corporatism and Change.* Ithaca, 1984.

Katznelson, Ira. *City Trenches: Urban Politics and the Patterning of Class in the United States.* New York, 1981.

Kaufman, Stuart. *Samuel Gompers and the Origins of the American Federation of Labor.* Westport, Conn., 1973.

Keller, Morton. *Affairs of State: Public Life in Late Nineteenth Century America.* Cambridge, Mass., 1977.

Kessler-Harris, Alice. *Out to Work: A History of Wage Earning Women in the United States.* New York, 1982.

Key, V. O. *Southern Politics in State and Nation.* New York, 1949.

Kipnis, Ira. *The American Socialist Movement, 1897–1916.* New York, 1952.

Kirkland, Edward C. *Industry Comes of Age: Business, Labor, and Public Policy, 1860–1897.* Chicago, 1967.

Kleppner, Paul. *Cross of Culture: A Social Analysis of Midwest Culture, 1850–1900.* New York, 1970.

——. *The Third Electoral System, 1853–1900: Parties, Voters, and Political Culture.* Chapel Hill, N.C., 1979.

Kleppner, Paul, ed. *The Evolution of American Electoral Systems.* Westport, Conn., 1981.

Kolko, Gabriel. *Main Currents in Modern American History.* New York, 1984.

——. *The Triumph of Conservatism.* New York, 1963.

Konesfsky, Samuel J. *The Legacy of Holmes and Brandeis: A Study in the Influence of Ideas.* New York, 1957.

Kraditor, Aileen. *Ideas of the Women's Suffrage Movement.* New York, 1981.

La Follette, Robert, ed. *The Making of America: Labor.* New York, 1967.

Lange, Peter, George Ross, and Maurizio Vannicelli. *Unions, Change and Crisis:*

French and Italian Union Strategy and the Political Economy, 1945–1980. London, 1982.

Laslett, John H. M. *Labor and the Left: A Study of Socialist and Radical Influences in the American Labor Movement, 1881–1924.* New York, 1970.

Laslett, John H. M., and Seymour Martin Lipset. *Failure of a Dream? Essays in the History of American Socialism.* Garden City, N.Y., 1974.

Lauck, W. Jett, and Edgar Sydenstricker. *Conditions of Labor in American Industries.* New York, 1917.

Lens, Sidney. *The Labor Wars: From the Molly Maguires to the Sitdowns.* Garden City, N.Y., 1973.

Leonard, Ira, and Robert Parmet. *American Nativism, 1830–1860.* New York, 1971.

Lescohier, Don. *The Knights of St. Crispin, 1864–1874.* Bulletin of the University of Wisconsin, no. 355. Madison, 1910.

Lescohier, Don, and Elizabeth Brandeis. *The History of the Labor Movement in the United States, 1896–1932.* New York, 1935.

Leuchtenberg, William E. *The Perils of Prosperity, 1914–1932.* Chicago, 1958.

Lichtman, Alan. *Prejudice and the Old Politics: The Presidential Election of 1928.* Chapel Hill, N.C., 1979.

Lieberman, Elias. *Unions before the Bar.* New York, 1950.

Lindblom, Charles. *Unions and Capitalism.* New Haven, 1949.

Link, Arthur. *Wilson: The Road to the White House.* Princeton, 1947.

——. *Woodrow Wilson and the Progressive Era, 1910–1917.* New York, 1954.

Lipset, Seymour Martin. *The First New Nation.* New York, 1963.

Lipset, Seymour Martin, and Earl Raab. *The Politics of Unreason: Right Wing Extremism in America, 1790–1977.* Chicago, 1978.

Lloyd, Henry Demarest. *A Strike of Millionaires against Miners.* Chicago, 1890.

——. *Wealth against Commonwealth.* New York, 1894.

Lodge, Henry Cabot. *The Restriction of Immigration.* March 6, 1896.

Lombardi, John. *Labor's Voice in the Cabinet.* New York, 1968.

London, Jack. *Valley of the Moon.* London, 1914.

Lorwin, Val. *The French Labor Movement.* Cambridge, Mass., 1954.

Lovestone, Jay. *The Government—Strikebreaker.* New York, 1923.

Lowi, Theodore J. *The End of Liberalism.* New York, 1969.

Lubell, Samuel. *The Future of American Politics.* New York, 1965.

Lubove, Roy. *The Struggle for Social Security.* Cambridge, Mass., 1968.

McConnell, Grant. *The Decline of Agrarian Democracy.* Berkeley, 1953.

——. *Private Power and American Democracy.* New York, 1966.

McCormick, Richard L. *From Realignment to Reform: Political Change in New York State, 1892–1910.* Ithaca, 1981.

McCraw, Thomas K., ed. *Regulation in Perspective: Historical Essays.* Cambridge, Mass., 1981.

McKelvey, Jean T. *AFL Attitudes toward Production, 1900–1932.* Cornell Studies in Industrial and Labor Relations. Ithaca, 1952.

McNeill, George E. *The Labor Movement: The Problem of Today.* New York, 1892.

McSeveney, Samuel. *The Politics of Depression: Political Behavior in the Northeast, 1893–1896.* New York, 1972.

McWilliams, Carey. *California: The Great Exception.* Westport, Conn., 1971.

———. *Factories in the Field.* Boston, 1944.

Mandel, Bernard. *Labor: Free and Slave.* New York, 1955.

Markovits, Andrei, ed. *The Political Economy of West Germany: Modell Deutschland.* New York, 1982.

Marx, Karl, and Friedrich Engels. *Ireland and the Irish Question.* New York, 1972.

———. *Letters to Americans: 1848–1895.* New York, 1953.

Mason, Alpheus. *Organized Labor and the Law.* Durham, N.C., 1923.

Michels, Robert. *Political Parties: A Sociological Study of the Oligarchical Tendencies of Modern Democracies.* New York, 1968.

Miller, Stuart. *The Unwelcome Immigrant: The American Image of the Chinese.* Berkeley, 1969.

Miller, Zane L. *Boss Cox's Cincinnati: Urban Politics in the Progressive Era.* New York, 1968.

Mitchell, Harvey, and Peter Stearns. *Workers and Protest: The European Labor Movement, the Working Class, and the Origins of Social Democracy, 1890–1914.* Itasca, Ill., 1971.

Mitchell, John. *Organized Labor: Its Problems, Purposes and Ideals.* New York, 1903.

Montgomery, David. *Beyond Equality: Labor and the Radical Republicans, 1862–1872.* New York, 1967.

———. *Workers' Control in America: Studies in the History of Work, Technology, and Labor Struggles.* New York, 1980.

Moore, Barrington, Jr. *Social Origins of Dictatorship and Democracy: Lord and Peasant in the Making of the Modern World.* Boston, 1966.

Morris, James O. *Conflict within the AFL.* Ithaca, 1958.

Mowry, George E. *The California Progressives.* Berkeley, 1951.

———. *The Era of Theodore Roosevelt and the Birth of Modern America, 1900–1912.* New York, 1958.

Murray, Robert K. *Red Scare.* Minneapolis, 1955.

Mushkat, Jerome. *Tammany: The Evolution of a Political Machine, 1789–1865.* Syracuse, 1971.

Nee, Victor, and Brett de Bary. *Longtime Californ': A Documentary Study of an American Chinatown.* New York, 1973.

Nelli, Humbert. *The Italians in Chicago, 1880–1930: A Study in Ethnic Mobility.* New York, 1970.

Nelson, Daniel. *Unemployment Insurance: The American Experience, 1915–1935.* Madison, Wis., 1969.

Olson, Mancur. *The Logic of Collective Action.* Cambridge, Mass., 1971.

Selected Bibliography

Ozanne, Robert. *A Century of Labor-Management Relations at McCormick and International Harvester.* Madison, Wis., 1967.

Paul, Arnold. *Conservative Crisis and the Rule of Law: Attitudes of Bar and Bench, 1887–1895.* Ithaca, N.Y., 1960.

Pelling, Henry. *A History of British Trade Unionism.* 3d. ed. New York, 1976.

——. *Origins of the Labour Party.* London, 1965.

Perkins, George W. *To the Officers and Employees of U.S. Steel.* December 31, 1902.

Perlman, Selig. *A History of Trade Unionism in the United States.* New York, 1923.

——. *A Theory of the Labor Movement.* New York, 1928.

Pessen, Edward. *Most Uncommon Jacksonians.* Albany, N.Y., 1967.

Pinkerton, Allan. *The Molly Maguires and the Detectives.* New York, 1877.

Piore, Michael. *Birds of Passage.* New York, 1979.

Piven, Frances Fox, and Richard Cloward. *The New Class War: Reagan's Attack on the Welfare State and Its Consequences.* New York, 1982.

——. *Poor People's Movements.* New York, 1979.

Pollack, Norman. *The Populist Response to Industrial America: Midwestern Populist Thought.* Cambridge, Mass., 1962.

Porter, Kirk, and Donald B. Johnson. *National Party Platforms, 1840–1960.* Urbana, Ill., 1961.

Post, Louis F., and Fred C. Leubuscher. *The George-Hewitt Campaign.* New York, 1887.

Potter, David. *People of Plenty.* Chicago, 1966.

Powell, Lyman, ed. *The Social Unrest.* Vol. 2. New York, 1919.

Powell, Thomas Reed. *Vagaries and Varieties in Constitutional Interpretation.* New York, 1967.

Ramirez, Bruno. *When Workers Fight: The Politics of Industrial Relations in the Progressive Era.* Westport, Conn., 1978.

Reed, Louis. *The Labor Philosophy of Samuel Gompers.* New York, 1930.

Rice, Stuart A. *Farmers and Workers in American Politics.* New York, 1924.

Richardson, James F. *The New York Police: Colonial Times to 1901.* New York, 1970.

Ricker, Ralph R. *The Greenback-Labor Movement in Pennsylvania.* Bellfonte, Pa., 1966.

Riis, Jacob. *How the Other Half Lives: Studies among the Tenements of New York.* New York, 1890.

Roberts, Peter. *Anthracite Coal Communities.* New York, 1904.

Robinson, Edgar. *The Presidential Vote, 1896–1932.* Stanford, Calif., 1947.

Rogin, Michael, and John Shover. *Political Change in California: Critical Elections and Social Movements, 1890–1966.* Westport, Conn., 1970.

Roosevelt, Theodore. *The New Nationalism.* (1910.) Englewood Cliffs, N.J., 1961.

——. *The Winning of the West.* 2 vols. New York, 1917.

Rosenblum, Gerald. *Immigrant Workers: Their Impact on Labor Radicalism.* New York, 1973.

Royce, Josiah. *California, From the Conquest of 1846 to the Second Vigilance Committee: A Study of American Character.* Boston, 1886.

——. *Race Questions, Provincialism, and Other American Problems.* New York, 1908.

Rundquist, Barry, ed. *Political Benefits.* Lexington, Mass., 1980.

Sandmeyer, Elmer. *The Anti-Chinese Movement in California.* Urbana, Ill., 1973.

Saposs, David. *Left Wing Unionism.* New York, 1926.

Saveth, Edward. *American Historians and European Immigrants, 1875–1925.* New York, 1948.

Saxton, Alexander. *The Indispensable Enemy: Labor and the Anti-Chinese Movement in California.* Berkeley, 1971.

Schattschneider, E. E. *The Semi-Sovereign People.* New York, 1960.

Schlesinger, Arthur M. *The Rise of the City, 1878–1898.* New York, 1933.

Schmitter, Philippe, and Gerhard Lehmbruch, eds. *Trends toward Corporatist Intermediation.* Beverly Hills, 1979.

Schorske, Carl. *German Social Democracy, 1905–1917: The Development of the Great Schism.* Cambridge, Mass., 1955.

Scisco, Louis Dow. "Political Nativism in New York State." Diss., Columbia University, 1901.

Shannon, David A. *The Socialist Party of America.* Chicago, 1955.

Shannon, William V. *The Irish Americans: A Political and Social Portrait.* New York, 1974.

Shinn, Charles Howard. *Mining Camps: A Study in American Frontier Government.* New York, 1885.

Shonfield, Andrew. *Modern Capitalism: The Changing Balance of Public and Private Power.* London, 1965.

Silbey, Joel. *A Respectable Minority: The Democratic Party in the Civil War Era, 1860–1868.* New York, 1977.

Silbey, Joel, and Samuel McSeveney, eds. *Voters, Parties and Elections.* Lexington, Mass., 1972.

Silbey, Joel, et al., eds. *The History of American Electoral Behavior.* Princeton, 1978.

Simons, H. J., and R. E. Simons. *Class and Colour in South Africa, 1850–1950.* Baltimore, 1969.

Skowronek, Stephen. *Building a New American State.* New York, 1982.

Solomon, Barbara. *Ancestors and Immigrants.* Cambridge, Mass., 1956.

Sombart, Werner. *Why Is There No Socialism in the United States?* (1906.) White Plains, N.Y., 1976.

Somma, Nicholas A. "The Knights of Labor and Chinese Immigration." Diss., Catholic University of America, 1952.

Selected Bibliography

Sowell, Thomas, ed. *Essays and Data on American Ethnic Groups*. Washington, D. C., 1978.

Spargo, John. *Syndicalism, Industrial Unionism and Socialism*. New York, 1913.

Spedden, E. R. *The Trade Union Label*. Johns Hopkins University Studies, ser. 28, no. 2. Baltimore, 1910.

Speek, Peter Alexander. *The Single Tax and the Labor Movement*. Bulletin of the University of Wisconsin. Madison, October 1917.

Stauffer, Alvin Packer, Jr. "Anti-Catholicism in American Politics." Diss., Harvard University, 1933.

Stedman, Murray S., Jr., and Susan W. Stedman. *Discontent at the Polls*. New York, 1950.

Stephens, John. *Transition from Capitalism to Socialism*. London, 1979.

Stephenson, George W. *A History of American Immigration, 1820–1924*. Boston, 1926.

Stockton, F. T. *The Closed Shop and American Trade Unions*. Johns Hopkins University Studies in Historical and Political Science, ser. 29, no. 3. Baltimore, 1911.

Suffern, Arthur. *Conciliation and Arbitration in the Coal Industry of America*. New York, 1915.

Sullivan, J. W. *The Trade Unions' Attitude toward Welfare Work*. New York, 1907.

Sundquist, James L. *Dynamics of the Party System*. Washington, D.C., 1973.

Taft, Philip. *Organized Labor in American History*. New York, 1964.

Thernstrom, Stephen. *Progress and Poverty*. New York, 1974.

Thomas, Harrison Cook. *The Return of the Democratic Party to Power in 1884*. New York, 1919.

Thomson, David. *Democracy in France since 1870*. New York, 1946.

Thorne, Florence C. *Samuel Gompers: American Statesman*. New York, 1957.

Tocqueville, Alexis de. *Democracy in America*. 2 vols. New York, 1945.

Tomlins, Christopher. *The State and the Unions*. New York, 1985.

Turner, Frederick Jackson. *The Frontier in American History*. New York, 1920.

———. *The Rise of the New West, 1819–1829*. (1906.) New York, 1962.

Urofsky, Melvin I. *Louis D. Brandeis and the Progressive Tradition*. Boston, 1981.

Van der Horst, Sheila. *Native Labor in Africa*. London, 1971.

Veblen, Thorstein. *The Theory of the Leisure Class*. New York, 1899.

Ware, Norman. *The Industrial Worker, 1840–1860*. Boston, 1924.

———. *The Labor Movement in the United States, 1860–1895*. New York, 1929.

Warne, Frank Julian. *The Immigrant Invasion*. New York, 1913.

———. *The Slav Invasion and the Mineworkers*. Philadelphia, 1904.

Webb, Sidney, and Beatrice Webb. *History of Trade Unionism*. Rev. ed. New York, 1920.

Weinstein, James. *The Corporate Ideal in the Liberal State, 1900–1918*. Boston, 1968.

———. *The Decline of Socialism in America, 1912–1925.* New York, 1967.

Weyl, Walter. *The New Democracy.* New York, 1912.

Wiebe, Robert. *Businessmen and Reform: A Study of the Progressive Movement.* Cambridge, Mass., 1962.

———. *The Search for Order, 1877–1920.* New York, 1967.

Wilensky, Harold. *The "New Corporatism," Centralization, and the Welfare State.* Beverly Hills, 1976.

———. *The Welfare State and Equality: Structural and Ideological Roots of Public Expenditures.* Berkeley, 1975.

Wilson, James Q. *Political Organizations.* New York, 1973.

Wilson, William Julius. *The Declining Significance of Race: Blacks and Changing American Institutions.* Chicago, 1978.

Wilson, Woodrow. *History of the American People.* New York, 1902.

———. *The New Freedom.* New York, 1913.

Witte, Edwin. *The Government in Labor Disputes.* New York, 1932.

Wittke, Carl. *Refugees of Revolution: The German Forty-Eighters in America.* Philadelphia, 1952.

Wolfson, Theresa. *The Woman Worker and the Trade Unions.* New York, 1923.

Wolman, Leo. *The Growth of American Trade Unions, 1880–1923.* New York, 1924.

Wood, Stephen B. *Constitutional Politics in the Progressive Era: Child Labor and the Law.* Chicago, 1968.

Woodward, C. Vann. *Origins of the New South, 1877–1913.* Baton Rouge, 1971.

———. *Reunion and Reaction: The Compromise of 1877 and the End of Reconstruction.* 2d ed. Garden City, N.Y., 1956.

———. *The Strange Career of Jim Crow.* New York, 1974.

Yearley, Clifton. *Britons in American Labor: 1820–1914.* Johns Hopkins University Studies in Historical and Political Science, ser. 75, no. 1. Baltimore, 1957.

———. *Enterprise and Anthracite: Economics and Democracy in Schuylkill County, 1820–1875.* Baltimore, 1961.

———. *The Money Machines: The Breakdown of Reform of Governmental and Party Finance in the North, 1860–1920.* Albany, N.Y., 1972.

Yellowitz, Irwin. *Labor and the Progressive Movement in New York State, 1897–1916.* Ithaca, 1968.

Young, Arthur Nicholas. *The Single Tax Movement in the United States.* Princeton, 1916.

Ziegler, Robert H. *Republicans and Labor, 1919–1929.* Lexington, Ky., 1969.

Index

Index

Index

Greene, Nathan, 33n48, 247n28
Greenstone, J. David, 15
Guttstadt, Herman, 96

Haight, Henry, 104n93
Hammer v. Dagenhart, 259n72
Handlin, Oscar, 234
Hanna, Marcus, 135, 137, 146
  and business-union alliance, 162–164,
    166, 167n17, 168, 170
  and coal strike, 173–174
  and new immigrants, 136, 141–142, 150,
    154
Harding, Warren G., 257
Hartz, Louis, 19–20, 28–29
Hayes, Max, 231
Hayes, Rutherford B., 89, 103–104, 136
Hays, Samuel P., 34n49
Haywood, Bill, 229–230
Hearst, William Randolph, 146n85
Hepburn Bill, 186n83, 241
Hill, David, 134n47
Hillquit, Morris, 230, 232
Hitchman Coal and Coke Co. v. Mitchell,
  246, 258
Hoar, George F., 103, 110
Hobsbawm, Eric, 50n14
Homestead strike, 33n46, 42n60, 171
Hoover, Herbert, 260
Hungary. *See* Immigration
Hunter, Robert, 233

Immigrant Aid Association, 75
Immigration, 9–10, 17, 40, 44, 67, 112,
  172, 178, 188n89
  changing nature, 29, 31, 38, 41–42
  effect on U.S. democracy, 65–66
  industrial class, 25, 42, 45, 68
  legislation and treaties
    anti-immigration, 92–96, 100, 104–
      107, 110, 113, 121, 130, 209n9,
      220, 260
    pro-immigration, 51, 53–54, 75, 78,
      80, 86, 101, 103–104
  link with racism, 17n5, 46–48, 52–53,
    67–68, 71–73, 75–76, 80, 85, 95–97,
    102, 104–105, 107–112, 122, 124–
    128, 221, 232–234
  male, 49
  mobility of immigrants, 27
  mobilization of new immigrants, 173,
    200–202
  recruitment of labor, 50–51, 53–54, 61–
    64, 75, 108–110, 194, 207
  restriction, 72, 185, 189, 195–198, 200,
    237

of Chinese, 30, 43, 50–51, 57–58, 71–
  113, 115, 121–122, 130, 140, 143,
  209n9, 220, 224–226, 229
of eastern and southern Europeans, 43,
  46, 57, 60, 62–63, 98, 100, 103,
  107–110, 122, 125–126, 196n113,
  224, 226, 229
of Japanese, 96–97, 220, 225–226,
  256n61
by literacy test, 124, 127, 128n29, 140,
  195, 211–212, 213n24, 217, 221–
  222, 246, 255–256
of public employment, 123
by type, 109, 122–127
under Wilson, 236–237, 241, 243–245,
  255–256
waves of, 33n47, 48, 51–52, 119, 165–
  166
See also Election of 1912; Nativism; System of 1896; Teutonic theory
Immigration Acts, 51, 53–54, 101
Immigration Bureau, 207–208, 236
Immigration Restriction League, 127
Industrial Workers of the World, 201, 208,
  234
In Re Debs, 133, 238
International Wire Workers, 143
Interstate Commerce Act, 133, 210
Interstate Commerce Commission, 134
Ireland. *See* Great Britain
Irish workers (in U.S.), 31, 52–53, 55, 60–
  61, 76, 80, 87–88, 114, 120, 124, 126–
  127, 135–137, 148, 150–154, 172. *See
  also* Democratic party
Irwin, William, 81
Italy. *See* Immigration

Japan. *See* Immigration
Jensen, Richard, 139
Johnson, Albert, 152n103
Johnson, Hiram, 219, 228

Kalloch, Issac, 86n49
Katznelson, Ira, 66
Kearney, Denis, 43, 77, 81–84, 86–88, 90–
  94, 99, 111, 113
Kelley, Florence, 184, 193, 250n38
Key, V. O., 18, 21, 113
Knights of Labor, 26n28, 63, 67, 87, 95,
  97, 113n1, 143
Knights of Saint Crispin, 56–57, 77–78
Know-Nothing party, 111, 114, 120–121

Labor, Department of, 236, 242–246, 252,
  256
Labor injunction. *See Buck's Stove and*

Index

Progressive Era (*cont.*)
  ty; Roosevelt, Theodore; Wilson,
  Woodrow
Progressive party, 214, 225–228
Prohibition, 53, 120, 128, 135–136, 260
Protective labor legislation. *See* American
  Federation of Labor; Kelley, Florence; Na-
  tional Civic Federation; Voluntarism;
  Wilson, Woodrow
Protestants, 52, 54, 120
Pullman strike, 129–130, 132–134, 137,
  144, 178, 237

Racism
  defined, 46n1
  in Democratic party, 80, 89–90, 102,
    104–105, 107–109, 111–112
  in Republican party, 105, 110–111, 221
  in Socialist party, 232–234
  in trade unions, 17n5, 46–48, 52–53, 67–
    68, 71–73, 75–76, 80, 85, 95–97, 101,
    122, 124, 128
  See also Nativism; Teutonic theory
Railroads, 58–59, 74–75, 80n26, 81, 84,
  103, 173, 176–177, 199, 211, 212, 255.
  See also Pullman strike; *entries for individual railroads*
Ramirez, Bruno, 167n18, 177n57
Reading Railroad, 58–61
Representative Assembly of Trades and Labor Unions, 86, 90–95, 99
Republican party
  displacement of Whigs, 21, 31
  free-labor coalition, 55
  and immigration, 54, 103, 105, 108, 121,
    139–141, 260
  and organized labor, 39, 162–165, 210–
    211
  reforms against working class, 34n49,
    152, 155, 157
  See also Election of 1896; Nativism; Racism; Roosevelt, Theodore; System of
  1896; Taft, William Howard
Richardson, James F., 76n15
Riemer, Jeremiah, 39n58
Rogin, Michael, 24–25, 37–38, 39n58
Roney, Frank, 81, 82n33, 84, 90–91, 93–
  94, 98–100, 111
Roosevelt, Theodore, 135
  campaigns of 1912, 225, 227, 228n76,
    243
  labor issues, 213–215, 218–222
  new immigrant support, 156, 226
  and coal strike, 175–176
  and National Civic Federation, 184,
    186n83, 206

social statism, 214, 218–219, 222
  trust regulation, 213–215
  views on immigration, 219–222
  See also Election of 1912
Root, Elihu, 175, 198n119
Rosenblum, Gerald, 65

San Francisco Chronicle, 82n83, 86, 131,
  147
San Francisco Federated Trades Council,
  96
San Francisco Morning Call, 94
Saxton, Alexander, 71, 97n82
Schattschneider, E. E., 35
Seamen's Act, 217n39, 246
Shefter, Martin, 17n4, 18n6, 149n97
Sherman Anti-Trust Act, 33n48, 36, 133n44,
  132, 163, 186, 210, 212, 238, 241, 245,
  258
Shoe-making industry, 56–58, 77–78, 92,
  94, 201n126
Silbey, Joel, 76n15
Skowronek, Steven, 17n4, 101n88
Smith, Al, 260
Social Democratic party (Germany), 16
Socialist party, 21, 243
  and AFL, 201–202, 208, 240–241
  and immigration policy, 228–235
  See also Debs, Eugene
Sombart, Werner, 18–19, 31n42, 265n6
South, the, 18, 34, 101, 104, 108, 127, 135,
  243, 252n48, 260
South Africa, 46, 48–49
Southern Pacific Railroad, 75, 78
Spargo, John, 231
Steel industry, 42, 150, 177, 179, 196. *See
  also* Homestead strike; McKees Rocks
  strike
Steffens, Lincoln, 178
Strasser, Adolphe, 79, 114
Suffrage, 20, 24, 26, 29–31, 68, 73–74, 98,
  115, 137n55, 185, 216
Supreme Court
  and anti-Chinese bill, 130
  Brandeis appointment, 242, 256
  centralization of political power, 33, 238
  federalization of immigration policy, 51,
    81, 102
  hostility to unions, 36, 43, 115, 133, 151,
    184–187, 211–212, 238–239
  and Taft, 210, 247
  and Wilson, 247–248, 257–259, 261–
    263
  in system of 1896, 34, 117, 164
  See also Laissez-faire constitutionalism;
  entries for specific decisions

Library of Congress Cataloging-in-Publication Data

Mink, Gwendolyn, 1952-
  Old labor and new immigrants in American political development.

  Bibliography: p.
  Includes index.
    1. Trade-unions—United States—Political activity. 2. United States—
  Emigration and immigration—History. 3. American Federation of Labor—History.
  4. Democratic Party (U.S.)—History. I. Title.
  HD6508.M584 1986   322'.2'0973   85-30963
  ISBN 0-8014-1863-1